Eurasian Maritime Geopolitics

Eurasian Maritime Geopolitics

THE UNITED STATES AND CHINA IN AN
AGE OF INDO–PACIFIC TRANSFORMATION

Kent E. Calder

BROOKINGS INSTITUTION PRESS
Washington, DC

Published by Brookings Institution Press
1775 Massachusetts Avenue, NW
Washington, DC 20036
www.brookings.edu/bipress

Co-published by Rowman & Littlefield
An imprint of The Rowman & Littlefield Publishing Group, Inc.
4501 Forbes Boulevard, Suite 200, Lanham, Maryland 20706
www.rowman.com

86-90 Paul Street, London EC2A 4NE

The Brookings Institution is a nonprofit organization devoted to research, education, and publication on important issues of domestic and foreign policy. Its principal purpose is to bring the highest quality independent research and analysis to bear on current and emerging policy problems.

British Library Cataloguing in Publication Information Available

Library of Congress Control Number: 2024949489

ISBN 978-0-8157-4074-2 (cloth)
ISBN 978-0-8157-4075-9 (paperback)
ISBN 978-0-8157-4076-6 (epub)

To the people of the Reischauer Center, past and present,
for their four-decade contribution to
international affairs.

Contents

Figures and Tables

TABLES

Preface

GEOGRAPHY IS PHYSICALLY ENDURING. And in classic geopolitical analysis, its functional significance is constant across the ages. Sir Halford Mackinder, father of geopolitics, saw Eurasia's Heartland as strategically central by virtue of where it lay, even as Nicholas Spykman, one of the founders of classical realism, prioritized its rimland periphery for similar reasons.

In reality, however, change is an unvarying aspect of our world. Human beings as a species are continually changing, as is the technology that enables us to continually navigate and make sense of our surroundings. As Heraclitus wisely observed, one cannot step into the same river twice.[1] And that is not only because *we* are changing. Human technology and interaction with the environment are changing as well.

What geography means in the contemporary world, how its practical significance changes over the years, and what such transformations ultimately mean for the nature of world affairs, have all been central concerns of my academic career for more than two decades. In thinking about the changing meaning of geography over time, I have been especially fascinated with implications for the structure and functional role in world affairs of Eurasia, the world's largest continent.

Eurasia, stretching from the Atlantic across the Middle East to China and the Pacific, is certainly expansive and centrally located in the global firmament. It is amply endowed with both resources and industrious inhabitants. And it is conspicuously a highly strategic segment of the globe of which the world's heretofore dominant superpower, America, is not physically part. Indeed, America is the *only one* of the five largest economies of the world—not to mention the five most populous—that is not located in Eurasia. Yet it has a vital interest, reflected in US grand strategy for more than a century, that no totalitarian power should gain consolidated dominance over the sprawling Eurasian land mass.

Eurasia, to be sure, has long been deeply divided internally, with major nations estranged and often divorced from one another. These persistent internal divisions prevented the massive continent from assuming the prominence on the global scene that Eurasia and its constituent nations otherwise would possess. Yet they did not preclude the possibility of greater cohesion, or negate the possibility that such cohesion could become the catalyst for broader systemic global change. Indeed, shifting assessments of Warsaw Pact solidarity; the Sino-Soviet split; and the collapse of the Soviet Union, as well as the broader significance of these developments, were a staple of international-affairs analysis as I was developing my own research agenda decades ago.

Sensing the potential global implications of a transformation in Eurasia's literally Balkanized political geography, I became intrigued with the ways in which that physically linked political-economic profile was beginning to change. From the very beginning, the changing functional role of the seas was central to my analytical concerns. In the spring of 1996, less than three years after China became an oil importer for the first time, I wrote "Asia's Empty Tank" for *Foreign Affairs*, and subsequently explored the geopolitical consequences for Asia's energy sea lanes between East Asia and the Persian Gulf in *Pacific Defense*.[2] In these early works, I found that high-speed economic growth was drawing the nations of Northeast Asia into fateful new relations with the Middle East, owing to the explosively rising energy demand across geopolitically strategic sea lanes spanning the Strait of Malacca. The United States, with its globally dominant naval forces, was a central intermediary in political-military terms, even though it had marginal energy imports from the region. Economic change on land, I concluded, was redrawing Eurasia's geopolitical map, particularly in China. Indeed, sea lanes were a vital, Promethian conduit through which that transformation of international power relationships was quietly occurring.

Sixteen years later, I returned to the reordering of Eurasian geography from a different, more terrestrial angle, in *The New Continentalism*.[3] As the ramifications of the Soviet collapse became clearer at the end of 1991, I set out to explore more concretely how politics, rather than economics in this instance, was transforming Eurasian geography—this time with a focus on changes in the functional role of land. I concluded that the Soviet demise was affording China more centrality and a chance to deepen ties across the continent, especially with Central Asia and the Middle East. Seventeen months after I wrote this assessment, Xi Jinping announced his Belt and Road Initiative.[4]

My latest exploration of geography and its real-world transformation, prior to the current work, was in *Super Continent: The Logic of Eurasian Integration*.[5] Once again, the central focus was on the dramatic transformations over land, in a post-Soviet, post–Cold War period when national borders and state regulation were changing dramatically. During the seven years following publication of *The New Continentalism*, I increasingly had come to appreciate the crucial role of technology and finance—those enablers of advanced infrastructure—in rendering the real-world meaning of geography highly malleable.

Dwelling particularly on innovations in transport logistics and infrastructure, together with streamlined physical infrastructure and border-clearance procedures flowing from expanded transcontinental political ties, I stressed how the economic feasibility of overland transport was rising. This technological change made transcontinental supply chains much more efficient and economical, thereby giving the relatively short overland (as opposed to maritime) distances across Eurasia, especially between China and Europe, enhanced geo-economic and ultimately geopolitical significance. China's explosive growth and geographic centrality within Eurasia further amplifies emerging overland relationships.

Super Continent naturally recognizes waterways in passing as an important dimension of the geographic links that bind the disparate parts of Eurasia, though it does not dwell on them.[6] It notes that sea transport has natural cost advantages over land. It also observes that for most of the five centuries and more since the demise of the classical Silk Road, sea transport has been the principal means of conveying goods and ideas across the vast distances separating Europe and Northeast Asia. All of these maritime realities have shaped my thinking.

After two major studies of overland transformations within Eurasia, my focus has returned more directly in this volume to the seas surrounding Eurasia and their rimlands, for three major reasons. First, and most importantly, the seas themselves are quietly changing in momentous yet unrecognized ways that demand urgent analytical attention. Their role as conduit for resource flows—as I was early to identify in the mid-1990s—has continued to grow, expanding beyond Northeast Asia and the Persian Gulf to involve Southeast Asia, South Asia, Australia, and Africa as well. Yet crucial new dimensions of oceanic life also have emerged, especially beneath the surface of the sea. Over the past decade, high-speed submarine fiber-optic networks have advanced rapidly, and deep-sea mining is now in imminent commercial prospect.

A second reason to focus attention on Eurasia's surrounding seas concerns the changing geo-economics and geopolitics of the sea lanes themselves. China's economic involvement within the sea lanes from Shanghai through Singapore to Suez and beyond is rising, even as the People's Liberation Army–Navy and its control over transit ports and fiber-optic communications also are growing. Similarly, the US-China rivalry is deepening, even as the stakes of European, Australian, and various other Asian actors in Eurasian sea-lane stability are rising.

I have one final motive, as an American, for pursuing an in-depth study of Eurasian sea lanes: their global geopolitical significance for America's standing in our twenty-first-century world. The United States, as noted above, is the only one of the major world powers that is not geographically a Eurasian actor in the narrow sense of the term. Some viable geopolitical presence in Eurasia, however, is crucial to America's global standing. In *Super Continent*, I concluded pessimistically that China enjoys centrality on land, with logistical, financial, and political changes on the continent likely to reinforce that dominance in coming years. I have come to realize that the Eurasian sea lanes connecting the rimlands of the continent provide the best option for sustaining an influential geopolitical role on the largest continent in the world, especially for a maritime power like the United States seeking to compensate for its lack of a direct territorial presence.

This volume will thus continue the exploration of Eurasian transformation that I began with *Pacific Defense*, *The New Continentalism*, and *Super Continent*, albeit from a new perspective. As in those three previous volumes, my concern is directed not only to developments within Eurasia itself, but equally to the implications of Eurasia's transition for America, and for the future US role in world affairs. Like the others, this book will transcend regional studies, into the insufficiently conceptualized functional examination of political geography itself.

In this research project, which has spanned nearly four years, I have been fortunate to have had the support of several gifted researchers, both at the School of Advanced International Studies at Johns Hopkins University and throughout the world. They have included Jonathan Canfield, Sir Michael Cianci, Vivian Chen, Yun Han, Dylan Harris, Amy Paik, Tom Ramage, Evan Sankey, Evan Wright, Luke Chen, Hana Anderson, Jada Fraser, Anu Anwar, Mika Mizobuchi, Shahad Turkistani, Monica Weller, Steven Wang, and Steven Zhang. Hal Brands, Toshiko Calder, Eliot Cohen, Andrew Erickson, Carla Freeman, Karl Jackson, Kenneth Juster, Jae-Seung Lee, Tom Mahnken, Jaehan

Park, David Sanger, David Shambaugh, Kotaro Shiojiri, and David Shear, among others, have provided especially useful comments. I am also indebted to Neave Denny, Devin Woods, Shannon Granville, Ezra Freeman, Shavanthi Mendis, and Yelba Quinn for important logistical and editorial support. Without all these people, this manuscript would be much the poorer, but, as the author, responsibility for any remaining defects must remain mine alone.

Although these words are the preface to a work, they also represent a conclusion, as they chronologically follow my last revisions. In a sentiment that I hope the reader will share, I have learned that, however peaceful and static the seas may at a distance seem, they are replete with energy and potential for sudden change. And I do believe that a deepened understanding of the often obscure yet increasingly dynamic developments on and under the seas of the world today will immeasurably enlighten our understanding of international relationships on land as well.

Kent E. Calder
Washington, D.C.
September 2024

Introduction

COULD THE SEAS BETWEEN YOKOHAMA AND SUEZ hold the key to the future of world affairs? Few observers three decades ago would have dreamed of such a prospect. Yet we live in a world of cataclysmic change, in which it is time to question longstanding verities from the past.

"Geography" and "transformation" are classic concerns of political and strategic analysis; both have given birth to major currents in recent thinking about international affairs. Yet these concerns are rarely linked to one another in contemporary discourse. Geography, as Yale Institute of International Studies founder Nicholas Spykman so often stressed, concerns itself with physical traits that change only slowly, though its broader sociopolitical implications have been an object of debate and research on multiple continents for 2,000 years and more.

Transformation is a sharply contrasting concept to geography. The former is a notion with classical roots, but of much more recent currency among international relations scholars than geography itself, reflecting the accelerating pace of change in our increasingly global world. Such myriad recent geoeconomic changes are fateful not only for the Eurasian continent but for world affairs as a whole.

Eurasia's sea lanes are, of course, a natural topic for global political-economic analysis, if only because of the massive scale of the adjacent continent. Eurasia is by far the largest land mass on earth, covering more than 40 percent of the entire globe's terrestrial surface. Literally a Super Continent, Eurasia is also home to well over half of the world's people, including the inhabitants of China, India, and Indonesia—three of the four most populous nations on earth. These countries naturally import explosively growing amounts of commodities, finished goods, and even information via the sea. Eurasia is likewise home to five of the eight nuclear weapons states worldwide, as well as to eight of the ten largest standing armies on earth. In addition, Eurasia also generates more than 60 percent of global gross domestic product (GDP).

Although Eurasia is a massive land mass, it also has a crucially important maritime dimension. The continent is surrounded, in intimate embrace, by the world's largest seas—in the east by the Pacific; in the west by the Atlantic; and in the south by the Indian, as indicated in Figure I-1. It is also bounded in the north by the still quiescent Arctic Ocean. And Eurasia's rimlands, especially those on the south and east, are among the most populous, rapidly growing, and ocean-dependent on earth. Maritime Eurasia is an arena where sea and land, in their dialectic, hold fateful keys to the global future.

China, as Figure I.1 suggests, holds a pivotal position on land within Eurasia, especially as its dominance over Russia and Central Asia rises in the face of Ukraine-related Western sanctions. The Eurasian seas—once a Western redoubt, when Britain ruled the waves—are now a much more complex picture whose future could determine global dominance. Western advantages, including America's blue-water navy (both above and beneath the surface of the sea) as well as strategic basing, are finely balanced against Chinese dual-use capabilities and dynamic expansion of shipbuilding, ports, and fiber-optic cable infrastructure. Russia's dominant presence in the Arctic could gain geopolitical consequence in future years, as global warming proceeds.

One might legitimately ask why the analytic focus on this work is Eurasian maritime politics, rather than those of the Indo-Pacific. The latter, after all, is currently the more fashionable and well-recognized term in popular discourse. There are three basic reasons, grounded in the distinctive analytic concerns of this volume. First, we are centrally concerned with the possible changes in world affairs that might critically challenge US global preeminence. Second, we are focused on how those adversarial relations play out on the sea and in its rimlands—not only or even centrally in the Indian or Pacific Oceans, but also in smaller, geopolitically contested maritime bodies, including the Mediterranean, the Red Sea, the Bay of Bengal, and even the Black Sea. Finally, we intend to systematically compare geopolitical developments on sea and on land, which is much more feasible when applying a common, well-developed concept in both instances, as I do in this volume and in *Super Continent*, my previous Eurasian study.[1]

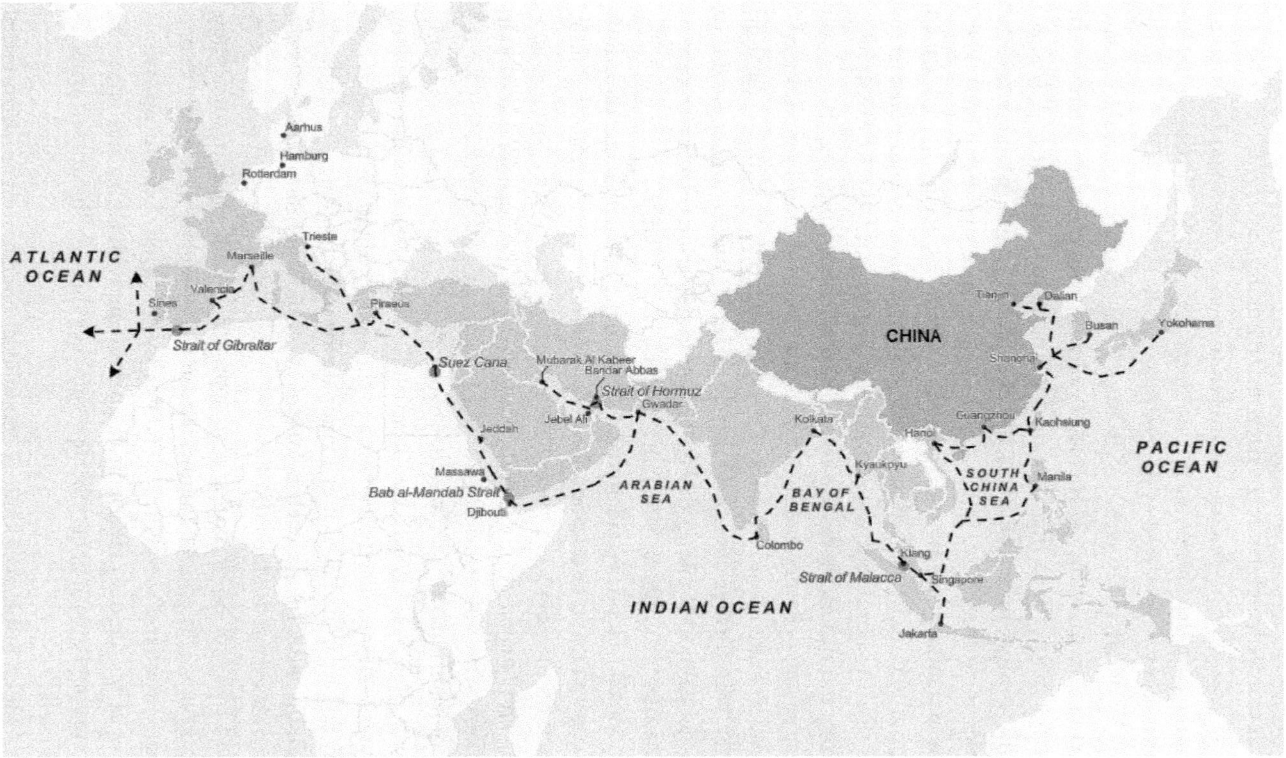

FIGURE I.I Maritime Eurasia and its adjacent sea lanes

SOURCES: Esri, HERE, Garmin, United Nations Food and Agriculture Organization (FAO), US National Oceanic and Atmospheric Administration (NOAA), US Geological Survey (USGS), © OpenStreetMap contributors, and the GIS User Community.

Literature Review

Geopoliticians with a global focus have thus naturally shown special concern for Eurasia, and must pay increasing attention to its sea lanes and rimlands in future. In the past, they were much more terra-centric. British geographer Sir Halford Mackinder conceived of the continent as the "world island," inevitably central to world affairs by virtue of its scale in the terrestrial world.[2] He saw the center of Eurasia, or the "heartland," as a literal pivot point for international relations as a whole. Even the renowned US naval strategist Alfred T. Mahan, despite his stronger maritime focus, did consider at length Asian continental geopolitics, including Central Asia and its importance to Russia. He understood the potential strategic importance of China, especially if well-armed and consolidated under unified leadership.[3] Mahan, however, also noted in his writings that the continent was chronically divided, and saw its divisions— prefiguring the observations of the political scientist Zbigniew Brzezinski three-quarters of a century later—as a strategic reality of global significance.[4]

Mackinder's logic was readily adopted by German geopoliticians, notably Karl Haushofer, who further developed the "heartland" concept and applied it to German geopolitical thinking during the interwar period. Haushofer stressed the notion of a "continental bloc," including Germany, Russia, and Japan.[5] The Germans took Mackinder's underlying insights in perverse and tragic directions, including as a strategic justification for their eastern policies, culminating in the 1941 attack on the Soviet Union and the Holocaust itself. Many Japanese neo-fascist thinkers likewise focused on the importance of the Eurasian heartland in global affairs, with militarist leaders using it variously as a justification for the invasion of Manchuria in 1931 and the attack on China proper six years later.[6]

For years after World War II, the "heartland" variant of geopolitical thinking about Eurasia fell into ill-repute, owing to the way in which militarists in both Germany and Japan had used it as a rationale for indiscriminate attacks on the Soviet Union and China as well as for the oppression of minorities across the continent. Heartland thinking did, however, regain some currency in the Soviet Union and later post-Soviet Russia as an approach to justifying Russian central-ity in world affairs. Alexander Dugin, for example, insistently stressed the notion of Russian "heartland" centrality, as did Sergey Karaganov.[7] Some also would see echoes of Mackinder in Vladimir Putin's entente with China and aggressive efforts to restore Russian geopolitical prominence through "heartland" consoli-dation as well.

In the United States, Mackinder's geopolitical emphasis on Eurasian global centrality also proved influential, but was taken in a very different direction, mainly by thinkers of European origin. The Dutch American geostrategist Nicholas Spykman accepted the general notion of Eurasian strategic central-ity, though he stressed the importance of nations at the edge of the continent, arrayed in a southerly crescent around the Eurasian heartland. He viewed this rimland, similar to our concept of Maritime Eurasia, as a crucial pivot region between the United States, located outside Europe, and the Eurasian heartland-based Soviet Union itself.[8] As Spykman noted, the rimland "functions as a vast buffer zone of conflict between sea power and land power."[9] Well over 30 years later, Zbigniew Brzezinski likewise recognized the importance of the Eurasian rimland. He also suggested the strategic necessity for the United States of balancing against that rimland through alliances such as NATO and various bilateral security arrangements across the Pacific.[10] Yet neither Brzezinski nor the other distinguished geostrategists mentioned above clearly foresaw the emergence of China as a primary strategic competitor to the United States, or the danger that it might closely align with other Eurasian powers, such as Russia and Iran.

The vigorous international-relations theoretical debate of the past five decades and more regarding hegemonic stability and global system transformation has run parallel to the largely terra-centric work of geopolitical thinkers regarding Eurasia, and only rarely have both concepts come near to intersecting.[11] How, scholars have been asking, does one system of international order transform itself into another? How and why do empires—and other hegemonic systems—from the Persian to the Roman, to the Anglo-American—rise and fall?[12] How can hegemonic stability in world affairs be sustained?

Classical global systems-transformation debates have been conducted mainly at a general, abstract level that transcends the empirical details of transition on any one continent. Robert Gilpin, for example, argued that major systemic changes necessarily occurred through hegemonic conflicts, from the Napoleonic Wars through World War II.[13] Robert Keohane contended that transnational understandings and the emergence of intergovernmental organizations (IGOs) could sharply reduce the likelihood of hegemonic conflict.[14] From an economic history perspective, Charles Kindleberger argued in complementary fashion that every international system requires a stabilizer, and that the global profile of system stability and transformation will be determined by the presence or absence of such a hegemonic power.[15] Looking at US-China relations, Graham Allison situated his analysis of the two countries in a broader analytical context, with major implications for the future of global affairs.[16] However, Allison did not have system transformation as a central focus or deal in detail with how developments in either the United States or China drive such an outcome. The emphasis rather is on the prospects for US–China conflict itself, not on likely outcomes or systemic implications.

Although grand theories of systems transformation in international political economy have given only limited consideration to concrete, geography-specific analysis, historical treatments have suffered from a converse failure to adequately consider the systemic implications of the phenomena they describe. Their analyses also have been consistently terra-centric. Cold War historians, for example, often direct attention to intra-Eurasian geopolitical developments, such as the Sino-Soviet split of the 1950s through the 1970s, and of efforts by American policymakers such as Henry Kissinger and Zbigniew Brzezinski to reshape that continental order. Others have examined the country-specific political-economic transformations unfolding on the continent. Those show, as we shall see, how the rising dependence of China on energy and trade along sea lanes to its west across the Indian Ocean generates new forms of geo-economic leverage and competition on and under the oceans that countervail trends on land.

Few analysts of any discipline have focused in holistic fashion on the linkage between discrete diplomatic initiatives and the macroscopic process of system change. This volume helps to complete the picture by providing insights into a crucial and long-neglected part of the Eurasian political economy—the geopolitics of the sea lanes, especially between Suez and Singapore, together with the global implications of their quiet recent transformation into a bustling thoroughfare for international trade.

A few Cold War historians have developed more holistic views of system maintenance and transformation, generally focusing on US policy.[17] Melvyn Leffler, for example, argued that US policy even before the conclusion of World War II envisioned an extensive system of overseas bases, a strategic realm of influence in the Western Hemisphere, and above all a balance of power in Eurasia. American policymakers, he contended, had come during the war to appreciate a disconcerting strategic danger—that an adversary or coalition of adversaries dominating Eurasia could integrate the resources, industrial infrastructure, and skilled labor of Europe and Asia into a war machine that could challenge the United States, wage protracted war, and gravely endanger American national security.[18]

The Problem for Analysis: America, Eurasia, and Hegemonic Stability

The copious recent literature on global system transformation naturally has focused on the United States and its changing role in world affairs—both because for close to a generation the United States was the world's sole hegemon, and also because such a large share of scholarship on such matters has been American. Yet the United States, despite its immense dynamism, comprises a declining share of global population and economic activity.[19] As the Cold War and its geopolitical correlate in the US-Soviet duopoly recede into history and new powers arise, analysts must search for new, less Washington-centric paradigms of global change. Could not the continent that is home to all the major global powers other than the United States instead become a central catalyst for systems transformation in world affairs?

Prospects for such a development depend on how coherent Eurasia itself is, or can become. Brzezinski posed the issue sharply in the mid-1990s when he observed that "cumulatively, Eurasia's power vastly overshadows America's. Fortunately for America, Eurasia is too big to be politically one."[20] Over the past three decades, however, much has changed both on the Eurasian continent and especially in its surrounding seas. China has risen, while Russia has grown both more truculent and more collaborative with China, as the dramatic February 2022 Xi Jinping–Vladimir Putin summit declaration of "unlimited partnership"—shortly before the Russian invasion of Ukraine—suggested.[21] Do the prospects of Eurasian disunion that Brzezinski so confidently foresaw in 1997 continue to prevail?

The Seas and Global System Transformation

Both *The New Continentalism* and *Super Continent* observed, somewhat pessimistically during the 2010s, that developments of the post–Cold War years have strengthened China's continental position on land and potentially in world affairs as a result.[22] This strengthening of continentalist trends long preceded Xi Jinping's Belt and Road Initiative (BRI) and its push for greater Chinese influence in Eurasia. The question remains, however, of whether developments by sea—where the Anglo-Saxon powers traditionally have been strong—can counterbalance this prospect. Surprisingly little research has been done on the geopolitical transformation of Maritime Eurasia: the continent's rimlands and surrounding seas. This area and the changes it has experienced are the point of departure for this book.

The seas, of course, have a different geopolitical consistency and relationship to grand strategy than the land. Unlike the land, as Julian Corbett has pointed out, the seas are not subject to ownership, as humans do not live there.[23] Conversely, the seas are naturally a realm of potentially intense competition, where technological competence can make its mark. The seas also can serve as critical enablers—indeed, determinants—of prosperity and even livelihood on land, making maritime access of critical economic importance, especially to populous and growing nations.

As Mahan suggested, the seas are thus "great highways," providing efficient transport across vast distances.[24] They can be powerful thoroughfares, both for food and energy flows above the surface and for information flows below. And the seas can also, as John Mearsheimer observes, serve conversely as geopolitically significant moats, critically shaping the strategy of nations along their shores.[25]

As we shall see in the coming pages, naval might, particularly in its subsurface dimension, is moving increasingly to the heart of competition in international affairs. Its dual-use correlates—ports, shipping, and the maritime defense-industrial base—are growing more important as well. As the land powers of Eurasia deepen their terrestrial ties, capabilities at sea, leveraged by the tactical flexibility that seapower provides, are becoming vital for maritime powers, including the Quad nations of the Indo-Pacific and likeminded regional powers.

This book's theoretical starting point is the work of Nicholas Spykman, who pointed to the amphibious nature of the rimland states of Eurasia, many of them populous and dynamic.[26] The pivotal positions of these Maritime Eurasian nations, sandwiched between land and sea, have created definite security challenges for them. Yet geography also has made such rimland countries natural entry points for intermodal transportation, including both ports and cable-landing stations, facilitating globalization and an explosive recent expansion of economic connectivity. Geopolitical positioning has thus made Maritime Asia a potentially central catalyst in the twenty-first-century struggle for economic development and efficient commercial exchange. Rimlands, after all, have prospective geopolitical flexibility in their international trajectory. They can orient toward either the land or the sea, adding to the global significance of their international decision-making.

In Spykman's World War II era lectures, delivered eight decades ago, he presciently identified the broader geopolitical importance of Eurasia's southern periphery—especially for a nascent superpower not territorially established on the continent, such as the United States. Modern audiences, however, might not ascribe as much importance to several of the areas he indicated as strategically vital rimlands, including monsoon-prone portions of South and Southeast Asia. Maritime Asia is rapidly regaining strategic importance, however, owing to its accelerating growth and rising population, as well as the deepening challenges that its growth poses to the global environment and to world energy and food supplies in particular. Nearby offshore neighbors to these rimland nations, including Britain, Japan, and Indonesia, which Spykman saw as part of the "outer crescent" rather than the rimland, have become more functionally important than even Spykman might have expected, in part because of their proximity to sea lanes.

Our most important difference with Spykman concerns the relative geopolitical priority he placed on land and sea. Like most geopolitical analysts, Spykman focused heavily on the functional importance of land areas in international affairs, even as he highlighted rimlands, and failed to fully appreciate the maritime.[27] Yet in the twenty-first century's global political economy—three-quarters of a century after Spykman was writing—the seas themselves are growing in functional importance globally for three major reasons. The first is the expansion of international commodity trade, especially in bulk commodities such as energy, food, and raw materials. Per-capita consumption is low but rising steadily across the densely populated South and Southeast Asian nations located astride the sea lanes, and their sizeable populations multiply the aggregate impact of any incremental increase. Indian oil import dependency, for example, rose from 77 percent in 2010 to 87 percent in 2023. India's aggregate oil demand is expected to reach close to 9 million barrels per day (bbl/day) by 2046.[28] All this energy commerce—like food and industrial commodities—flows in and out over the seas.

The second reason the Eurasian seas are steadily growing more important geo-economically is the expansion of trade in manufactures, fueled by the rise of container shipping. This growth is further enhancing the commercial importance of the sea lanes, especially those to and from China. Technological developments, ranging from the advent of robotics and advances in submarine technology to the coming of the internet, are a third factor to consider in the world beneath the seas in both economic and military dimensions. More than 95 percent of global internet traffic, for example, flows physically beneath the seas via fiber-optic cables, thereby enhancing the importance of the world beneath the seas in both economic and military-strategic dimensions.

All these trends are pronounced in the Eurasian sea lanes, bordering the most populous, rapidly growing, and most energy-consuming continent in the world. Eurasia is now home to more than 5 billion people—greater than 70 percent of the human race. Most live in close proximity to the sea, and they are now beginning to experience the internet-driven information revolution. The continent is also home to four of the six largest energy-consuming countries in the world—all of the top global consumers apart from the United States.[29] And these consumers overwhelmingly source their energy through seaborne imports, mainly from the Middle East.

Two authoritarian states, China and Russia, are consolidating land power on this largest continent. When coupled with the underlying advantages of sea power relative to land, including transportation cost and flexibility of destinations, it is especially pressing to understand geopolitical dynamics in Maritime Eurasia—which includes the continent's surrounding seas and their adjacent rimlands. Many states have economic and strategic incentives to use the seas where possible. The geo-economic and geopolitical role of the waterways circumnavigating continents like Eurasia from both the south, across the Indian Ocean, and in future from the north, across the Arctic, makes the pivotal role of the sea lanes in Eurasia's emerging geopolitics a topic of paramount analytic importance. It is in Maritime Eurasia—the pivotal rimland nations along the west, south, and east of the continent—where the rising weight on land of the authoritarians can be most effectively balanced and offset. As Mahan pointed out at the turn of the twentieth century, "land power is modified by the proximity of the sea."[30]

An Emerging Agenda for Research: Geo-Economic Implications of Land vs. Sea

To fully appreciate the important role of sea lanes—peripheral to the rimlands, yet interacting intimately with them—one must first consider the contrasting geo-economics of land and sea transport. Both have very different costs and benefits. The geo-economic meaning of land transport and communications, as opposed to sea, can be conceptualized in useful transactional terms.[31] The infrastructure required for overland transport—railways, highways, or pipelines, for example—entails considerable capital expenditures. It also commits the user to a fixed geographic route and creates the strong probability of iterated transactions along such a route. With overland infrastructure comes trade, and often regulations, as well as taxation. Maritime transport, by contrast, implies freer and less constrained patterns of economic interaction. Once maritime passengers or cargo leave a given port, their transactional options are far broader than on land. Even where routing is relatively fixed, as by fiber-optic cable, commodity flows (in this case, information) are largely unconstrained by national regulation. The ability of governments to regulate maritime interactions of virtually all varieties tends to be limited. And bulk transportation by sea—crucial for energy, food, and raw materials—tends to be much cheaper and often more efficient than overland alternatives.

In the Eurasian context, land transport has a few latent advantages that may countervail the flexibilities, economies, and freedom provided by its maritime counterpart. As I found in *Super Continent*, the major coastal ports of Western

Europe and Northeast Asia, such as Shanghai and Rotterdam, are as much as 30 percent closer by land than by sea. Overland transport costs per physical unit conveyed, however, inevitably are much higher than for sea transport owing to the nature of the transport itself. Even in 2020, the cost of shipping one 20-foot standard cargo container (known as a twenty-foot equivalent unit, or TEU) from China to Europe was around $20,000 by air and $7,500 by rail, but only $1,500 by sea.[32] Following the COVID crisis, similar ratios also prevailed in 2024.[33]

The speed and convenience of overland transport has improved somewhat over the past decade. Political obstacles to transcontinental trade, including tariffs and border clearance restrictions, have fallen sharply. Meanwhile, containerization, internet communication, real-time inventory management, and improved infrastructure have improved both delivery times and predictability while significantly reducing costs.[34] Today, rail transport from Europe to China takes only eleven to eighteen days, compared with thirty days by sea.[35] These overland dynamics have, however, been complicated since early 2022 by the Ukraine conflict and the resulting sanctions against Russia. Both the NATO (North Atlantic Treaty Organization) members and the major democratic states of Northeast Asia have terminated most financial transactions and transit trade with Russia and Belarus. Some overland service between East Asia and Europe via Kazakhstan has continued, but rising transaction costs and proliferating regulations have inhibited, at least temporarily, the expansion of overland Eurasian trade.

The Enduring Importance of the Seas

Overland transport and intellectual exchange within Eurasia, so actively promoted by China's BRI, thus faces enormous challenges from maritime competitors concentrated in the rimlands and operating in the peripheral seas. Maritime Eurasian commercial operators like Maersk, many traditionally based in Europe, enjoy incomparable flexibility and freedom in defining their political-economic options, as do their naval counterparts. Warships can be engaged in friendship diplomacy one day and fighting pirates or terrorists the next.

Water transport also enjoys an uncontestable underlying cost advantage relative to overland transport in terms of weight; it is hard to conceive of how that cost advantage could be overcome. From an integrated transport cost/elapsed time perspective, overland rail is now competitive with air but still a long way from being competitive with sea. And fiber-optic cables beneath the sea have formidable, enduring advantages in the informatics sphere that would be very difficult to overcome.

Because it is possible to transport even extremely heavy cargo, including virtually any type of bulk commodity, by water over long distances cheaply, conventional water transport still has considerable potential scale economies. Across the post–World War II period, innovations already have reduced long-distance water-transport costs remarkably. Indeed, the advent of 300,000-ton supertankers carrying upward of 2 million barrels of oil, and massive ore carriers of similar scale have made it economically feasible to transport oil, bauxite, and iron ore by water halfway around the world, from the Persian Gulf and the Amazon, to efficiently fuel the refineries and blast furnaces of the industrialized world.[36] This unprecedented economy of bulk marine transport steadily fueled the explosive growth of basic industry along Eurasia's eastern rim over the past three decades. And unexploited potential economies still remain in port construction and scale, related logistics, and other dimensions of both shipping and shipbuilding.

Economies of scale and speed of transmission are multiplied manyfold in underwater fiber-optic transmissions that move virtually with the speed of light, and are ideal for iterative transactions with sophisticated data centers located even thousands of miles distant. Technical innovations since the late 1980s are making undersea internet communication ever more financially attractive, compared to satellite alternatives.[37]

Eurasia's own distinctive socioeconomic transformation over the past three decades has greatly enhanced the importance of the sea lanes, both within Eurasia itself and in international affairs more generally. To understand why the sea lanes have risen so sharply in importance, it is important to recall not only technological change, but also the continent's demography and population distribution. China, India, Indonesia, Pakistan, and Bangladesh—five of the six most populous nations in the world—are Maritime Eurasian and concentrated almost next to one another along the Indo-Pacific sea lanes. All have low but rapidly rising propensity to consume energy, feed grains, and manufacturing-related bulk commodities. They also have relatively low rates of internet penetration. Their use of the Eurasian sea lanes for consumption, as well as industrial and informational purposes, is thus destined to grow, not least because of their general proximity to the sources of supply.

The same revolution in transport logistics that radically altered the cost calculus of overland transport in the first decade of the twenty-first century has likewise revolutionized the "last mile" of maritime container transport, between the water's edge and inland conveyance. This change has provoked major changes in port configuration across Maritime Eurasia, as well as in the design of shipment containers. Such infrastructural improvements, where realized, are helping to restore an uneasy balance between land and sea transport costs for longer distances as well.

In important areas such as port management practices, containerization, and intermodalism, the same technological advances in logistics that have radically reduced the cost of overland transport over the past ten to fifteen years also are creating new opportunities for maritime alternatives.[38] These new advances in logistics, if implemented in the major ports of the world, may help repel the assault by long-distance overland transport on the sea's traditional dominance in shipping and usher in a more complex era of intermodal transport. Logistical progress at strategic nodal ports such as Singapore, Colombo, Port Said, and Piraeus—all astride major Indo-European supply lines—are of special relevance to sea-lane competitiveness.

The Information Revolution amplifies the importance of the seas still further. For the past three decades, internet transactions have flowed with increasing intensity beneath the oceans of the world, as a proliferation of landing stations and overland cables has broadened the access they provide. The transformative effect of subsea cables on international connectivity and economic progress is especially pronounced in developing rimland Eurasian countries like Pakistan, Myanmar, Bangladesh, and Sri Lanka, as their internet connectivity rises from an extremely low base.[39]

Sea Transport and Geopolitics

The land-sea transport debate naturally has a geopolitical dimension, with important Eurasian dimensions, as noted above. Of late, the most dramatic complicating effects are on land. The geopolitical aspects are clearly manifest within Eurasia. Overland transport moves primarily by rail across soft authoritarian states (China, Russia, and Central Asian nations) into Europe, giving such states leverage over land-based international commerce. Within Europe itself, those most receptive to overland routes are also semi-democratic or soft authoritarian states, such as Serbia, Hungary, and Belarus, that either are outside the European Union or stand precariously within it.

The Ukraine conflict has begun to seriously disrupt several of the overland routes, especially those passing through Russia. It also has hampered the use of the energy pipelines between Russia and Europe, making Europe much more dependent on the sea lanes for energy supply. As the resulting sanctions and enduring political tensions of the Ukraine conflict cause serious harm to the global standing of the authoritarians in Russia and Belarus, their ability to serve as distribution centers for the surrounding regions likewise may be affected.

Because land transport moves directly across political boundaries, it is deeply interrelated with the domestic politics of individual nation states. And the jurisdictions it traverses are, in the main, antagonistic to or at most only loosely aligned with American security interests. Those inside the European Union and NATO have the capacity to serve as veto players within Western institutions, depriving those institutions of resilience in responding to challenges from the East. The problems alliance leaders in Brussels and Washington encounter in dealing with recalcitrant national politicians in Ankara and Budapest are only illustrations of the larger problem inherent in relying on the goodwill of individual states where collective action is required.

Contrasting to the situation across land, Maritime Eurasian commerce is growing more rapidly, driven by the commodity trade required to service the large and growing populations in developing Asia. Maritime commerce also is stimulated on the European side by overland pipeline disruptions caused by the war in Ukraine, such as the termination of the Nord Stream 1 and 2 energy pipelines under the Baltic Sea. As the Ukraine conflict has shown, the sea lanes between Europe and Northeast Asia, like those across the Atlantic, generally are less vulnerable to geopolitical disruption than the land routes. Those sea lanes are also (so far) clearly the province of the great maritime powers, preeminently the United States and the United Kingdom. Given the deepening estrangement of the G-7 powers from the Eurasian continental states, especially Russia, and the intensification of Sino-American tensions, this Western dominance of the sea lanes is of increasing global strategic importance even as developing nations' economic reliance on the seas continues to grow.

The global economy's heavy dependence on the Eurasian sea lanes for energy imports flowing from the Persian Gulf—as well as for broader commercial requirements, including food supply—makes this Western maritime dominance of continuing international geo-economic relevance and strategic importance. At present, these sea lanes operate primarily around the southern rimland of Eurasia, linking the Mediterranean to the Persian Gulf and ultimately to the East China Sea. In the coming years, they also could span the Arctic seas to the north of Eurasia as global warming continues to melt the polar ice.

The Eurasian sea lanes are not, however, without their own geopolitical complexities, especially beneath the waves. Even though the seas, as Corbett points out, may not be subject to national ownership, precisely for that reason they are unusually vulnerable to hybrid action by gray-zone actors. Undersea cables or pipelines can be tapped or cut easily, and often surreptitiously. As their geo-economic importance grows, such gray-zone activities become increasingly attractive forms of hybrid warfare, especially as nuclear escalation grows more and more constrained.[40] These critical sea lanes connecting the east and west of Eurasia, especially between Suez and Singapore, thus clearly appear as the strategic core of any Eurasian political economy capable of assuming regional coherence. The fate of those sea lanes, in both surface and subsea dimensions, will profoundly shape the future of the continent as a whole. They will be especially central to Eurasia's transcontinental connectivity.[41]

Those sea lanes and their adjacent littoral are, in reality, the functional equivalent today of Spykman's rimland in years past. From the Napoleonic Wars until 1945, the preeminent rimland power was Great Britain. Since World War II, that fateful mantle within Eurasia has devolved upon the United States, even though it is an extracontinental power. Simply put, America's sea lane preeminence preserves the formidable rimland linkages between Western Europe and Northeast Asia that prevent a powerful counterweight to US influence from emerging within the contiguous geographic core of Eurasia itself. The future of Maritime Eurasia, in the face of China's rising presence, could thus profoundly shape the stability of the world as we will know it in future years.

The Eurasian Sea Lanes and American Globalism

In light of expanding Chinese influence across Eurasia on land in response to China's centrality, economic dynamism, and grand strategy through the BRI, key geopolitical questions for the twenty-first century emerge: Can America respond by sea? And if so, what might its response strategy be? And how might that strategy involve key Asian stakeholders?

Few would question the current dominance of the US Navy on the deep-blue waters of the world, including the Indian Ocean. With eleven aircraft carriers supported by sophisticated carrier battle groups, the US Navy has global blue-water capabilities incomparably superior to those of any other major power. With a powerful submarine fleet and advanced sonar technologies, as well as expertise with unmanned submersible vehicles, it also retains superior capabilities in the increasingly important underwater dimension.

China is a rising runner-up, but in Eurasian maritime affairs it remains less influential at present than the United States. In terms of blue-water capabilities, Beijing has two operational aircraft carriers—less than a fifth of America's total.[42] Those assets are far less sophisticated than the US version, even though China is building more advanced carriers, including nuclear-powered models that it had not possessed before. China's submarines are likewise slower and noisier, with weaker sonar-detection capabilities. Even though China and Russia show signs of deepening naval collaboration and related technological transfer, the US-China asymmetries in naval capacity along the Eurasian sea lanes continue to be substantial, especially west of Singapore.[43]

Apart from raw naval capabilities, the United States also has a basing structure that dominates important maritime chokepoints across Maritime Eurasia and powerfully complements its imposing hardware.[44] This basing network generates powerful leverage against China, constraining the latter's strategic options and undercutting its power-projection capability at sea. The US basing structure in the Indo-Pacific is anchored in the east at Pearl Harbor, home to the Pacific Fleet. Another formidable pillar is Yokosuka, once the headquarters of the Imperial Japanese Navy at the entrance to Tokyo Bay. Yokosuka also is now the home port of the US carrier *George Washington*, an indicator of the sharp transformation in Japan's geopolitical role across the twentieth century.[45] America's basing profile also includes powerful air bases along the periphery of China, at Kadena in Okinawa and Osan in Korea, as well as naval support facilities at White Beach in Okinawa. Further south, the United States has ship-repair facilities and equipment prepositioning capable of servicing carriers in Singapore, and a formidable southern strongpoint at Diego Garcia, deep in the Indian Ocean. America's western anchor is the Fifth Fleet, based in Bahrain, together with an outpost in Djibouti, and the Sixth Fleet, commanding the Mediterranean.

Complementing the formidable US basing network and hardware capabilities as tools for dominating the Eurasian sea lanes are the United States' broader system-dominance capabilities. There is the United States' global satellite surveillance network, with the US-owned Global Positioning System (GPS). There is American control of global finance, through the SWIFT financial reporting system. There is American dominance of undersea fiber-optic networks. Moreover, there is the nuclear dimension, including potent US undersea capabilities. US nuclear submarines—including ballistic-missile submarines (SSBNs), cruise-missile submarines (SSGNs), and fast-attack submarines—project power beneath the seas for long periods.[46] Many of them also pack more firepower than their surface-fleet counterparts, even as they maintain far greater invulnerability.[47]

In the years to come, US military capabilities will be further enhanced by alliance arrangements such as the AUKUS agreement among the United States, the United Kingdom, and Australia.[48] US strengths in regional theaters such as the Indo-Pacific are complemented by dominant potential at the global level as well. American defense spending, after all, is greater than that of the next ten nations combined.[49] And that pattern of US preeminence has persisted for decades.

The Challenge of Allied Indo-Pacific Maritime Defense

For all its capabilities, however, US naval power confronts deepening challenges, as we shall see in this volume. A peer competitor is rising, in the form of the Chinese People's Liberation Army–Navy (PLA-N), which increasingly is allied with its Russian counterpart. This Chinese competitor now has the largest fleet of naval vessels on earth. Although it is inferior qualitatively to the United States and lacks real combat experience, it has the luxury of being able to concentrate on nearby hotspots like Taiwan, while its US counterpart confronts a more global range of tasks. The United States is also plagued by budgetary shortfalls and an aging fleet, even as it enters a perilous period later this decade of refurbishing its strategic forces.[50]

Parochial US economic interests, furthermore, do not center on the Eurasian sea lanes. Remarkably little American commerce, other than military procurement, flows by sea to destinations between Suez and Singapore. Indeed, only 2 percent of US imports and 2 percent of US exports flow to and from the strategically important Persian Gulf nations. US petroleum imports from Gulf countries—the core of American trade with the Gulf—have fallen steeply since 2010, to around 10 percent of total US petroleum imports in 2023.[51]

The primary commerce in the Eurasian sea lanes today, conversely, is the export of Persian Gulf oil and gas to Asia, and secondarily to Europe. In this respect it is thus China and Maritime Eurasia—*not* the United States—that are most heavily economically engaged. And that imbalance of flows is increasing, as a growing Asia draws in more commodities. Northeast Asia, especially Japan and Korea, remains deeply dependent on the Gulf for crude oil and liquefied natural gas (LNG). Similar trends are emerging in South and Southeast Asia as well.

The energy-rich United States, however, responds to a different equation. In 2023, for instance, Japan and South Korea procured 95 percent and 74 percent, respectively, of their crude oil imports from the Persian Gulf, compared with China's Gulf-sourced import dependency of over 48 percent. Persian Gulf LNG dependency for the three were 9, 33, and 26 percent, respectively.[52] The United States, by contrast, imports fewer and fewer hydrocarbons, and conversely is becoming the world's largest LNG exporter, accounting for 21 percent of prospective global exports in 2023.[53] The bulk of those US exports flow eastward to Europe, rather than westward to Asia. Precisely because of Maritime Eurasia's continuing dependence on these Eurasian sea lanes, as well as the United States' central role in assuring smooth, uninterrupted navigation there, the US maritime-security role in the Eurasian sea lanes generates important influence with its allies, and other rimland states as well. The shared interest in freedom of navigation—and in the question of whether US leadership can sustain it—is pervasive.

China's Competing Vision at Sea

As suggested above, China's geo-economic concerns in the Eurasian sea lanes differ greatly from those of the United States. In an economic sense, China's needs are much more immediate: it is the largest oil importer in the world, taking in over 11 million bbl/day in 2023.[54] The ratio of such offshore Chinese dependency is steadily rising. By 2030, the International Energy Agency predicts that China will import around 13 million bbl/day, comprising close to 80 percent of its domestic consumption.[55]

Apart from resource import commitments, China is rapidly gaining the panoply of disparate overseas obligations that major powers around the world acquire as their overseas presence matures. Large powers typically have citizens overseas who require protection from turbulence abroad—in recent years, for example, China has been forced to evacuate its citizens from local instability in Libya, Yemen, and Ukraine.[56] Also high on Beijing's priority list are pressing Taiwan toward reunification; along with expanding PLA-N capabilities closer to those of the US Navy in order to redress the continuing strategic imbalance between the two nations.[57]

For the past two decades, as its economy has grown and its energy consumption has risen, China has faced the deepening challenge of the Malacca Dilemma. The oil it imports from the Persian Gulf must traverse the Indian Ocean and pass through the Strait of Malacca to reach Chinese ports. China has struggled mightily to find ways around this dilemma, such as by investing in its China–Pakistan Economic Corridor (CPEC) alliance with Pakistan and a pipeline across Myanmar to Yunnan, by exploring possibilities for a Northern Sea Route in the Arctic, and by considering proposals for Kra Canal across Thailand as potential long-term options. All of these alternatives, however, confront political-economic obstacles, leaving the United States and its allies with continuing maritime leverage against China.

China's Malacca Dilemma has a new twenty-first-century dimension: information sovereignty. More than 95 percent of the world's internet traffic, including that of China, flows through fiber-optic cables beneath the oceans. These undersea cables are laid through the same strategic chokepoints, including the

Strait of Malacca, used by Chinese ships, and largely are under the control of Western multinational high-tech firms. Achieving sovereign control over information flows for both security and economic purposes is another deepening maritime challenge for Beijing.

Under Xi Jinping, China has moved in recent years to arrest its growing dependence on resource imports and foreign undersea cables. It has done so through structural transformation toward a less resource-intensive economy; expanded digital infrastructure construction; and policies of "dual circulation," intended to delink the traded and nontraded components of the Chinese economy.[58] Such policies have begun to blunt the rapid rise of an interdependence with the world that otherwise would deepen China's strategic vulnerabilities, particularly with respect to energy, microchips, and other advanced technology. Yet the pace of Chinese growth and rising domestic consumption have made it painfully difficult to avoid its heavy dependence on global networks beyond its control—a determined shift toward alternate energy notwithstanding.

For China, in short, the Eurasian sea lanes—especially those between Shanghai and the Persian Gulf—have an immediate geo-economic importance that they do not hold for the United States. Over the longer term, they also are a crucial link for China to the Eurasian rimlands of South and Southeast Asia, the Persian Gulf, and Western Europe, all of which are crucial to global leverage with the United States. That importance of the rimlands may well grow should Chinese per-capita commodity consumption continue to rise. Yet China lacks the offshore national-security infrastructure, namely the overseas military bases and dedicated military communications networks, to adequately support its rising overseas commitments. This imbalance has inspired a determined Chinese effort to expand defensive capabilities across the Indo-Pacific in both the military and political-economic spheres, provoking a deepening and broad-based maritime competition with the United States.

New imperatives of maritime defense are arising below the seas, as well as on their surface. These flow from the changing strategic balance, in which China has rising strength in its nearby seas and adjacent rimlands. Defense imperatives also flow from new countervailing opportunities beneath the sea itself. These are epitomized in the collaborative AUKUS project, linking US, British, and Australian submarine development, production, and deployment activities, with a special focus on the Indo-Pacific.

How that US-China competition in the Eurasian sea lanes will evolve, from Yokohama to Southampton, and what the most appropriate US response should be, are key concerns of our research here. These sea lanes, like the Eurasian continent itself, are far from American shores. And the domestic American resources to respond to new challenges are limited. Yet a collective response with hybrid military and nonmilitary dimensions, conducted jointly by the United States and key Indo-Pacific allies, could well significantly shape the global future. Such a response will need to include a combination of credible threats and credible assurances, as game theorist Thomas Schelling suggested decades ago.[59]

Key Concepts in Eurasian Maritime Geopolitics

The central analytical concerns of this volume are macropolitical: understanding the post–Cold War transformation in Eurasia's sea lanes between Northeast Asia and Europe, while assessing the global implications thereof. To systematically assess the geopolitical implications of these historic political-economic transformations, however, it is useful to employ some mediating concepts. These concepts help link the economic and the geopolitical realms while highlighting the functional role that specific geographical bodies play in global geo-economic systems more generally.

This research employs seven central concepts that have special heuristic value in assessing the geopolitical implications of the enormous economic and technological changes now underway across Eurasia's sea lanes:

(1) *Chokepoints:* Narrow locations on the sea where passage for vessels and undersea cables is sharply constrained. Examples are the Strait of Malacca, the Bab al-Mandab, and the Suez Canal.

(2) *Transit seas:* Smaller bodies of water notable primarily for their functional role of linking and providing access to larger bodies of water and to land masses. Cardinal examples are the Red Sea and the South China Sea.

(3) *Maritime bastions:* Water bodies that may have political-military roles, including as strategically important staging areas for submarines. A wide range of water bodies can have such roles for various reasons. The South China Sea (for China) and the Sea of Okhotsk (for Russia) often are considered to play such geopolitical roles.

(4) *Enclosed bays:* Maritime bodies extending deeply into continents but not fully enclosed by chokepoints. Examples include the Bay of Bengal.

(5) *High seas:* Maritime bodies, distinctive for their scale, that play multiple geopolitical functions, including transit and bastion roles. Examples are the Indian and Pacific Oceans.

(6) *Emerging sea routes:* Maritime bodies that may not yet be navigable in some dimension but may have strong future prospects. An example

would be the Northern Sea Route along Russia's Arctic Sea coast between Europe and Asia.

(7) *The Malacca Dilemma:* The challenge that China faces as economic growth stimulates rising energy imports and intensified transport reliance on the Strait of Malacca.

In Conclusion

"Geography" and "transformation" have both been classic topics in international political economy for decades. Rarely, however, have changes in the political configuring of geographic units such as continents and the functional role of oceans been seen as related to major transformations in the international order. This book explores such fateful interactions, with a special focus on the seas and the surrounding rimlands that link Europe and Northeast Asia, the antipodes of Eurasia as a whole.

This volume continues the exploration of Eurasia's changing geopolitics that began with my *Super Continent* volume in 2019. That previous volume focused on overland developments; this one focuses on the maritime, and particularly on the peripheral sea lanes, circumnavigating the south and increasingly the north of the world's largest continent. It considers both their conventional elements and the increasingly important subsea dimension, through which more than 95 percent of internet traffic now flows. Maritime Eurasia—both the sea lanes and their littoral— comprises a strategically critical periphery to the continent whose evolution ultimately will determine the continent's geopolitical fate. This research thus draws on the conceptual contrast of "heartland" and "rimland" developed by Nicholas Spykman, but broadens Spykman's rimland variable to include developments on and below the peripheral seas.

After chronicling the transformation of Maritime Eurasia, in both its oceanic and terrestrial dimensions, this book will consider global implications and policy prescriptions. Given China's strategic centrality and rising preeminence on land within Eurasia, it is particularly critical for the United States and allies to hold their own at sea. To do so, however, the United States will need the support of allies in more carefully defined federative relationships, as well as sensitivity to the growing importance of commodity trade and the broader nonmilitary dimensions of security. We will explore all these Maritime Eurasian dimensions in the pages to come.

1

The Strategic Geography of Eurasia's Sea Lanes

Geography is the most fundamental factor in foreign policy, because it is the most permanent.

—Nicholas J. Spykman, *The Geography of the Peace*[1]

SPYKMAN'S PRESCIENT OBSERVATION in *Geography of the Peace*, published a year after his passing, was at once both profound and misleading. Geography is indeed fundamental, in the sense that physical location of geophysical features such as mountains or bodies of water are virtually impossible to change. The *functional* significance of any given place on earth, however, can change profoundly over time. One need only ask elderly pearl fishermen of the Persian Gulf, or their Philippine counterparts in search of South China Sea marlin, about the changing meaning of place.[2]

Physical locations on both land and sea share this paradoxical dualism—they have both an enduring physical configuration and a protean functional nature. Eurasia is the largest continent on earth, yet it is at the center of an even larger group of surrounding seas. To the east lies the Pacific, the largest ocean on earth; to the west is the Atlantic, the second largest; and to the south is the Indian Ocean in third.[3] To the north lies the Arctic—a small ocean, but highly consequential in strategic terms.

Eurasia's rimland sea lanes, which naturally connect the disparate corners of the continent, are our central analytical concern here. Their geopolitical configuration shapes the ability of the various components of the continent to connect with one another, and that continuity in turn powerfully configures the continent's influence in global affairs. As rimland sea lanes, they commonly are discussed as an undifferentiated unit. To the British Empire in its Victorian heyday, they were the All Red Line from Southampton to Singapore.[4] To the Chinese today, they are the Maritime Silk Road. In reality, however, each segment has its own unique strategic geography and security challenges. Discrete sea lane segments affect the ways in which maritime Asia is able to balance rising Chinese influence on land with countervailing US and allied preeminence at sea.

As with all other forms of political geography, the functional role and relative importance, including enduring physical contours, of specific bodies of water within the broad sea lanes from Europe to Northeast Asia varies over time. As global warming makes the polar seas more navigable, for instance, the economic importance of the Arctic Ocean could rise. The strategic importance of each maritime segment relates also to surrounding landscape configurations. Yet the maritime geographical features themselves have a continuing and all too often neglected significance that compels us to recount in some detail their configuration, and the means by which physical geography in turn helps shape political, military, and diplomatic roles.

The Western Pacific

Furthest to the east, from the perspective of Eurasia's sea lanes, lies the western edge of the world's largest ocean. With 45 percent of the world's water surface and 32 percent of the entire surface of the earth, the Pacific Ocean dwarfs the earth's combined land areas. Much of that vast sea, from the areas washing the shores of both North and South America to those extending from the Arctic 12,500 miles south to the Antarctic, is largely irrelevant to the Eurasian sea lanes. The actual areas touching the greater Pacific Ocean region extend from Japan southwest across the Strait of Malacca, the Indian Ocean, the Red Sea, and the Mediterranean Sea, and around the southern rim of Europe. Nonetheless, the Pacific as a whole is distinctly relevant to the Sino-American strategic rivalry at the heart of the story.

The most strategically consequential parts of the Pacific Ocean, from a Eurasian geopolitical standpoint, lie in close proximity to the Eurasian continent, within the so-called First and Second Island Chains. The three major island complexes of the Pacific's western perimeter, depicted in Figure 1.1, are important to mention at the outset for two key reasons: their proximity to major land features of Eurasia itself, in this aerospace era of vast distances, and the potential role of those island complexes as points of contention in future Indo-Pacific struggles, including potential US-China confrontations. Certainly, in an age of increasing missile capabilities, the US Indo-Pacific Command (INDOPACOM) and the National Security Council have had to contemplate the role of the Pacific islands bordering Eurasia in the future of global geopolitics.[5]

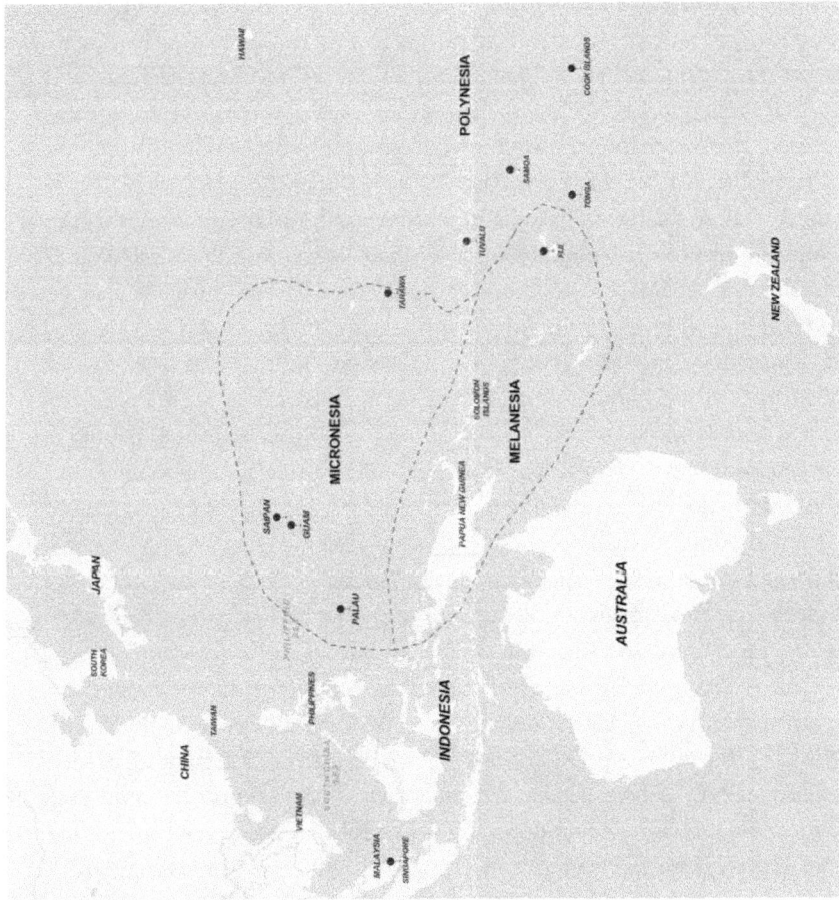

FIGURE 1.1 Three main island complexes of the western Pacific
SOURCE: Author's illustration.

Furthest east, and most distant from the core of the Indo-Pacific itself, lies Polynesia. This far-flung island grouping in the central Pacific stretches 5,000 miles from Hawai'i in the north to New Zealand in the south. It includes such island complexes as Samoa, Tonga, Tuvalu, and the Cook Islands, several of which are strategically important to the nearby ANZUS (Australia, New Zealand, and the United States) nations.[6] However, despite its immense size, Polynesia is the Pacific island complex least relevant to Eurasian maritime geopolitics.

A second important Pacific island complex, to the southeast of Japan and east of the Philippines, is Micronesia. This group of islands north of the equator and west of the International Date Line is closer to Eurasia, and highly relevant to its geopolitics in the space age. Micronesia includes the Mariana Islands in the northwest, the Caroline Islands in the center, the Marshall Islands to the east, and the islands of the Republic of Kiribati—including the World War II battlefield atoll of Tarawa—to the southeast. The Marianas in particular are well within missile range of the Asian continent. Guam has served as America's most important air and naval strongpoint in the western Pacific since the days of the Vietnam War, and looms ever larger, strategically speaking, in the era of supersonic and hypersonic weaponry. Palau, southeast of Taiwan and the Philippines, and even closer to Asia than Guam, is also growing in strategic importance.

The third major Pacific island complex, and the most important geographic and cultural connector between the Indian and Pacific Oceans, is Melanesia. This portion of the western Pacific, as it begins to merge with the Indian Ocean, includes at its heart New Guinea, the world's second-largest island after Greenland and by far the largest of the Pacific islands.[7] The Solomons, where US Marines thwarted Japan's efforts to establish military stepping stones to Australia during World War II, are also there. Melanesia likewise includes Fiji, which has a substantial population of ethnic Indians as a legacy of British colonial rule.[8] Like Micronesia, Melanesia also has recently become part of the Eurasian strategic equation in the age of missile defense and submarine ascendancy, as recent frenzied visits by senior White House staffers suggest.[9]

The unique strategic importance of the western Pacific is very much a function of its geography, given special relevance by technological change. The Pacific's vastness, its proximity to areas of major political-economic importance on the western rim of Asia, and the ease of entry and exit make it an important staging area for SSBNs. These same traits conversely endow many of the islands in the western Pacific with strategic significance as potential military bases, listening posts, provisioning centers, and demarcation sites determining exclusive economic zones (EEZs). A proliferation of fiber-optic cables—the backbone of global information society, with unique strategic importance of its own—also runs beneath the Pacific's waves.

Strategic Island Chains

The geopolitical significance of Pacific geography is a subtle subject that has fascinated American students of world affairs for a century and more.[10] The shores of the Pacific, after all, are home to the most dynamic nations of the twenty-first century in world affairs. These countries, however, simultaneously have complex, often contentious mutual relations with one another, dominated increasingly by the deepening US-China rivalry.

One of the most acute and consequential past characterizations of Pacific geography was John Foster Dulles's 1952 description of the strategic island chains, as he unveiled his strategic rationale for the San Francisco Peace Treaty framework that formally ended World War II in the Pacific.[11] The island-chain concept—originally formulated in the midst of the Korean War as a US strategy for surrounding the Soviet Union and the People's Republic of China by sea—also would be used by Chinese analysts to substantiate their fears of encirclement by American forces.[12] Figure 1.2 presents the essential distinctions that Dulles made, which have been influential with both US and Chinese strategists since the 1950s.

As the map suggests, a group of islands stretching southwest from Guam through Palau to the western tip of New Guinea, including parts of both Micronesia and Melanesia, serves as a potential rear-area defensive line for Western forces in the Pacific. These islands provide rapid access to the Asian continent by air or missile as well as strategic depth within the broader Pacific. Collectively, this island group is often known as the Second Island Chain. Closer to the Asian continent, on a southwesterly line from the Kuril Islands, through Japan (including Okinawa) to Taiwan and the Philippines, ending in the South China Sea, lies an even more strategic forward-defense perimeter—the First Island Chain. A crescent of American military bases along this line, operated by the US Navy, US Air Force, and US Marine Corps within a few hundred miles of China's major population and economic centers, inevitably shapes Beijing's calculations. Control of these two island chains, to the extent that it prevails, powerfully reinforces US leverage in relation to Eurasian continental powers such as China and Russia, by either constraining or facilitating their access to the blue waters of the open Pacific.

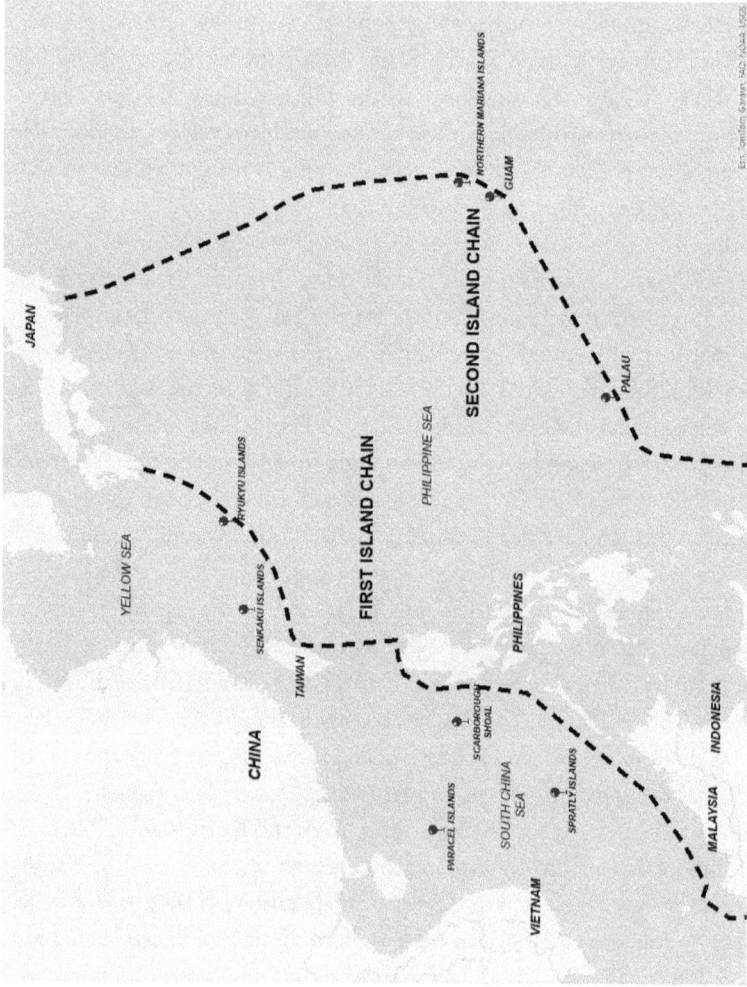

FIGURE 1.2 Strategic island chains of the Pacific

SOURCE: Office of the Secretary of Defense, *Annual Report to Congress: Military and Security Developments Involving the People's Republic of China 2012* (US Department of Defense, July 2012), 40, https://dod.defense.gov/Portals/1/Documents/pubs/2012_CMPR_Final.pdf.

The East China Sea

For China and Japan, the second- and third-largest economies in the world, the most important segment of the Eurasian sea lanes is doubtless the adjacent East China Sea, at the heart of the First Island Chain. (See Figure 1.3.) Unlike the western Pacific, which is relatively amorphous, peripheral, and sparsely populated, the East China Sea is compact, enclosed, and geopolitically central. Although small for a sea, at less than 1.3 million square kilometers (smaller than the Gulf of Alaska), it is surrounded by arguably the most highly developed manufacturing complex in the world and by nations with an aggregate population approaching 2 billion people. Only through narrow passages passing in close proximity to Japan and Taiwan do Russia, mainland China, and Korea have access to the open sea.

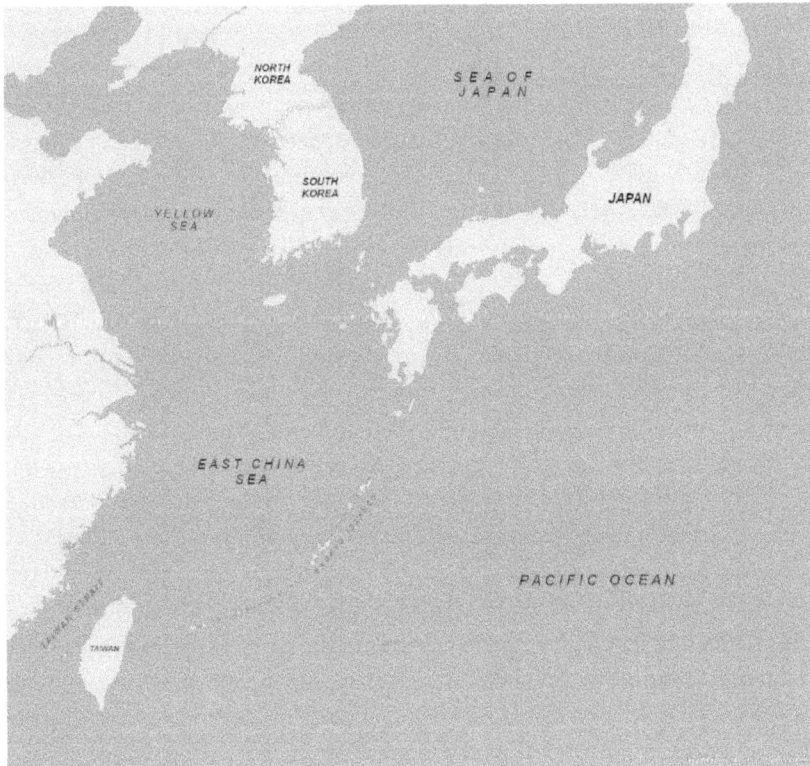

FIGURE 1.3 The East China Sea

SOURCE: US Energy Information Association (EIA), "East China Sea," September 17, 2014, https://www.eia.gov/international/analysis/regions-of-interest/East_China_Sea.

Because the East China Sea is adjacent to many large and powerful nations, the chokepoints at its entry and exit, as well as island barriers to broader ocean access for coastal nations, are geopolitically important and historically contested. At the northern end of the sea lies Tsushima, the Japanese island commanding the Strait of Tsushima where the climactic battle of the Russo-Japanese War was fought in 1905. To the east is the Ryukyu island chain, with Okinawa, the site of a climactic final battle of the Pacific War, at its center. To the south is Taiwan, a major geopolitical flashpoint of global affairs ever since the PLA's 1949 triumph on the Chinese mainland. (Chapter 9 will look more closely at Taiwan's circumstances.)

The East China Sea is the natural focal point for Sino-Japanese military confrontation, a proclivity that has played out repeatedly across history. In 1873, only five years after the Meiji Restoration gave birth to the modern Japanese nation state, Japan launched a punitive invasion of Taiwan. Two decades later, the First Sino-Japanese War (1894–1895) broke out, leading to the Treaty of Shimonoseki that ceded the island of Taiwan to Japan. Four decades later (1937–1945), China and Japan became central protagonists in the bloodiest conflict of East Asian history, during which between 14 and 20 million people died.[13] Since World War II, the tensions have continued to simmer, with Taiwan at the heart of controversy.[14] Following Japan's surrender in 1945, the Kuomintang, the Chinese Nationalist political party, reoccupied Taiwan. In the late spring of 1950, Taiwan became the PLA's final major target in creating a China unified under Communist rule, following Mao Zedong's declaration of the People's Republic of China on October 1, 1949, and the liberation of Hainan, completed the following May 1.[15] Then, following the outbreak of the Korean War less than two months later, US Far East Command leader General Douglas MacArthur interposed the US Seventh Fleet in the Taiwan Strait, perpetuating a division that has persisted, however precariously, for the past seven decades.

The political-military profile of the East China Sea and the strategic First Island Chain at its periphery flow easily from the sea's geography. This strategic body of water lies directly adjacent to China's most advanced industrial centers, including Shanghai. These centers are highly export-oriented, as their products flow out to the broader world through the narrow passageways out of the sea—which are controlled by Japan.[16] This geo-economic location naturally creates incentives for China to maintain strong and easily reactive military forces along its shores. China's heavy military presence along the shores of the East China Sea, conversely, presents a tangible threat to Japanese forces, US forward-deployed contingents, and international shipping. Mutual tensions persist, although the danger to Japan is moderated somewhat because Japanese political-economic power centers mainly on the Pacific Ocean, making the East China Sea effectively Japan's "back door." Nonetheless, the East China Sea provides Japan's most direct sea lanes to Singapore and beyond. Territorially disputed islands and resource deposits are additional bones of contention that not only pit China and Japan against one another, but also involve South Korea. The East China Sea without question remains an area of considerable geopolitical tension when both China and Japan are strong, especially when China is assertive, rising, and connected economically to the broader world.

The South China Sea: Blue Chinese National Soil?

A thousand nautical miles to the southwest, beyond the Taiwan Strait, lies the South China Sea—sometimes known as "China's Caribbean," owing to its proximity to Chinese shores.[17] Like the East China Sea, this enclosed body of water is clearly important to Chinese national security and the Chinese economy.[18] The South China Sea provides a natural shield for China's southeast, its most densely populated and economically developed region, as suggested in Figure 1.4. The sea also appears to harbor significant offshore oil deposits. It is the home port of some of China's most important naval bases, including advanced submarine facilities at Yulin Harbor, as well as communications and intelligence-gathering infrastructure.[19]

The South China Sea, however, is in no sense a Chinese lake. It is a crucial international commercial shipping route for all of Northeast Asia, supplying Japan and Korea, as well as China itself, with Persian Gulf oil and European manufactures.[20] Indeed, the South China Sea carries well over $3 trillion in international shipping annually—more than 20 percent of total global commerce, and an estimated one-third of the world's maritime trade by value.[21] It carries close to 20 percent of Australia's trade.[22] The sea is also a primary transit route for naval forces, including those of the United States, between the North Pacific and the Indian Ocean.

The underlying geopolitics of the South China Sea are thus intrinsically complicated, naturally pitting China and its Northeast Asian neighbors against one another in an open playing field competition for both resources and navigation access. Historical and contemporary conflicts have exacerbated these implicit tensions. Territorial disputes within the region complicate the situation still further, as do Chinese efforts to assert hegemony even in the face of these strains. The contentious circumstances of Taiwan, immediately to the north, overshadow all of these issues. Far from being "China's Caribbean," the sea

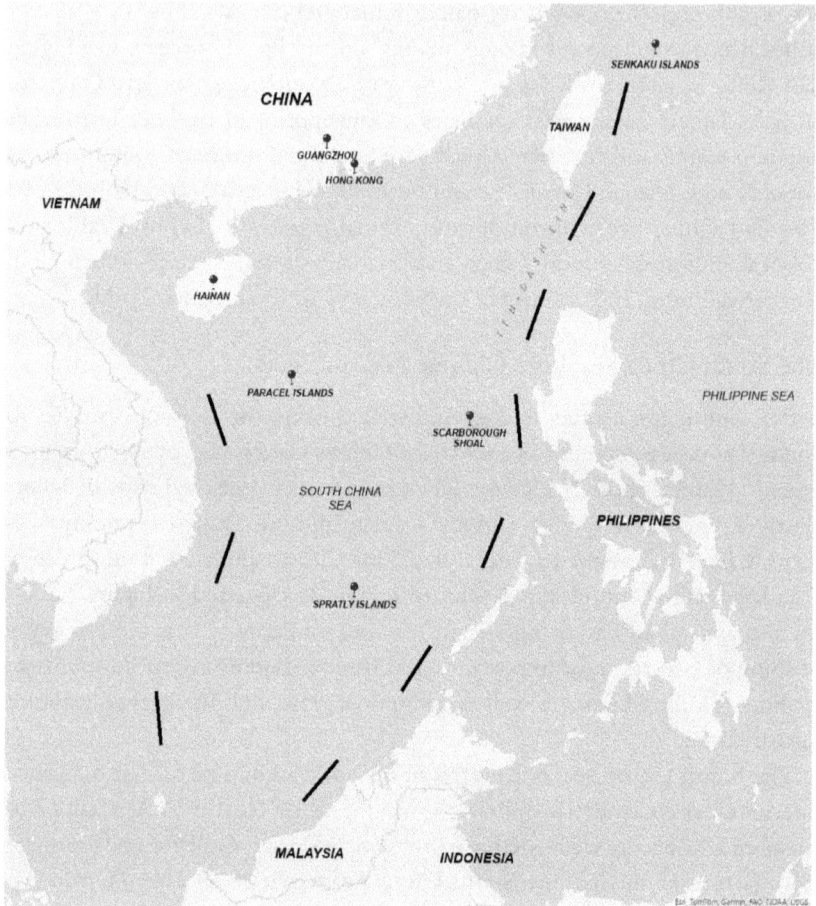

FIGURE 1.4 China's claims extend deep into the South China Sea

SOURCE: United Nations Convention on the Law of the Sea (UNCLOS) and Central Intelligence Agency (CIA), in "What Is the South China Sea Dispute?," BBC, July 7, 2023, https://www.bbc.com/news/world-asia-pacific-13748349.

might equally be known as "Asia's Cauldron"—a natural receptacle for heated and potentially explosive conflict.[23] And as if the South China Sea were not explosive enough already, it lies astride the strategic First Island Chain, directly adjacent to its Taiwanese linchpin.

Japan's history of imperial expansion in Southeast Asia is one significant historical irritant, still a concern for China, Korea, and some groups in Southeast Asia. Yet more relevant today is China's recent claim, stressed ever more insistently since the 1970s, to nearly 80 percent of the South China Sea, under the "ten-dash line" concept.[24] Based on the Chinese government's markings on its official maps, China's current territorial claims extend to within 200 miles of Kalimantan (Indonesia), within 50 miles of Palawan (Philippines), and within 50 miles of Sarawak (Malaysia). Chinese claims also directly conflict with those of Vietnam, the Philippines, Malaysia, and of course Taiwan.

China has conceded that its ten-dash line concept does not translate into full sovereignty over the entire South China Sea. Years ago, Beijing occasionally was willing to compromise on territorial issues; in its 2004 maritime boundary agreement with Vietnam, for instance, it conceded more than 53 percent of the Gulf of Tonkin to the Vietnamese.[25] In April 2012, however, Chinese maritime surveillance vessels seized Scarborough Shoal from the Philippines, prompting that nation to bring a case against China at the Permanent Court of Arbitration in The Hague.

China has become even more assertive on issues of South China Sea security since around 2015, especially in its steady construction of artificial islands in disputed waters near the heart of the sea. Three geopolitical motives have been inspiring Beijing over the past decade. First, China has been striving to reinforce the credibility of its self-declared ten-dash line, claiming sovereignty over 90 percent of the South China Sea. A second related driver has been litigation at the Hague Tribunal on Law of the Sea, which in 2016 declared China's claims illegitimate, spurring defensive efforts at re-assertion. A third motive has been more narrowly strategic. China's artificial islands are being tied to the buildup of its anti-access/area-denial (A2/AD) systems. On its outposts in the South China Sea, China has been installing antiship cruise missiles and surface-to-air missiles.[26]

In the course of its buildup, China has built military bases on Fiery Cross Reef, Mischief Reef, and Subi Reef within the Spratly Islands, including large airstrips, logistics facilities, communication towers, and surface-to-air missile emplacements. It has established elaborate submarine monitoring facilities around the artificial islands and connected them by secure undersea cable with military facilities on the Chinese mainland.[27] It also has deployed a network of floating surveillance platforms and sensors in the South China Sea, a part of its Blue Ocean Information Network. These Chinese surveillance systems are of two varieties: floating integrated information platforms and island reef-based integrated information systems. Some are located in international waters, but most have been placed between Hainan and the Paracel Islands, in the northern part of the South China Sea. Their locations are indicated in Figure 1.5.[28]

The broader international community, particularly the United States, has been actively involved in the South China Sea controversy since July 2010, when US Secretary of State Hillary Clinton asserted at the Hanoi APEC (Asia-Pacific Economic Cooperation) summit that the United States had a

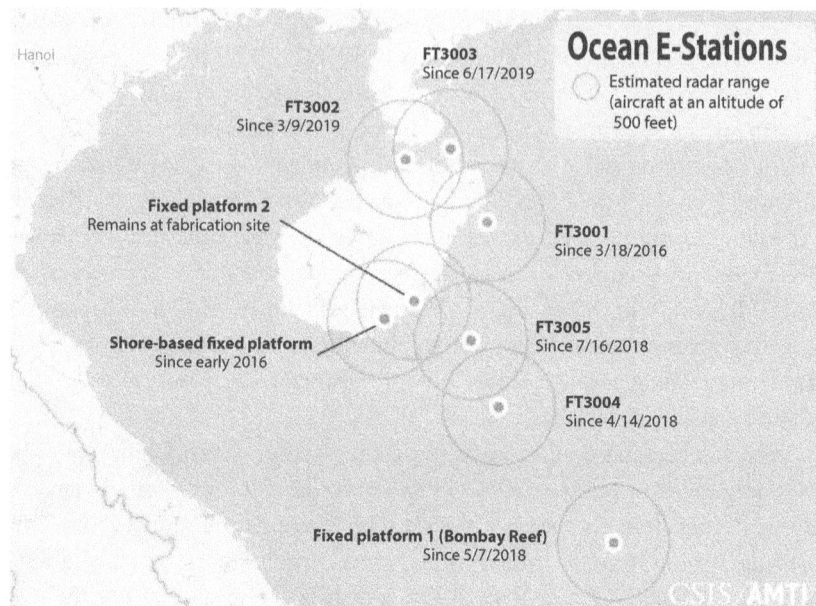

FIGURE 1.5 China's ocean e-stations

SOURCE: CSIS Asia Maritime Transparency Initiative, "Exploring China's Unmanned Ocean Network," June 16, 2020, https://amti.csis.org/exploring-chinas-unmanned-ocean-network/.

"national interest" in the South China Sea.[29] In January 2013, the Philippines took China to the Permanent Court of Arbitration in The Hague over its expansive South China Sea claims, and received a favorable ruling regarding those claims in 2016.[30] China did, however, continue to build artificial islands in the midst of the sea lanes, and to systematically militarize them.

Beijing has continued its militarization efforts to this day. Those initiatives have naturally raised the South China Sea's global importance and the geopolitical stakes of conflict in its waters. Over the past several years, the Chinese military also appears to have been constructing an "Underwater Great Wall" in the South China Sea—a string of submerged sensors, buoys, and drone submarines, as discussed above—to enhance its antisubmarine warfare (ASW) capabilities close to Chinese shores.[31]

Technological advances and expanding maritime claims both seem to be driving these new ambitions, many of which have dual military and civilian-use dimensions. The fruits of such efforts are by no means complete. By 2025, China reportedly hopes to complete construction of its Blue Ocean Information Network in "key maritime areas of (Chinese) jurisdiction." By 2035, it is proposing to build out the "Belt and Road" marine network on a more international scale, and by 2050 to expand construction to an "oceanic polar information" network, leading development of the "global ocean information industry."[32]

The South China Sea is thus one of the most volatile and consequential flashpoints along the entire Eurasian sea lane route from Southampton to Yokohama, and a maritime arena with broader global significance. It abuts the heartland of mainland China and serves as the back door to Taiwan. Not surprisingly, Taiwan finds itself increasingly vulnerable to the PLA's growing short-range power-projection capabilities. The South China Sea likewise directly adjoins many ASEAN (Association of Southeast Asian Nations) member countries and serves as an important transit sea route for nations throughout the world—not just the northeast Asian allies of the United States but European powers as well.[33] For the United States, which has significant foreign direct investment stakes in Singapore and the Philippines, not to mention Japan and South Korea, its major geo-economic and geopolitical interests are at stake. For all the major parties concerned, this large yet strategic body of water—three times the size of the East China Sea—almost certainly will be a realm of globally fateful great-power confrontation in future years.[34]

The Strait of Malacca

Heading westward from the South China Sea toward the oil fields of the Persian Gulf, and then onward to Europe, the Eurasian sea lanes wend their way through a critical chokepoint: the Strait of Malacca. This narrow stretch of water, only 550 miles (890 kilometers) long, runs between the Malay Peninsula and the Indonesian island of Sumatra. It takes its name from the Malacca Sultanate, which ruled over the area between 1400 and 1511 when the Portuguese became the first Europeans to set foot in the region. At its narrowest, in the Phillips Channel just south of Singapore, the Strait is only 1.5 nautical miles (2.8 kilometers) wide. It is also relatively shallow, at places only 82 feet (25 meters) deep. Yet close to 100,000 vessels traverse the Strait every year, including some of the world's largest supertankers and bulk carriers, making Malacca the busiest waterway of its kind in the world.[35]

The Strait of Malacca carries over a quarter of the world's traded goods by volume, including everything from crude oil, coal, palm oil, and Indonesian coffee, to Chinese manufactures. More than 16 million bbl/day of crude oil pass through the Strait, amounting to more than a quarter of all the oil traveling by sea worldwide, including almost 90 percent of Japan's oil supply and nearly 70 percent of South Korea's.[36] Almost 40 percent of global LNG trade also passes through the South China Sea, including two-thirds of China's imports and 90 percent of Taiwan's, as well as more than half of the goods that Japan secures from abroad.[37] Thirty percent of total global trade passed through the Strait in 2024, according to a recent calculation.[38]

Given both its palpable narrowness and its global economic importance, the Strait of Malacca holds a geopolitical significance that naturally renders it highly strategic from a security standpoint. Singapore, now a diminutive city-state lying at the eastern entrance to the Strait, thus lies astride a chokepoint of global importance. In 1905, British First Sea Lord John Fisher recognized it as one of the "Five Keys that lock up the world for the Royal Navy."[39] For decades a primary anchor for powerful dreadnoughts such as the *Repulse* and the *Prince of Wales*, Singapore was a principal target of Japan's 1942 Southeast Asian invasion, together with the nearby Sumatran oil fields.[40]

Today, Southeast Asia's "poisonous shrimp," as Singapore is often called, spends well over $10 billion a year—twice the comparable expenditures of Vietnam—on defense.[41] The island state also maintains strong, albeit discreet, security relationships with the United States, as well as remarkably stable, candid, and pragmatic relations with neighboring China, India, and Indonesia. Since the end of the Cold War, Singapore has served as the venue for multiple major cross-strait meetings between mainland Chinese and Taiwanese leaders, as well as the 2018 summit between former US President Donald Trump and North Korean leader Kim Jong Un.

Dominating the northwest approach to the Strait of Malacca, as that narrow waterway broadens toward the Indian Ocean, lie India's Andaman and Nicobar Islands (ANI). The remote 750-kilometer-long archipelago is a chain of 572 islands, located around 1,200 kilometers across the Bay of Bengal from mainland India. Only recently were its wired telecommunications connected to the mainland by Japanese optical fiber.[42] Yet despite its economic and cultural detachment from the Indian mainland, ANI's strategic positioning is extraordinary. It lies not only at the mouth of the Strait of Malacca, but also in close proximity to several major Southeast Asian nations, as indicated in Figure 1.6. The Andamans, for example, are less than 40 kilometers from Myanmar territory, 135 kilometers from Indonesia, and 550 kilometers from Thailand. India's southernmost possession, Indira Point in the Nicobars, is only 135 kilometers north of Indonesia's northernmost holding, Rondo Island.

Adding to ANI's strategic location is their close proximity to the very deepest sections of the eastern Indian Ocean, one of the world's most attractive basing areas for nuclear submarines of multiple nations. Their location is also highly

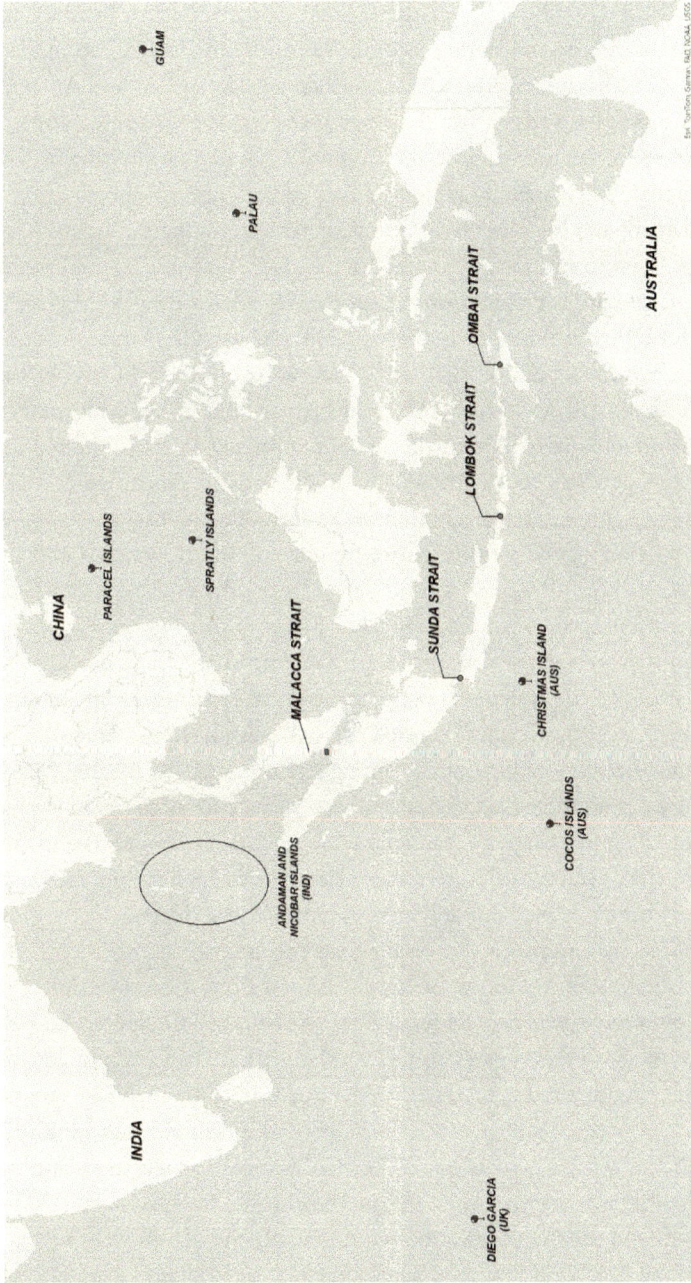

FIGURE 1.6 The western entrances to the Strait of Malacca

SOURCE: Author's illustration.

complementary, in strategic terms, to Australia's Cocos Islands. Together with Australia's nearby Christmas Island, the Cocos chain commands Indian Ocean entrances to the Sunda and Lombok Straits south of Sumatra, as also indicated in Figure 1.6. Although nearly 2,000 miles apart, the Indian and Australian island territories just west of the Strait of Malacca provide important ASW listening points for monitoring the movement of hostile maritime traffic. Their strategic importance is steadily rising as sonar technology advances.

The Andamans and Nicobars have held geopolitical importance for a thousand years. The Chola Empire, led by Rajendra Chola I (1014–1042), used them as a strategic naval base for operations against the Srivijaya Empire of Java. The sea lanes through these islands retain notable and growing strategic significance today, not least because they are a favored route for Chinese, US, and other nuclear submarines headed for the deep, vast, and inaccessible waters of the eastern Indian Ocean. Around $3 trillion annually in international trade also passes through the south Andaman Sea around the Andamans, en route between the Indian Ocean and the Strait of Malacca. That transit traffic includes around 40 percent of the world's entire freight volume flowing to and from China, Japan, and South Korea. Crude oil outbound from the Persian Gulf is one important component of this trade, but by no means the only one.

There are two important routes though the Andaman Sea, connecting the Strait of Malacca to the Indian Ocean. The so-called Ten Degree Channel, also known as the Great or Grand Channel, passes between the Andamans to the north and the Nicobars to the south. Seemingly remote, the Ten Degree Channel is nevertheless a heavily traveled shipping lane, especially for traffic headed up the Bay of Bengal. The Six Degree Channel, to the south of the Nicobars and virtually within sight of Indonesia, is narrower and has even higher shipping density with similarly immense global strategic importance. More than 60,000 commercial vessels annually traverse these two channels combined.[43]

The Andamans and Nicobars, however isolated from mainland India, have attracted substantial international attention across the years. Organized European colonization began with settlers from the Danish East India Company, who arrived in the Nicobars in 1755. Austria tried unsuccessfully to establish a competitive presence between 1778 and 1784, but Denmark persisted until 1868, when it sold the Nicobar Islands to Britain. The British incorporated the islands into British Indian territory a year later. During World War II, Japan occupied both the Andamans and the Nicobars, although nominally the islands were under the authority of the Azad Hind provisional government of Subhash Chandra Bose.[44] Underlining the isolated status of the islands at that point, the Japanese did not formally surrender the Andamans to British forces until October 7, 1945, more than a month after the definitive proceedings in Tokyo Bay.

The strategic importance of ANI has become clearer globally over the past two decades, as the volume of trade between East Asia and points west of Malacca has steadily risen and India's involvement in regional security cooperation has deepened.[45] Indian trade with Australia, for example, grew from $10 billion in 2007 to over $45 billion in 2023, driven by raw material and service-trade expansion.[46] Ever since the mid-1990s, as China became a net oil importer increasingly reliant on the Persian Gulf, the Pentagon has been quietly pressing India to upgrade India's own military presence there. In 1995, following a closed-door meeting in Washington between then Indian Prime Minister P.V. Narasimha Rao and US President Bill Clinton, India established a Far Eastern Naval Command and the United States pressed the Indian government to set up a naval base on the islands.[47] In 2001, the Indian Armed Forces established the Andaman and Nicobar Command, the Indian military's first and only tri-service theater command, based at Port Blair. The command reported directly to the chief of the Defense Staff in New Delhi, with responsibility for preventing smuggling, piracy, drug and gun trafficking, and illegal immigration in and around the Malacca Strait. It also was in a position to help coordinate Indian involvement in multilateral security ventures at the gate to the Indian Ocean, as well as to monitor Chinese activities.[48]

Given the importance of the Indian Ocean to global shipping, and the sheer size of that immense maritime body, it is attractive for nuclear submarines. Consequently, chokepoint gateways to the Indian Ocean, such as the ANI, have a particular importance to ASW and related surveillance efforts. As noted above, the Chinese have been suspected of establishing listening posts in the area. In March 2020 the Indian Navy actually discovered twelve Chinese underwater drones deployed for gathering oceanographic naval intelligence in the Andamans.[49]

Responding to increasing Chinese activity in the area, India has joined the US-Japan "Fishhook SOSUS" system of sonar detection, in which arrays of hydrophones and magnetic anomaly detectors on the seabed work in coordination with reconnaissance aircraft to enable a multitier ASW system.[50] Pointing to the deepening security ties between India and the United States, as well as the strategic importance of the Andamans, in July 2020 India purchased six additional P–8 Poseidon ASW aircraft from the United States. The following month, amid Sino-Indian frictions in the Himalayas, a US P–8 Poseidon ASW aircraft landed and refueled in the Andamans.[51]

China has not been passive in the face of efforts by the United States, India, and like-minded nations to capitalize on the chokepoint potential implicit in the geographic location of the Strait of Malacca and the nearby ANI. Apart from the surveillance efforts described above, China has begun building dry docks at Myanmar Navy shipyards, and is reviving plans for a $7.3 billion deep-water port at Kyaukphyu on the Andaman Sea. This could enable it to base PLA-N forces, including submarines, on both sides of the Strait, and thereby position itself to contend with the elaborate chokepoint monitoring capabilities that the United States, India, and Australia are building in the area.[52]

Crossing the Bay of Bengal

From the Strait of Malacca and the Andaman/Nicobar archipelago chokepoints, the massive Indian Ocean, the third-largest maritime body on earth, opens to the view. The next portion of the westward voyage traverses the southern fringes of the Bay of Bengal, technically a northern extension of the Indian Ocean. This bay, 1,000 miles wide and roughly 2.6 million square kilometers (1 million square miles) in area, is the largest body of water of its kind in the world. As an enclosed sea, it is bounded by thousands of miles of coastline—on the west by India and Sri Lanka, on the north by Bangladesh, and on the east by Myanmar and the northern reaches of the Malay Peninsula, as noted in Figure 1.7. Many of the great rivers of Asia empty into the Bay of Bengal, including the Ganges, the Brahmaputra, and the Salween.[53] The bay is also of strategic importance, with its shores close to China's back door from the south.[54]

Nature in the Bay of Bengal is unusually turbulent. The Indian tectonic plate and the Burma microplate meet under the bay, near ANI. Their mutual friction, particularly where they confront the Sunda plate, has created a subterranean volcanic arc subject to periodic tremors and occasional violent eruptions.[55] In December 2004, for example, a rupture more than 100 kilometers wide on the floor of the Andaman Sea provoked a massive undersea earthquake and related tsunami that killed more than 250,000 people along the nearby coastlines.

Apart from earthquakes and tsunamis, the Bay of Bengal is also subject to unusually heavy monsoons, whose intensity stems from the area's proximity to the sheer mass of the world's largest mountain chain, the Himalayas.[56] The Tibetan plateau heats in summer, drawing in moist winds from the bay; in winter, cool, dry air conversely blows outward from the continent back to the humid, warmer bay, with its greater capacity than land to store heat.

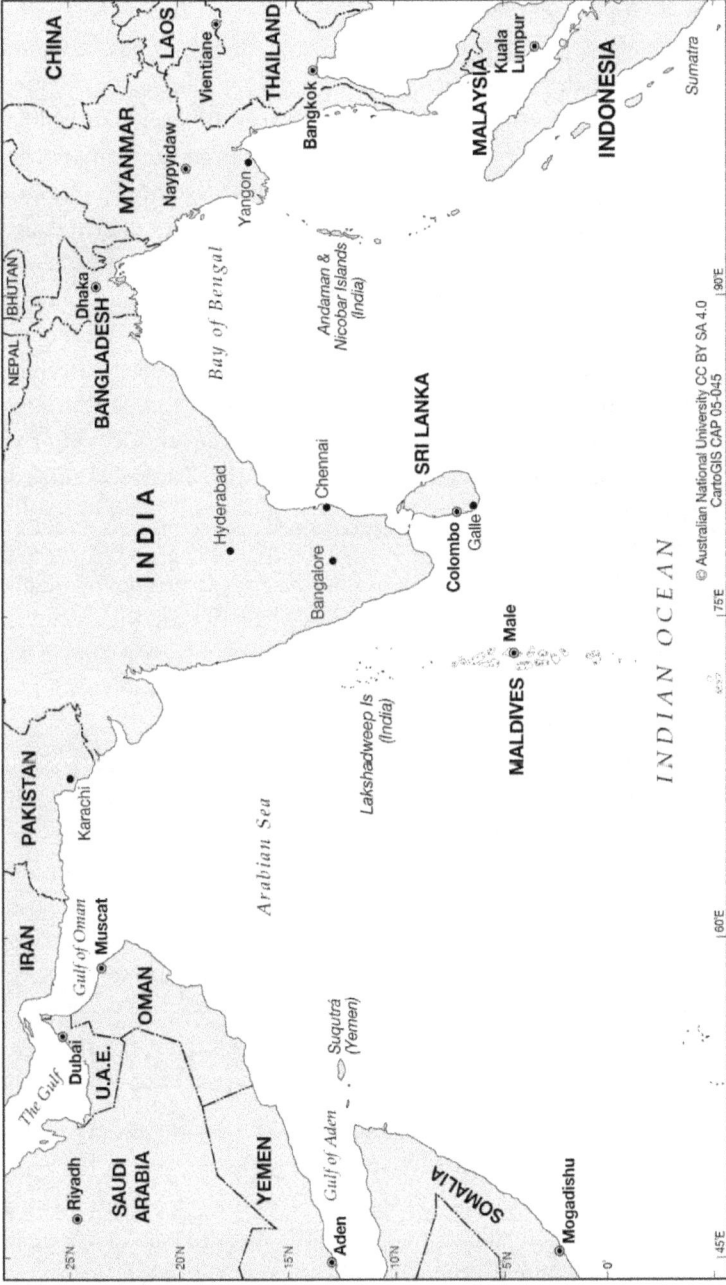

FIGURE 1.7 The Bay of Bengal with the Indian Ocean

SOURCE: Author's illustration.

In addition to heavy monsoons, the Bay of Bengal experiences spring and fall cyclones, as tropical storms with rotating winds are known in this part of the world. These weather systems can often provoke intense winds and floods, especially in October and November. In May 2008, for example, the disastrous Cyclone Nargis hit Myanmar, fronting on the Bay of Bengal, killing almost 140,000 people and inflicting more than $12 billion in damage. In May 2020, Cyclone Amphan inflicted over $13 billion in damage and ninety deaths in India's West Bengal alone, while rendering 500,000 families in Bangladesh homeless.[57]

Several of the littoral nations fronting on the Bay of Bengal are also politically turbulent and easily prone to ethnic violence. Sri Lanka is still recovering from a bloody sixteen-year civil war (1983–2009) between the Buddhist Sinhalese and the Hindu Tamils, which left an estimated 100,000 dead and another 20,000 missing.[58] It also recently has suffered major terrorist violence, including Islamist Easter Sunday suicide attacks on three Colombo churches and three major hotels in 2019 that killed 269 people and injured more than 500.[59] Myanmar has similarly experienced troubling ethnic violence between militant Burmese Buddhists and the Muslim Rohingya, exacerbated by military atrocities, as well as protracted ethnic civil wars involving the Karen and the Kachin minority peoples. India and Bangladesh, of course, have bitter memories of past communal violence as well.

Together with its multifaceted turbulence, the Bay of Bengal enjoys geostrategic importance that is not lost on major powers, including India, China, and the United States. The bay lies at the confluence of South and Southeast Asia, and offers an extensive coastline with extensive offshore natural gas reserves. The bay extends deep into the interior of the Eurasian continent, butting up against China. Its northern reaches, easily penetrable by submarine, lie less than 400 miles as the crow flies from China's Yunnan Province, and only 1,900 miles from Shanghai, China's largest city and one of its most important industrial centers.[60]

Blue Water: The Vastness of the Indian Ocean

The Indian Ocean covers more than 70 million square kilometers (27 million square miles) and holds nearly 20 percent of the water on the earth's entire surface. This broad ocean stretches across seven time zones and crosses almost half of the world's latitudes.[61] Thirty-eight nations share Indian Ocean coastlines. Its geography, as Admiral James Stavridis has pointed out, is one of vast, open space.[62]

Strangely, despite its vastness, the Indian Ocean has been a connector more than a divider across the centuries—a zone of trade, rather than an arena of conflict, to a greater degree than either the Pacific or the Mediterranean.[63] As early as the first century CE, Indonesian seafarers crossed the ocean westbound to settle Madagascar, off the eastern coast of Africa, where their descendants remain dominant to this day. During the first and second centuries, extensive trade relations developed between Roman Egypt and the Tamil kingdoms of southern India.

Over the centuries, Indian Ocean waters became a sociocultural conduit. The ocean's maritime trade routes enabled Islam to spread in its early days first to the Indian subcontinent and then onward to Indonesia. From around the year 800 up to 1873, when the Sultan of Zanzibar finally outlawed the slave trade under British pressure, Muslim merchants sold thousands of African captives annually to littoral markets across South and Southeast Asia. And Chinese seafarers, most notably the Muslim eunuch Zheng He, similarly ventured forth from their homeland through the Strait of Malacca, and across the Indian Ocean to Zanzibar, on trading ventures in the early fifteenth century.[64]

Neither the Atlantic nor the Pacific Oceans have enjoyed this historic role of connector nearly as long as their Indian Ocean counterpart. Christopher Columbus did not cross the Atlantic until 1492, nearly a century after Zheng He's voyages began. And despite vague stories of Polynesian voyages across much of the Pacific in antiquity, the first confirmed circumnavigation of the Pacific was by the Spanish fleet of Ferdinand Magellan from 1519 to 1522.[65]

The Powerful Influence of Geography

Civilizational forces unique to the Indian Ocean rimlands have supported this longstanding connectivity, and yet the region's underlying physical factors clearly are fundamental. Unlike the Atlantic, the Pacific, or the Mediterranean, the Indian Ocean experiences strong monsoon winds, which in the era of sailing ships made long-distance travel much easier than elsewhere. From April to September, summer monsoon winds blow persistently eastward, from Africa's east coast across the Indian Ocean and the Indian subcontinent. The winds then reverse direction in the fall, owing to temperature differentials between land and sea. From October to April, dry prevailing winds (the winter monsoon) blow outward from China and Mongolia, toward Southeast Asia and ultimately Australia.[66] This predictable seasonality helped seafarers from early times plan for and undertake long voyages, trusting the monsoon winds to speed them onward to their destination.

Other traits of the Indian Ocean also make it conducive to connectivity and to commerce. It is the warmest of the major global bodies of water, and it has warmed 1.2 degrees Celsius (°C) over the past century, between 1901 and 2012.[67] It also is well populated with marine creatures that thrive in its warmer waters, notably tuna and shrimp.

The Indian Ocean is also, finally, configured geographically in an unusual fashion that is conducive to the unique socioeconomic connectivity that it has enjoyed over the centuries. It is an "embayed ocean," with large, semi-enclosed bodies of water along its periphery.[68] The largest of these bodies, the Arabian Sea to the west of the Indian peninsula and the Bay of Bengal to the east, made east-west travel along the ocean's perimeter easier, throughout the era of wind power, than it would have been otherwise. Simple, smaller craft without strong ocean-going capacity have been able to travel considerable distance along the Indian Ocean rimlands by hugging the coastline—something they could not do easily in most other parts of the world during the era of sail.

Connectivity with the Broader World

Connectivity has thus been unusually high within the Indian Ocean region across the centuries, compared to patterns around most major oceans of the West. Yet it was not until the age of European empires in Asia, from the arrival of Vasco da Gama at Calicut (Kozhikode) in what is now India in 1497, that the Indian Ocean became a *globally* significant strategic thoroughfare. The ocean's sea lanes held early political-military significance for Portugal, with its outposts in Malacca, Macao, and Calicut; then for the Dutch, as they established bases in Sri Lanka and likewise colonized the East Indies; for the French at Pondicherry and then Indochina; and even for the Danish and the Austro-Hungarians in the Nicobars. Finally, however, it was the British, expanding east from Gibraltar following the Napoleonic Wars of the early nineteenth century, who came to hold the most substantial imperial stakes in the Indian Ocean, as will be described in future chapters.

For many years, the Indian Ocean was of little significance to the United States on the opposite side of the world. Until the early twentieth century, and in many ways until mid-century, the United States was highly resistant to the temptations of global involvement, preferring generally to focus on its own hemisphere. Indeed, until the 1960s the United States was not even seriously considering a basing presence in the Indian Ocean.[69] Yet as the United States acquired global geopolitical stakes across the 1950s and 1960s, with both the US military and American allies such as Japan and Korea increasingly coming to rely on the Indian Ocean sea lanes for energy supplies from the Persian

Gulf, a more robust Indian Ocean military presence could not be avoided. That presence, however, remained more a concession to allies and a manifestation of global commitment than a reflection of parochial national interests.

The United States ultimately did establish one of its most globally significant interservice military basing complexes on the centrally located Indian Ocean island of Diego Garcia, 3,000 miles south of the Persian Gulf, commissioned in 1973. Yet planning, legitimating, and completing that complex took more than a decade to achieve, and its expansion in the post–Vietnam War years of the mid-1970s was highly controversial at home.[70] It was not until 1986 that the entire complex at Diego—with a 12,000-foot runway to accommodate B–52 bombers, a lagoon that could accommodate a full aircraft carrier battle group, and the naval and aviation fuel-oil storage capacity to support such a massive task force for a full month—finally materialized.

The Rising Role of Energy Trade

The US military, together with Japanese corporations, became major customers for Persian Gulf oil in the 1950s. South Korea joined them in the late 1960s. Since the early 1990s, the Indian Ocean has come to play another important strategic function in world affairs: a transit seaway for rising Chinese oil and LNG importation from the Persian Gulf. As late as 1990, China was exporting over $1 billion in crude oil annually to Japan alone. By the fall of 1993, however, rapid domestic growth had led it to become a net global oil importer. In 2017, China surpassed the United States in annual gross crude-oil imports.[71] By 2019, China was importing more than 4 million barrels a day from the Gulf alone—around 55 percent of its total imports from nations within the Organization of the Petroleum-Exporting Countries (OPEC)—primarily traversing the Indian Ocean sea lanes.[72] And in 2021 China became the largest LNG importer on earth, with a significant share of this same supply flowing from the Persian Gulf.[73]

Political-Military Dimensions

The position of Diego Garcia, directly south of the Persian Gulf, made that small, geographically remote atoll an ideal strongpoint for American aerial operations in both the Middle East and South Asia. Together with the massive US aircraft carrier fleet of eleven carriers and their associated battle groups, Diego has played a key role in assuring the security of the energy sea lanes. It had a central role in the United States' conflicts in Afghanistan (2001–2021) and Iraq (2003–2015). The vastness of the Indian Ocean also made the area ideal for US strategic submarine operations, including those targeting Russia

and China. For similar reasons, its chokepoint entryways became priority locations for surveillance of potential adversaries.

Although the United States, with its formidable carrier fleet and base at Diego,
has unrivalled political-military leverage in the blue waters of the Indian Ocean,
the region remains remarkably decentralized politically and in some ways it is
unstable. Unlike both the Pacific and the Atlantic, it is not home to any rival
global powers. Yet the Indian Ocean is central to global Islam, with more than
90 percent of the world's Islamic population living in its basin.[74] Unfortunately,
the region has considerable experience with piracy, as well as ethnic conflict,
and reportedly is home to multiple terrorist groups. There is major potential
for trouble here along these energy sea lanes of global importance. India in
particular has been responding to this prospective threat: it has one aircraft
carrier in service and a second commissioned in September 2022.[75] India is
also growing its fleet of nuclear submarines, including boats capable of launching nuclear missiles.

The Arabian Sea and the Persian Gulf: A Tale of Two Seas

Every single day, the energy sea lanes carry around 21 million barrels of oil across
the world's waterways, outward from the Persian Gulf, the massive energy reser-
voir that harbors nearly half of the world's oil reserves.[76] More than three-quarters
of that volume typically flows to Asian markets.[77] On their way from the Gulf
to the Indian Ocean, the supertankers pass through the Arabian Sea, one of
the most strategically significant of the seas traversed by the Eurasian sea lanes.
Located between the Persian Gulf and India, for more than 3,000 years the
Arabian Sea has served as a fundamental conduit of commerce and cultural
exchange, with South Asia's powerful and persistent monsoon serving as an
insistent facilitator.

Both the Persian Gulf and the Arabian Sea have long enjoyed close ties
with India, particularly from colonial days. Both regions lived for long periods
under British rule, until 1947 in the case of the Indian subcontinent and until
the 1970s in the case of many parts of the Gulf. As a consequence, the rimlands
of these two seas have strong mutual trade relations, substantial South Asian
expatriate populations, a common English-speaking tradition, and extensive
political-military interaction.

The two bodies of water are sharply divergent in size—the Arabian Sea is
more than fifteen times as large, at 3.8 million square kilometers. As indicated
in Figure 1.8, the Persian Gulf is an enclosed water area, with traffic constricted
by the narrow Strait of Hormuz chokepoint, only twenty-one miles wide at

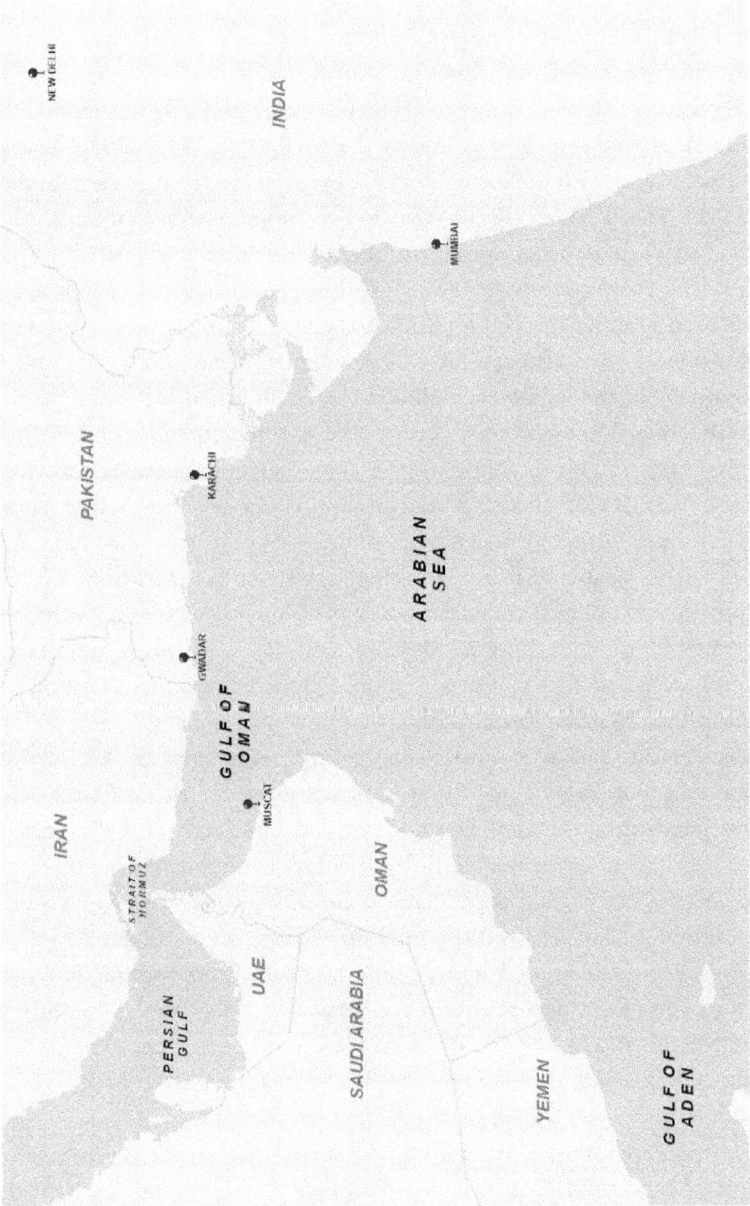

FIGURE 1.8 The Persian Gulf and the Arabian Sea

SOURCE: Author's illustration.

its narrowest point. The Arabian Sea, by contrast, has an open aperture almost 1,500 miles wide at its base, into which maritime traffic can virtually enter at will.

The surrounding political-economic context of the two seas is also instructive, especially in comparative context. Both are surrounded by Muslim nations, several of which—Yemen, Iraq, Iran, and Somalia come to mind—are or have been in recent years politically unstable. The littoral nations of the Persian Gulf are by and large exceedingly wealthy on the strength of their extraordinary energy reserves, and with the exception of Iran generally are aligned with the United States. Those bordering the Arabian Sea are in general more unstable, and in many cases have become hotbeds of terrorism, piracy, or both.

For all of the above reasons, the Persian Gulf has major strategic importance as a destination in different ways for both Asia and the industrialized West. For Asia and to a lesser extent Europe the Gulf is a source of energy; for the United States, especially in the era of shale oil and gas, its importance is more derivative and strategic, flowing from America's role as a preeminent global power. The United States, after all, is little more than 10 percent dependent on Gulf oil even as a share of its declining overall crude-oil imports, compared to many times as high a proportionate dependence in the cases of Japan and Korea.[78] Yet as both an ally to Japan and Korea, as well as a strategic competitor to China, US diplomatic and political-military roles in the Gulf are central in sustaining America's credibility with those nations and with the world as a whole. As in the Indian Ocean, America's presence in the Gulf is more a manifestation of its globalism than of more parochial interests.

It is the Persian Gulf, of course, that is a major repository of the oil and natural gas that fuels so much of the world's economy. Northeast Asia is particularly dependent on the Gulf: Japan, Korea, and Taiwan are virtually devoid of local oil and gas reserves, which the Gulf enjoys in abundance. All three of them are well over 70 percent dependent on the Gulf for their entire oil supply, and for a substantial, if significantly small share of their natural gas as well.[79] China is more diversified, with more domestic hydrocarbon production, but it is close to 50 percent dependent on the Persian Gulf for current imports.[80] For all of Northeast Asia, imports from the Gulf have major importance, both economic and strategic; all those imports must pass through the Arabian Sea, en route outbound from the Strait of Hormuz.

The strategic importance of the Arabian Sea is thus in part derivative— a function of the importance that the energy-rich Persian Gulf itself holds today for Asia, Europe, and the United States. Its simple scale also provides strategic depth, and its geographic configuration offers an attractive flexibility for naval forces, especially for aircraft carriers. They can come and go flexibly, and operate at close proximity to both the Gulf and surrounding territories in Iran, Iraq, Pakistan, Afghanistan, or even Somalia. All these areas are volatile politically, and in some cases havens for terrorism and piracy.

Not surprisingly, the Arabian Sea has been one of the most frequent operational destinations worldwide for the US Navy, across the three decades of Middle East regional conflict since the 1991 Gulf War with the US response to Iraq's invasion of Kuwait. Reflecting the region's rising political-military importance, the US Navy Fifth Fleet was reactivated in 1995 and head-quartered in Bahrain. Command difficulties during the 1991 Gulf War—when the Mediterranean-based Seventh Fleet was forced to take command of US naval forces in the Gulf, owing to insufficient US senior naval staffing in the Gulf itself—were an important factor behind this decision.[81]

The Approaches to Europe

From the Indian Ocean, the Eurasian sea lanes divide. One avenue, filled with supertankers, runs northwest toward the Strait of Hormuz and the Persian Gulf. The other runs further west, through the Gulf of Aden to the eighteen-mile-wide Bab al-Mandab chokepoint. From there, it proceeds up the Red Sea toward the Suez Canal and the Mediterranean, as indicated in Figure 1.9. The westward route carries less energy—only around 5 million barrels a day through the Bab al-Mandab, or one-quarter as much as through the Strait of Hormuz.[82] It does, however, carry a large and growing load of Chinese manufactures, bound largely for Europe.

Located virtually astride the strategic Bab al-Mandab chokepoint, where the Red Sea meets the Gulf of Aden, is the tiny city-state port of Djibouti. It has a population of only 884,000, but it plays an important regional trans-shipment role, serving as port of entry for 86 percent of Ethiopia's foreign trade. Five nations have already established military facilities there, nominally in connection with regional piracy and counterterrorism operations.[83] Those of France, the former colonial power, date from 1932; the United States set up facilities in 2003, followed by Japan in 2011, Italy in 2013, and China in 2017.[84]

From Djibouti, the Eurasian sea lanes flow 1,400 miles (2,250 kilometers) up the excruciatingly hot and salty Red Sea, the northernmost tropical sea on earth, along the coasts of Saudi Arabia, Eritrea, and Sudan to Port Suez. Substantial transit trade, deepening outside-power political-military involvement, and new deployment of major submarine cable lines make the Red Sea of increasing geopolitical importance.[85] Regional powers, especially Saudi Arabia

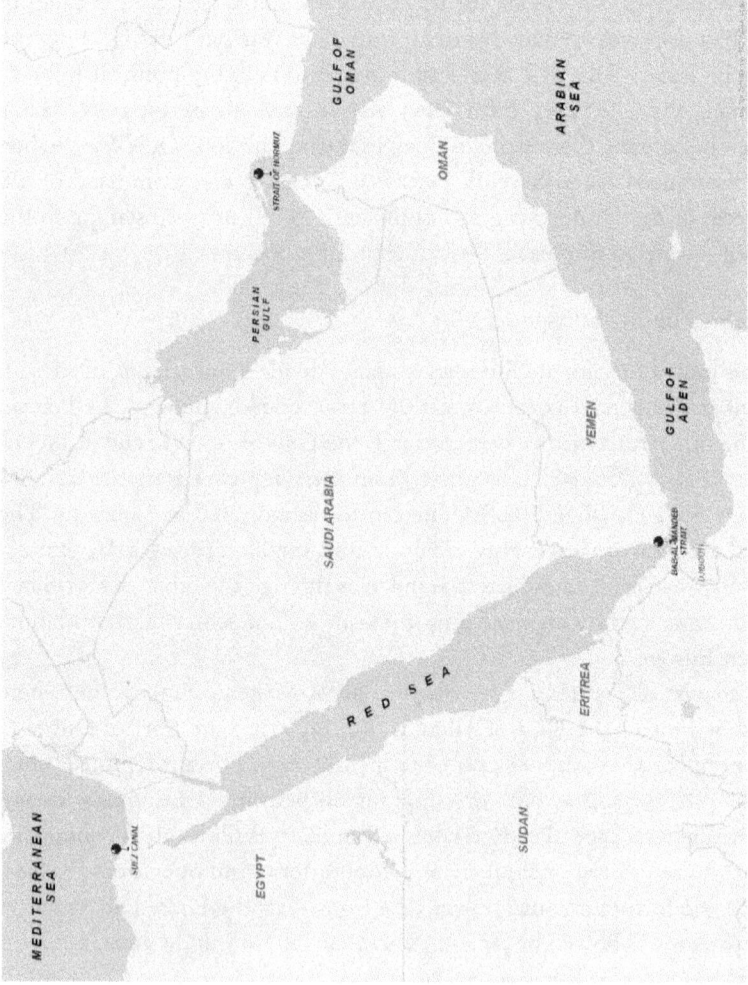

FIGURE 1.9 From the Indian Ocean to the Mediterranean

SOURCE: Esri, HERE, Garmin, FAO, NOAA, USGS, © OpenStreetMap contributors, and the GIS User Community.

and the United Arab Emirates, are also assuming more proactive roles, driven by civil conflicts in Yemen, Sudan, and the Horn of Africa during the early 2020s.

From Port Suez, vessels enter the Suez Canal for a twelve- to sixteen-hour transit voyage to the Mediterranean. This transit cuts around 8,900 kilometers (5,500 miles) off the distance of an alternate journey around South Africa's Cape of Good Hope. Since 2015, a major renovation has nearly doubled the capacity of the canal, from forty-nine to ninety-seven ships per day, with a heavy share of the incremental traffic originating in China.[86] At Port Said, the northern terminus to the canal, shipping heads out into the broad waters of the Mediterranean. The first major port of destination for many is Piraeus, the port of Athens since ancient times, and the scheduled home port for a US Navy Sixth Fleet aircraft carrier during the early 1970s—the same period that the USS *Midway* was assigned to Yokosuka, Japan. From late 2021, the port of Piraeus—third largest in the world—has been 67 percent majority owned by COSCO, China's largest shipping company.[87]

The Northeast Passage across the Arctic: The Strategic Sea Lane of Coming Years?

Throughout recorded history, seafarers plying the rimlands of Eurasia have taken the southern route from Europe to Asia, via the Suez Canal and around India. The Arctic sea lanes around the north of the continent are roughly 40 percent shorter on voyages between the centers of political-economic power on both sides of the continent.[88] Those centers, with their associated industrial cores, are concentrated north of 30 degrees latitude in both Western Europe and Northeast Asia, as well as in North America.[89] There would thus be a natural potential economic attraction to northern sea lanes, even if they were not also the shortest.

Serious interest in a Northeast Passage across the Arctic from Europe to the Far East is well over five centuries old. Sir Hugh Willoughby captained an expedition financed by London merchants to find a new route to the riches of Asia in 1553. Forty years later, starting in 1594, the Dutch explorer Willem Barents crossed the Arctic Ocean from Norway to Russia (now called the Barents Sea), discovering Spitsbergen in the Svalbard archipelago. In 1728, Vitus Bering of Denmark conducted a voyage from the Siberian peninsula of Kamchatka through the Bering Strait that separates Asia and North America, into the Arctic Ocean, searching for a way into the Northeast Passage from the east.[90] It was not until 1878–1879, however, that Swedish explorer Adolf Nordenskiöld, traveling eastward from Europe to Asia was able to navigate the Northeast Passage as a whole.[91]

The obstacle for centuries to even exploratory transit of the geographically efficient northern sea lanes around Eurasia, of course, was climate. Throughout recorded history, the northern sea lanes have been forbiddingly icebound. Yet with temperatures in the Arctic now rising twice as fast as the world average, global warming is beginning to suggest a potentially different future equation.[92] Between 1982 and 2015, the Arctic warmed an estimated 4°C. Over the coming decade the region may well warm by 2°C annually, approximately twenty-five to fifty years before the world as a whole reaches those average rates of increase.[93] This steady Arctic warming is already beginning to open the northern sea routes to both commercial passage and natural-resource exploitation.

The Arctic Ocean along which the major northern sea routes traverse is actually more like a large sea, geographically speaking, than one of the major oceans of the world. It has a surface of 14 million square kilometers, or 1.5 times the surface area of the United States. That is only one-fifth the size of the Indian Ocean, however, and at an average depth of 1,200 meters the Arctic Ocean is not particularly deep. Yet it does have massive resources ripe for exploitation. It is home to 240 species of fish, and reportedly holds 13 percent of global oil, 30 percent of the world's entire reserves of natural gas, and 20 percent of global LNG.[94] In total, the Arctic accounts for an estimated 22 percent of the world's undiscovered resources.[95] Global warming makes such exploitation increasingly feasible, particularly given the limited dimensions of the Arctic Ocean itself.

It is important to recognize the geopolitical implications of the Arctic's new vitality. As indicated in Figure 1.10, well over half of the Arctic shoreline lies next to Russia, but less than 4 percent of that fronts on the US coast.[96] The sea lanes in close proximity to Russian shores are those most rapidly becoming ice-free, or at least ice-unencumbered. Russia actively has been trying to "de-ice" the Northeast Passage in order to extract resources and to facilitate oil and gas transportation from the Arctic to new markets in the Pacific.[97]

Russia, it is important to note, is highly conscious of the potential strategic opportunities that the Arctic affords, as well as the emerging reality that nature likely affords it the earliest and most substantial opportunities of any nation to exploit Arctic resources. It was the first nation to make major territorial claims there, dropping a titanium Russian flag, for example, on the seabed of the North Pole itself in August 2007.[98] Today, it claims rights to more than half the floor of the Arctic Ocean.[99] Moscow has developed sixteen deep-water ports along its northern coast, as well as numerous military bases.[100] It has also built over forty icebreakers, two with nuclear-powered capabilities, to facilitate

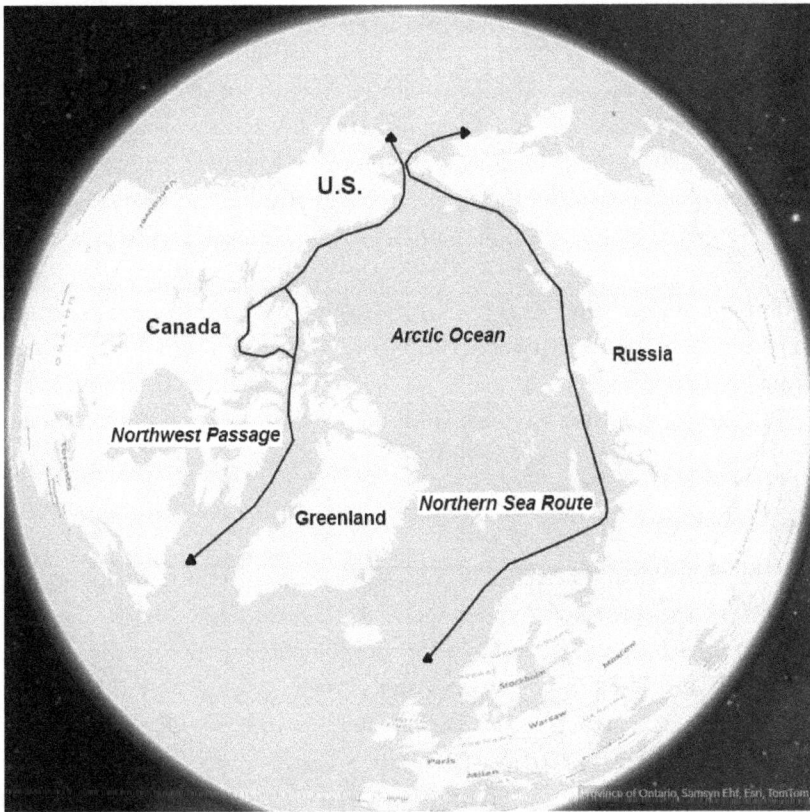

FIGURE 1.10 The emerging Arctic sea lanes
SOURCE: Author's illustration.

seaborne transportation in the Arctic, compared to only five such icebreaking vessels owned by the United States.[101]

Russia is engaged in massive resource development in the Arctic. A $27 billion LNG plant, for example, is being constructed on the eastern coast of the Yamal Peninsula on the Barents Sea by a multinational consortium including Russia's Novatek, China's CNPC (China National Petroleum Corporation) and CNOOC (China National Offshore Oil Corporation), and France's Total. China in particular has played a central role in these endeavors as part of its "Polar Silk Road" program (2021–2025) of accelerated infrastructure building and resource extraction. Its firms own 30 percent of the Yamal project, with COSCO Shipping also playing a key role in transporting the gas to Asian markets in a fleet of ice-breaking LNG tankers. Another massive project (LNG II) is also underway nearby.[102] These Arctic projects have, over the past decade, become a crucial support for Russia's economy as a whole. The Arctic region now produces 70 percent of Russia's oil and 95 percent of its natural gas, along with 90 percent of its platinum, 90 percent of its nickel, and 99 percent of its diamonds.

Although Russia and China are formidable players in the Arctic, especially in combination, the United States also enjoys advantages through its extensive alliance network. Five of the eight Arctic Council nations are longstanding NATO allies.[103] And two more, Finland and Sweden, joined NATO following the Russian invasion of Ukraine in February 2022.

In Conclusion

Geography, Spykman noted, is the most fundamental factor in foreign policy, as it is the most permanent. Most geopolitical analysis deals with the configuration of the land, and national location, but the configuration of the seas and related sea lanes also are important. The Eurasian sea lanes are especially significant from a global perspective because they are the most cost-effective and least politically constrained means of transport between two of the three largest global economic centers—Europe and East Asia. Precisely for that reason, their evolution is critical to the third side of that triangle, the United States, which has been militarily dominant in these sea lanes since 1945.

Although the Eurasian sea lanes are collectively important in global terms, to understand implications of their geography it is important to disaggregate the sea lanes themselves and the seas through which they pass. This chapter has examined in detail and comparatively the geographic profile and associated geopolitics of the western Pacific; the East and South China Seas; the Andaman, Arabian, and Red Seas; and the Indian Ocean. It also has considered the positioning of key chokepoints and military outposts, such as Singapore, Diego Garcia, the Andaman Islands, and Djibouti, as well as the geopolitical significance that flows from the location of each.

The chapter began by noting that Pacific island configurations far from Asian shores, including Micronesia and Melanesia, significantly influence Asian geopolitics in the twenty-first aerospace age. It also observed, however, how the island chains closer to Asian shores profoundly configure the region's geopolitics and animate US–China competition. Within the First Island Chain, closest to China itself, geography naturally favors China most strongly.

Westward from the Strait of Malacca, the geography of the sea lanes has different geopolitical implications. The vast blue waters of the Indian Ocean, as well as the expansive Arabian Sea, favor global maritime powers with expeditionary capabilities, like the United States. Strongpoints such as Diego Garcia, in the depths of the Indian Ocean, reinforce that blue-ocean dominance. Meanwhile, chokepoints such as the Straits of Malacca and Hormuz, as well as the Bab al-Mandab at the southern entrance to the Red Sea, have major geopolitical significance where they potentially constrict significant trade flows. Since the early 1990s, China increasingly has relied on imported oil and other raw materials, even as its manufactured exports have expanded. Rising trade flows of increasingly vital commodities naturally have made these chokepoints of increasing importance.

Embedded Western political-military presence generally has enabled these chokepoints to be a pressure point of US leverage. Yet that US presence is now facing Chinese contestation, caused by the sea lanes' deepening geo-economic importance for China. Although America's blue-water dominance is a major feature of the Eurasian sea lanes west of Malacca, the economically vital maritime routes run remarkably close to land. This geographic reality renders the Eurasian sea lanes vulnerable in substantial measure to the local politics of rimland nations—a delicate topic to be considered further in Chapter 3.

The Eurasian sea lanes connect Europe and Northeast Asia, in a world where for the past three-quarters of a century the US role also has been central. Two key questions for Eurasian sea lane geopolitics, therefore, are what strategic role these three protagonists perceive the sea lanes to play, and how global strategies regarding the Indo-Pacific sea lanes have evolved over the years. These points will be the central concern of the pages that follow.

2

The Changing Geo-Economics of the Sea Lanes

EURASIA'S SEA LANES VIRTUALLY ENCIRCLE the globe. Some of the most important routes, such as those across the Pacific, connect Eurasia with other continents and are globally consequential in manufactured trade. It is the sea lanes within Eurasia itself, however—particularly those from Shanghai to Suez—that could well play the more subtle yet determinative role in shaping the geopolitical future of the continent. After all, those intra-Eurasian sea lanes traversing the South and Southeast Asian rimland have the greatest potential strategic significance. They ultimately determine whether a potential Eurasian Super Continent, even one dominated by an aspiring land power like China, will be able to cohere in the face of powerful global cross-pressures.

The Eurasian sea lanes described above, as this chapter also will show, are more circuitous geographically than the overland transcontinental routes, yet they enjoy considerable cost advantages over land transport. They also are growing steadily more important for conventional commerce, energy trade, resource development, and fiber-optic information flows. Continentalist pressures are strong on land, especially in the face of China's BRI, as I have noted elsewhere.[1] Nonetheless, the power that is able to dominate the Eurasian sea lanes—especially the space between Suez and Singapore—will enjoy a formidable competitive advantage against land-based competitors, as maritime transport is so much more cost-effective, especially for commodities.

Geo-Economic Functions of the Eurasian Sea Lanes

The sea lanes of Eurasia have a distinctive geographic configuration and economic profile. They extend more than 7,000 miles along an east-west axis, connecting the economic antipodes of the continent in Western Europe and Northeast Asia with their rapidly deepening interchange. Sea-lane security at present, however, ultimately is assured by an external hegemonic power—the United States—whose geographic base lies far outside Eurasia itself.

Despite its enormous influence in the sea lanes and commitment to freedom of navigation worldwide, the United States has surprisingly few domestic political-economic reasons to play an ambitious political-military role in the Indian Ocean between Suez and Singapore. The United States trades and invests much less in that broad area on the opposite side of the globe than with the G-7 nations. Apart from oil, parochial American interests are distinctly limited. Yet Washington has global system-maintenance concerns and strategically important alliance partners (Japan and South Korea, as well as NATO) for whom the Indo-Pacific sea lanes are the site of indispensable trade flows, especially for energy. Washington's commitment to Eurasia's sea lanes is thus a litmus test of an American globalism that transcends narrow interest. To further complicate the geo-economic picture, since the 1990s China has grown more dependent on the sea lanes to the Persian Gulf and is becoming ever more uncomfortable with the prevailing realities of unilateral American political-military dominance there.

Over the centuries, Eurasia's sea lanes—stretching at their greatest extent from Northeast Asian ports like Yokohama, Shanghai, and Pusan to counterparts in Europe and the Middle East—have filled five central political-economic functions: commerce, imperial control, energy supply, communications infrastructure, and information-society catalyst. Where a given function has been important regionally, and where there have been synergies across Eurasia, the implications have been significant for the broader world. Geo-economic functions have been added to the Eurasian sea lanes chronologically in the sequence outlined above.

The importance of those sea lanes in global terms has risen over the years as Asia has grown, increasing both global connectivity and hydrocarbon dependence. China's greater reliance on imported oil and gas from the Persian Gulf has been particularly fateful. Given rising Chinese geopolitical preeminence in continental Eurasia, geo-economic prospects in the Eurasian sea lanes, where US dominance has been traditional, will be critical to the future of Indo-Pacific rimland politics and of American geopolitical influence across Eurasia.

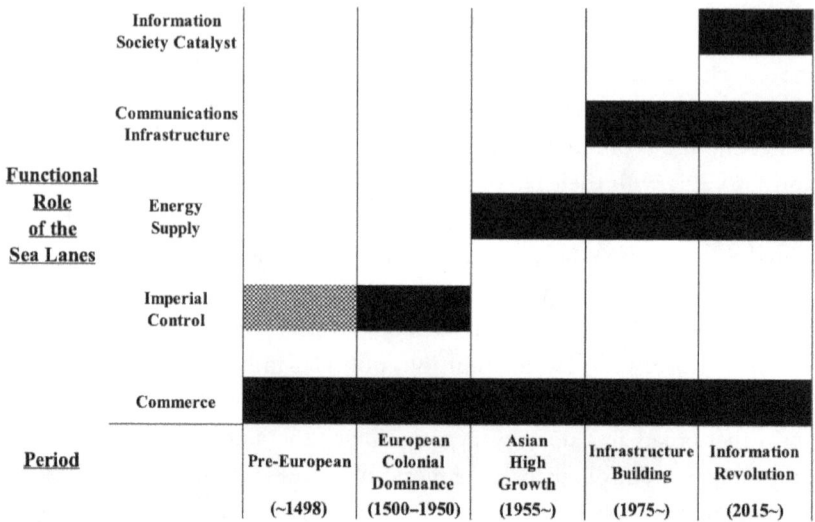

FIGURE 2.1 Broadening geo-economic functions of the Eurasian sea lanes
SOURCE: Author's conceptualization.
NOTE: The "Asian High Growth" period was also one of major related energy demand growth.

The configuration of these five geo-economic functions of the sea lanes has followed a broad evolutionary course historically, as suggested in Figure 2.1. As new functions have been added, the relative importance of each variable has oscillated over time, both for the key Asian nations involved and for their partners outside the region. The ways in which the importance of the five functions has changed for individual nations, and for their relationships, will be considered in more detail later in this volume. Yet the broad collective evolution and the consequences of change in individual indicators for more general future prospects in the sea lanes are clear, as the following pages will show.

Historical Evolution

The Eurasian sea lanes were born in the pre-Columbian era, over five centuries ago, as a vehicle for purely regional commerce. They were then connected functionally to the global system through imperial rule, linking European colonial powers and Asian colonies. As the global political economy grew and became more transregionally connected during the 1960s and beyond, energy and then information began flowing more intensely across the rimland sea lanes, endowing the maritime routes between Europe and Northeast Asia with unprecedented geostrategic importance for both Asia and the broader world. This contemporary reality of connectivity can be understood most clearly by tracing its gradual emergence across history.

Pre-European Era (Before 1498)

"The second half of the 13th century," as Janet Abu-Lughod observed, "was a remarkable moment in world history. Never before had so many regions of the Old World come in contact with one another."[2] In that period, Eurasia's sea lanes first began to assume wider global importance. Imperial Rome and imperial China, to be sure, had been in indirect contact around the beginning of the Christian era; the Muslim conquests of the seventh and eighth centuries also temporarily enhanced interdependence across much of Eurasia. Those early connections, however, were fleeting and involved only limited parts of the world, with little impact on the broader course of world affairs.

What happened in the thirteenth century was different and especially fateful for the Eurasian sea lanes. The Levant and India, of course, had enjoyed significant commerce through the Persian Gulf as early as around 3000 BCE. This trade continued, as "Sindbad's Way," until the Mongol conquest of Baghdad in 1258 CE.[3] From the mid-thirteenth century, however, a more intense, wide-ranging, and integrated "three-circuit" Asian sea trade system began to evolve, involving indirect trade from Europe to as far as China, based on the highly predictable winter and summer monsoons of the continent. This cosmopolitan three-circuit trade, involving Muslim, Hindu, Southeast Asian Buddhist, and ethnic Chinese communities, substantially increased both commerce and prosperity across the Indian Ocean region.[4] Mongol hegemony, as well as Venetian and Egyptian commercial acumen, facilitated and complemented these trading patterns.[5] The Persian Gulf and Arabian Hadramut traded with India's Gujarat and Malabar Coast through Muslim networks. Hindus and other groups in turn traded across the Bay of Bengal with Malacca and Palembang. These Southeast Asian centers in turn conducted commerce, mediated largely by ethnic Chinese with ports in China from Canton to Hangchow, as indicated in Figure 2.2.[6]

Among the earliest Western accounts of the three-circuit sea-lane system is that of Marco Polo.[7] He returned to Venice from the court of Kublai Khan between 1292 and 1295, largely by sea. In his book *Il Milione* (commonly known in English as *The Travels of Marco Polo*), he describes sights corresponding realistically to Vietnam, Java, Sumatra, the Andaman Islands, and Sri Lanka, en route to Hormuz at the entrance to the Persian Gulf. Although Polo's

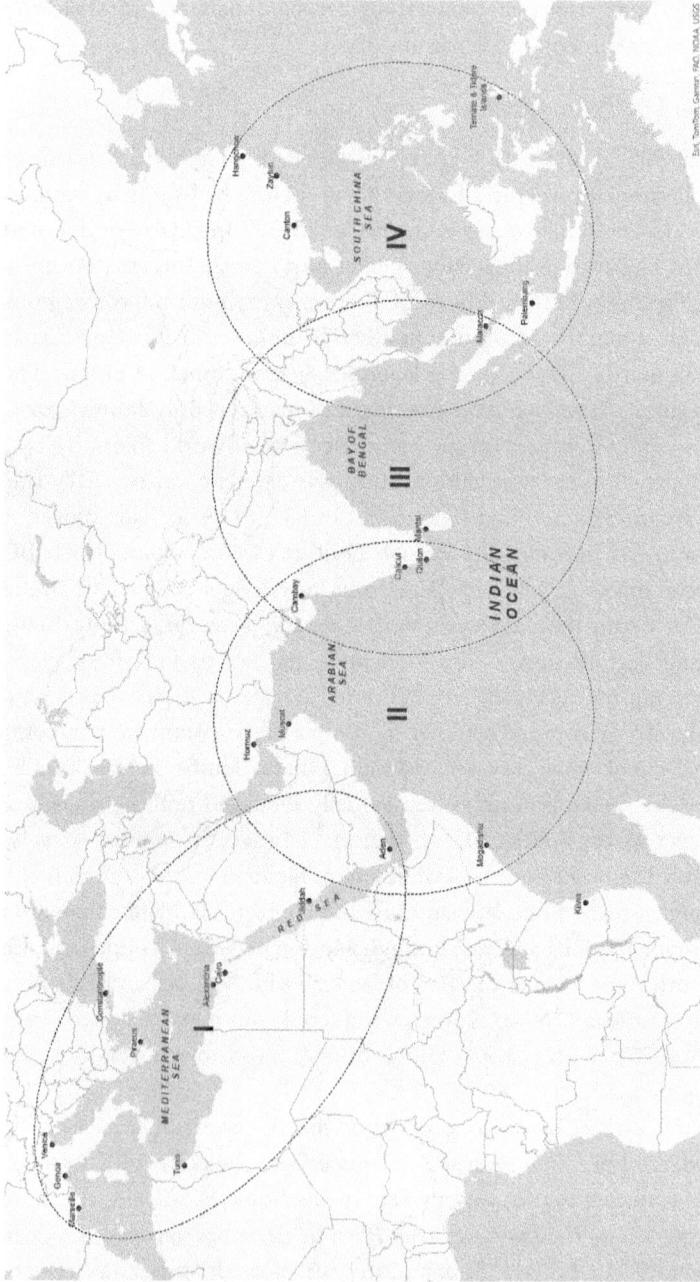

FIGURE 2.2 The "three circuit" trading system of the medieval Indian Ocean

SOURCES: Esri, HERE, Garmin, FAO, NOAA, USGS, © OpenStreetMap contributors, and the GIS User Community.

return journey to Venice occurred solely within the Eurasian rimland sea lanes, mainly across the Indian Ocan, the transregional interaction in which he participated had broader regional and even global implications.

Polo's accounts of his travels later gave Christopher Columbus the goal for his own 1492 journey of reaching Japan, a plan that unexpectedly ended up taking Columbus instead to the Americas. Polo's book also motivated European merchants to break the Arab monopoly on trading spices that Polo described in his treatise. His vivid recounting of Asian riches, however embroidered, inspired future European explorers and colonists to exploit and subdue the vigorous pre-Columbian worlds of both Eurasia and the Americas, which were at a technological disadvantage to the West, particularly in military terms.

The bulk of east-west Indian Ocean sea-lane interaction during the Middle Ages remained commercial. Relations between the rimland antipodes of Europe and East Asia largely were indirect, and invariably involved middlemen of some kind. In contrast to conditions on the Eurasian continent, where the Mongols decisively if ephemerally concentrated power on land, sovereignty over the seas was diffuse. Unregulated commerce prevailed. A small number of maritime forays held broader geopolitical aspirations, such as the seven voyages of Ming Dynasty official Zheng He, dispatched by Emperor Zhu Di.[8] Zheng He traveled explicitly as a government envoy with a massive entourage, promoting a "homage and tribute" system of government-controlled overseas trading.[9] This sort of state-driven commerce, however, was unusual.

Arabs, Chinese, and various Indian ethnic groups did create colonies of ethnic kinsmen in disparate trading cities across the Indian Ocean, as the Japanese and Chinese did in Southeast Asia. Yet these were simply trading networks devoid of broader geopolitical implications. To the extent that government intruded into such matters during medieval days, it was often to tax and inhibit trade, as the late Ming dynasty in China or the Tokugawa Shogunate in Japan (1603–1868) were prone to do.

European Colonial Dominance (1498–1945)

For millennia, the Eurasian sea lanes remained a mechanism of transport within a limited region with greatly restricted global implications. Yet the arrival of Vasco da Gama at Calicut in 1498, following a tortuous passage from Portugal around Africa's Cape of Good Hope, presaged a new era for the Eurasian sea lanes—more systematically immersed in the increasingly global international political economy. Although da Gama had come to India ostensibly to trade, he brought military support and a desire for political dominance that largely had been missing from pre-European commercial forays in the Indian Ocean. The Portuguese pursued a system of state capitalism whereby the royal family maintained a monopoly on Portuguese trade at the country's commercial footholds as well as a monopoly over the spice trade.[10] Commerce in spices like cinnamon, nutmeg, and cardamom was so lucrative that it configured Portugal's quest for imperial possessions so as to protect royal taxation prerogatives. Those possessions thus shadowed the spice supply chain from the Moluccas in the Indies via a series of bases, including Malacca, Goa, Hormuz, Mozambique, Angola, and Cape Verde, all the way back to Lisbon itself.[11]

In short order, da Gama and his Portuguese colleagues established a trading presence, buttressed by military support, in Goa (1510), Malacca (1511), Hormuz (1514), Guangdong (1514), and finally Macao (1557).[12] Ultimately, the Portuguese explicitly annexed Macao, Goa, and East Timor as colonies.[13] The Eurasian sea lanes in turn became a colonial lifeline for lucrative spice trade, to the distinct benefit of the metropole.

A stream of similarly mercantilist European rivals followed the Portuguese into Asia. First came the Spanish, with Ferdinand Magellan claiming the Philippines for Spain in 1521 in the course of a round-the-world exploratory mission whose conclusion he did not live to see. In 1569, a Spanish expedition fleet led by Miguel Lopez de Legaspi landed on Samal Island in the Philippines to revive Magellan's claims, seizing Cebu and Panay. In 1571, de Legaspi moved on to capture Manila, declaring it capital of the Philippines, under Spanish dominion.[14]

In 1602, the Dutch East India Company (*Vereenigde Oostindische Compagnie*, or VOC) was founded, receiving exclusive rights from the Dutch sovereign to deal in East Indian military issues on behalf of the Crown. The VOC went to work immediately, at the high noon of mercantilism, to sabotage the commercial activities of its Portuguese and Spanish competitors, and at the same time establish a dominant Dutch presence in the Spice Islands (part of present-day Indonesia). The Dutch then founded Batavia, now known as Jakarta, at the very heart of the East Indies, almost equidistant between India and Japan.

For over three centuries up to 1949, except for the World War II interlude of Japanese occupation, the Dutch retained dominance there. In 1624, the Dutch invaded Taiwan as well, which they held until 1662, and then again from 1664 to 1668. That presence afforded the Dutch a strategic position for trade with both Japan and Southeast Asia. Trade with Japan in particular became extremely lucrative for the Dutch. Silver was uncommonly cheap in Japan relative to gold, and the Dutch faced no competitors there.[15] The Japanese, owing to their self-imposed isolation, were either unaware of the differentials in pricing or unable to capitalize on them. From 1727, the Dutch also had active commercial chambers in Guangzhou, although trade between the West and the vast, prospering Chinese nation was far less lucrative than with the isolationist Japanese. As with the Portuguese, the sea lanes across the Indian Ocean became critically important to the Dutch both to protect their new colonies and commercial interests as well as to ensure the prosperity of their motherland. This situation persisted for well over two centuries.

The British were the late bloomer among European imperial powers in Asia. To be sure, the British East India Company was founded relatively early (1600), and for fifteen years it held exclusive trading rights to all British trade with Asia. In 1715, it was able to establish an official chamber of commerce in Guangzhou, but failed to achieve much early financial success elsewhere across the region, particularly in China.[16] By the early nineteenth century, however, Britain's involvement in Asia began to deepen substantially and assumed an explicitly imperial cast. Through the 1814 Treaty of Paris, near the end of the Napoleonic Wars, Britain gained Malta, the Seychelles, and Mauritius as possessions, adding to Gibraltar, which it had occupied a century earlier. In 1819, the British colonial official Sir Stamford Raffles founded Singapore, ignoring objections from the Dutch in nearby Batavia, who had long aspired to a Spice Islands monopoly. Five years later, an Anglo-Dutch treaty, sensitive to Britain's rising global role, left Malaya and Singapore unambiguously within the British sphere of influence. In 1842, Britain triumphed in the infamous Opium Wars and annexed Hong Kong Island. In 1858, the private East India Company was abolished, with the Crown succeeding to its possessions across the Indian subcontinent. The Crown also annexed the Strait Settlements (Penang, Malacca, and Singapore) in 1867, and Burma in stages between 1826 and 1886.[17]

With India as the jewel of Queen Victoria's imperial crown, and a string of possessions stretching out to the antipodes that had come to serve as sources of raw materials and important markets for British manufactures, the Eurasian sea lanes from Southampton to Singapore became central to British national security. The completion of the Suez Canal in 1869, followed by the British occupation of Egypt itself in 1882, only intensified this priority. The All Red Line from Suez to Singapore and beyond, linking British industry to far-flung resources and markets, was crucial to maintaining this empire.[18] Protecting its imperial sources and markets was Whitehall's central concern.

Both France and Germany came even later than Britain to the Asian colonial game. France established suzerainty over Indochina between 1858 and 1893.

Meanwhile, Germany occupied New Guinea (1884), the Bismarck Archipelago in the South Pacific (1884), and Tsingtao in China (1897).[19] For these latecomers—as for the British and other colonialists who had gone before—the strategic logic was similar: the Eurasian sea lanes connected Asian possessions that provided resources and revenues in peace, as well as manpower in war, to their respective metropoles.[20]

Conspicuously, the Asian nations that remained uncolonized during Eurasia's imperial interlude—Japan, China, and Thailand—nevertheless retreated geopolitically from the sea lanes. Failing to contest the seas, both China and Japan went into formal isolation, dealing with the domineering Westerners at a distance through entrepot trading centers like Nagasaki and Canton. Japan went so far as to ban the construction of sailing ships for over two centuries.[21]

Energy to Fuel High-Speed Growth (1955–present)

Until World War II, it was primarily colonial ties that bound Europe to Asia across the Eurasian sea lanes. In the early postwar years, however, the major colonies in Asia became independent: the Philippines in 1946, India and Pakistan in 1947, Burma and Ceylon in 1948, Indonesia in 1949, and Malaya in 1957. Within a decade thereafter, East Asian economic growth also began to accelerate—starting with Japan, then the Asian Tigers, and finally China itself, under Beijing's Policy of Reforming and Opening Up.[22]

With rapid economic growth came a rising energy demand. First, there was need for petrochemical-based fertilizers and plastics as well as energy-intensive construction materials, including steel and aluminum.[23] Growing consumer affluence created demands for energy-consuming automobiles, air conditioning, and air travel. On the wings of rising consumption by both industry and individual consumers, East Asian energy demand began to soar from the mid-1950s on, recording a more than threefold increase between 1971 and 2014.[24]

This rising Asian energy demand was not entirely commercial, however; military uses of energy were also substantial. Less than a year after the conclusion of the Chinese civil war (1946–1949), the Korean Peninsula exploded in conflict (1950–1953), with an energy-intensive air war above the peninsula being a major dimension. The protracted Vietnam War (1965–1975) was likewise energy intensive, with air power and the extensive movement of military vehicles stimulating explosive aviation and diesel fuel demand. Technological advances in warfare had heightened, not lessened, the energy demands of military conflict. During US General George Patton's armored offensive across France in late 1944, for example, his Third Army of 400,000 men used around

400,000 gallons of gasoline daily. Six decades later, in May 2005, the Pentagon maintained around one-third of that number of troops deployed in Iraq, yet those forces used four times as much fuel relative to force strength as Patton had used for his push into Europe.[25]

East Asia itself was by no means devoid of energy resources. Japan had been a major coal supplier to Western steamship lines until early in the twentieth century, while China continued as a net crude oil exporter until the fall of 1993. The region's explosive economic growth, however, rapidly depleted local energy supplies, provoking a hunger for imports. East Asia's primary energy demand more than doubled in fifteen years, from about 1,000 million tons of oil equivalent (MTOE) in 1990 to 2,059 MTOE in 2005, and will likely double again to almost 3,800 MTOE by 2030.[26] As virtually all forms of energy are bulk commodities, by far the most cost-effective means of importing energy— coal, oil, and LNG—into Asia has been by sea.

Before World War II, Japan imported oil extensively from the United States. Southeast Asia had also been a key source of supply for Japan and, to the extent that other nations required and could pay, for the region as a whole. By the end of the 1950s, as regional demand began to outstrip supply, East Asia cast its gaze increasingly westward on energy matters, across the Indian Ocean, toward the Persian Gulf.

The first step in East Asia's deepening embrace of Middle Eastern energy was actually taken by the US military. In all of America's overseas conflicts through World War II, American military needs for energy had been fueled onshore, preeminently from the massive and seemingly inexhaustible East Texas oil fields. By the end of the 1940s, however, that pattern had begun to change. From 1946 to 1950, for example, between 30 and 42 percent of the petroleum products moved by the US Navy were actually sourced from the Persian Gulf.[27] And the American war effort during the Korean War was heavily fueled from Persian Gulff refineries as well.[28] Korean War offshore procurement massively stimulated the Japanese economy also, and following a brief postwar recession Japanese demand for offshore oil began to accelerate once again during the late 1950s.

High-speed growth brought spiraling energy demand that neither a Japan devoid of hydrocarbons nor even traditional Southeast Asian fields could supply. Japanese energy demand doubled every five years from the 1950s into the 1990s; the Persian Gulf, only 5,000 nautical miles away and possessed of the largest hydrocarbon reserves on earth, became a convenient supplier.[29] Japan thus naturally sought out oil supplies from the Persian Gulf, and Korea, Taiwan, and ultimately the People's Republic of China soon followed. After

Million barrels per day (MBD)

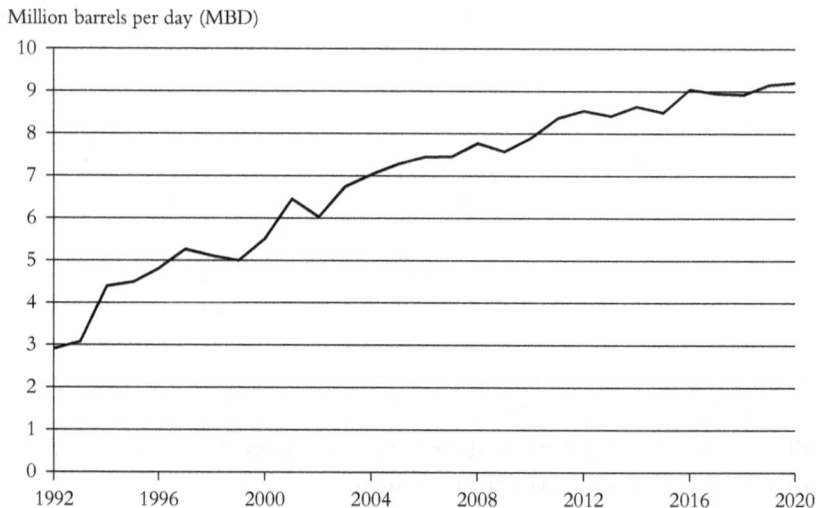

FIGURE 2.3 Rising Northeast Asian oil imports from the Persian Gulf (1992-2020)

SOURCES: BP, *BP Statistical Review of World Energy*, 2021 edition. International Energy Agency (IEA), IEA Oil Information Statistics (database), 2021 edition. United Nations, Commodity Trade Statistics, http://comtrade.un.org. Million barrels per day (MBD) estimates calculated from *BP Statistical Review of World Energy*'s "Approximate conversion factors."

NOTE: Northeast Asian importing destinations include China, Japan, and Korea. Persian Gulf countries include Kuwait, Iran, Iraq, Oman, Qatar, Saudi Arabia, and the United Arab Emirates.

growing beyond purely domestic supplies, Northeast Asian oil imports more than tripled between the early 1990s and 2020, as indicated in Figure 2.3.

From the 1950s on, Northeast Asia built high-growth, energy-intensive industries such as steel, shipbuilding, and petrochemicals. Consumer interest in cars, air conditioners, and other energy-consuming devices provoked substantial demand for natural gas as well. Japan and South Korea, isolated from continental energy sources, elected for LNG. Environmental considerations intensified this demand, as LNG was less polluting than other hydrocarbon alternatives. As with oil, the Persian Gulf (together with Southeast Asia) loomed large as a major potential LNG supplier to Northeast Asia. As shown in Figure 2.4, demand for LNG across the Indo-Pacific sea lanes from the Persian Gulf to Northeast Asia has risen sharply since the 1960s, fueled by high-speed growth.[30] This pattern seems likely to continue, especially in China, as LNG displaces more environmentally unfriendly fuels.

China's rising imports of oil and gas from the Persian Gulf have been especially notable, both in geo-economic terms and quantitatively across the past three decades. China, a near-peer competitor of the United States in the political-military realm, imports hydrocarbons across many of the same Eurasian sea lanes

Million cubic meters

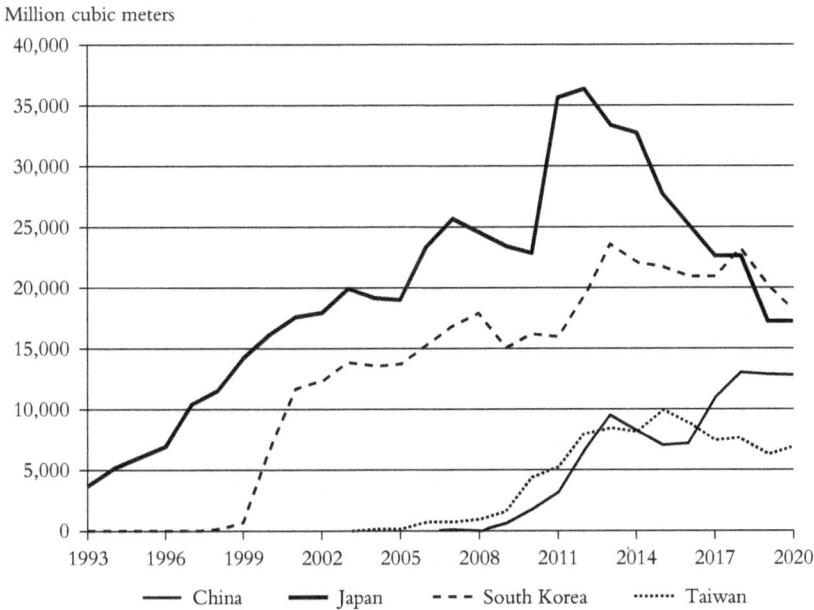

FIGURE 2.4 Rising seaborne Asian LNG imports from the Persian Gulf (1993–2020)
SOURCE: IEA, *IEA Natural Gas Information Statistics* (database), 2021 edition.
NOTE: Asian importing destinations include China, Japan, South Korea, and Taiwan. Persian Gulf countries include Oman, Qatar, and the United Arab Emirates.

as do American allies Japan and Korea.[31] China's dependence on the Gulf itself for around half of its oil imports is somewhat lower than that of Japan and Korea. Yet it also is dependent on Africa for around 20 percent of its hydrocarbons, and these commodities flow across Indian Ocean sea lanes that, like the sea lanes to the Gulf, continue to be dominated by the United States.[32]

In sum, over the past three decades, East Asia's strategic interest in the sea lanes across the Indian Ocean to the Persian Gulf has been fueled by the energy that has driven Asia's rapid growth. That interest has continued to deepen for more than half a century, as Asian crude oil imports have risen to well over half of the Gulf's total exports.[33] International Energy Agency projections suggest that Asian seaborne imports from the Gulf will rise to the year 2030 and possibly beyond.[34]

In more recent years, the Ukraine and Gaza conflicts of the early 2020s also have quickened European interest in the Eurasian sea lanes to and from the Persian Gulf. Moscow's full-scale invasion of Ukraine in February 2022 ruptured intimate energy ties between Russia and most of the European subcontinent, with European nations turning to the Gulf and the United States for LNG resources.[35] Access to US-sourced LNG was, however, constrained in early 2024 by US environmental policies that limit LNG export licensing. In January 2024, for example, US Energy Secretary Jennifer Granholm announced that the United States would be pausing new LNG projects in order to evaluate their potential impact on climate, energy security, and LNG prices.[36] From October 2023, the Gaza conflict and the resultant attacks on Red Sea commerce by Hamas-allied Houthi militants in Yemen led BP, MSR, and other large European energy and shipping firms to reroute their vessels around Africa and to explore alternatives to the Gulf dependence that they had so recently cultivated.

Infrastructure Building (1975–present)

As discussed above, one central dimension of East Asia's deepening transregional attraction to the Middle East has been the procurement of energy supplies. In many cases, that attraction has led to East Asian firms directly participating in both upstream energy operations and infrastructure building in the Gulf. Japan's Arabian Oil Company (Araseki) began oil production and supply-chain development in 1958, followed by first Korean and then Chinese firms.[37] Major East Asian construction companies, such as Korea's Hyundai Construction, have also been deeply engaged in the region, supported by the massive petrodollar wealth of the Gulf states. Hyundai built the massive Jubail industrial complex in Saudi Arabia's oil-rich eastern province following the 1973 Oil Shock.[38] Similar projects have proliferated across the states of the Gulf Cooperation Council (GCC). Saudi Arabia's Yanbu complex on the Red Sea, for example, now generates a quarter of Saudi industrial output, employs 55,000 workers, and includes the fourth-largest oil refinery in the world.[39]

Developments in postwar Iraq have been especially striking. By 2014, as the Islamic State was beginning its rise in the region, three Chinese firms were present in five of the country's major oil fields, either independently or in joint-venture arrangements. China was buying half of Iraq's oil, and an estimated 10,000 Chinese nationals were working in the country. CNPC was participating in three oil fields of southern Iraq, two of which were in partnership with third-country firms, including British Petroleum. CNOOC undertook a joint venture in the Missan oil fields with a Turkish firm, while Sinopec concluded a contract in Kurdistan.[40] During 2018 and 2019, China added seven more oilfield-development, oil-refining, petrochemical, and natural gas-processing projects. Between 2021 and 2024, it expanded its presence further, adding potential dual civilian-military use infrastructure, such as the Dhi Qar airport in southern Iraq, to expand integrated gas and oil concessions. In early 2024, for example, Petrochina took over Exxon Mobil's operator role in the giant West Qurna 1 oil field, and also was awarded a contract for the development of the large Nahr bi Umar gas field in Basra, southern Iraq.[41]

Asia's rapid growth, its resource deficiencies, and the Middle East's ample reserves have thus created over the past six decades a historic and steadily deepening energy and infrastructural interdependence that is central to the modern geo-economics of the Eurasian sea lanes. Every day, more than half of the 21 million barrels of oil and two-thirds of the LNG flowing in international trade move across Eurasian sea lanes from the Strait of Hormuz to Shanghai, Pusan, Yokohama, and nearby energy terminals.[42] This energy trade is a core geo-economic reality of the Eurasian sea lanes, and likely will persist for at least the coming decade.

Ever since the two oil shocks of the 1970s, Asian relationships with the Gulf have transcended simple import-export energy trade. Such trade has remained fundamental, as suggested above, but the scale of Asia's energy imports and its manufacturing and construction prowess naturally has led to massive infrastructure building and downstream investment. Over the past decade in particular, China's BRI, as well as competitive Japanese and Korean programs, have expanded the scope of these countries' investments in Asia to include the ports, roads, and railways that facilitate growing east-west regional sea lane trade.

The Information Revolution: The Sea Lanes as a Communications Channel (2015–present)

As we have seen, the sea lanes of the twenty-first century are a key waterway for commodity trade, including massive flows of oil and LNG. Yet they also double as an increasingly important if little-known conduit for telecommunications. In the early 2020s, more than 570 active or planned submarine cables—bundles of fiber-optic lines that traverse oceans along the seabed—carried over 95 percent of all intercontinental voice and data traffic worldwide, rendering those cables crucial to the economies and national security of nations everywhere.[43] The rapid expansion of the industrial internet, including the Internet of Things; the resulting increase in the number of devices and people connected online; and the increasing speed and capacity of telecommunications enabled by 5G technology are making both high-speed communications and the undersea cables that are their principal conduit ever more vital to the world economy as a whole.[44]

Undersea cables were considered strategically important from their very
inception in the mid-nineteenth century, 150 years before the coming of the
internet. For a full century thereafter, Britain insisted on running its global
cable connections exclusively on British territory and the connecting seas as
a means of ensuring the security of the British Empire.[45] The United States,
as it became a world power, was less able to be particular on the territorial
dimension of the undersea cables it laid, as it lacked the global sweep of Britain's
possessions. It did, however, insist that its cable station operators be American
citizens, and it considered undersea cable control to be a critical national
security issue.

Following the end of the Cold War and the privatization of many telecommunications companies worldwide, undersea cable construction and management became a more purely commercial enterprise. Recently, however, marine
cable networks have begun once again to assume a more geopolitical character,
owing to their role as an indispensable conduit for the internet traffic that is
in turn vital to twenty-first-century economic life. Dedicated secure cables
naturally have direct military utility as a means of linking far-flung installations,
but even civilian-use cables can have geopolitical implications when they open
parts of the world that have lacked extensive advanced communications both to
the Information Age and to one another.

The rise of China and the active entry of America's most powerful high-
tech enterprises into this realm have intensified the revived geopolitical cast to
undersea cables.[46] China's role has been especially important over the past
decade in linking hitherto unconnected parts of the developing world, such
as Africa and Latin America, directly to each other without passing through
Western-dominated communications hubs. China also has been important in
shaping the development of information societies in strategically crucial nations
like Myanmar, Sri Lanka, Pakistan, and even Saudi Arabia on Beijing's terms.[47]

The major telecommunications cables of the world, so vital to the internet,
run almost entirely beneath the sea lanes. Even with their practical importance
to the functioning of the internet, and hence of the highly interconnected global
economy, they are remarkably inconspicuous. Being submerged beneath the
sea, ambiguously situated in the global commons, they are detached from most
political controversy as well as from regulation and taxation. This submarine
geo-economic positioning that cables enjoy also affords their makers and owners,
variously including Western national governments and major multinationals like
Microsoft, Google, Meta, and Amazon, considerable flexibility in configuring
both construction and maintenance.[48] For a century and more, that low-profile

existence aided first Great Britain and then the United States, as well as their multinationals, in sustaining hegemonic global communications supremacy. Fiber-optic cables transmitting data under the oceans at the speed of light gave US firms network supremacy that reinforced US global geopolitical dominance.

Undersea cables today carry virtually all of the world's intercontinental internet traffic. These cables emerge from the sea at roughly 1,000 coastal landing stations worldwide. At these stations, the submarine cables interface with land-based networks, allowing information to flow pervasively through local societies. Network management software, connected to the stations, routes the internet communications that flow through the stations to facilitate efficiency—and potentially divert or monitor communications along the way.[49]

Today, these cables are undergoing a period of unparalleled structural trans-formation. Rapid technological upgrading and infrastructural expansion are extending the benefits of internet interconnection in unprecedented new ways. Undersea cable networks are durable, structurally conservative systems that are physically capable of lasting for generations and are technically difficult to restruc-ture because of their mostly underwater location.

Since the advent of optical-fiber transmission in the late 1980s, however, technological change in the submarine-cable sector has led to shortening cycles of obsolescence and the persistent need to upgrade. During the late 1980s, then-new optical-fiber cable technology was rapidly adopted worldwide, driven by accelerating demand for international calls as well as the availability of a new, cost-effective type of cable-laying ship ordered by major firms such as the US subsea cable manufacturer SubCom. As optical-fiber cable technology improved, the length of cable capable of transmitting signals effectively without repeaters likewise increased, so companies often opted to lay these improved cables on the sea bed, next to older ones.[50]

These technological and economic pressures for upgrading appeared first among the advanced industrial nations across the North Atlantic and the Pacific, particularly the United States, Japan, and Australia. America's Big Four informatics firms were and continue to be involved with these efforts; today, they own or lease nearly half of the world's undersea bandwidth, mainly through cables linking the traditional industrial democracies.[51] These firms are only beginning to focus on connecting locations in the developing world, where China conversely has placed a clear strategic emphasis.[52]

In the Information Age, US dominance of fiber-optic undersea cables is a basic pillar of broader US geopolitical supremacy. For China to offset this dominance, it would need an independent cable network connecting core areas of the world directly with China. Direct links to Europe and the Middle East would be particularly important owing to the global geo-economic importance of that nexus.[53] Over the past decade, new patterns of optical-fiber construction have begun to emerge along Eurasia's rimland sea lanes, often along routes connecting East and Southeast Asian nations.[54] The highly populated littorals of the Indian Ocean and connected seas, ranging from East Africa across India and Indonesia to China, house the bulk of the next 4 billion Internet users who soon could be brought into global connectivity, further broadening the geographic range of activity along Eurasian cables.[55] With rates of Internet connectivity still low in Eurasian rimland states, such as Myanmar, India, Sri Lanka, Bangladesh, and Pakistan, the future configuration of cables beneath the sea lanes could have a profound influence on the profile of emergent information societies in these nations as well.[56]

The fastest, cheapest, and most efficient approach to connecting the Internet systems of emerging Eurasian rimland nations is unquestionably via undersea cable. The 5G and Internet of Things technological innovations, as noted above, will intensify this imperative over the coming decade. Global warming, which will open functional routes across the Arctic, also could help deepen undersea cable ties between East Asia and Europe.[57] China, through its Digital Silk Road program, is emphasizing the importance of submarine fiber-optic cables and channeling special attention to direct connections with Europe, the Gulf, and Africa beneath the sea lanes. Across Asia as a whole, China in 2019 owned or assisted in building nearly 30 percent of existing cables, and recently has projected an imposing majority share in all planned future cables.[58] In China's efforts, the Chinese multinational Huawei has an especially central role, as it is involved directly or through affiliates in fully a quarter of the world's cable construction and repair. Huawei arguably is involved in a majority of cable projects in the developing world, including both undersea cables and landing stations.[59]

China's submarine cable strategy in the Eurasian sea lanes has two principal geopolitical dimensions: extend flexible outreach to areas with low internet penetration, to induce them to enter the internet economy on terms conducive to China's interests; and create a transregional information network architecture conducive to Chinese interests by deepening direct contacts with China and also by connecting areas, especially in the developing world, that are friendly to China but do not have direct links to one another.[60] Myanmar and Sri Lanka, for example, are low internet-penetration nations that China has helped bring into broader international contact through undersea cables. Transregional architecture favorable to China has been promoted recently by two ambitious undersea cable projects: a 3,750-kilometer line from Brazil to Cameroon in Africa, which significantly increases South-South connectivity; and the highly ambitious, Eurasia-centric PEACE (Pakistan and East Africa Connecting Europe) project, recently extended eastward to Singapore.[61] HMN Tech, formerly Huawei Marine, is involved in roughly 100 of the 400 undersea cable networks operating worldwide and is the driving force beyond this important transcontinental marine-cable system.[62] Both projects work more systematically than most Western alternatives to include Africa in global information society—albeit on Chinese terms.

The PEACE project is particularly relevant to the future of Eurasia's sea lanes. A 15,000-kilometer-long submarine cable system, it provides ostensibly open, flexible, and carrier-neutral services for its customers.[63] Since its completion in November 2022, it has connected Pakistan's Gwadar Port, which China has been developing since 2002 as a potential dual civilian-military use facility, to a landing point near Mombasa in Kenya. Other spurs from Gwadar connect it to the Red Sea via Djibouti, where China established its first overseas base in 2017, and ultimately to southern France. A Phase 2 connection will also stretch down the Indian Ocean littoral to Durban, South Africa, with linkages to Singapore and the Maldives.[64] This undersea cable, interconnected with direct links across the Tian Shan Mountains through Pakistan from China, provides the shortest direct optical-fiber route in the world from China outward to both Africa and Europe. Via the Eurasian sea lanes, it will reinforce deepening ties between China on the one hand and potential partners in South Asia, Africa, and Europe on the other. It will likewise provide secure transcontinental communications for Chinese firms and government agencies, thus giving the Eurasian sea lanes new and heretofore unanticipated geo-economic meaning in the Internet Age.

Emerging Western alternatives such as the expanding SEA-ME-WE-6 cable network, which is moving toward completion during 2025, provide an instructive contrast to China's efforts. SEA-ME-WE-6 will consist of ten fiber pairs using the latest SDM technology, stretching more than 19,200 kilometers from Singapore to Marseilles, only crossing land in Egypt.[65] The US company SubCom is the prime contractor for the SEA-ME-WE-6 cable consortium, but it also includes partners from thirteen nations along the cable route from Singapore to France. Unlike the PEACE cable, it has connections in India and Bangladesh, as well as in Italy, a key NATO member. SEA-ME-WE-6 does not, however, connect to Africa, which is a major objective of the PEACE Cable.

US-China competition in fiber-optic undersea cable construction between Singapore and Suez seems likely to intensify in coming years. In April 2023, China's largest telecommunications companies announced plans for a second Europe–Middle East–East Asia cable to rival SEA-ME-WE-6. This $500 million cable is expected to would link Hong Kong, Hainan Island, Singapore, Pakistan, Saudi Arabia, Egypt, and France, and would be laid by HMN Technology, which lost out on the SEA-ME-WE-6 contract to SubCom.[66]

Moving to the future, Eurasia's sea lanes also may be home to substantial undersea resource-development projects. Significant undersea exploration has identified cobalt, manganese, titanium, and rare-earth elements as among the most prominent minerals available.[67] Several of these minerals are critical in making electric-car batteries, wind turbines, and other high-tech products essential in reducing fossil-fuel reliance and in combatting climate change.[68] Japan has already tapped successfully into a deposit of mineral resources 1,600 meters off the coast of Okinawa.[69] China is planning a manned experimental base below the South China Sea that would exploit mineral resources, as well as assert Chinese sovereignty.[70]

Several Eurasian nations, including Japan, South Korea, Australia, India, Russia, and China, have concluded agreements with the International Seabed Authority, established under the International Law of the Sea Convention, to undertake deep-sea mining once a global framework for exploiting such resources in an environmentally acceptable manner has been worked out.[71] China has been especially active in this area and is by far the leader in concluding contracts.[72] Corporate and island-state pressures for extraction to begin during 2024–2025 are strong, and a new battlefield for US-China maritime competition is looming.[73] All of these activities herald new eras for Eurasia's sea lanes, along multiple dimensions.

A new era for strategic competition beneath the seas, fueled by the information revolution, resource competition, and transformative changes in microelectronics, is also dawning. Submarines are growing stealthier, more versatile, and more lethal, even as advancing missile technology increases the vulnerability of surface ships. This quiet transformation beneath the seas has major implications for great-power competition, as well as the rising importance of maritime issues in world affairs, as future chapters will show.

In Conclusion

Eurasia's sea lanes, which Zheng He once traveled many centuries ago, still stretch over 4,100 nautical miles from Ningbo to Hambantota, and thence to

Zanzibar and Mombasa. From Gwadar, those sea lanes still extend more than 4,800 nautical miles northwest, across the Gulf of Aden and up the Red Sea, to the shores of Provence. Yet although the physical geography may well remain constant, the economic configuration and functional role of Eurasia's sea lanes in the broader geopolitics and geo-economics of world affairs have changed profoundly. Those changes, and their implications, are what concern us now.

Eight centuries ago, the Eurasian sea lanes were only sporadically travelled, and socioeconomic connectivity was low. Today, the integration and the long-distance interactions along sea-lane routes are far more intense. Eight centuries ago, transregional energy flows were minuscule and the undersea dimension of the sea lanes was nonexistent. Even sixty years ago, these patterns largely had not changed. Yet today, technical advances in communications, electronics, and robotics, driven by economic needs and security concerns, are rapidly transforming the undersea world. Undersea cables are one crucial dimension, with unmanned underwater vehicles (UUVs), advanced sonar devices, and various undersea resource-extraction technologies becoming important as well.

The character of the Eurasian sea lanes, in economic and technological terms, thus has seen great changes over the years. The political, diplomatic, and military implications of that transformation are similarly historic. Particularly in an era when China has begun to radically alter the geopolitical nature of the Eurasian continent on land through the BRI, parallel pressures for transformation beneath the sea—as well as the global stakes of such a transformation—are on the rise.

Eurasia's sea lanes are thus no longer simply the monsoon-dependent waterways of a millennium past, bringing fine silks east and spices west. Today, their surfaces teem with supertankers carrying the energy lifeblood of half a continent. Meanwhile, their depths harbor optical-fiber cables that power the Information Revolution, as well as myriad sonar listening devices and UUV robots with defense applications. Eurasia's sea lanes, in short, are giving birth to the powerful synergies and tensions that quietly animate the growth and transformation of the world's most dynamic continent. It is to that process of growth and transformation, along the rimlands of Eurasia's strategic sea lanes, that we now turn.

3

Linking Land and Sea
The Transformation of Eurasia's Rimlands

Who controls the Rimland rules Eurasia; who rules Eurasia controls the destinies of the world.

—Nicholas Spykman, *The Geography of the Peace*[1]

ALONG MULTIPLE POLITICAL-ECONOMIC DIMENSIONS, the Eurasian sea lanes from Suez to Singapore and beyond have changed profoundly over the past three decades. They have become much more important as a means of conveying energy resources from the Persian Gulf to the growing nations of Asia. They carry more foodstuffs to nourish their increasingly affluent populations. And, quietly, they have become a key conduit for the Information Revolution as optical fiber cables proliferate beneath the waves, together with submarines and a variety of sonar listening devices. China and the United States are the protagonists in provoking the epic maritime changes now underway.[2]

This transformation in the sea lanes and the adjacent littoral nations, coupled with the rise of China as a Eurasian land power following the collapse of the Soviet Union, is incomparably historic. These changes are casting into sharp relief the pivotal geopolitical importance of the unstable buffer coastal areas separating the continent from the sea, which Nicholas Spykman termed the "rimlands."[3] Although Spykman was writing eight decades ago, reflecting presciently on the impending US-Soviet conflict following the end of World War II, his geopolitical theorizing has considerable relevance for similarly bipolar US-China tensions today.

Focusing on the interaction of land and sea powers, Spykman assumed that land powers would make active efforts to gain access to the sea, and thus to threaten arteries of commerce and communication vital to the sea powers. He also assumed that such land powers would strive to capitalize on the commercial opportunities provided by access to the maritime world, an economic realm naturally free of major political constraints. In such efforts to secure maritime access, the orientation of nations standing between land and sea—the rimlands—would be crucial.

As Spykman astutely noted, there has never been a simple land power vs. sea power opposition across modern history.[4] The persistent historical alignment, both in peace and war, always has been between dominant great powers of land or sea, with the "amphibian" rimland nations in between expressing naturally mixed allegiance. The orientation of the amphibians has thus been geopolitically pivotal. In Spykman's day, the pivotal rimland powers facing the Soviet Union were in Western Europe, Northeast Asia, and certain Central Eurasian nations such as Turkey and Iran. Today, in relation to China, the geopolitically relevant rimlands border the Indo-Pacific sea lanes from Greece through Suez, Djibouti, Colombo, Singapore, and onward to Shanghai and Yokohama. These twenty-first-century rimlands and peripheral islands include many of the most rapidly growing and changing nations of Eurasia.

Just as the Eurasian sea lanes are being steadily transformed in the economic realm by energy and cybernetic flows, the politics and foreign policy of key rimland countries—India and Indonesia among them—are changing as well, owing to their proximity to sea lanes and potential affinity with great powers seeking to dominate and unify Eurasia.[5] Within key nations, including the rimlands, such local political-economic evolution is to a significant degree domestically driven. However, larger external forces can also affect and potentially reconfigure the course of events, with global implications. China's BRI and the Information Revolution are two such example of these overarching external forces.

In *Super Continent*, I identified four critical junctures—short, sharp periods of transition with transcendent systemic consequences—that have transformed the Eurasian political economy on land over the past half-century.[6] Those junctures were (1) China's Four Modernizations of the late 1970s, (2) the collapse of the Soviet Union in late 1991, (3) the global financial crisis of 2008, and (4) the Crimean crisis of 2013–2014. The last of these involved sharp domestic political transformation within Ukraine, followed by Russia's annexation of Crimea in March 2014.[7] These four critical junctures, I argued, played a central role in the emergence of the "Super Continent" phenomenon that has begun to materialize on land.

Only one of these four critical junctures, the Four Modernizations, was a development explicitly internal to China. Yet all four helped profoundly to reshape China's role in the broader world. Collectively, they created the international conditions within which Xi Jinping's BRI could become a promising Chinese global grand strategy, and one with special relevance for the Eurasian rimlands, including Pakistan and Myanmar, standing between a growing China and the southern sea.

Since *Super Continent* was published in May 2019, another sharp, sudden external shock has beset the Eurasian, and indeed the global, political economy. As with the previous four critical junctures, this latest trauma is exerting strong pressure for structural change on the continent, including its rimlands. That fifth and most recent critical juncture has been the Ukraine war, in its multifaceted military, political, and social dimensions. The war, precipitated by Russia's invasion in late February 2022, initially provoked severe political-economic consequences, especially in the Maritime Eurasian rimlands. Embargoes and wartime dislocations spurred sharp increases in food and energy prices worldwide—even in the affluent, commodity-rich United States—precisely because commodity trade is so closely linked to the sea. Maritime Eurasia, especially the countries of the Mediterranean rim and South Asia, is heavily populated and short of energy and grain supplies, as well as foreign exchange, as suggested in Table 3.1. The distinctive resource and demographic endowments of these nations made conflict-induced commodity price rises especially painful. Nations such as Egypt, Sri Lanka, Pakistan, and Myanmar faced wrenching social dislocation and unrest as a consequence, and dislocations proved painfully enduring.[8]

Super Continent detailed the structural implications of the first four critical junctures on land, which collectively aided the rise of China. China's Four Modernizations were instrumental in transforming the country into a massive market for transcontinental imports, especially oil and other raw materials; they also made China the world's top manufacturer, and generated the financial resources enabling the BRI. The collapse of the Soviet Union at the end of 1991 then opened a power vacuum within the continent's heartland into which China could readily expand. The 2008 global financial crisis prompted massive fiscal spending in China. That spending led, in turn, to rapid domestic development in China's west and a new role for China as market of last resort for the Eurasian continent as a whole. The Crimea crisis of 2014 also deepened Russian dependence on China, as Russia's broader European and trans-Atlantic ties were fatally disrupted.

These four critical junctures, as I argued in *Super Continent*, strengthened the overland ties between China on the one hand and Central Asia, Russia, and ultimately much of Europe on the other. The junctures also aggravated local

TABLE 3.1

Maritime Eurasia's socioeconomic profiles

Countries	Population (million)	Energy Imports (%)	Food Imports (%)	Foreign Exchange Reserves (billion USD)	GDP (billion USD)	Debt (% of GDP)	Unemployment (%)	CPI Inflation (%)
Bangladesh	167.0	17.0	17	33.75	446.35	28.20	5.23	9.5
Djibouti	1.0	29.0	29	0.59	3.870	47.10	28.39	2.6
Egypt	109.5	-7.0	21	32.14	398.40	87.20	9.33	34.6
Eritrea	6.3	22.0	46	1.91	2.38	164.00	8.05	7.5
Ethiopia	116.5	6.0	24	3.05	155.80	31.40	3.69	28.3
India	1,400.0	34.3	5	638.48	3730.00	89.36	6.40	5.6
Indonesia	279.5	-103.0	11	137.22	1420.00	39.90	3.50	2.6
Myanmar	58.0	-33.0	12	7.70	74.70	62.50	1.50	28.6
Pakistan	247.7	24.0	13	9.93	340.60	89.00	6.30	29.7
Philippines	116.4	46.0	14	96.04	435.70	60.90	3.40	3.9
Sri Lanka	23.3	50.0	14	3.13	76.20	114.00	5.39	4.0

SOURCES: World Bank (food and energy and GDP data series), https://data.worldbank.org; *The Global Economy* (foreign exchange reserves), https://www.theglobaleconomy.com; and *World Population Review* (debt to GDP, unemployment, and CPI inflation), https://www.worldpopulationreview.com.

NOTES: (1) Sources are the latest available for the data series in question. (2) The data base years are as follows: food and energy (2015); GDP and foreign-exchange reserves (2022–2023); debt/GDP ratio (2022); unemployment (2022); and CPI inflation (2023).

indebtedness in developing rimland nations, as they stimulated BRI-related infrastructure spending. This leverage, much of it seemingly beneficial at first, intensified longer-term dangers of financial crisis in the event of global interest-rate and commodity-price increases. Unfortunately for populous, energy-poor developing nations like Pakistan, Sri Lanka, and Egypt, the Ukraine war and broader global trends between 2022 and 2024 stimulated inflationary pressures that provoked precisely these perverse consequences.

Our central concern in this volume, of course, is understanding developments at sea and in Eurasian rimland countries, in an effort to assess whether occurrences at sea offset those on land, and in turn help to sustain the broader global preeminence of maritime nations such as the United States and Japan. The Eurasian seas naturally have been subject to the same global and regional shocks as the Eurasian continent. Yet the seas are situated somewhat differently in geographic terms and are impacted differently by political forces. The Maritime Eurasian rimland states, experiencing generally high levels of economic interdependence with the broader world, also have been unusually exposed to overseas price fluctuations. What was the impact of these external shocks on Rimland Eurasia and the adjacent sea lanes? That is our analytical concern across the following pages.

Critical Junctures and the Rebirth of Maritime Eurasia

As noted in Chapter 1, there is a long history of interaction across the Eurasian sea lanes, stretching from the Mediterranean and the Red Sea to the Indian Ocean, the Strait of Malacca, and beyond. China, especially during the fifteenth century, played a major role in this classical interchange, as manifest in the well-known voyages of Zheng He. From the abrupt end of China's voyages of exploration in the mid-Ming period until the recent past, however, the Eurasian sea lanes have been dominated by European colonial powers and the United States. For more than five centuries, until the 1990s, China had little interaction with Eurasia's sea lanes beyond the waters adjacent to its shores.

China's Modernizations

The critical junctures of the past four decades have begun to transform that longstanding pattern of Western dominance. The first of those junctures, China's Four Modernizations, introduced the Middle Kingdom once again as a major player in the sea lanes—over three decades before the BRI began. Initially, China's expanded role in the sea lanes was almost purely a matter of market demand, driven by the rise in its energy imports from the Persian Gulf and its own need for foreign markets. The principal intermediaries were Western; Chinese investors, shipping companies, and military interests were only marginally involved. Gradually, maritime relationships came to involve more actors, including many from China, and assumed a much clearer geopolitical dimension, as Chapter 5 explains in detail.

The evolving role of the COSCO Shipping Group and other Chinese corporations in the Eurasian sea lanes, and in global shipping generally, is illustrative. Founded in 1997 by the Chinese government as a state-owned enterprise, COSCO grew rapidly after China joined the World Trade Organization in 2001. It exploited synergies between China's growing export-manufacturing capacity and innovations in global shipping—many of them, such as container shipping, originating in the United States.[9] In 2005, COSCO's container subsidiary, China Shipping Container Lines, was named the most profitable container line in the world by *American Shipper*, a pattern that persisted thereafter for several more years.[10]

Thanks to heavy capital investment, a series of state-sponsored mergers, and opportunities flowing from China's dominant role in global manufacturing, the COSCO shipping conglomerate of 137 vessels had by September 2020 become the largest shipping company in the world in overall capacity, and third in container capacity.[11] In 2023, it also ranked fourth in actual cargo tonnage.[12] COSCO's control of key ports, including Shanghai, Colombo, and Piraeus, enabled it to introduce scale economies and other innovations in container shipping that greatly enhanced its dominance in the Eurasian sea lanes.[13] In late 2024, it extended its influence in the Pacific as well, as President Xi Jinping opened South America's first port to receive megaships at Chancay, Peru.[14]

COSCO is by no means the only major Chinese firm that handles shipping-related matters.[15] China Merchants Port (CMPORT), with which COSCO has complementary relations, accommodates 60 million containers around the world. Among its current major project is a $10 billion port in Bagamayo, Tanzania, projected to be the largest in Africa.[16] A third major Chinese firm, Hutchison Ports, is also Hong Kong–based, and a private-sector affiliate of the Hutchison Whampoa conglomerate. All of China's Big Three rank among the world's leading terminal operators, and together control 81 percent of the ninety-six Chinese company ports.[17]

The Collapse of the Soviet Union

A second global critical juncture, the dissolution of the Soviet Union at the end of 1991, led to sweeping retrenchments across the Eurasian land mass. Yet it also had a profound maritime dimension. Perhaps most importantly, the Soviet collapse led to the virtual disappearance of the Soviet Navy from Eurasian waters. The Russian fleet retreated from key Asian anchorages such as Cam Ranh Bay in Vietnam, as well as Aden, Yemen; Hargeisa, Somalia; and Massawa, Eritrea—not to mention Alexandria, Egypt, further along the Eurasian sea lanes to the west. By 2015, the Russian navy had shrunk to little more than a quarter of its size in 1990, prior to the Soviet collapse, with a heavy share of the contraction along the Eurasian sea lanes.[18]

This collapse of Soviet naval power also led, for more than two decades, to Pentagon strategists giving the Eurasian sea lanes less priority than they had had during the Cold War, when the Soviets had been America's only peer competitor. To be sure, the United States held fast to its strongpoint at Diego Garcia and frequently maintained carrier battle groups on station in the Arabian Sea to cope with Saddam Hussein's Iraq and an intermittent Iranian threat. The global strategic environment, however, was transformed markedly by Moscow's demise, which benefited the United States and induced a strong sense of self-confidence (as well as passivity) in Washington toward Eurasia's sea lanes. Despite the uncertainties induced by aggressive nonstate actors—including terrorists, smugglers, and pirates—as well as a proliferation of aspiring new rimland states in the Indian Ocean, the absence of peer competitors naturally lulled US concerns.

Paradoxically, the collapse of the Soviet Union also provoked subtle changes in the responsiveness of some key Maritime Eurasian rimland nations toward China. Indonesia in particular had been China's most intransigent opponent in Southeast Asia since the Untung coup of 1965, which had been inspired by China-friendly communist sympathizers and had resulted in the death of Indonesia's top military leadership. In 1991, however, transcending resentments of the past, Jakarta suddenly recognized Beijing, just as the Soviet Union was collapsing. That bold step led, early in 1992, to Singapore's decision to recognize the People's Republic. To allay fears within ASEAN that its ethnic Chinese majority would overly influence its dealings with Beijing, Singapore had promised to be the last nation in ASEAN to recognize China, and was at last able to do so.

A second major consequence of the Soviet collapse for Eurasia's sea lanes was a new maritime role for former Soviet client states. Most important to sea-lane geopolitics was the shifting position of Vietnam, a key rimland state, with its extensive sea front of over 2,000 miles along the South China Sea. Hanoi had been a major regional ally for Moscow during the Cold War, providing basing facilities for the Soviet fleet at Cam Ranh Bay in return for substantial Soviet subsidies. Those supports naturally disappeared in the early 1990s, and within less than a decade Vietnam reoriented toward Japan and the United States, its major sources of development assistance and strategic reassurance in the post–Cold War world.[19] Japan provided nearly $20 billion for Vietnam between 1992 and 2011, and after the 2014 oil-rig confrontation with China it provided patrol vessels and training for the Vietnam People's Navy as well.[20] The United States also supplied increasing amounts of aid after 1991, in the areas of education, environment, health, and security, while also supporting Vietnam diplomatically.[21] For both historical and geopolitical reasons, Beijing was not a preferred option for Hanoi, even though the People's Republic had provided substantial support for North Vietnam during the Vietnam War (1965–1975). Relations spiraled downward especially rapidly during and after the Sino-Vietnamese War of 1979.

Far to the west, Ethiopia—which, at this time, had extensive sea coast including Eritrea—had, like Vietnam, been a coastal state closely allied with the Soviet Union during the Cold War. It responded to the Soviet collapse, first of all, with domestic change. The collapse of the Soviet regime in Moscow led rapidly to the end of its client Mengistu government in Addis Ababa, and to improved relations with the United States. Nearby Djibouti, on the Bab al-Mandab at the Red Sea's entrance, also reoriented toward Washington.

Although several of the smaller Soviet client states along the sea lanes abruptly shifted their diplomatic orientation following the Soviet collapse and of necessity began cultivating the United States, during the early post–Cold War years Washington was reluctant to embrace them. Turbulence in Somalia, Yemen, and Rwanda inhibited the Clinton administration from broader commitments. Meanwhile, a financial crisis in Mexico added to America's burdens close to home. When the Asian financial crisis broke out in June 1997, the United States washed its hands of rimland Eurasia. Only a financial meltdown in Korea, a top 20 economy in the global context, made the broadening geo-economic turbulence in Seoul too dangerous for Washington to ignore. So as China began to rise across the following decade, many smaller rimland nations along the Eurasian sea lanes were both economically vulnerable and also lacked a clear external patron.

The Lehman Shock and Beyond

The global financial crisis of 2008 had major political-economic impact within China itself, spurring a massive $586 billion public works program.[22] Through its far-sighted Western Development Strategy, expressed in the form of concrete construction projects such as high-speed rail, that fiscal stimulus laid the groundwork for the ambitious transcontinental infrastructure initiative that would become Xi Jinping's land-based "Belt" Initiative in September 2013.[23]

The 2008 financial crisis and China's response, however, also had fateful implications for the sea lanes and for the rimland nations of Maritime Eurasia bordering them. China's Maritime Silk Road initiative, unveiled before the Indonesian parliament in October 2013, would be a driving force.[24]

The contrasting continental and maritime prongs of China's BRI have both had major implications for the Maritime Eurasian rimland states, and also illustrate the centrality of BRI in Chinese grand strategy as a whole. The Maritime Silk Road, as its name implies, has involved investments in port facilities and shipping infrastructure along sea coasts and their hinterland. The Belt construction projects, and their predecessors in the Western Development Strategy of Jiang Zemin and Hu Jintao, supported the development of China's western hinterland, but also linkages between the interior regions of China and the rimland states to the south. Among those linkage projects were the CPEC between China and Pakistan, the China-Myanmar Economic Corridor, and the Bangladesh-China-India-Myanmar Economic Corridor.

The Maritime Silk Road, a key dimension of China's signature BRI, had major political-economic implications for rimland countries along the Maritime Eurasian sea lanes.[25] Domestically within China, it involved a substantial economic development program for Hainan, China's southernmost province, as well as numerous ports along China's southeastern coast. These efforts had both economic and strategic implications. In May 2020, for example, China's State Council announced plans to convert the whole of Hainan into China's largest Special Economic Zone, with zero tariffs.[26] The government also embarked on a five-year, $35 billion investment in Hainan's highway system.[27] It also refurbished the Yulin Naval Base, near Sanya, an installation equipped with *Shang*-class nuclear submarines and fronting on the South China Sea.[28]

The Maritime Silk Road likewise has provided major infrastructural support for rimland states along the Eurasian sea lanes. Myanmar, Bangladesh, Sri Lanka, Djibouti, Eritrea, Egypt, Greece, Slovenia, and even Italy have been included in China's ambitious program, as we shall see in more detail in Chapter 5. The Maritime Silk Road has also nurtured a string of dual-use port facilities, as in Djibouti and Gwadar, with both potential military implications and economic connections to strategic hinterland areas, as suggested in Figure 3.1.

The former client states of the Soviet Union, which the United States had failed to woo before the global financial crisis and which it remained unable to support amid that crisis, were among the first affected by China's new initiative. The clearest case was Sri Lanka, where the financial crisis compounded the domestic turmoil of a civil war that had been ongoing since 1993. Repelled

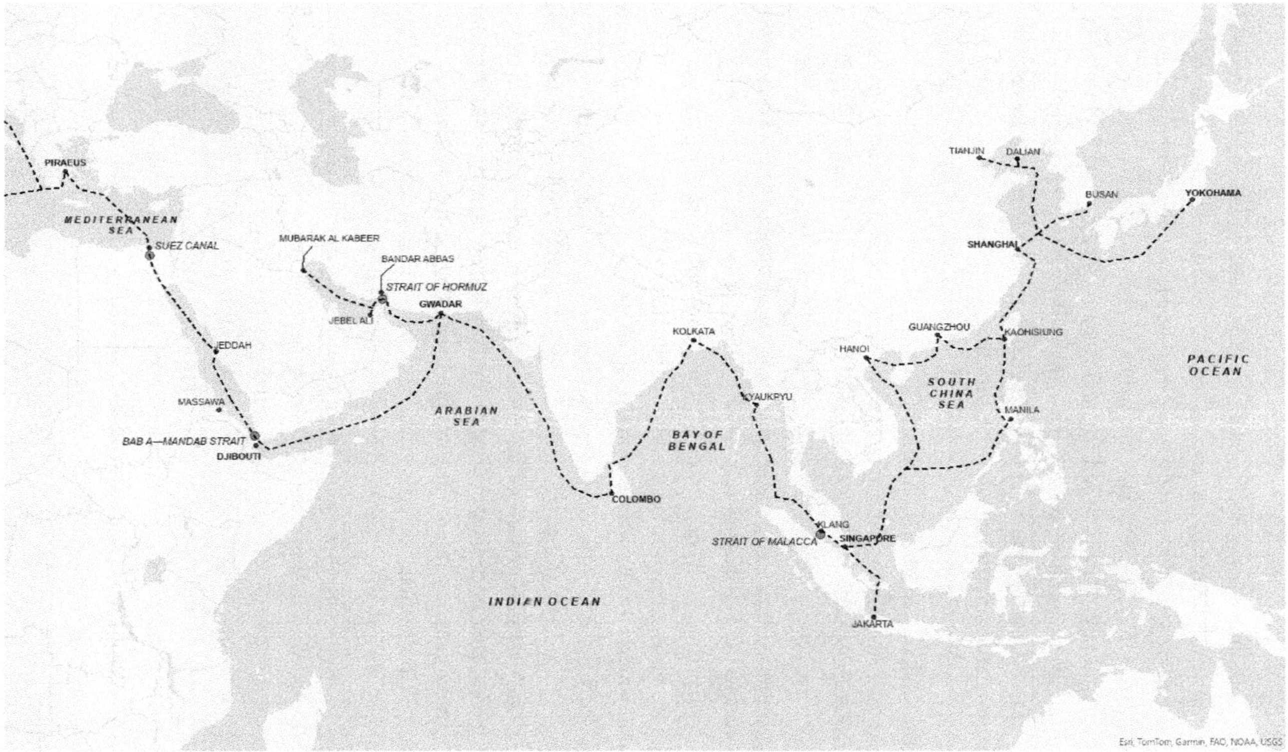

FIGURE 3.1 Key rimland port facilities along the Maritime Silk Road

SOURCES: Esri, HERE, Garmin, FAO, NOAA, USGS, © OpenStreetMap contributors, and the GIS User Community.

by both the brutality of the conflict and the associated costs, neither Japan, a traditional donor, nor the United States felt inclined to intervene. China, flush with funds, and intent on geopolitical aggrandizement, intervened aggressively to support the Sinhalese, tipping the military scales and ensuring their victory in the civil war in 2009. This triumph, regrettably, laid the seeds for the political-economic crises that would ravage Sri Lanka in the early 2020s.

The Rajapaksa family, which led the victorious Sinhalese side, was thereafter both politically advantaged within Sri Lanka and permanently beholden to Beijing. China later bolstered the Rajapaksa political fortunes in return—while helping itself geopolitically—by building a massive port and airfield at Hambantota, near Rajapaksa's hometown on Sri Lanka's southern coast, in literal sight of supertanker sea lanes. The airfield's single runway measures 3,500 meters (almost 12,000 feet), making it capable of receiving the world's largest passenger aircraft, the Airbus A-380, as well as large military transport planes.[29] The alliance with the Rajapaksas provided a durable beachhead for Beijing in the South Asian rimland periphery, until sharp spirals in commodity prices amid the Ukraine war abruptly forced the Rajapaksas from power in early July 2022.[30]

China's surprising buoyancy following the 2008 global financial crisis echoed resoundingly across those sea lanes and their rimland, replicating patterns within continental Eurasia. In the Mediterranean, Spain, Italy, and Greece were among the most badly shaken by the crisis, and all began forging deeper ties with China. So did Egypt, Sudan, Ethiopia, Djibouti, and Saudi Arabia along the Red Sea littoral. All these nations needed China as both a market and an investor. In Egypt, for example, China became the largest investor in the Suez Canal Corridor, investing more than $20 billion in multiple large, state-of-the-art container terminals, as well as manufacturing facilities in such sectors as fiberglass. China State Construction Engineering has also become the lead investor in development of Egypt's new $45 billion administrative capital, which will include the Iconic Tower, Africa's tallest building, as well as twenty other skyscrapers.[31]

Across the Arabian Sea, Oman has joined Beijing's longstanding ally Pakistan in support of China, following Sri Lanka's example. Iran and China have large cooperative projects in progress, as is well known. These include Chabahar Port, only 100 miles from the Pakistani border—a potentially important transshipment center directly south of Afghanistan and Central Asia.[32] Bangladesh and Myanmar, which also recently have strengthened their ties to China, also both signed on to the Maritime Silk Road in 2016.[33]

Ultimately, China's formidable ability to withstand the 2008 global financial crisis, and to continue its steady growth from 3 percent of global GDP in 2000 to more than 18 percent in 2020, transformed its position along the Eurasian sea lanes more than any single political-economic development of the past half-century.[34] Its rapid, sustained economic growth made it an attractive customer for the raw materials of Southeast Asia, Africa, and the Middle East. Its growing industrial capacity enabled it to function as a supplier of price-competitive middle-range manufactured goods, which were highly appreciated across the largely middle-income rimland nations of Maritime Eurasia. And its own growing affluence, greatly enhanced by the 2008 critical juncture, made it an attractive potential source of development assistance and markets, while generating fiscal resources—the dividends of rapid economic growth—that supported its military expansion at the same time.

Crimean Aftershocks

The 2014 Crimean crisis generated major shockwaves across Europe. Russia's annexation of the Crimea, after all, had been the first unilateral attempt to alter national boundaries on the continent since World War II. Most Western nations found this unprecedented unilateral move patently unacceptable. Moscow was ostracized and subjected to broad-based Western sanctions. This Western backlash forced Russia into the arms of a less-judgmental China, with major perverse implications for the autonomy of continental (especially landlocked) nations such as Mongolia and nearby states in Central Asia, as well as even North Korea. The maneuvering room long accorded these small "balancers" in the face of Sino-Russian tensions abruptly was reduced as those bilateral tensions between the Eurasian continental giants themselves subsided.

The Crimean crisis had a more indirect impact on the maritime rimlands than on land, as there were fewer Russia-China balancers like Mongolia along the sea lanes. The crisis did, however, further enhance the standing of China, which already had risen substantially following the 2008 global financial crisis. As in the case of Mongolia inland, smaller states along the sea lanes lost their ability to balance between China and Russia, or indeed to balance at all, unless the United States actively joined the geopolitical game. Yet a complacent Washington, decisively ascendent in a unipolar post–Cold War world, did not deign to do so, despite the strategic importance of the rimland nations in play.[35]

During this remarkable interval of American inattention, China, under a new president, Xi Jinping, began an unprecedented diplomatic offensive. Beijing's efforts shrewdly exploited both Russia's weakness, flowing from the 2014 Crimean crisis, and the newfound strengths of China's economic position from the lingering effects of the financial crisis. Xi announced China's land-based initiative, the Silk Road Economic *Belt*, on September 7, 2013, at Nazarbayev University in Astana, Kazakhstan.[36] He presented the parallel maritime initiative, the 21st Century Maritime Silk *Road*, less than a month later, on October 2, 2013.[37] The Maritime Silk Road thus was unveiled shortly before the political unrest in Ukraine that would lead to the Crimean crisis. Although the two events were not directly related, Russia's subsequent isolation from the West gave new leverage to Beijing not only in relations with Moscow itself but also with Russia's allies and erstwhile client states. China thus emerged from the Crimean crisis with enhanced geopolitical and geo-economic momentum on the Eurasian sea lanes, as well as with littoral states.

The Ukraine Conflict: A Fifth Critical Juncture

On February 24, 2022, Russian forces invaded Ukraine in by far the largest cross-border military action in Europe since World War II. Although the invasion failed in its early days to achieve a "decapitation strike" against Ukraine's capital, Kyiv, by mid-2024 it had already cost well over half a million lives. Ukraine incurred more than $410 billion in estimated physical damage during the first year of the war alone, with over 20 percent of farmland wrecked and 30 percent of the country littered with land mines or unexploded ordnance. By early 2024, the estimated costs of rebuilding Ukraine had risen to around $1 trillion, with over $10 billion of damage each month being accrued.[38]

Rebuilding costs continued to rise, reaching $10 billion a month as the war dragged on into its third year in late February 2024.[39] More than 6 million Ukrainians had fled abroad as refugees and over 5 million had been displaced domestically.[40] The invasion likewise provoked major dislocations in the global economy, far beyond Ukraine's shores, with major implications for the Eurasian sea lanes.

The dislocations from the 2022 Ukraine invasion, with their serious effects on the global economy, had two basic origins. Most obviously, sweeping G-7 sanctions against Russia, covering most trade and investment ties apart from limited energy flows, disrupted traditional commodity transactions. The disruption led to spiraling prices for food, energy, and basic commodities, ranging from aluminum to fertilizer.[41] Sanctions-related dislocations were compounded by wartime destruction in Ukraine, as well as Russian blockades of Ukrainian Black Sea ports. Ukraine's inability to actively use Odesa, once the busiest port in the entire Soviet Union, was especially constraining, although Ukraine's remarkable naval counteroffensive relieved pressure on Odesa and neighboring ports by early 2024.[42]

The global implications of wartime sanctions against Russia were especially pronounced in the energy sphere. Both the United States and Great Britain totally banned the import of Russian hydrocarbons, and Germany terminated the Nord Stream 2 gas pipeline from Russia. As Western firms withdrew from most energy-development projects in Russia, the European Union also devised a plan for phasing out gas imports from Russia as well.[43] Developing countries such as China and India absorbed a substantial part of diverted Russian energy supplies. Yet market dislocations, combined with broader global inflationary pressures, nevertheless provoked a rise of more than 40 percent in global oil and gas prices during the first three months of the conflict alone.[44] This increase was a particularly heavy burden for non-energy-producing developing nations.

The global implications of the conflict itself were most tragically felt in the food-supply area, where the impact fell heavily on the poorest of the poor. Before the war, Ukraine alone generated over 10 percent of the world's entire exports of feed grains. In 2020, Ukraine and Russia together exported 28 percent of the wheat, 26 percent of the barley; and 16 percent of the corn being exchanged in international trade.[45] Further, Odesa, Ukraine's largest port, was also one of the largest grain-export sites in the world—constrained by Russian missile threats from supplying global grain shortages worldwide.

The 2022 Ukraine critical juncture thus struck a savage blow to the Eurasian sea lanes and their associated rimland, from the early days of the conflict. Many of the developing nations along the sea lanes were both populous and major importers of food and energy, as indicated earlier in Table 3.1. Sri Lanka, for example, faced major social unrest and a deteriorating balance of payments situation during late April and early May 2022 that precipitated a large-scale political transformation, bringing down both the prime minister and the president.[46]

Political-economic shock waves shook other heavily populated developing nations of Maritime Eurasia as well. The impact was especially strong in Egypt, a nation of over 104 million people and one of the world's largest wheat importers; in 2021, 85 percent of its grain supply came from Ukraine and Russia.[47] (China, currently the largest wheat importer in the world, also was affected by the constraints in food supplies.[48]) With the onset of war, wheat prices rose 44 percent and sunflower oil (another commonly imported commodity) rose 32 percent. Much of the economic burden fell on the Egyptian government, which heavily subsidizes key food items such as *eish baladi*, a traditional flatbread used as a staple in home cooking, especially by the poor.[49] These food and energy price hikes, coupled with spiraling fiscal deficits and currency depreciation, stimulated severe consumer price inflation.

In Pakistan, the severe economic shocks provoked by the Ukraine war were intensified by underlying weaknesses and political-economic turmoil provoked by the COVID-19 pandemic and massive floods before the conflict began. Spiraling public debt and its broader consequences, including currency depreciation, were one major problem. Pakistan is largely self-sufficient in wheat (92 percent), but heavily dependent on imports for edible oils (71 percent), fertilizer (60 percent), and petroleum (60 percent). Sharp global price rises in these commodities, provoked by the war and intensified by currency depreciation, dealt a crippling blow to Pakistan's already fragile economy and exacerbated poverty in the country.[50]

In Conclusion

Half a century ago, the rimlands of Maritime Eurasia included, as they do today, vital sectors of the global political economy. There were the manufacturing centers of Europe. There was the oil-rich Persian Gulf. And there were also the teeming population centers of South and East Asia, with their immense growth potential but with an ominous degree of related resource vulnerability.

Five critical junctures since 1978—China's Four Modernizations, the 1991 collapse of the Soviet Union, the 2008 global financial debacle, the 2014 Crimean crisis, and the 2022 Ukraine conflict—have forced a new and more concrete Eurasian continental connectivity. China, most importantly, has grown large economically and powerful militarily, but also fatefully dependent on the energy and the markets provided by the Eurasian sea lanes. The rimlands adjacent to those sea lanes consequently have experienced much deeper maritime interaction than they had previously. Russia's overland presence, once substantial, has been reduced, while both China's land and sea presence has expanded, especially since the 2008 financial crisis. Even China's tilt toward Russia on the eve of the 2022 Ukraine conflict could not disrupt broader Chinese influence across the Eurasian rimlands, ranging from South Asia to the Mediterranean.

Some aspects of the rising interdependence among the Eurasian rimland nations are similar to what is transpiring in the continental core. Economic interdependence is increasing across sectors ranging from energy to information. And the critical junctures of the past half-century progressively have enhanced the geo-economic role of China across rimland countries, reinforcing China's influence further inland as well.

The tension between geopolitical stability and China-oriented change, however, is by no means resolved. Spiraling debt problems, especially for the populous food and energy importers, create further uncertainties. The contours of the deepening challenges within Maritime Eurasia, and the options for a Western policy response, are outlined in the chapters to come.

4

Guardians at the Gate
The Anglo-Saxons and the Indo-Pacific

Control of the sea by maritime commerce and naval supremacy means predominant influence in the world . . . because, however great the wealth of the land, nothing facilitates the necessary exchanges as does the sea.

—Alfred Thayer Mahan, *The Influence of Sea Power upon History*[1]

FOR THE PAST SEVENTY YEARS AND MORE, the United States has loomed large as guardian of the market economies clustered along Eurasia's eastern and western rims, from Southampton to Shanghai and Yokohama. In between, across the continent, stretches a vast overland expanse of largely authoritarian states, including China, Russia, and the Central Asian near abroad. To the south lie sea lanes—vital, liberating, and for many years the exclusive lines of both military communication and civilian commerce between the non-Communist nations of east and west. In the teeming Maritime Eurasian rimlands westward from China, adjoining the Indian Ocean and adjacent seas, live well over a third of the people on earth—many in functioning democracies and producing more than a sixth of global GDP.[2]

Over the three decades since the collapse of the Soviet Union, the geopolitics and geo-economics on land of Eurasia have changed markedly, influenced by the steady rise of China.[3] The middle of the continent has demonstrated far more cohesion than was formerly the case—a circumstance propelled by the palpable isolation, intensified by the Ukraine conflict, of Russia from the west, as well as the measurable strengthening of railways, roads, and pipeline networks supported by China's BRI.[4] Political-economic ties between China and parts of the so-called New Europe, the former Warsaw Pact members who were close to Beijing in Cold War days, also have revived even in the face of rising local suspicion in the West of Sino-Russian ties.[5] Along the Eurasian sea lanes to the south of the Eurasian continent, however, America appears to have retained its preeminence.

Singapore to Suez: The Far Side of the World

The United States has not always dominated the Eurasian sea lanes and their adjacent rimland. It is, of course, a young nation compared to several of the veteran resident powers of Asia. In particular, China's history with the adjoining sea lanes extends back more than a thousand years. And America's history of dominance in the Eurasian sea lanes is short even in terms of its own national story.

For the first two-thirds of its history, the United States lay diplomatically in the shadow of its British cousins, not only regionally within Eurasia but also globally. Although the United States has been an itinerant, marginal maritime player even from the early days of its existence, it lies, as geography inevitably reminds us, on the far side of the world from Eurasian waters. The Bay of Bengal and the Strait of Hormuz are both well over 7,000 miles distant from Washington, D.C. Eurasia's sea lanes also generally traverse a part of the world with which, for most of its first two centuries, the United States had remarkably little interaction. The major centers of early American political-economic power were on the Atlantic coast, almost exactly halfway around the world from India or Singapore. In contrast to the European powers, the United States held no colonial possessions in Asia until it acquired the Philippines from Spain in December 1898. And even then, the United States could achieve any potential access to Asia most easily across the Pacific, especially following the completion of the Panama Canal in 1914.

Reflecting the long but narrow nature of America's Eurasian sea-lane association, it was only in 1800, barely a generation after American independence, that Captain Edward Preble's frigate *Essex* became the first US Navy warship to enter the Indian Ocean during the undeclared "Quasi-War" with France.[6] In 1833, the United States established its first ties to the Persian Gulf, concluding a Treaty of Amity and Commerce with the Sultanate of Oman. Over the following decade, it achieved a virtual monopoly of trade with Zanzibar, so extensive that British visitors in to the sultan's palace in 1841 were astounded to encounter lively prints of US victories over the Royal Navy in the War of 1812 decorating the walls as they arrived.[7]

America's early Eurasian associations extended into Southeast and Northeast Asia, as well as the Middle East and Africa's periphery. Further east along the Eurasian sea lanes, the United States nurtured early ties with Thailand, with the two countries signing a Treaty of Amity and Commerce in 1833 just as Washington also was establishing ties with Oman. China was next, through the Treaty of Wanghia in 1844, soon after the Opium Wars. The Treaty of Kanagawa established US relations with Japan in March 1854, a few months after Commodore Matthew Perry's "black ships" first dropped anchor in Japanese waters. An American commercial treaty with Persia followed in 1856. Though the United States, like other Western powers, adopted high-handed tactics at times, Washington was late to formal imperialism and sparing in its overseas military deployments.

After an early start in establishing Eurasian ties, the United States turned inward during its Civil War in the 1860s, causing a hiatus in America's relations with the Indo-Pacific. Although William Henry Seward, President Abraham Lincoln's secretary of state, maintained an active wartime foreign policy, that diplomacy was directed mainly toward keeping the Atlantic powers from intervening on behalf of the Confederacy in America's civil conflict. For the beleaguered US government, Pacific affairs were not a central focus. Incongruously, the most dramatic early American naval involvement with the Indian Ocean came not from the United States of America, but from the Confederacy. From September to November 1863, the Confederate raider CSS *Alabama* staged a 4,500-mile Indian Ocean expeditionary raid from South Africa to the East Indies and back, evading the US Navy's gunship *Wyoming* and taking three Union shipping prizes near the Sunda Strait and the Java Sea.[8] Neither the Union nor the Confederacy, however, appears to have had a clearly articulated strategy toward the Indian Ocean.

By the late 1870s, with the Civil War behind it, a more outward-facing America was ready to explore commercial opportunities more actively across Maritime Eurasia. In 1879, Commodore Robert Shufeldt, commanding the man-of-war *Ticonderoga*, circumnavigated the Indo-Pacific in the course of his historic round-the-world voyage. After visiting Muscat to renew American ties, Shufeldt traversed the Strait of Hormuz, commanding the first American naval vessel to enter the Persian Gulf. After visiting Bushire and Basra, and steaming seventy miles up the Shatt-al-Arab, he sailed eastward from the Gulf—as supertankers were to do a century later—across the Indian Ocean and through the Strait of Malacca as well as the South China Sea. Upon reaching Northeast Asia, Shufeldt laid the groundwork between 1880 and 1882 for an unprecedented Treaty of Commerce and Amity with Korea.[9]

Britain's Deep Early Engagement

In contrast to the United States, Britain engaged deeply with the Eurasian sea lanes from its earliest days of exploration—first economically and later politically, nearly two centuries before the United States itself was founded.

That British involvement was first spearheaded by the East India Company, a private "national champion" with both monopoly powers and active support from the Crown, founded in 1600 to participate in the spice trade.[10] After vanquishing the Portuguese in India in 1612, the East India Company wrested trading concessions from the Mughals and steadily expanded its political-economic influence on the Indian subcontinent, gaining control of Bengal in 1757. The Company also traded tea, cotton, silk, and opium with China and others across the region, before ceding its official responsibilities to the British Crown following the Indian Mutiny of 1857. Private entrepreneurs also played a central role in Britain's early Eurasian engagements, particularly up to the 1880s. Apart from the East India Company, Stamford Raffles in Singapore in 1819, Jardine Matheson in Hong Kong in 1842, Rupert Brooke in Brunei in 1842, and Ferdinand de Lesseps in Egypt in the 1860s were instrumental in furthering the British presence along the sea lanes. None served formally as government officials.[11]

Behind this salient early role for entrepreneurs and adventurers, of course, were powerful political-economic forces. From the mid-eighteenth century on, Britain's demand for both raw materials and markets for its goods grew explosively, fueled by the Industrial Revolution. India and China as markets, together with Australia and Southeast Asia as raw material sources, became increasingly important for Britain, with the sea lanes an essential transmission mechanism. Those sea lanes also served as a conduit for the flows of civilian labor and conscripts outward from India that strengthened the empire in multiple dimensions.[12]

J. R. Seeley remarked in the 1880s that the British Empire "conquered and peopled half the world in a fit of absence of mind."[13] Indeed, the historical record suggests that the political dimension of Britain's involvement with the sea lanes and their neighboring rimlands was driven more by short-term crisis and expediency than by a long-term strategy of extending formal state dominance. The Crown's first strongpoint along the sea lanes was Gibraltar, acquired in 1713 through the War of Spanish Succession. Malta, Ceylon, Mauritius, the Seychelles, and the Cape of Good Hope were acquired in 1814 through the Napoleonic Wars, a conflict largely on the European continent. Singapore (1819), Hong Kong (1842), and Egypt (1882) came under British control through special circumstances only loosely related to national strategy. It was the accelerating geopolitical rivalries with France, Russia, and Germany at varying periods from the 1880s on that drove Britain to the dominant global hegemonic position—and, arguably, overextension—that it acquired at the height of the Victorian Age.

At its height, Britain was virtually omnipresent along the Eurasian sea lanes, as suggested in Figure 4.1. India was the key: the most populous component of the Empire, affording an impressive market despite its poverty, not to mention inexhaustible source of sepoy troops. As Lord Curzon, viceroy of India (1899–1905) and later foreign secretary (1919–1924) put it in 1901: "As long as we rule India, we are the greatest power in the world. If we lose it, we will drop straight away to be a third-rate power."[14] Apart from India, Australia, Singapore, Malaya, and a major neocolonial presence in China, anchored by Hong Kong, were all crucial dimensions of Britain's global power in Eurasia. In its heyday, Britain also enjoyed one other incomparable strategic advantage in the Eurasian sea lanes: control over the key chokepoints for maritime traffic between Europe and the Far East. As First Sea Lord Sir John Fisher put it in 1904: "Five keys lock up the world. Singapore. The Cape. Alexandria. Gibraltar. Dover."[15] Political control over these chokepoints, combined with Britain's naval strength, gave the Crown a dominance over the Eurasian sea lanes that no rival could match easily.

By the end of the nineteenth century, however, Britain faced a rising challenge to its global naval dominance from the potential alignment of three antagonists: France, Russia, and Germany.[16] In response, British Foreign Secretary Lord Landsdowne in January 1902 took a step unprecedented in modern diplomatic history: he signed the Anglo-Japanese Naval Treaty with the Japanese diplomat Hayashi Tadasu, who later would become foreign minister. Alliance, rather than the splendid isolation that former Foreign Secretary Lord Palmerston had so prized only decades previously became a central tool of both British diplomacy and Eurasian sea-lane geopolitics, with notable implications for the future.

For over twenty years, the Anglo-Japanese alliance proved strategically beneficial to both countries. For the Japanese, it provided an invaluable counter to tsarist Russia, allowing Japan to launch and win the Russo-Japanese War in 1904–1905, thus mitigating its nearest major threat.[17] And Tokyo also aided the British in World War I, during which the Imperial Japanese Navy convoyed British troop ships across the Indian Ocean, helping the British Empire to deploy more than a million Indian soldiers to the trenches in France. Following World War I, however, the geopolitical logic of the Anglo-Japanese alliance unwound, and it was terminated in 1923.[18] Britain's own role in the sea lanes declined, most dramatically with its defeats in Malaya, Singapore,

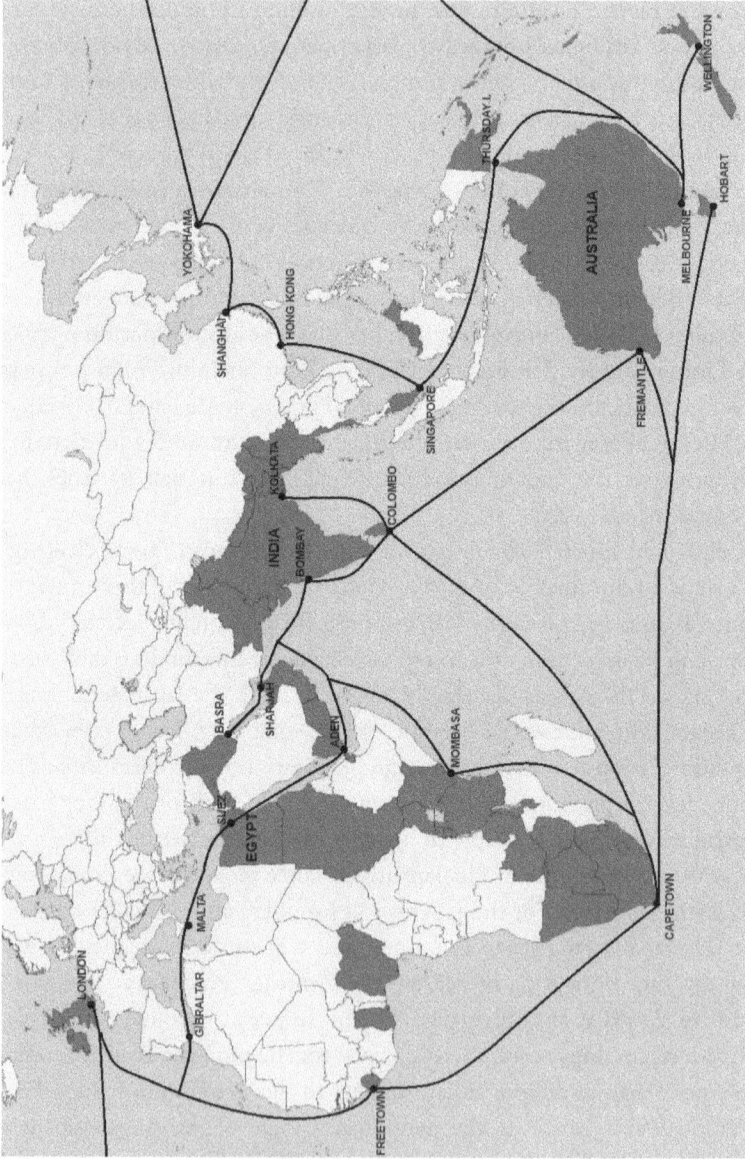

FIGURE 4.1 Eurasian sea lanes as lifelines to the British Empire (1930)

SOURCE: Author's illustration.

Burma, and the Andamans during early 1942. Despite victory over Japan in 1945, the Empire had been fatally undermined—the independence of India and Pakistan (1947), as well as Ceylon (1948), Burma (1948), Malaya (1957), and the Persian Gulf states (1960s), added to the toll. Finally, in January 1968, Prime Minister Harold Wilson declared the end of Britain's military presence east of Suez, which had been so prominent for over two centuries.[19]

An Emerging American East Asia Focus

For most of the first two centuries of American independence, during the vigorous years that the United States industrialized and rose to global prominence, its relations with the Eurasian sea lanes centered largely on East Asia. The United States opted to leave South and Southeast Asia, as well as the Persian Gulf, to the British and other European colonial empires. In April 1898, during the US war with Spain, Commodore George Dewey triumphed at the Battle of Manila Bay, beginning a turbulent half-century of US involvement—mostly colonial—in the Philippines. Even after the Philippines achieved independence on July 4, 1946, the United States continued to maintain a major military presence in the islands, with two of its largest overseas bases at Clark Field and Subic Bay until 1992.[20] Since the late 1990s, Washington has concluded a series of less elaborate military-access agreements with the Philippines.[21]

Diplomatically, America's core Eurasian concerns lay in China. Militarily weaker than many global powers of the day; less invested economically in Asia; and geographically distant across the Pacific, the United States could not dominate China directly. America therefore saw its geopolitical interests best served by the concept of an "Open Door," a notion articulated by Secretary of State John Hay in a series of diplomatic notes during 1899–1900. Hay proposed a free, open market and equal trading opportunities for merchants of all nationalities operating in China, suggesting that Chinese tariffs apply universally and be collected by the Chinese themselves, rather than by foreign powers. Hay also noted the importance of respecting the "territorial and administrative integrity" of China.[22]

Behind Hay's "Open Door" approach, which dominated US grand strategy in Asia for more than three decades, was a strategic calculation shared with Presidents William McKinley and Theodore Roosevelt, as well as the influential naval strategist Alfred Thayer Mahan. Their consensus view was threefold: (1) America's preeminent geostrategic challenges lay in Asia, rather than the Atlantic or the Western Hemisphere, (2) China's prospects were central to the future of Asia, and (3) the United States lacked the political and military capacity to unilaterally determine outcomes.[23] Accordingly, it made strategic sense for the United States to focus on three goals: (1) secure Pacific and Western Hemispheric defense, to the exclusion of more ambitious global concerns, (2) reinforce US preeminence at strongpoints such as Hawai'i and the Philippines, and (3) inhibit other major powers or coalitions of powers from establishing dominance in China itself.

US grand strategy of the early twentieth century toward Asia was thus an emphatically Sino-centric approach, dramatically different from the broader Indo-Pacific focus of later years. Maritime involvements between Singapore and Suez, by this logic, made little strategic sense for the United States. That region, after all, was a British sphere of influence in which the United States had only limited geo-economic stakes until the commercial development of Persian Gulf oil began in the 1930s. Further, the British enjoyed the embedded capabilities and prerogatives of empire, which the Americans in general still lacked, especially along the Indian Ocean littoral.

American concerns about the sea lanes connecting Europe and Northeast Asia thus remained muted throughout the first third of the twentieth century and well beyond. Washington's priority focus on the Pacific, as opposed to the Indian Ocean, was reinforced by three factors: (1) the early strategic calculations about East Asia's importance outlined above; (2) limited American political-military resources in the region; and (3) the riveting impact of actual military conflict—first with Japan (1941–1945); then China and North Korea (1950–1953); and finally with North Vietnam (1965–1973). Yet changing strategic calculations in the Middle East, driven by energy, mandated marginally increased attention there as well.[24] Both the Mediterranean and the Persian Gulf became new arenas of enhanced US concern largely unrelated to Asia, and the United States approached them primarily from the Atlantic rather than across the Indian Ocean.

A Middle East Anglo-American Fixation

Energy and geostrategy ultimately would drive the United States toward an obsession with the Middle East. Yet those dual concerns were surprisingly slow to emerge in Washington, D.C., during the early twentieth century. The nation of Israel, later to become a major US strategic ally in the region, did not yet exist, and oil was only gradually emerging as a strategic commodity. In World War I, motorized vehicles and aircraft became important in a major conflict for the first time, with naval vessels shifting rapidly from coal to oil as well.[25] Of the world's most prominent military and industrial powers on the eve of the war, only the United States and tsarist Russia were major producers and exporters of oil. All the other major powers, including Britain, Germany, Japan, and France, relied heavily on imports, principally from America. Indeed, more than 90 percent of the fuel powering Allied victory in World War I came from the United States.[26] Yet it was Britain, which acutely lacked domestic oil resources, that spearheaded these momentous geopolitical transformations and led the West's initial penetration of the Middle East.

For the first three decades of the twentieth century, Britain exerted overwhelming dominance in the oil industry of the Persian Gulf, based on early and lucrative positions in Persia and Iraq.[27] By the early 1930s, however, American oil companies had broken the British monopoly, gaining a foothold first in Bahrain. From that initial strongpoint, the United States soon expanded into controlling interests in Kuwait and Saudi Arabia.[28] The US government forcefully supported these efforts of private American firms, giving them enhanced leverage with local governments in the Gulf.[29]

World War II greatly magnified the emerging strategic importance of the Persian Gulf in the world of energy, as oil-burning vehicles, ships, and planes became more prominent in warfare. To be sure, the United States still supplied 80 percent of the oil fueling the Allied war effort—close to the share it had provided during World War I.[30] Yet denying rising Middle East oil supplies to nearby Axis-friendly nations, including Turkey, was a crucial Allied strategic objective. Around the same time, Persian Gulf refinery capacity, as well as crude production dominated by US-run multinationals, was rising rapidly, making supplies from the Middle East lucrative for Western firms as well.

These multifaceted changes opened important new possibilities for a globalist postwar future encompassing both Europe and Asia. It would be a future mediated by US firms and protected by American arms, though the continental United States itself continued to be self-sufficient in energy production.[31] However, even if the postwar geopolitical framework was otherwise increasingly American, the provision of Middle Eastern energy supplies remained for years an Anglo-Saxon operation. Five of the major petroleum companies that made up the so-called Seven Sisters global energy oligopoly were American, but two—Shell and British Petroleum, formerly the Anglo-Iranian Oil Company— were British. Moreover, as a longstanding colonial power with deep-seated socio-economic ties to the region, Britain also retained a degree of residual political influence in the Gulf, even as its role as formal protector waned during the 1960s and 1970s.

Military Conflict, Energy, and the Rising Strategic Importance
of Eurasia's Sea Lanes

The recent strategic importance of the Eurasian sea lanes for the United States,
and secondarily Britain, has passed through three historical phases. During the
first period, beginning with the start of the Korean War in 1950, the sea lanes
out of the Persian Gulf became a crucial energy-supply route for offshore US
military forces, as well as for the growing economies of US allies in Europe and
Northeast Asia. During the second phase in the 1960s, 1970s and 1980s, these
sea lanes also became a zone of fierce competition with the Soviet Union, as
the advent of satellites and nuclear submarines globalized formerly parochial,
Eurocentric confrontations. Finally, across the 1990s, Eurasia's sea lanes became
a realm of deepening competition with and leverage over China, as the Chinese
energy imports from the Persian Gulf began to rise along precisely the same
access routes as those of US allies.

US competition with China in the sea lanes, of course, remained a distant
prospect in 1945. The immediate issues then were America's own narrower
concerns, as well as those of its primarily Western allies. As peace and a modi-
cum of prosperity began returning to the industrialized West in the late 1940s,
for the first time in a generation, it was clear that the world beyond America's
shores would need more oil and that the United States alone could not supply it.
With Russia out of the equation amidst the Cold War, the obvious emerging
alternative was the Persian Gulf. Between 1945 and 1950, America's domestic
share of global petroleum production declined from 70 percent to 51 percent,
with the Gulf share more than doubling in this same period from 7 percent
to 16 percent.[32] An increasing portion of this supply, flowing up the Red Sea
to the Mediterranean, went to Europe. Yet few serious observers saw Asia as a
major energy customer. Nor did the sea lanes flowing eastward from Hormuz
to Malacca look like conduits for major hydrocarbon flows.

The Korean War and Rising Energy Demand, Military and Civilian

It was military necessity that first caused Washington to truly appreciate the
strategic importance of the Eurasian sea lanes—initially in the context of the
Korean War. As that conflict exploded on the world stage in June 1950, and
then escalated, oil stockpiles in Korea remained painfully limited. Middle East
procurement offered the quickest and most efficient way to supply US forces
in Asia. The refineries of the US Gulf Coast, after all, lay much farther from
the conflict zone than the Persian Gulf, and any oil shipments would have to

make a time-consuming passage through the Panama Canal and across the broad Pacific.

From the latter half of 1951, the Pentagon sourced almost all of its diesel oil and Navy standard fuel oil for the Korean conflict from the Persian Gulf.[33] Beginning in 1952, a substantial amount of the jet fuel used by the US military in the Far East—both Korea and Japan—also originated there. And by the last months of the Korean conflict, the Gulf provided the United Nations allies, as well as US forces, with all of its black oil, roughly a third of its jet fuel, a quarter of its motor gasoline, and more than half of its diesel oil.[34] Only aviation gasoline remained a fuel sourced exclusively from domestic US sources, and Middle Eastern refineries were developing capabilities to produce that as well.

The Korean War was thus a critical turning point in US policy toward the Eurasian sea lanes, caused by a critical shift in US operational military interests and a parallel devolution toward an integrated strategic view of the Middle East and East Asia. The Pentagon became conscious that sea routes from the Persian Gulf and across the Indian Ocean to Northeast Asia could be important to addressing the energy concerns of US forces deployed in Korea, Japan, and Southeast Asia, especially in the event of military conflict. This lesson also proved useful more than a decade later during the Vietnam War (1965–1973). That conflict further intensified American defense interest in the sea lanes west of the Malacca Strait, and their direct geographic linkage to more traditional areas of US strategic concern in the Far East. Together, America's first two major post–World War II conflicts thus gave the Pentagon a strategic energy interest in the Indo-Pacific sea lanes that it previously had lacked.

US geo-economic interests from the Korean War on in Persian Gulf oil supply also felicitously coincided with the civilian energy needs of US allies—first Germany and Japan, and later South Korea, among others. These countries all were growing rapidly, led by energy-intensive manufacturing sectors producing steel, ships, automobiles, and petrochemicals. The demand of these allied nations for hydrocarbons paralleled that of the US military, giving the United States, for the sake of its global alliances, still another reason to serve across the Eurasian sea lanes as a new Anglo-Saxon guardian at the gate.

Cold War Confrontation Broadens American Sea-Lane Involvement

The deepening Cold War conflict with the Soviet Union, from the 1950s through the 1980s, was a second major driver of broadened US strategic interests in the sea lanes between Suez and Singapore. One influential strand of American strategic thinking in the early postwar years, epitomized in the work of diplomat

George Kennan, had been that the Soviet threat was geographically and situationally limited.[35] Kennan considered Europe and Northeast Asia to be the central theaters of confrontation, with South and Southeast Asia distinctly peripheral. For Kennan, there was no clear reason for US-Soviet confrontation to become a global concern.

The contrasting view, epitomized in top State Department official Paul Nitze's April 1950 National Security Council policy paper NSC 68, was a more expansive notion: the Soviet threat required global containment.[36] The Korean War, exploding suddenly in the middle of 1950 on the opposite side of Eurasia from Europe, strongly reinforced Nitze's broader, more integrated view, although local political countercurrents in the rimlands periodically challenged this line of thinking. In 1951, for instance, the United States and Britain faced a surge of nationalist sentiment in Iran catalyzed by Prime Minister Mohammed Mossadeq, prefiguring the 1979 Islamic revolution led by Ayatollah Ruhollah Khomeini. Various US-sponsored multilateral security schemes in the Middle East and Southeast Asia, including the Baghdad Pact (which later would become the Central Treaty Organization, or CENTO), and the Southeast Asia Treaty Organization (SEATO), also collapsed. Regional instability thus perpetuated a geopolitical vacuum in the South Asian and Middle Eastern rimlands that challenged broader American Cold War aspirations to contain the Soviet Union.

Technological changes of the 1950s, particularly in two crucial dimensions, supported Nitze's globally oriented concerns.[37] The first was the advent and rapid technical advance of nuclear submarines. In January 1954, the United States launched the USS *Nautilus*, its first nuclear submarine. Later in the 1950s, it introduced the *George Washington* class series of submarines, capable of firing the progressively longer-range Polaris (December 1957), Poseidon (1972), and Trident (1979) missile families.[38]

The second technological advance, similarly propelling a global competition with the Soviet Union, was the dawn of the Space Age. In late January 1958, the United States launched its satellite, *Explorer I*—almost four months behind its Soviet predecessor, *Sputnik I*.[39] In December of the same year, the United States launched an Atlas missile containing the experimental SCORE communications satellite.[40] In July 1962, America's first active communications satellite went into orbit.

Within five short years, the United States (and, not long after, Soviet Union) thus gained the ability to hide their awesome nuclear power in the depths of the sea and simultaneously to deliver nuclear weapons accurately against adversaries thousands of miles away, provided that defense communications were adequate. These new capabilities, especially important for the non-aligned "far side of the world" stretching across South and Southeast Asia, to which strategic rivalry previously had not extended, fueled a broad Cold War competition that inevitably became global in scope. The ominous new potential of advanced weaponry in a nuclear age spawned a geopolitical rationale for more intense cooperation with local partners capable of providing basing, servicing, and logistical support. That logic has endured across the years, despite changing geo-political circumstances. The recent US-UK-Australia naval partnership (AUKUS) pursues similar logic in mid-twenty-first-century maritime geopolitical relations with China.

US imperatives for maintaining both nuclear and conventional deterrence intensified over the 1970s, as the Soviet Navy became increasingly active and capable in the Eurasian sea lanes. Under the command of Admiral Sergey Gorshkov, the Soviet Union placed particular emphasis on countering US aircraft carriers through an extensive building program for missile-equipped Soviet destroyers, cruisers, and long-range naval aviation.[41] To showcase its efforts to the Politburo, in 1970 the Soviet Navy held "the largest peacetime naval exercises ever conducted, with phases in the North Atlantic, the Mediterranean, the Indian Ocean, and the western Pacific, as well as in seas adjacent to the Soviet Union."[42] Major naval bases at Berbera, Somalia, and Socotra, Yemen, as well as an air base in Aden, Yemen, anchored this emerging Soviet activity along the Eurasian sea lanes. The Soviet presence significantly inhibited US freedom of action, as evidenced during the independence struggle in East Pakistan during 1971 that created the nation of Bangladesh.[43] Soviet intervention and support for the Bangladesh independence movement prevented the United States from preserving the integrity of its regional ally Pakistan, or dictating the terms of regional relationships surrounding an independent Bangladesh that were to follow.

Soviet intervention in the rimlands of South Asia during the 1960s and 1970s had a consequential impact on regional security for three major reasons. First, it strengthened the hand of India by providing both armaments and diplomatic support. Second, it weakened Pakistan's leverage in the region by facilitating the loss of East Pakistan—one-fifth of Pakistan's entire territory—which had provided a strategic edge in previous conflicts with India. This new weakness in turn encouraged the Pakistani government to support asymmetric terrorist activities that harmed the interests of India, and later the United States, in Afghanistan and elsewhere. Finally, it divided South Asia into two rough configurations—one inclined toward the United States and China, and the other toward the Soviet Union and India. The new South Asian regional equation initially encouraged rimland states such as Sri Lanka, the Maldives, and Bangladesh to align with India, with whom they shared both geographic proximity and cultural ties. This tendency, which lasted until around 2000, provoked an ambivalent stance toward any US presence in the region.[44] Over the past two decades, however, the rise of China and more positive US engagement have created a more fluid geopolitical picture.

China's Deepening Persian Gulf Energy Import Dependence:
New Leverage for the United States?

With the waning of the Cold War following the Soviet collapse, America's guardianship role in the sea lanes faced a fresh challenge across the 1990s and beyond: the rise of China and its deepening energy dependence on the Persian Gulf. From the early 1980s on, the Chinese economy grew at close to double-digit rates, concentrated in energy-intensive sectors like steel, shipbuilding, and petrochemicals. Energy demand rapidly outstripped China's domestic supply. Beginning in the fall of 1993, China emerged as a growing importer of Gulf-supplied oil and ultimately LNG as well.[45] China's oil imports continued to rise steadily for close to three decades, reaching more than 12 million gross bbl/day by 2020, as indicated in Figure 4.2.[46] Chinese LNG imports grew as well, especially during the 2010s.[47] These developments created important new Chinese dependencies and tensions with Beijing's neighbors that would factor into America's evolving guardianship role.

America's Post–Cold War Guardianship Role

The classical Cold War with the Soviet Union ended with the Soviet collapse of December 1991, less than two years before China became a net energy importer. Although their effects were not apparent at the time, these two developments would fundamentally transform both the functional importance of the sea lanes to the Gulf for China and the geo-strategic meaning of America's naval presence in those sea lanes. The US role evolved from being one of security guarantor for its allies with regard to the Soviet Union to a new yet parallel role of providing re-insurance against a rising China.

The future challenge to America's guardianship role in the Eurasian sea lanes lies in the enormous political-economic complexity of the ambivalent rimland nations between Singapore and Suez that separate longstanding American allies

Million barrels per day (MBD)

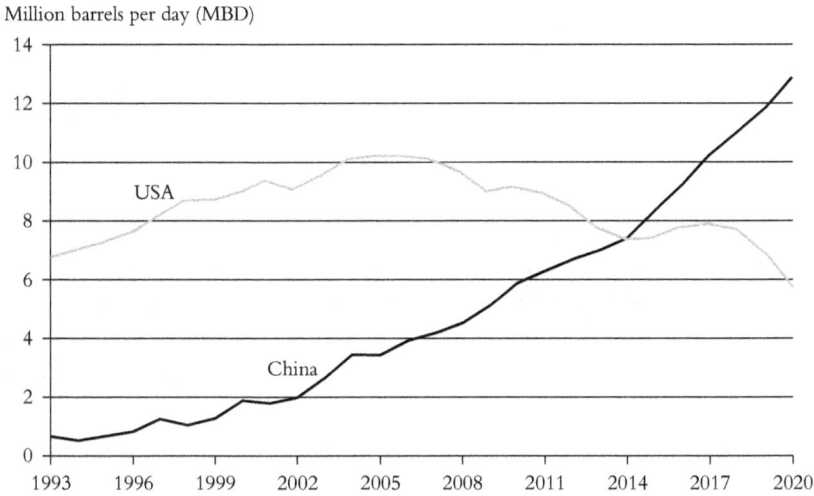

FIGURE 4.2 China's steadily growing gross oil imports (1993–2020)
SOURCE: IEA, *IEA Oil Information Statistics* (database), 2021 edition.

in Europe geographically from those in Northeast Asia. The vast expanse across the Indian Ocean and the Red Sea—around 5,000 nautical miles—passes predominantly through the Muslim world or the environs of India. Both areas, for historical, political, and cultural reasons, find the notion of Anglo-Saxon (including specifically American) guardianship problematic. This ambivalence creates significant challenges for an active US role in the rimlands, particularly with the complex aspects of deepening Chinese involvement there as well.

Within the Muslim world, a persistent complication facing a US guardianship role for the past many decades has been American support for Israel. Although the United States did support the creation of Israel in 1948, Washington was highly ambivalent about Israeli actions as late as the Six-Day War in 1967. Nevertheless, domestic political considerations pulled the United States into deepening support for Israeli military action that culminated in the Nixon administration's fateful decision to send weapons and supplies to Israel during the Yom Kippur War of 1973, and the ensuing Arab oil embargo on petroleum exports to the Netherlands and the United States, both seen as allies of Israel.[48] Washington once again supported Israel in a series of conflicts across the ensuing four decades, culminating in the Gaza conflict of 2023–2024.

US strategists, following Spykman, have not been myopic regarding the importance of the Eurasian rimlands astride the sea lanes. During the Eisenhower years, US Secretary of State John Foster Dulles did cobble together the Baghdad Pact and SEATO as strategic groupings in the region, and reworked the former as CENTO following the military coup and overthrow of the Iraqi monarchy in 1958. Yet none of these US-inspired multilateral alliances proved enduring, not least because problems in US relations with the Islamic world persistently complicated American initiatives.

Given the delicate ties between the Arab world and the United States—as evidenced in tensions surrounding the 1958 Iraqi coup, the regional backlash against a US military intervention in Lebanon around the same time, and the bombings of US diplomatic and military installations in Beirut during the early 1980s—the United States avoided a major forward-deployed presence in the Arab world until the Iraqi invasion of Kuwait in 1990. Until that time, the scant US naval basing presence along the sea lanes between Suez and Singapore was a small location in Bahrain, which it had maintained since 1941; the Diego Garcia base deep in the Indian Ocean; and the periodic presence of highly mobile US aircraft carriers, flexibly deployed from the Mediterranean.[49] To this day, the formal American military presence in the Eurasian rimlands remains politically complicated.

A second, more recent challenge to US relations with the Muslim world has been the US-led "war on terrorism" following the al-Qaeda terrorist attacks on New York and Washington on September 11, 2001. Whatever their view of the original attacks, many Muslims criticized the protracted US military actions that followed in Afghanistan and Iraq, with some likening those actions to the Christian Crusades of the Middle Ages. Such sentiments were especially strong among younger Muslims in developing rimland nations across the Middle East and South Asia, who often also suffered personally from low economic growth and extensive youth unemployment.

Without a significant direct US military presence in the heart of the Islamic world during the Cold War, the importance of Diego Garcia as a core element of the US guardianship role in the region has long loomed large strategically. As has been noted, this strongpoint in the heart of the Indian Ocean was conceived in the 1960s and fortuitously consolidated in the mid-1970s, after the fall of Saigon in 1975. Figure 4.3 illustrates its incomparably strategic location 2,500 miles south of the Persian Gulf. This position is enhanced by the proximity of nearby islands in friendly hands—India's Andaman and Nicobar Islands, as well as the Cocos Islands of Australia—that together control the eastern approaches to the Indian Ocean.

The island of Diego Garcia itself is part of the British Indian Ocean Territory, devoid of local politics.[50] Although this arrangement was created at significant

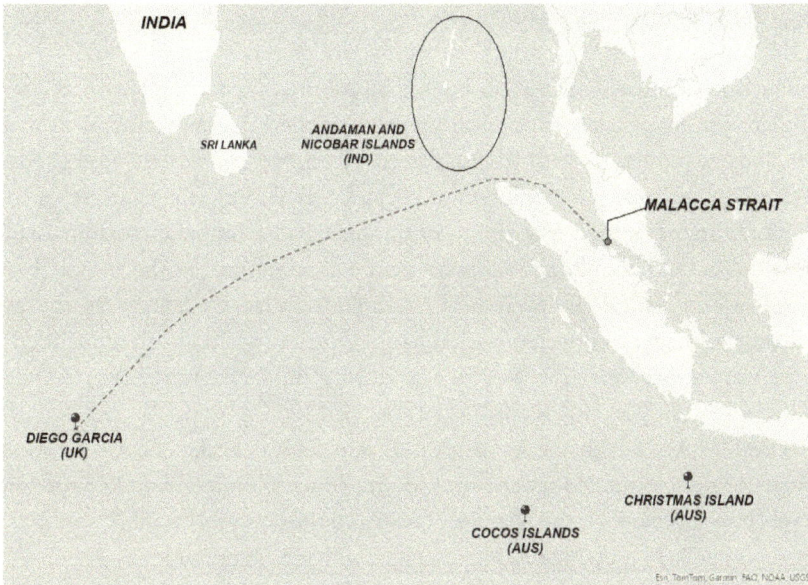

FIGURE 4.3 Diego Garcia in strategic context

SOURCES: Esri, HERE, Garmin, FAO, NOAA, USGS, © OpenStreetMap contributors, and the GIS User Community.

cost to previous inhabitants, it has provided the basing complex considerable operational flexibility. Given its location and its relative detachment from local political pressures, Diego is well suited to flexibly perform a wide range of military roles. It continues to host extensive US Air Force, Navy, and Marine Corps facilities, as well as large stores of prepositioned equipment and munitions, making it a powerful instrument of US security policy and a source of diplomatic leverage within AUKUS, and within the Quad as well.[51]

Political turbulence in the Middle East has forced the United States to contend with complex diplomatic situations that have challenged its military presence along the Eurasian sea lanes. Across the 1960s and most of the 1970s, as the global strategic importance of Persian Gulf energy reserves rose, the United States employed a "Twin Pillars strategy" that relied heavily on Iran as a regional proxy for American security interests and on Saudi Arabia to supply its energy needs.[52] Particularly after the 1973 oil shock and the ensuing Yom Kippur War, the United States greatly accelerated arms shipments to Iran. Key leaders in Washington, including the preeminent geo-strategist Henry Kissinger, supported the shah's self-assumed role as the de facto guardian of the Gulf, even as Britain downsized what had been a powerful presence east of Suez.[53]

The 1979 Iranian Revolution consequently presented a fundamental challenge to the American geopolitical presence in the Eurasian rimlands, even as US allies in both Europe and Asia, driven by energy concerns, found the sea lanes to be of increasing strategic importance. Following the collapse of the shah's regime in Tehran, Washington no longer had a proxy, apart from Israel, on which it could confidently rely for geopolitical support in the Middle East. This loss of a critical ally periodically created logistical challenges for the US military, as it lacked convenient local basing options when events demanded a more immediate American presence, as during the "reflagging" controversies of the Iran-Iraq War (1980–1988).[54]

The US presence in the rimlands thus remained episodic and intermittent, involving no systematic forward deployment of naval forces. The US Sixth and Seventh Fleets, based in the Mediterranean and the western Pacific, respectively, were compelled to operate at a distance or on only temporary assignments to the region. This proved to be a major tactical handicap, given both local political volatility and the high strategic stakes for Washington that were involved.

The Iraqi invasion of Kuwait in 1990 profoundly reconfigured the political-military equation in the Persian Gulf. Iraqi President Saddam Hussein's attempt to seize the productive Kuwaiti oil fields gave birth to the sudden, disturbing prospect of a sweeping geopolitical change in that strategic region, even as long-standing American allies had come to rely heavily on Gulf energy resources and thus on the Eurasian sea lanes. Equity markets in Tokyo, Seoul, and Singapore, not to mention New York, shuddered in response. The day after Saddam's invasion, Tokyo's Nikkei fell 1.9 percent, London's FTSE dropped 1.5 percent, and the New York Dow Jones average declined 1.2 percent.[55]

During the fall of 1990, the United States took up a more explicit guardianship role in the Persian Gulf by launching Operation Desert Shield—a "line in the sand" to defend Saudi Arabia that had more to do with allied energy interests than America's own domestic concerns. In the wake of the actual liberation of Kuwait during Operation Desert Storm, the United States established an unprecedented presence in the Gulf with boots on the ground and an enhanced maritime commitment, as indicated in Figure 4.4. The US naval presence, both at Bahrain and in the Arabian Sea outside the Gulf, expanded significantly, as did US Army presence in Kuwait. Following the US invasion and occupation of Iraq in 2003, the US further strengthened this physical presence in the Gulf, with increased American air power in Qatar and the

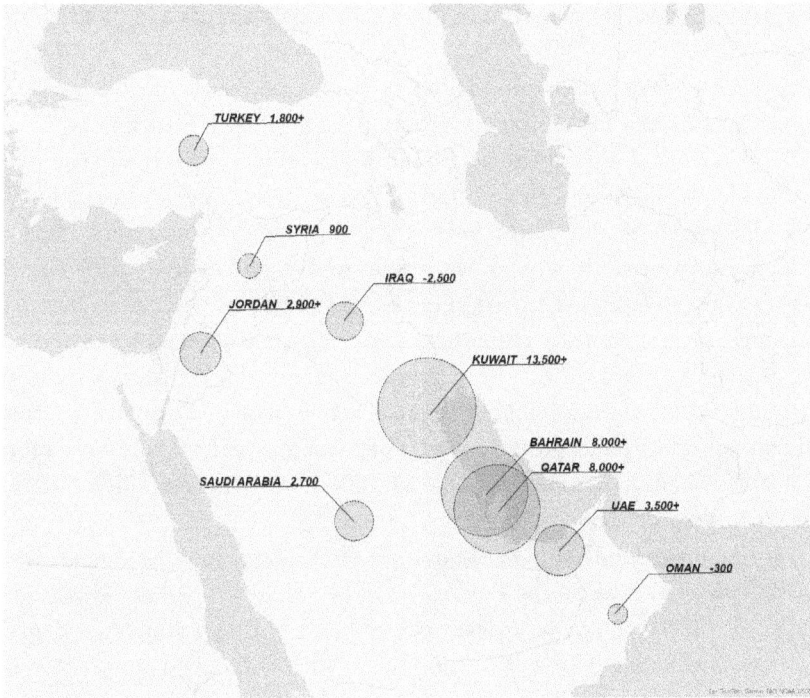

FIGURE 4.4 US military presence in the Persian Gulf (2023)

SOURCE: US Defense Manpower Data Center, March 2024 (for Turkey, Kuwait, Bahrain, UAE, Oman, and Qatar); Joseph R.. Biden Jr., "Letter to the Speaking of the House of Representatives and President pro tempore of the Senate – War Powers Report," White House, June 7, 2024, https://www.whitehouse.gov/briefing-room/presidential-actions/2024/06/07/letter-to-the-speaker-of-the-house-of-representatives-and-president-pro-tempore-of-the-senate-war-powers-report/ (for Jordan and Saudi Arabia). Created with Datawrapper.

United Arab Emirates (UAE). That robust Gulf presence has endured even after large-scale withdrawals from both Iraq and Afghanistan over the past decade.

Despite the end of combat operations in Iraq and Afghanistan, the United States continues to deploy around 40,000 troops in the US Central Command (CENTCOM) area of operations, stretching from Egypt to Afghanistan.[56] US deployments in the Middle East were at roughly half of deployment levels to Europe.[57] Bahrain, Qatar, and the UAE provided the backbone for US naval and air forces, with US ground forces concentrated in Kuwait.

The US naval presence onshore in the Gulf, unaffected by the US withdrawal from Afghanistan in 2021, is now more substantial than it has ever been. Bahrain hosts the headquarters of the Fifth Fleet and around 9,000 US personnel. The UAE's Jebel Ali port, which can handle vessels up to the size of aircraft carriers, hosts more US Navy ship visits than any port outside the United States.[58] And Oman has emerged, following a strategic port deal in March 2019, as an important additional destination, providing US warships enhanced access to the Gulf region outside the Strait of Hormuz.

Despite some marginal strengthening of US presence in the Persian Gulf, the challenges to America's continuing role in the Islamic world as a whole remain clear: the sociopolitical heritage of "9/11" and the ensuing decade of US combat presence in Muslim lands from Afghanistan to Iraq and Syria. US complicity with Israel's 2023–2024 Gaza incursion has also been an irritant. Yet as China's economic stakes in the Islamic world rise, the United States also has opportunities in relation to China, including support for the human rights of Muslim minorities from Xinjiang to the Rakhine state of Myanmar. To meet China's regional challenge, the support of Muslim maritime rimland nations such as Indonesia, Bangladesh, and the Maldives could have a significant impact on the future of Maritime Eurasia.

Fifteen hundred miles further east from the Gulf lies the Indian subcontinent—another waystation along the Eurasian sea lanes where US political-economic stakes and influence have historically been limited. The subcontinent, of course, was the crown jewel of the British Empire, which naturally marginalized any prospective US role. Following its 1947 partition and continuing to this day, India, with its massive demographic scale, remained defiantly nonaligned and skeptical of the need for alliance relationships, despite the Cold War and China's invasion of a disputed border region in 1962.[59]

The United States recently has become an important market and source of inbound direct investment for India, although US exports to India lag behind.[60] Meanwhile, China recorded more than $118 billion in bilateral trade with India in 2023–24, surpassing the United States as India's largest trading partner.[61] Defense procurements from the United States have totaled nearly $20 billion since 2008, and are rising.[62] Nevertheless, procurements from the United States are still greatly surpassed by those from Russia, even though dependence on the Russians is declining.[63] India for years also benefited from major Russian technology transfers and licensed production agreements, although these have been complicated since February 2022 by the Ukraine war and corresponding Western pressure.[64] Nearly two-thirds of Indian military aircraft in place, including nearly half of submarines and warships, continue to be Russian made.[65]

With its socialist tradition and embedded institutions, India remained decidedly ambivalent about both market-oriented foreign investment and multilateral agreements. Although a maritime nation, it elected not to rely on US naval preeminence and developed a substantial blue-water navy of its own, including two aircraft carriers.[66] It remained distinctly noncommittal, even though it was an indispensable anchor for any meaningful balancing coalition among maritime democracies against Eurasian continental powers. And its nonalignment became especially glaring in 2022 during the war in Ukraine, when it expanded energy imports from Russia in the face of Western embargoes.[67]

In Conclusion

As we have seen, the Anglo-Saxon geopolitical role in the Eurasian sea lanes has changed profoundly since the East India Company first set foot on local shores in 1608. The lengthy British interlude at the outset was explicitly imperial. Only in 1947 did the Indian subcontinent achieve formal independence, and only from the 1960s did it attain meaningful strategic autonomy.

America's role in the sea lanes and the adjacent rimlands between Suez and Singapore was distinctly secondary to that of Britain until long after World War II. The US maritime presence between Suez and Singapore gained a strategic rationale for the Pentagon during the Korean War—the first American overseas conflict fueled out of the Persian Gulf. The dawn of the Space Age and the advent of nuclear submarines also created global Cold War strategic imperatives that directed new attention to the Eurasian sea lanes, especially as the Soviet Union from the mid-1960s on began active involvement in Eurasian waters. The British withdrawal from east of Suez across the 1970s intensified the Pentagon's sense that the United States would need to take over this guardianship role. A final US strategic imperative in the Eurasian sea lanes has been the region's own internal energy trade. From the late 1950s, rapid growth in Japan and Western Europe, and then in South Korea, triggered a growing dependence across Eurasia on the Persian Gulf and its energy supplies, even as the United States itself remained largely self-sufficient. From the early 1990s, China also began to depend on the Persian Gulf. The steady rise of China, and its deepening maritime energy dependence, would become a major source of Washington's geopolitical leverage on Beijing.

The Anglo-Saxon guardianship role in the sea lanes, between Suez and Singapore particularly, has always been distinctive. It has its roots in empire—the British Empire, which dominated the sea lanes from the seventeenth century until after World War II. Since the 1980s, however, the United States has almost exclusively played the guardianship role, but it has been operating with a limited basing network between Japan and the Persian Gulf apart from Diego Garcia. And US guardianship stands outside the clearcut alliance frameworks prevailing in Europe and Northeast Asia. Consequently, the United States is by no means Britain's straightforward neocolonial successor. Furthermore, the United States has lacked the massive trade and foreign-investment stakes along the Eurasian rimland periphery typical of its involvement in Europe, Latin America, or (ironically) in China. Even in energy, US trade dependence on the Eurasian sea lanes, in the era of shale gas, is limited and declining.

How then, will America's guardianship role in the Eurasian sea lanes evolve? Is it an object example of the sort of overextension in which Britain engaged during the early twentieth century, which ultimately led to its international decline? How adequately is America's precarious rimland role configured to the challenges of the future?

Four key points are in order. First, the United States has formidable embedded defense capabilities in the Indo-Pacific, a legacy of its past activities. Most importantly, its strongpoint at Diego Garcia stands optimally astride the blue waters of the Indian Ocean. It is only 2,500 miles straight south of the Persian Gulf; less than 2300 miles southwest of Singapore, and directly astride the sea lanes from China and Singapore to South Africa. Diego, a British Indian Ocean Territory, holds minimal political risk and is admirably secluded—a perfect, confidential staging area for submarines, attack aircraft, aircraft carriers, pre-positioned equipment, and rapid-deployment forces. Felicitously, the local facilities were all completed over a generation ago, and so incur limited capital costs today.

America's embedded capabilities as the guardian of the Eurasian sea lanes have another formidable dimension: US aircraft carriers. The Pentagon has eleven of these worldwide. China, the runner-up, has only two that are currently operational, and both are of markedly inferior quality to those of the United States. Carriers, to be sure, have their weaknesses as well as strengths. They are enormously expensive—advanced *Gerald Ford*-class carriers cost over $13 billion each, or the price of almost 1300 anticarrier cruise missiles, not including the cost of the roughly twenty support ships in a carrier battle group.[68] Carriers are also already increasingly vulnerable to missile attack from such weaponry as the PLA-N's Dong Feng-21 and Dong Feng-26 ballistic missiles, not to mention hyper sonics now under development.[69] However, in the blue waters of the Indian Ocean, and in addressing natural disasters or dealing with nonpeer competitors, these carrier capabilities are a powerful American advantage, as are advanced US submarine and acoustic-detection capabilities.

A second American strength in a future guardianship role is Washington's extensive network of strategic alliance relationships. NATO allies in Europe, together with bilateral allies in Northeast Asia (Japan and Korea), as well as Australia, all rely on energy from the Persian Gulf, and as a result have economic incentives to support a US security role in the Eurasian sea lanes. Even more importantly from an operational standpoint, Great Britain and Australia have joined the United States in the strategically important AUKUS partnership, directed to multifaceted maritime defense cooperation across the Indo-Pacific. This partnership could complicate the strategic calculations of a rising China, as it gives the United States and its allies greater submarine resources and enhanced operational capabilities in the Indo-Pacific region.[70] In addition, India has joined the United States, Japan, and Australia in the looser, broader, yet complementary economic and security partnership known as the Quad.

In the aggregate, these defense-related networks are a central dimension of America's guardianship role in the sea lanes. The AUKUS partnership provides the hard-security base: dispersed, "federated defense" capabilities able to offer service and support hubs for naval power on multiple continents, with the Indian Ocean at the center. The submarine technology focus is particularly strategic, reflecting the increasing importance for the Anglo-Saxon allies of subsurface defense—in which the United States excels—as improved Chinese missile capabilities threaten to erode the relative potency of surface ships.

A third dimension of America's emerging guardianship role is its remarkably minimalist use of formal military bases, in contrast to their central role in traditional US positioning in Europe and Northeast Asia.[71] Most conspicuously, US forces recently have withdrawn from long-held positions in Iraq (2003–2013); and Afghanistan (2001–2021). The Pentagon now has formal bases along the sealanes between Europe and Japan only in the Persian Gulf (Bahrain, Qatar, the UAE, and Kuwait) and in Djibouti, limited repair and resupply facilities in Singapore, and the all-important strongpoint in Diego Garcia.

Although formal US basing arrangements along the sea lanes remain modest, especially in the Indian Ocean, Washington's defense network ties have allowed it to retain powerful influence over maritime chokepoints through which military and civilian transport of all nations must pass. The more extensive China's activity in the sea lanes becomes, the more important for both the United States and its allies this chokepoint presence also becomes as a source of leverage. In particular, the synergistic combination of Indian and Australian cooperation provides important geographic coverage of chokepoints at the eastern entrance to the Indian Ocean, including the Malacca, Sunda, and Lombok Straits. India's Andaman and Nicobar Islands, as well as Australia's

Cocos and Christmas Islands, are all important in the regard. Recent advances in hydrophones, robotics, and sonar monitoring, especially in the United States, are synergistic with Quad partner geographic positioning.

The US presence astride Eurasia's sea lanes, in short, has been reconfigured significantly over the past decade. The massive military presence in rimland nations like Iraq and Afghanistan is no more. Forward-deployed basing in Maritime Eurasia is more limited than previously. Yet Washington's Diego Garcia strongpoint, together with its blue-water carrier capability and chokepoint access, remain a consideration for any potential rival to American power. Key alliance structures such as AUKUS continue to strengthen the United States' vital undersea capabilities.

The continental United States remains, of course, on the far side of the world from the most strategic and politically volatile stretches of Maritime Eurasia. Direct US ties from Singapore northeast to Japan are more substantial, but there are sharp contrasts between US political, military, and economic involvement west and east of the Malacca Strait. Nevertheless, owing to its European and East Asian allies' ongoing need for stable access to the energy and commerce flows along those sea lanes—and for global strategic stability more generally—America is thrust into the incongruous role of maritime guarantor in a relatively unfamiliar part of the world.

How enduring can America's guardianship role in the Eurasian sea lanes and their rimlands be, as China rises? In the First Sea Lord John Fisher's day, more than a century ago, the Royal Navy confidently believed that it held the keys that could lock up the maritime future for Britain. Does the US Navy of the twenty-first century still command those powers, solidifying America's dominant geopolitical role within Maritime Asia and beyond, as China rises?

5

The Challenger

China and Eurasia's Sea Lanes

The primary objective should be to subjugate other states without actually engaging in armed combat, thereby realizing the idea of complete victory.

—Sun Tzu, *The Art of War*[1]

WITHIN THE EURASIAN CONTINENT, China enjoys a geographic centrality, coupled with scale, that in times of strength justifies its traditional appellation of "Middle Kingdom." It lies in the center of the habitable and heavily populated eastern core of the continent, surrounded by fourteen land neighbors and six others in close proximity by sea. China also has the largest population in its neighborhood, and until 2023 it was the most populous nation in the world.

Across the past four decades, China not surprisingly also has recorded the most rapid economic growth of any large nation on earth. Yet that growth has been driven not by continental ties with neighbors, but by commercial ties to nations far away, connected mainly by the seas. The United States, Japan, and Germany have been among its largest trading partners. Saudi Arabia, Angola, Australia, and Brazil all have been large commodity suppliers—necessarily delivered over maritime routes. Chinese exports, conversely, have accounted at times for close to 40 percent of its GDP, with seaborne trade dominant.[2]

Although seaborne trade has been central to China's recent economic rise, and the Middle Kingdom has grown to be heavily dependent on bulky raw materials imported by ship, its military has been configured along strikingly different lines than its economy. The People's Liberation Army, born of the civil war and the revolution that created the People's Republic of China itself, has always been far more developed than China's navy.[3] And that navy, until the mid-1990s was configured more for coastal defense than for global power projection, despite China's deepening interdependence with countries

all around the world. Only in 2015, with the introduction of its Near Seas
Defense and Far Seas Protection Strategy, did the PLA-N begin to fully globalize
its operations.[4]

For many years, therefore, economic pressures have been driving China's
increasingly ambitious definition of its political-military role in the Eurasian
sea lanes. Over the past decade, political priorities in Zhongnanhai appear
to have given this naval expansion more momentum. As one expression of
this trend, in December 2023 former PLA-N Admiral Dong Jun was named
Minister of National Defense, the first naval officer to hold that position.[5]
Naval expansion, to the degree that it materializes, also increases prospects for
tension with the United States and its sea-lane-dependent allies, most notably
Japan. China's growing offshore economic stakes from the Persian Gulf to the
South China Sea, together with its scale and autarkic great-power security
aspirations, easily make Beijing the primary challenger to US preeminence in
the Eurasian seas.

China's Maritime Heritage

China, to be sure, has a long history of engagement with its southern ocean
stretching across the South China Sea to the Strait of Malacca and beyond. It
has powerful reasons, driven by its explosive economic growth, for increased
involvement with the sea lanes, especially those from China to Europe, which
PLA-N analysts have termed "China's Maritime Lifeline."[6] China is already
more dependent on the sea lanes for its international trade than the global
average.[7] Manufactured exports as well as commodity imports will continue
to deepen this maritime dependence in future years.[8]

Although confronting a period when its maritime orientation will likely
intensify, China thus also builds on a longstanding maritime heritage. The
Middle Kingdom has been a central part of trading networks through the
South China Sea as well as intermittently a major production network for
them since at least the Han Dynasty. Chinese traders and vessels started directly
sailing in the South China Sea during the Song period (960–1279 CE).[9] As
we shall see in this chapter, China's shipbuilding industry also has as much as
700 years of tradition.[10]

Flowing from the traditional Confucian disdain for trade, as well as China's
all-consuming centrality on the continent, much of the early maritime interchange between China and the broader world was mediated not by Chinese but
by foreigners, including Srivijayan traders from what is present-day Sumatra.[11]
By the fifth and sixth centuries, however, Chinese vessels were sailing beyond

the Strait of Malacca in coastal voyages conveying Buddhist pilgrims to India and back, while also dabbling in commerce.[12] Between the tenth and thirteenth centuries, the Song dynasty began building its own trading fleets, in part because continental trading options had been foreclosed by its loss of access to the overland Silk Road. Chinese fleets then began hesitant trading expeditions to the *nan hai* (southern seas) during the fourteenth and fifteenth centuries, venturing as far south as the Sulu and Java Seas.[13] Chinese trading colonies in Southeast Asia also were founded during this period of outreach, and classic trading ports along the Fujian and Guangdong coasts began to prosper—including some like Guangzhou, which had been a bustling center of trade for several centuries.[14]

During the 1370s, following disastrous setbacks in struggles with the Mongols, as well as increasing attacks by Japanese pirates, the Hongwu emperor abruptly declared a *haijin*, or a ban on seaborne trade, directly particularly at private commerce. This ban continued in various forms, with varying degrees of implementation, until 1567. Both foreign trade and even at times the construction of sailing ships were strictly prohibited.

During the reign of Emperor Yongle (1402–1424), however, the Ming dynasty did launch the seven voyages of Zheng He (1405–1433) in a mercantilist effort to induce kingdoms south and west along the sea lanes to resume "tribute" to the Ming court. Given their geo-economic objectives, Zheng He's "tribute-diplomacy" fleets were purposely awe-inspiring. They included massive treasure ships, some more than 400 feet in length, with nine masts, and weighing over 1,200 tons.[15] Zheng He's 1405 maiden voyage included nearly 28,000 men, 62 treasure ships, and 200 ships of other sizes. His venture was the culmination of an era—over seven centuries long—during which China prevailed as the preeminent naval power in the world.[16] The formal ban on private trading continued until 1567, when foreigners once again were allowed to enter Chinese trading ports and Chinese traders permitted to venture overseas.[17] Even after the end of the trade ban, the new Qing dynasty continued to fear the subversive influence of expatriate Chinese, who numbered over 100,000 in Jakarta alone.[18] The Kangxi emperor banned trade with the "Southern Ocean" in 1717 and instituted tighter port inspections and travel restrictions within China itself. In 1757, the Qianlong emperor declared that Canton would be the only Chinese port open to foreign traders, thus initiating the Canton System of restricted trade that continued until the Treaty of Nanking concluded the first Opium War in 1842.

Over the generations of Song, Ming, and Qing regulatory ambivalence toward the sea lanes, alternately encouraging and banning foreign trade, a considerable

Chinese diaspora slowly began to cohere outside China itself. Populated heavily by commercial refugees from isolated trading communities along China's southern coast, between Shanghai and Hong Kong, communities of expatriates had been gathering in Southeast Asia since the end of the Warring States period (476–221 BCE).[19] Following the collapse of the Tang, Song, and Ming dynasties, as well as during surges of restriction or oppression of seafarers, emigrants from China steadily increased. In the late nineteenth century, the opening of the Suez Canal and a surge in Southeast Asia's economic development, coupled with British tolerance of unrestricted immigration into its Asian colonies, led to an overseas Chinese population in Southeast Asia by 1907 of nearly 7 million—the vast majority of all overseas Chinese.[20] By 1995, their numbers had grown sixfold to more than 30 million people, and the collective GDP of overseas Chinese in Southeast Asia had come to rival that of the People's Republic of China itself.[21]

China's Rising Maritime Economic Stakes

Given the huge and growing Chinese diaspora in Southeast Asia, accompanied by rapidly deepening trade and investment, both economic and cultural interaction across the East and South China Seas have expanded over the past century and more. Recent economic growth, however, has provoked a discontinuous shift. Following adoption of Deng Xiaoping's reform and opening policy in 1978, foreign direct investment (FDI) from the Chinese diaspora became highly influential in China's development, profoundly shaping policies toward foreign capital. By 1993 China had become the largest recipient of FDI in the developing world, with the Chinese diaspora contributing the bulk of the financing. Indeed, between 1978 and 1993, for example, the Chinese diaspora provided more than 88 percent of all FDI into China.[22]

Energy

Since the early 1990s, propelled by rapid economic growth, China has become increasingly reliant on the energy resources delivered over the Eurasian sea lanes from the Persian Gulf. Until the fall of 1993, China was a net oil exporter, but by 2023 it was importing more than 11 million bbl/day.[23] Its reliance on the energy sea lanes from the Gulf, and across the Indian Ocean from Africa, is liable to deepen still further. The International Energy Agency forecasts, for example, that Chinese seaborne oil imports will reach 15 million bbl/day by 2030, with the bulk flowing from the Gulf and from Africa.[24] China also is becoming a major importer of LNG across those same sea lanes from the Gulf.

Industrial Raw Materials

Energy is by no means the only raw material that the sea lanes bring back to China. China's massive industrial plant, which churns out half of the world's steel, imports huge amounts of iron ore, manganese, copper, and other minerals. The wide-ranging activities of Chinese multinationals, under the "going out strategy" of overseas investment and resource acquisition that has prevailed over the past decade, are facilitating imports from Africa, Latin America, and the Middle East. That said, structural shifts toward knowledge-intensive sectors are moderating these commodity-import flows. Insatiable raw-material demand is also driving China's extensive efforts in undersea resource development, as described in Chapter 2.

Food Supply

China's resource imports across the sea lanes are by no means limited to commodities such as food, industrial raw materials, and energy. China is also deeply linked to the sea lanes through its enormous fisheries production and trade. It has, first of all, the largest marine-capture production in the world, comprising 15 percent of the global total in 2020. Chinese fisheries production is rapidly growing; in 2020, it reached 308 percent of its 1980 levels.[25] Chinese fishermen also are venturing further and further afield, particularly since the 1980s, when an extensive distant-water fishing (DWF) subsidy program was introduced. In those years China also began to provide tax-exempt status, fuel subsidies, insurance support, and diplomatic cover to promote the expansion of DWF operations.

In addition to being the world's largest fish processor, China also has been the largest national marine-products exporter since 2002. At the same time, since 2011 it likewise has become the second-largest importer for this category in terms of value.[26] The European Union, as a collective of twenty-seven nations, looms somewhat larger than China in global import and export shares, but China has significantly larger shares along both dimensions than does any individual nation.[27]

Equally relevant to China's role in the sea lanes to its enormous shares in global fisheries markets is the huge size of its fishing fleet, and that fleet's relentless upgrading. In 2010, China had more than 675,000 fishing boats, with a total tonnage of 8.8 million tons.[28] By 2019, more than 90 percent of those vessels were motorized, and their average scale was steadily increasing. This fleet naturally includes the geopolitically relevant scope of China's DWF fleet, which is orders of magnitude larger than its US or European competitors. Chinese official statistics reported 2,551 registered DWF vessels and 177 approved DWF enterprises in 2022.[29] New research by the Overseas Development Institute in London, however, indicates that China's DWF is actually five to eight times the reported size, with around three-quarters of the fleet actually located outside internationally recognized Chinese waters.

The vast DWF fleet apparently holds three purposes for China. First, it is primed to meet a growing demand for seafood at home: currently, Beijing requires its fleet to return nearly two-thirds of its catch to Chinese markets. Second, it helps in asserting territorial control over historic claims, particularly in the South China Sea and often with the support of Chinese coast guard vessels. Finally, it helps to promote national governmental interests associated with the BRI.[30]

Confronting the Malacca Dilemma

In dealing with the very real energy and food-supply challenges of a nation of 1.4 billion people who have benefited from the high-speed economic growth and rising affluence of the past four decades, China faces a sharpening dilemma. At least 90 percent of its trade is seaborne, as noted earlier, and it is particularly dependent on the sea lanes to the Strait of Malacca and beyond to the Persian Gulf and Europe.

As President Hu Jintao pointed out in November 2003, given the country's need to control its own destiny even in the face of rising energy imports, China must decide how to respond to the efforts of "certain powers" to control navigation through the Strait of Malacca and beyond.[31] This dilemma came to a head explicitly early in this century, as energy imports through the Strait of Malacca grew even as US military forces entered Baghdad in April 2003. Yet the challenge itself has much deeper origins.

Modern China's apprehensions about adversarial control of its southwestern sea lanes to Malacca and beyond long predate its dependence on imported oil from the Persian Gulf. Those fears had geopolitical origins rooted in history, with Japan and the Soviet Union, in addition to the United States. In June 1971, for example, weeks before Henry Kissinger's secret visit to Beijing, Chinese Premier Zhou Enlai condemned "Japanese reactionaries" who were attempting to revive the old dream of a Greater East Asia Co-Prosperity Sphere by "brazenly claiming" that territories all the way to the Strait of Malacca were Japan's lifeline.[32] The Chinese leadership persistently attacked Japanese Prime Minister Sato Eisaku both for his support of Taiwan and for his allegedly expansionary designs on Southeast Asia, in cooperation with the United States.[33]

For close to two decades from 1979, China also was deeply suspicious of Soviet designs on the Strait of Malacca. It asserted that the Soviets pursued a "dumbbell strategy" of attempting to dominate the Indo-Pacific, with Malacca as a critical link.[34] Beijing saw Soviet naval activism in the Indian Ocean as a dangerous counterpart to Moscow's pressure on China's northern border, aimed at encirclement of China.

Following the Soviet collapse in 1991 and the end of the Cold War, China's concerns about its sea lanes to Malacca apparently receded for close to a decade. Indeed, across the 1990s geopolitical concerns about the Strait of Malacca were more common in Washington than Beijing, revolving about a postulated but as yet unestablished Chinese threat.[35] Deterioration in US-China relations early in the George W. Bush administration, however, provoked by the Rumsfeld-Wolfowitz strategic vision of US global hegemonic dominance, and intensified by the April 2001 aerial confrontation over Hainan, in which a Chinese fighter pilot was killed, revived Chinese geo-economic concerns about Malacca once again.[36]

By the early 2000s, however, rising energy imports across the oceans had become an important economic backdrop to Chinese policymaking. In August 2002, a *People's Daily* report on the Fourth Asian Middle East Association conference first connected the Strait of Malacca to Chinese energy security.[37] The following year, China established its National Petroleum Reserve Office and started to build its first strategic oil reserves. The US intervention in Iraq, where China had major energy investments, in that same year intensified Beijing's geo-economic concerns.

President Hu Jintao reportedly first articulated the concept of the "Malacca Dilemma" at China's Central Economic Work Conference on November 29, 2003. The Chinese government initially disseminated the message through unofficial channels, likely to avoid provoking foreign stakeholders in the Asia-Pacific region. The first article to authoritatively use the phrase "Malacca Dilemma" appeared around a week after Hu's reported address.[38] The following month, a pro-Beijing, state-owned Hong Kong newspaper, *Wen Wei Po*, elaborated that Hu had further demanded that his colleagues "formulate new oil and energy policies from a strategic viewpoint."[39] And from 2004, China began expanding its naval capacities, transferring the converted Soviet carrier *Vartag* to a Dalian drydock in 2005 and launching its first domestically produced aircraft carrier, the *Shandong*, in 2017.[40]

Hu's Malacca Dilemma continues to be a core issue in Eurasian maritime geopolitics to this day, and a central concern of this chapter. China is adopting a hybrid approach to this question with both civil and military dimensions. Even as it expands its naval and paramilitary capabilities, including its coast guard, China is developing overseas port facilities in Myanmar and Pakistan, as well as overland infrastructure connecting the Indian Ocean to western China, to reduce overall national reliance on the Strait. It is also aggressively pursuing alternative energy policies, including rapid expansion of electric vehicles, to the same effect.

China's approach over the past two decades to its deepening Malacca Dilemma—a problem ironically fueled by its own prosperity—is fourfold. It has expanded its navy significantly, with a related comprehensive strengthening of civilian and military domestic security infrastructure. These shifts are especially pronounced in areas adjoining the sea lanes, especially in China's southernmost province of Hainan. China also, however, nurtures gray zones where its economic and geopolitical interests converge, such as development of its massive blue-water fishing fleet. It has been developing hybrid strongpoints along the sea lanes to Malacca, and beyond to Europe, that combine trade, information processing, and ultimately military functions. And it has been working intensively to develop industries that help reduce foreign energy and raw-material reliance, including electric vehicles and solar power.

Rising Formal Chinese Naval Strength: Myth and Reality

There is little question that formal Chinese naval strength, as distinct from the substantial gray-zone and quasimilitary capabilities outlined above, also has risen steadily and substantially in recent years. During the late 1960s and the 1970s, China passed first France and then Great Britain in naval tonnage. Early in the twenty-first century (2004–2014), the PLA-N also markedly extended its operational ambitions from "near-sea defense" to "far-sea protection."[41] As it began building aircraft carriers and expanding its fleet of other capital ships, such as cruisers and destroyers, China passed Russia in naval tonnage around 2015. Soon, it had developed by a significant margin the largest and most powerful navy in Indo-Pacific waters, apart from the United States. Indeed, over the 2010s decade alone (2010–2019) the PLA-N grew by 200,000 tons, or an amount equal to the displacement of the entire British Royal Navy. China's navy today is almost twice as large as Japan's by tonnage, and well over twice the size of India's, as indicated in Table 5.1. As the table suggests, China's naval strength looms large relative to that of other major Asian powers, even without

TABLE 5.1

Chinese naval expansion in comparative perspective (1980–2019)

	1980	1990	2000	2010	2019
	(Unit: % global naval tonnage)				
United States	43	41	45	45	41
China	1	2	5	7	10
Russia	32	33	11	9	8
Japan	1	2	4	5	5
India	1	2	3	3	4
Great Britain	6	4	4	3	0

SOURCES: Brian Crisher and Mark Souva, "Power at Sea: A Naval Power Data Set, 1865–2011," *International Interactions* 40, no. 4 (2014): 602–29, http://www.briancrisher.net/naval-data-project; and IISS updates.

the substantial "gray" capabilities outlined above. Russia's navy has declined substantially in absolute terms since the end of the Cold War. Japan's Maritime Self Defense Forces has grown since the 1980s, but it has not done so nearly as rapidly as China. Neither has the Indian Navy.

By some measures, China's navy now even rivals or exceeds that of the United States in scale. Its surface fleet in 2025, for example, is expected to reach 395 ships, considerably larger than the US Navy's 2024 figure of 292.[42] And the PLA-N naturally has a far-greater concentration of its fleet in the Eurasian sea lanes, as US naval operations are considerably more global than those of China.[43] Further, many Chinese naval vessels are produced domestically at a much lower cost than similar procurement in the United States, with all but top-line vessels arguably comparable in quality to at least those of Asian regional navies.

China's surface ship force does include a heavy share of small vessels chronically ill-suited for global power projection, so a strictly numerical comparison with US naval strength would be misleading. The PLA-N has, however, improved markedly in qualitative terms, especially over the past decade. It has two operating aircraft carriers, commissioned in 2012 and 2019, respectively, and a third has been formally launched.[44] There are also plans for a fourth carrier, which is likely to be nuclear-powered and well-suited for extended long-range deployments.[45] The PLA-N likewise is deploying an innovative group of multi-mission craft, including a hybrid amphibious assault ship/aircraft carrier capable of launching combat drones and fighter jets, as well as transport helicopters and amphibious assault troops. Such multipurpose vessels will enable Beijing to project power far from its shores sooner than conventionally expected.[46] And China is significantly improving the PLA-N's antiship, ASW, and air defense capabilities through innovative, highly mobile vessel development and rapidly improving A2/AD missile capabilities.

China clearly seems to be stressing defensive capabilities in its naval procurement, striving first of all to repel US naval power in maritime areas that China claims as its own, both surrounding Taiwan and including most of the South China Sea. The PLA-N has developed a variety of antiship missiles, including the CJ–1; CX–1; and YJ–12 versions, well as the highly advanced YJ–18 supersonic anti-ship missile.[47] It also has developed two types of antiship ballistic missiles (ASBMs), designed to hit and destroy surface ships, including US aircraft carriers. Its inventory includes the road-mobile DF–21D, with a range of 1,500 kilometers, as well as the multirole DF–26 intermediate-range missile, with a range of 4,000 kilometers.[48] These growing capabilities render US surface-ship access to waters near China problematic in case of contingency, increasing the importance of submarines and long-range surface capabilities for both countries.

Although the East and South China Seas, directly adjoining China's most important population and industrial centers, are of greatest strategic concern to China, Beijing can by no means ignore the Bay of Bengal.[49] The apex of the bay in Bangladesh lies extremely close to major industrial centers in Yunnan and Sichuan Provinces, and its deep, temperate waters and complex hydrology make it ideal for submarine operations, including strategic deployments. Local differences over water rights, Exclusive Economic Zones, and Rohingya refugees, with Sino-Indian geopolitical rivalries in the background, introduce elements of conflict. Responding to intraregional tensions, both Bangladesh and Myanmar, with the support of China and India, deploy submarines and engage in active ASW operations there.[50]

China, of course, includes a long-range submarine force in its naval arsenal, including six *Jin*-class nuclear SSBNs, each carrying up to 12 JL–2 submarine-launched ballistic missiles. The JL–2 missile appears to have a range of just over 5,000 miles. The PLA-N's Yulin naval base, where the bulk of the advanced *Jin*-class submarines are based, lies some 5,000 miles from Alaska, nearly 6,000 miles from Hawai'i, and more than 7,000 miles from the West Coast of the mainland United States. Consequently, China's SSBNs appear to have at best only a marginal deterrence capacity from their home staging areas in the South China Sea.[51]

At present, China also appears to lack the capability to challenge the United States on the blue waters of the Pacific or the Indian Ocean. Although its rising missile capabilities and land-based air defense give it clear advantages in any prospective combat close to its frontiers, outside the First Island Chain in the Pacific it also is disadvantaged geopolitically by US dominance along its periphery.[52] The PLA-N fully operates only two carriers—conventionally powered rather than nuclear at present, and relatively elemental ones at that—compared to eleven for the United States. And China has not developed America's formidable carrier battle groups to support the carriers that it does have.[53] It has, however, stressed submarine development and has been making sustained technological advances.[54] It appears to have been making particular progress in developing autonomous underwater vehicles (AUVs) for marine surveillance and reconnaissance, although the United States still has major advantages in undersea surveying and mapping.[55] As of 2023, the PLA-N had only a modest fleet of six nuclear-powered ballistic missile subs, compared to eighteen more capable *Ohio*-class SSBNs in the United States.[56]

Although China clearly has long-term aspirations to develop powerful blue-water capabilities, its short-term security concerns are clearly defensive and directed closer to home. Taiwan undeniably is a top priority, with implications to be considered in depth in future chapters. Suffice it to say here that any shift in the broad sea-lane balance of power south and west from the Taiwan Strait undermines the stability of the Cross-Strait status quo as well.

Along China's coasts and in the South China Sea, an important development since 2010 has been the emergence of a Chinese-built "Underwater 'Great Wall'" of hydroacoustic sensors and related sonar countermeasures and autonomous undersea gliders, located at depths of up to 3,000 meters.[57] This formidable infrastructure likely is directed against sophisticated American underwater capabilities. Located in part on military bases on artificial islands recently built in the Spratly Archipelago, the sensors reportedly feed into fiber-optic cables on the same reefs, housing the latest missiles.

The new Great Wall appears to have three major strategic goals: (1) monitoring vessels passing through contested waters; (2) raising the costs of intervention in a conflict in the South China Sea, especially over Taiwan; and (3) intimidating or spying on other states.[58] China thus appears to be developing a comprehensive network of undersea devices, exploiting the latest artificial-intelligence and robotics technology that it has available. The network appears designed primarily to assert A2/AD preeminence over US or allied forces around the periphery of Taiwan. It also, however, could constrain Japanese and South Korean sea lanes to Southeast Asia and the Persian Gulf in the event of conflict.

China's Expanding Naval Base Network

China's major established naval bases are concentrated at home, along its 9,000-mile-long eastern coastline. The most historically important strongpoint, often termed the "city of the navy," is arguably the northeastern city of Lüshun, known before World War II as Port Arthur. Lüshun is the home port of many of China's most modern destroyers, submarines, and escort vessels, and was the initial home port of the *Liaoning*, China's first aircraft carrier. Strategically positioned on the Bohai Strait, next to the important commercial port of Dalian, as indicated in Figure 5.1, Lüshun controls access from the Yellow Sea to strategic power centers of China, including Beijing and Tianjin, and suggests the embedded defensive orientation of China's navy—especially its forces deployed in the north of the country.

Another historically important naval base in China's north is Jianggezhuang, fifteen miles east of Qingdao on the Yellow Sea, and the headquarters of the PLA-N's Northern Theater Navy. Before World War I, Qingdao was a German concession and a strongpoint for German naval operations. The Jianggezhuang Naval Base contains training schools for pilots, submariners, and other specialists. It is one of China's three major submarine bases, home to both Type 092-class SSBNs and also Type 091-class nuclear attack submarines.[59] Nearby Qingdao is also the headquarters of China's major undersea natural-resource development program.

China's Eastern Theater Navy is headquartered at Ningbo, once the Ming Dynasty sea port from which Zheng He sailed as far as Zanzibar. Nearby is the Dinghai naval base, which houses the many mobile frigates that make up the bulk of the Eastern Theater Navy. Commanding the northern approaches to the Taiwan Strait, this base houses China's most state-of-the-art guided missile destroyers, whose deployment suggests the high priority that Beijing places on the Taiwan issue.

Some of China's most important naval bases are in the southeast, reflecting the rising strategic importance of the South China Sea and the sea lanes southwestward to Singapore and onward to the Persian Gulf. Zhanjiang, about 150 miles southwest of Hong Kong, is the headquarters of China's Southern Theater Navy. With a natural deep-water harbor, it is one of only a few Chinese ports accessible to large vessels at all stages of tide. It is also home to the PLA's Strategic Support Force—the cyber, space, and electronic-warfare service branch of the PLA. Yulin Naval Base, located on the south shore of Hainan Island fronting on the South China Sea near Sanya, arguably is the Southern Theater Navy's most important support facility. Construction began in 2000 and has been continuing since then; the facility already contains four submarine piers capable of handling any submarine in the PLA-N's service, as well as berthing facilities for two aircraft carriers and for amphibious assault

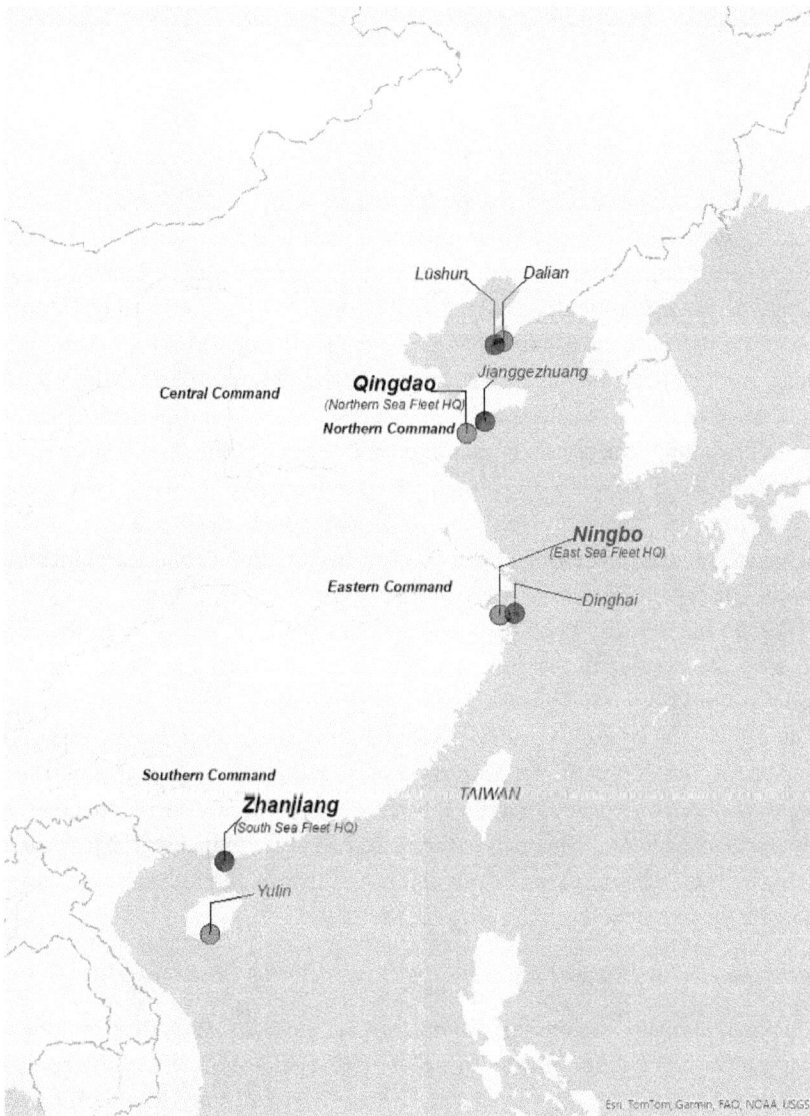

FIGURE 5.1 China's major domestic naval bases and their strategic orientation

SOURCES: US Department of Defense and author's illustrations, with Esri, HERE, Garmin, FAO, NOAA, USGS, © OpenStreetMap contributors, and the GIS User Community.

NOTE: Major bases and military commands noted in bold.

ships. Beijing also reportedly plans to homeport all of China's largest and most advanced *Jin*-class nuclear submarines at Yulin in secure underground facilities.[60]

Reinforcing the Potential of China's Southern Territories

China's Eurasian sea lanes curve southward across the South China Sea, before heading westward from the Strait of Malacca to the Persian Gulf. Near the tip of the spear, pointed southward, lies Hainan, a major target of China's strategically driven domestic developmental ambitions. With 9.5 million people, the island has twice the population of Singapore, but it is spread across almost fifty times as much land and has ample room to grow economically.[61] China clearly intends to transform Hainan, once a quiet subtropical backwater, into a strategic military and economic waystation on the Maritime Silk Road. Since 2000, the island has hosted the abovementioned dynamic Yulin Naval Base. Since 2016, Yulin has been connected by underwater fiber-optic cable to Woody Island in the disputed Paracel chain.[62] The Lingshui and Qionghai naval bases also lie nearby, on Hainan's eastern and southeastern coasts.

Hainan has recently been elevated by Beijing to a high priority in the economic realm, facilitating its role as a link to the southern seas, Southeast Asia, and the world beyond. In June 2020, the whole island was designated a free-trade zone—the largest of around 2,500 such designated zones across China. To facilitate its development, the government has launched a five-year, $35 billion highway development program for the island.[63] Income and corporate taxes are capped at 15 percent for Hainan residents and eligible companies.[64] Meanwhile, most of China's claims in the South China Sea are asserted to be appendages of Hainan, further enhancing the status of the province.

Venturing Westward Beyond Malacca

China traditionally has refrained from formal overseas basing, including naval bases, in favor of more ambiguously defined dual-use facilities. More than two decades ago, Pentagon strategist Andrew Marshall, and then a later 2007 Department of Defense contract report from Booz Allen Hamilton, described these facilities as a "string of pearls" across the Indian Ocean.[65] Several of the key locations—trading ports with geopolitical importance, stretching from China to the Mediterranean—are noted in Figure 5.2. In the aggregate, these ports represent an important dimension of Chinese sea-lane strategy, especially in dealing with peacetime contingencies.[66]

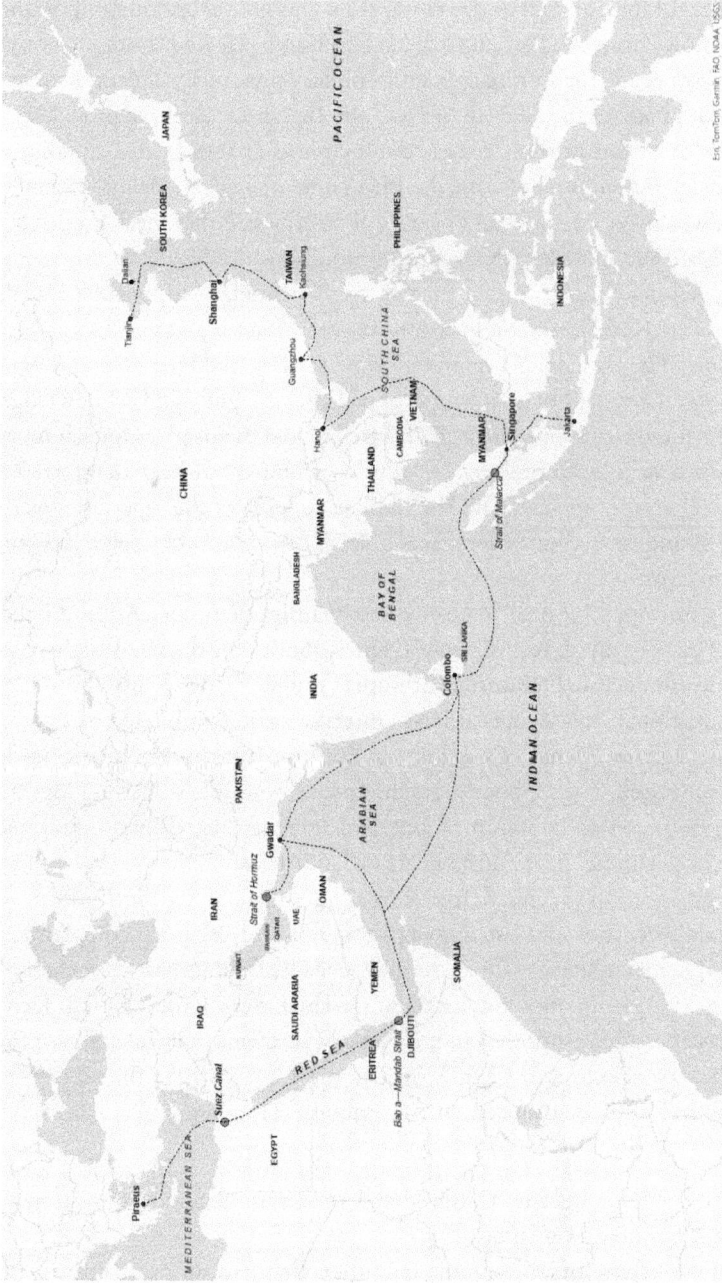

FIGURE 5.2 Chinese strategic strongpoints along the Eurasian sea lanes

SOURCES: Esri, HERE, Garmin, FAO, NOAA, USGS, © OpenStreetMap contributors, and the GIS User Community.

The exigencies of evacuating Chinese and other civilians from political crises in Yemen and Libya, as well as the rising scale and geo-economic importance of energy flows from the Persian Gulf back to China, created strong incentives over the past decade for a more explicitly military presence.[67] The intermittent challenge of piracy in the Arabian Sea and the Indian Ocean have provided the pretext for more ambitious Chinese deployments farther from China's own shores. During the summer of 2014, the PLA's new strategic guidelines expanded significantly its previous sphere of operational priorities, so that "near-sea defense" (*junhai fangyu*) also included "far-seas protection" (*yuanhai huwei*).[68]

In 2017, China opened its first formal overseas military support base at the entrance to the Red Sea in Djibouti, on a ten-year lease at an annual lease fee of $20 million.[69] The Chinese government originally described the base as a "logistical support facility," although it later dropped the ambiguity and acknowledged it as an actual military support base.[70] This facility, and the nearby Doraleh multi-purpose port, were both built by DP World of Dubai but later transferred to China Merchants to operate, with the implicit support of the Djibouti government. DP World sued China Merchants in local courts, but they ruled in China Merchants' favor.[71]

China's port in Djibouti is connected seamlessly to the Addis Ababa–Djibouti Railway, an almost entirely Chinese-built and financed high-speed railway line connecting Djibouti to Ethiopia's capital.[72] The facility also is connected operationally by secure undersea internet cable (completed by Huawei Marine in 2021) to China's strongpoint in Gwadar, Pakistan, and thence overland to China itself. The Djibouti port thus provides seamless dual-use logistics, including both secure communications and transport, to Chinese diplomats and military personnel deep in the heart of East Africa.

Although Djibouti is China's first formal naval base along the Eurasian sea lanes, it is unlikely to be the last, with a panoply of dual-use ports complementing the explicitly military.[73] Over the past decade, Beijing has been carefully cultivating a range of nations along these sea lanes, steadily developing deeper ties that over time have assumed an increasingly clear-cut political-military cast. One such example close to China's own home waters, where the conversion to military use is quite advanced, is in Cambodia. The progression has been as follows:

(a) In 2012, China became Cambodia's largest arms supplier, a position that it has held ever since.

(b) In 2016, China and Cambodia held their first in a series of annual bilateral military exercises, known as the Golden Dragon.[74]

(c) In June 2018, during a visit to Phnom Penh to attend a China-Cambodia military exhibition, China's Defense Minister Wei Feng pledged $100 million in unrestricted military aid to the Cambodian government.[75]

(d) In July 2019, the *Wall Street Journal* reported on a secret agreement between China and Cambodia granting thirty-year use of the Ream Naval Base, near Sihanoukville on the Gulf of Thailand, to post military personnel, store weapons, and berth warships, with automatic renewals every ten years.[76] By 2024, Chinese naval vessels were regularly and overtly docking there at dedicated piers, often coinciding with broader people-to-people exchanges and commercial activities.[77]

In Cambodia, as in Djibouti and Pakistan, China has thus proceeded through an incremental progression from economic assistance and trade to rather explicit provision for military basing, progressing over a period of several years.

Gray-Zone Capabilities: Where Economic and Geopolitical Interests Converge

As we have seen, China has had enduring maritime interests across the centuries, focused precisely on what are now the Eurasian sea lanes. These interests have deepened substantially since the early 1990s, propelled by rapid growth, demand for raw materials, and the development of overseas markets for China's manufacturers. This heightened economic interdependence has in turn given rise to new security imperatives, within the context of a global maritime regime dominated by China's principal rival, the United States.

One primary element of China's security response in the sea lanes has been the development of gray-zone capabilities that are nominally civilian but can perform as effective political-military tools without provoking an undesired military response.[78] China has worked to amplify the legitimacy of these gray-zone capabilities and tactics by building domestic legal institutions, bureaucratic structures, and enforcement mechanism that make them appear legal.[79] This approach has been especially prominent in waters adjacent to China, such as the East and South China Seas, and against five US allies and strategic partners: Japan, Vietnam, Indonesia, the Philippines, and Taiwan. Chinese maritime militia and coast-guard forces are assuming such gray-zone roles as well.

FISHING FLEETS

Since the mid-1980s, China has placed special emphasis on developing a market-oriented yet state-supported fisheries program that is able to operate competitively on a global basis. As China's own maritime stakes have grown at the national level, this program has come to serve geopolitical as well as human security purposes. In May 1982, the Fifth National People's Congress eliminated the Sixth Ministry of Machine Building, which had supervised fisheries under the previous socialist system, and established the China State Shipbuilding Corporation (CSSC) as an alternate supervisor. The 1982 NPC decision "corporatized" all state shipbuilding activities, including construction of fishing boats, under the CSSC, and authorized an unprecedented degree of market-based economic autonomy.[80] In 1985, the relaxation of fishery price controls further strengthened market incentives. Between 1991 and 1997, as China grew more dependent on offshore economic connections, a series of new Chinese government subsidies and training programs, as well as diplomatic support for agreements with promising fishery partner nations, encouraged DWF in the Indian Ocean and in African waters.[81]

As China's fishing fleet grew larger and more robust technologically, and more linked to the government, during the early post–Cold War years, its expansion began to assume the above-described geopolitical implications. It also has begun to assume the capacity to play significant political-military roles.[82] This capability has become especially important in disputed waters of the East and South China Seas close to China itself, where fishing boats periodically have been important in asserting controversial Chinese territorial claims. Nonofficial craft such as fishing vessels can give Chinese authorities latitude to engage in strategically ambiguous actions that delegitimate their rivals in territorial claims— including Japan, South Korea, the Philippines, Taiwan, Vietnam, and Malaysia— by informally backing what Chinese fishermen claim as legitimate economic rights, as fish is a major element of the Chinese diet. Such apolitical representations help reduce foreign pushback while garnering domestic political support for future gray-zone activities.

Maritime Militia

The maritime militia, a separate organization from both the PLA-N and the China Coast Guard, is composed of citizens working in the marine economy who receive training from both organizations. They are prepared for border patrolling, surveillance and reconnaissance, search and rescue, and other auxiliary tasks that would support naval operations in wartime.[83] The maritime militia ultimately are responsible to China's State Council and the PLA's Central Military Commission, as well as to local governments on more operational matters, through dual civilian-military command structures at each level of authority.

TABLE 5.2

Chinese Coast Guard force levels (2005–2020)

Type (tonnage)	2005	2010	2017	2020	15-Year Net Increase
Oceangoing patrol ships (2,500–10,000)	3	5	55	60	+57
Regional patrol ships (1,000–2,499)	25	30	70	80	+55
Regional patrol combatants (500–999)	30	65	100	120	+90
Subtotal: Ships that can operate offshore	*58*	*100*	*225*	*260*	*+202 (+350%)*
Coastal patrol craft (100–499)	350	400	450	450	+100 (approx.)
Inshore patrol boats/minor craft (<100)★	500+	500+	600+	600+	+100 (approx.)
Total: All China Coast Guard	900+	1,000+	1,275+	1,300+	1400 (approx.)

SOURCE: Andrew S. Erickson, Joshua Hickey, and Henry Holst, "Surging Second Sea Force: China's Maritime Law-Enforcement Forces, Capabilities, and Future in the Gray Zone and Beyond," *Naval War College Review* 72, no. 2 (2019), https://digital-commons.usnwc.edu/nwc-review/vol72/iss2/4; and author assessment.

Given information-access problems and the limited government control actually exercised over Chinese fisherman, it is difficult to assess the extent to which Chinese authorities actually control fishermen operating in the South China Sea. Some fishermen have collaborated with the China Coast Guard and/or the PLAN in gray-zone operations, indicating that the maritime militia does exploit the plausible deniability afforded by the dual identity of its members as both military personnel and civilian mariners. From the evidence provided in authoritative Chinese-language sources, however, it is unrealistic to portray the maritime militia as a coherent body with adequate professional training, or as a body that systematically has conducted deceptive missions in close collaboration with the PLAN and the coast guard.[84]

The China Coast Guard

Conventionally separate from military service, but more systematically attached to government than the maritime militia, is the China Coast Guard. With more than 1,300 ships, this powerful modern force is by a substantial margin the largest body of its kind in the world, and over time it has been taking on more of an explicit national-security role. Table 5.2 indicates its rising degree of scale and sophistication over the past decade.

As seen in the table above, by 2020 the China Coast Guard had 140 vessels of 1,000 tons or more, reaching a scale four times its level for these categories in 2010, just before President Xi Jinping came to power. During the 2010–2016 period, its tonnage increased by 73 percent, substantially exceeding the 50 percent tonnage increase recorded by the Japanese Coast Guard during the same period. Over those same years, its $1.74 billion budget exceeded that of its Japanese counterpart by 15 to 20 percent, leading to rising Chinese pressure in disputed waters.[85] China's coast guard today includes 10,000-ton-plus ships equipped with 76-millimeter guns—bigger than those of the largest naval vessels owned by either the Philippines or Indonesian navies, which are competing claimants to China's PLA-N in the South China Sea.[86]

Though the China Coast Guard is not formally part of the PLA-N, its remit has drifted into that sphere of military administration. Until 2018, it was under the civilian control of the State Oceanic Administration, led from 2013 to 2017 by Meng Hongwei.[87] Since 2018, however, the Coast Guard has been under the overall command of the Central Military Commission, chaired by President Xi Jinping himself, and operating under the intermediate supervision of the People's Armed Police.

In late January 2021, China enacted the Coast Guard Law of the People's Republic of China. This law explicitly grants broad powers to that body and confirms its quasimilitary status. The coast guard was authorized for the first time "to carry out defense operations" under the orders of the Central Military Commission, and under certain circumstances to fire on foreign ships.[88] It also was empowered to forcibly dismantle unapproved structures built by foreign countries in waters claimed by China, which are numerous in the South China Sea. The Coast Guard is therefore becoming a second navy, rivaling some regional navies in terms of displacement, weapons systems, and functional role, although Chinese authorities remain cautious about making such a characterization explicitly.

Building Hybrid Strongpoints: The Sinews of Future Sea-Lane Dominance

As this chapter has shown, China has been developing a substantial military presence in the Eurasian sea lanes—one that appears imposing to most of the regional powers in Asia, including India, Australia, and Japan, although arguably less so to the United States. Much more substantial, in the long run, is the transformation underway in dual military-civilian use infrastructure. This historic structural change could support both economic prosperity for the nations along the Indo-Pacific sea lanes, especially those that are home to the relevant facilities, and also expanded Chinese military capabilities. Included in this important category of dual-use capabilities are port facilities, submarine cable systems, last-mile logistics, shipping, and hinterland infrastructure, including railways and other transport lines connecting into key multidimensional hubs.

These strongpoints—generally situated where the land meets the sea—connect overland commerce to the sea lanes, exploiting logistical advances in robotics and digital communication to make the ports themselves increasingly efficient and competitive. Over time, as at Djibouti and Gwadar, an explicitly military dimension often is added.

From Gibraltar to a New Paradigm: Exploiting Twenty-First-Century Seashore Synergies

At the heart of China's soft approach to sea-lane dominance is the notion of "strategic strongpoints." These are by no means the statically militarized "five keys that lock up the world" in First Sea Lord John Fisher's parlance, as Gibraltar was in his day. Instead, China's strongpoints represent a softer, dual-use functional equivalent suited to the twenty-first century, in which the geo-economic significance of the sea and the seashore rimland relative to the continental interior are changing in ways that even the far-sighted Nicholas Spykman would not recognize.

China's real and putative "string of pearls" strongpoints along Eurasia's sea lanes are a heterogenous range of facilities. One—Djibouti, at the confluence of the Red Sea and the Gulf of Aden—is China's first formal overseas military base. Others, such as Gwadar in Pakistan, clearly combine military and civilian functions without an explicitly military designation. Piraeus in Greece, Colombo in Sri Lanka, and even Algeciras in Spain—in the literal shadow of Gibraltar—currently have exclusively economic roles, although they are receptive to Chinese military ship visits. The commonality is strategic location along routes of mixed military and commercial significance that strikingly parallel the British Empire's All Red Line a century ago. Given the twenty-first-century importance of internet communications, container-port transshipment, and LNG processing, multipurpose coastal strongpoints arguably are more important in global geo-economic affairs than ever.[89]

In contrast to Britain at Gibraltar in Victorian and Edwardian days, China's emerging strongpoints do not involve overt territorial military conquest. The strongpoints are sea-coast cities, opportunistically chosen in response to local rimland political-economic circumstances. Those futuristically configured strongpoints can synergistically link trade, information processing, and explicit but low-profile national security functions. Geographical location that maximizes the integrated and rapidly changing economic and security advantages of sea-shore proximity are a priority, as at Gibraltar, but the circumstances are configured for twenty-first rather than eighteenth-century imperatives.

China's quiet cultivation of strategic strongpoints along the Maritime Eurasian rimland has been proceeding with increasing intensity for two decades. It often has occurred, as noted above, in response to local suggestions, just as was true of the British Empire in the eighteenth and nineteenth centuries. Local interests have wanted new technology, financing, or political-economic support against local rivals.

The evolution of China's Gwadar facility is a case in point. In 2001, China and Pakistan signed an agreement for the two countries to jointly develop a major new Arabian Sea port at Gwadar, 250 miles from the entrance to the Strait of Hormuz. Pakistani President Pervez Musharraf, rather than the Chinese, initiated the request.[90] Like his predecessor Ayub Khan, Musharraf was interested in enabling Pakistan to become an Indian Ocean power with strong links to the nearby Persian Gulf.[91] Phase I construction at Gwadar was completed in June 2006, and the deep-water port opened a year later under Port of Singapore Authority management. However, the facility failed to meet the lofty goals initially set by Musharraf and subsequently lay largely unused until just before the Xi Jinping government announced the creation of CPEC in 2013.[92] China Overseas Port Holdings, a Hong Kong registered firm with close ties to China, took over Gwadar in 2013, with the understanding that it would inject money into the port. Since then, Gwadar has taken on new functions with geopolitical significance for the Chinese, especially in the secure communications area.[93]

China accelerated its development of strategic strongpoint projects, under a variety of largely nonmilitary pretexts and often at outside suggestion, during and after the global financial crisis of 2008 (from which China largely was insulated). In 2008, the state-affiliated Tianjin Economic Development Authority concluded an agreement to establish a Suez Special Economic Zone in Egypt, astride the Suez Canal itself, during a period of Egyptian financial constraints. That same year, the China Development Bank began lending to support the Hambantota port development project in Sri Lanka, located midway between China and the Persian Gulf. And in 2009, China's COSCO state-owned shipping line, now the fourth largest in the world, concluded its first lease in Piraeus, the port of Athens, Greece, as the Greek financial crisis worsened. Many of these local projects were in desolate locations, but all had access to the coasts, exploiting potential synergies between land and sea implicit in the BRI concept. Spykman would have understood.

Ever since President Xi Jinping announced the BRI in the fall of 2013, strategic strongpoint projects have proliferated. In 2014, Myanmar invited bidders for its Kyaukphyu deep-port development project on the Bay of Bengal, the sea-lane connection point for the 1,700-kilometer-long China-Myanmar Economic Corridor. The project would link Kunming, Yunnan's capital, with the strategic bay, and serve as a connection point for a pipeline pumping over 400,000 bbls/day directly to southeastern China, thus helping to finesse the Malacca Dilemma.[94] Two years after the gas pipeline went into operation in 2013, CITIC (formerly the China International Trust Investment Corporation) won the tender at Kyaukphyu for a combined deep-water port capable of berthing supertankers and an industrial park. In April 2017, the crude oil pipeline also commenced operations, with CITIC managing the integrated transport and value-added industrial project.

All of the above locations have comprehensive economic and military significance. In addition to these possibilities, experts from the PLA-N–affiliated Chinese Naval Research Institute have listed the Seychelles and East African coastal locations as additional possible candidates for hybrid Chinese seashore facilities.[95] Mombasa in Kenya, on the Indian Ocean, is already a terminal point for the Chinese PEACE undersea cable route direct from China via Pakistan, as Chapter 6 will discuss.

Local demands often have been important catalysts in the establishment of these Chinese outposts. Yet their geographic distribution, as suggested in Figure 5.2 above, shows a remarkable concentration along the Eurasian rimland littoral, exploiting a new twenty-first-century synergy between land and sea. They stretch in a line along the sea lanes, from the Strait of Malacca westward toward Europe, with an additional spur southward to economically strategic locations in East and Southern Africa.

Piraeus in Greece; Djibouti; Gwadar in Pakistan; and Colombo in Sri Lanka concretely illustrate the broader twenty-first-century seashore developmentalist logic with which China quietly has begun to challenge the United States. China's new strongpoints, to be sure, are not Gibraltars, and there is no Diego Garcia. They do not yet have the visually formidable, narrowly military configuration of the imposing Anglo-American bases that have dominated Eurasia's sea lanes for two centuries and more. Yet they are strategically placed, close to chokepoints, markets, and transshipment centers, to maximize Chinese geoeconomic interest.[96]

China's new strongpoints do, however, represent many aspects of China's subtle, incremental, and creative emerging challenge to US-centric dominance of the Eurasian sea lanes. In the following pages, we will present the key elements of China's hybrid emerging paradigm and the ways in which it has been replicated across the Eurasian sea lanes. In conclusion, we will consider how China's quiet approach capitalizes on a new, technologically driven synergy between sea and land, replete with strategic implications, that is implicit though not directly expressed in the BRI concept. That Chinese challenge to longstanding Anglo-Saxon Eurasian sea-lane dominance has been incubating over the past decade and could well burst forth more openly in coming years.

Strongpoint Function 1: Supporting Trade

China is the largest trading partner of most nations along the Eurasian sea lanes, and its market is becoming more attractive as it continues to grow.[97] That dynamic encourages host countries, especially developing ones, to accommodate Chinese presence along the sea lanes. Strikingly, it is almost invariably the host side that requests Chinese involvement at the strongpoints, not least because state-of-the-art ports invite greater trade. Rapid recent technical increases in port efficiency and scale, on which China has capitalized, together with Chinese financial support under BRI, have intensified this trend toward increased trade through mega-ports, and bad-debt problems have not reversed it.

Piraeus is one of the most strategic Chinese strongpoints along the Eurasian sea lanes, in part because of its proximity to major political-economic centers in Europe and because Greece is a member of both NATO and the European Union. Chinese diplomats have called Piraeus a "dragon head," or position of synergistic regional importance.[98] The United States also once recognized the significance of Piraeus; in 1972, the Nixon administration proposed to home-port a US aircraft carrier there.[99] It remains the closest major European port to Asia, and the terminus of the Sea-Land Bridge from Asia to the heart of Europe. Greece is also home to firms that manage 20 percent of global shipping.

In 2009, COSCO first bought into the Piraeus port complex in Greece, in the shadow of the 2008 global financial crisis. And in 2016, with Greece again in financial difficulty, its government offered COSCO control of the whole port. COSCO ultimately invested well over $1 billion in the port and its amenities.[100] In addition, developers in Piraeus added a hotel and shopping mall complex to cater to Chinese tourists, a counterpart to the purely maritime Chinese infrastructure intended to exploit synergies surrounding core port investments.

Meanwhile, within the decade following the 2008 financial crisis, container traffic through Piraeus rose almost thirteenfold, driven by COSCO's substantial modernizing investments. Other service income, include tourist-related revenue, also soared.[101] By 2020, Piraeus had become the largest container as well as passenger port in the Mediterranean. It was also handling more than 10 percent of China's exports to Europe, and had become the fourth-busiest container port on the continent. Piraeus also had a much broader commercial and strategic focus than Rotterdam, Antwerp, or Hamburg, Europe's largest northern ports, and was set to capitalize on new growth possibilities in the Balkans and Central Europe, supported by BRI-related infrastructure funding.[102]

Greek leaders of contrasting political persuasions have consistently cultivated China in recent years in the hopes of stabilizing their country's financial fortunes. Both the left-oriented populist Prime Minister Alexis Tsipras, who spoke prominently at Xi Jinping's first Belt and Road Forum, and the more conservative Kyriakos Mitsotakis, a Harvard College/Harvard Business School graduate and former McKinsey consultant who hosted Xi's 2019 visit to Athens, have supported deeper ties with China. And China's investments in the Piraeus port, providing much needed capital inflow while facilitating Chinese trade flows through Greece across the Mediterranean and Central European regions, played a key role over the past decade in mitigating Greece's financial woes and promoting Sino-Greek relations.

From a modest role beginning in 2007, COSCO's role at Piraeus has grown to the point where it now holds 67 percent of total equity in the container port. Transformed by heavy Chinese investment and deepening trade relations with China, including tourism and service trade, Piraeus has assumed a central role in eastern Mediterranean commerce as a whole. Between 2010 and 2020, container-shipping throughput at Piraeus increased more than sixfold, from less than 900,000 TEUs to over 5.4 million.[103] COSCO management enabled Piraeus to become the largest container port in the entire Mediterranean by 2020.[104]

Further to the west, China has been simultaneously pursuing trade and geo-strategy that links land and sea. In the Adriatic, it has focused on Trieste in Italy and Koper in Slovenia, encouraging both Italy and Slovenia to join the BRI in March and June 2019, respectively.[105] The COVID pandemic slowed Chinese progress on the ground, with German and Italian enterprises taking pre-eminent positions in the Trieste port-logistics platform.[106] In December 2023, moreover, Italy did not renew its formal participation in the BRI. Yet China's long-term strategic intent to assert its presence at the head of the Adriatic, and in Central Europe, remained clear.

Still further west, China has made active inroads in Spain through port acquisitions and infrastructure upgrading that have helped Spanish ports increase their productivity significantly, especially through innovations in container shipping.[107] One port, at Algeciras, lies in the literal shadow of Gibraltar.[108] More than 35 percent of the containers moving through Spanish ports now originate in China.[109] China thus now operates trade-centric strongpoints all the way across the Mediterranean to the Strait of Gibraltar, while developing railroads, freight-forwarding centers, and other sea-land linkages to support this trade.

China has also begun nurturing other hybrid strongpoints across the Indian Ocean, the Red Sea, and the Mediterranean, using leverage from trade to strengthen its broader geo-economic position along the sea lanes linking Europe and Asia. Among the clearest and most classical outposts is Suez City, located astride the Suez Canal, which was a central British imperial concern from the 1860s until Gamal Abdul Nasser nationalized Anglo-French interests in 1956. In 2008, China—Britain's lineal commercial successor in Egypt—established a Suez Special Economic Zone alongside the canal, followed by a Suez Canal Corridor project in 2014. In the wake of a major 2016 visit by Xi Jinping, the state-owned China Harbor Engineering Corporation began work on a major container terminal in the corridor.[110] By 2019, China had invested between $16 and $20 billion in Egypt, mainly in Suez Canal Zone projects strategically located along the corridor. The canal is one of the most important chokepoints in east-west Eurasian shipping because it links the Mediterranean Sea and the Indian Ocean. Prominence at Suez is thus central to China's transformation from being a purely East Asian to becoming an authentically Eurasian power.[111]

The previously mentioned Gwadar, another strongpoint 2,600 miles to the east, lies only 250 miles from the Persian Gulf, where China procures roughly half of its massive oil imports. Gwadar's proximity to the Gulf also gives it potential—attractive from the host Pakistani standpoint—as a service center for the Gulf, in hybrid economic and military dimensions. Gwadar also feeds into the ambitious CPEC project in that it helps link the Gulf directly overland to China itself, promoting Chinese commerce with the Middle East that side-steps the Malacca Dilemma.[112] Recently, however, Gwadar and its Baluchistan periphery have been plagued by separatist unrest.[113] Activists who have criti-cized China's failure to address local concerns have been elected to key local positions in Gwadar itself.[114] Yet the strongpoint is becoming increasingly strategic for China as its economic ties with the Persian Gulf deepen, and as infrastructure building, both above and below the seas, continues apace.[115]

Strongpoint Function 2: Information Processing

Imperial Britain naturally appreciated the strategic importance of submarine cables, and began operating a cable line to Gibraltar in 1870. Gibraltar then served as a critical connection for the All Red Line extending across the Eurasian seas to Australia.[116] Yet despite its formidable political-military profile, Gibraltar has never been able to fill the multifaceted political-economic functions that Piraeus, Djibouti, Gwadar, and similar strongpoints have managed to occupy in the Information Age.

Undersea cables today are the preeminent avenue of global communication in both civilian and military dimensions. They are far more cost-effective than any other communications medium, including satellite communications, and they handle more than 95 percent of internet traffic worldwide. Magnifying the geo-economic importance of cables today, the internet plays much broader sociopolitical roles in advanced and even developing societies than cable traffic did a century and more ago.[117] A robust cable network today is especially vital to the development and healthy functioning of competitive service industries, especially finance. Because these cables interconnect to overland communication at seaside locations like Piraeus, Djibouti, and Gwadar, they are especially important to the littoral nations bordering on the Indian Ocean, the Red Sea, and other parts of the Eurasian sea lanes. For societies that are just breaking into the Internet Age, this information infrastructure is vital to their economic development.

Broadband infrastructure is critical to economic development along the Eurasian rimlands, particularly populated nations of South and Southeast Asia, owing to the network externalities generated by such infrastructure. The greater the number of users, the more value is derived by *other* users. Further, investment returns, in terms of economic growth, may be higher than in other forms of infrastructure because of the impact of broadband on information diffusion, industrial productivity, and organizational efficiency.[118] China thus has acknowledged that it can reap immense economic and potentially geopolitical returns by creating information societies in developing Eurasian rimland nations, especially since most other advanced industrial nations have been ignoring such opportunities.

Autonomous undersea cable-communication networks are also critical in security terms for China. Most of global communications, both through satellites and through submarine cables, are dominated by Western multinationals—particularly the powerful technology majors such as Facebook, Microsoft, and Amazon—or by the US government. These multinationals have not, however, been as active beneath the Eurasian sea lanes, especially between Singapore and Suez, where they do not have dominance and which have less of a commercial attraction than their existing investments in the Atlantic and the Pacific. Filling this information gap west of Singapore provides an opportunity for China to be autonomous from Western information networks, and to dominate—through informatics—a strategic yet neglected part of the globe.

China has been actively pursuing informatics opportunities in Greece, an underserved corner of Europe, using its substantial port presence in Piraeus as a point of departure. Huawei is by far the largest telecommunications firm, and is a major employer in Greece, enjoying recent annual double-digit sales increases as well.[119] More importantly, however, Huawei's local activities are part of a larger, regionwide approach. Chinese firms like Huawei use Greece as a stepping stone to activities in the Balkans and Hungary, taking advantage of BRI-related infrastructure connections in both communications and transportation.[120]

China has adopted a parallel, strategically oriented regional approach to informatics development in Saudi Arabia, one of Maritime Eurasia's most geo-economically significant nations. As in Greece, Huawei is the linchpin.[121] During Xi Jinping's December 2022 visit to Saudi Arabia, Huawei concluded multiple informatics deals in areas such as cloud computing, and explored moving its Middle East regional headquarters to Riyadh.[122] It followed up with the elaborate LEAP 2023 event in the Saudi capital, showcasing its next generation carrier networks, including 5.5G, as well as Cloud-Network Express and related applications available to the Saudis.[123]

Over two thousand nautical miles away across the Eurasian sea lanes lies Gwadar, in Pakistan. Desolate as Gwadar is in conventional economic terms, it offers China an unusual, little-appreciated opportunity in the information-technology sphere. It is the seaside landing point of a now-completed optical-fiber telecommunications line, extending overland from Beijing and then onward (via Gwadar) beneath the seas to both Europe and Africa. Gwadar is the perfect location as the terminus for a connection to a far-ranging China-centric undersea cable network. It is a catalytic locale where the synergies implicit in a holistic approach to land and sea—to the BRI—can be efficiently realized. This strongpoint plays a central if little-recognized role in a broader Chinese initiative that in coming years could be the most globally compelling dimension of Beijing's involvement in the Eurasian sea lanes. It is the physical connecting point from China, as noted above, for the PEACE Cable project, a 15,000-kilometer undertaking under the BRI, connecting Asia, Africa, and Europe via submarine cables. Its first stage was completed in November 2022, with Huawei Marine Networks and the Hengtong Group serving as the major contractors.[124] In April 2023, China's largest telecommunications firms also announced a $500 million Europe–to–Hong Kong cable to rival the US-backed SeaMeWe-6 project, as noted earlier.[125]

The PEACE Cable parallels in important respects the "string of pearls" network of economic/military strongpoints that characterizes China's hybrid strategy toward the Eurasian sea lanes. In addition to facilitating (and potentially monitoring or structuring) social communication along "South-South" lines centrally involving China, the PEACE cable network can foster trade and the related production and service networks. China-related manufactures, which are strongly price competitive, are especially likely to benefit. China-related services, notably in finance, also are poised to benefit from the information-sector upgrading, the related real-time interactions, and the exclusive, direct connection to China itself.

These considerations are the logic behind the ambitious Port City Colombo project in Sri Lanka, where the China Communications Construction Company and China Harbour Engineering Company are building a futuristic financial city with advanced communications links that is the size of Sri Lanka's existing national capital city itself.[126] Following China's aggressive expansion efforts in the Colombo area, Japan canceled its light-rail line connecting Port City to downtown Colombo. In November 2023, the United States also announced plans to develop a major rival container port terminal in Colombo, raising fears of excess capacity at Port City.[127] Nevertheless, for China the locational logic of Colombo for broader Indian Ocean trade, services, and information flows definitely remains.

The PEACE Cable connects Gwadar with Mombasa, Kenya's largest port, across the Indian Ocean, and Djibouti, at the entrance to the Red Sea. From Djibouti, the cable proceeds beneath the Red Sea to Egypt and from there across the Mediterranean to Marseilles, France, as indicated in Figure 5.3. At Gwadar, the PEACE Cable also connects into the overland optical fiber line to China. The hybrid sea-land network as a whole thus provides Beijing with a secure, Chinese-built and operated high-speed communications system potentially capable of both economic and defense applications. Significantly, it also connects many of the other prospective strongpoints in Beijing's evolving Eurasian network, all the way to Europe. Before the Digital Age, dawning in the 1990s, this multi-faceted web of connectivity would have been patently impossible.

The evolving PEACE Cable network is attractive to Pakistan, as to the other host nations involved, because it serves as an entry card to the global information society of the twenty-first century, regardless of its Sino-centric bias. Pakistan ranked only 79th out of 100 economies on the Economist Intelligence Unit's Inclusive Internet Index for 2022, and even lower (96th) in access and usage.[128] Only 17 percent of its population used the Internet, with only 14 percent on

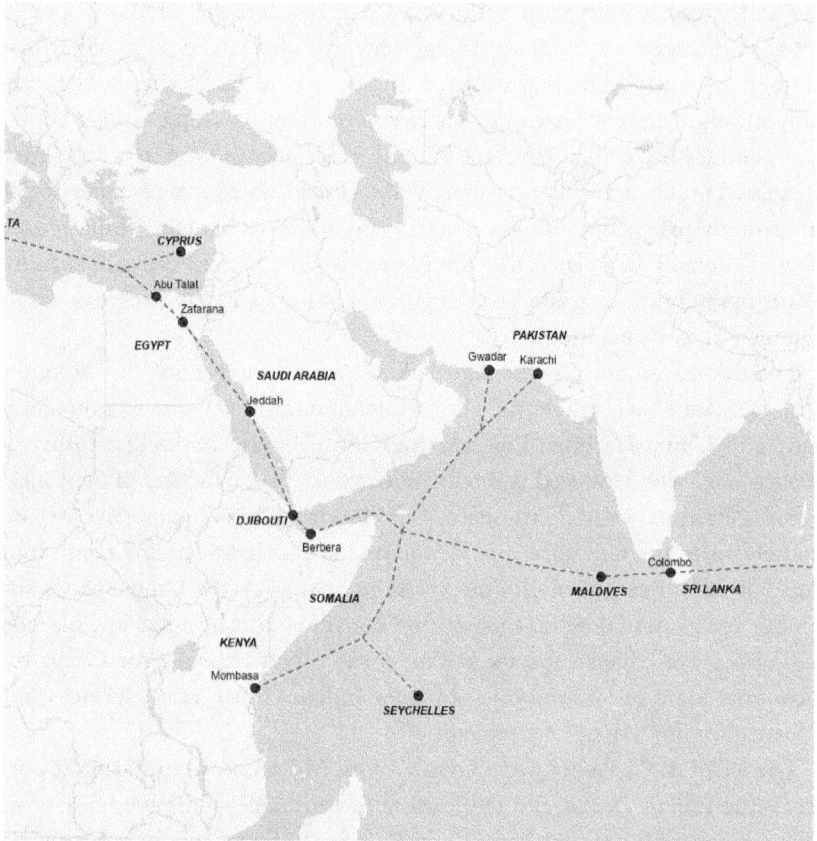

FIGURE 5.3 The emerging PEACE Cable Euro-Asian communications network
SOURCES: PEACE Cable International Network and Government of Pakistan.
NOTE: The section from Kenya to South Africa is a further extension that will start operating later than other segments of the network.

social media. Literacy and content available in local languages also were low. Many of these problems are common in other sea-lane strongpoint nations that China recently has begun to actively link through submarine cable programs.[129]

Strongpoint Function 3: National Security

China's systematic accumulation and reinforcement of low-profile strongpoints along the Eurasian sea lanes reinforces its long-term national-security interests, even as it generates increased trade flows of goods, services, and information. This is most dramatically evident in Piraeus, formerly a US naval base, where

COSCO's rising commercial involvement has facilitated ship visits by the PLA-N.[130] These visits originally took place in connection with the PLA-N's role in combating international piracy in the Gulf of Aden around 2008, but have continued in more recent years under other auspices.

Despite the ship visits and Huawei's dominant role in Greek telecommunications, the hard security dimension is not prominent in Chinese activities at Piraeus. Greece is, after all, a NATO member. Security is more salient for China elsewhere along the sea lanes. In the case of Gwadar, the deep-water port allows contingency docking and supply support for PLA-N surface ships and submarines, in close proximity to the Persian Gulf, even if the port does not operate formally as a naval facility. China's presence there also helps geopolitically to keep India, with whom China has tense relations across the Himalayas, in check.[131]

Other Chinese strongpoints west of Malacca, which are largely connected with one another and with China itself through Chinese-built, dedicated optical-fiber submarine cables, have similar strategic profiles. Djibouti lies at the Bab al-Mandab, controlling the entrance to the Red Sea through which close to 20 percent of world trade flows, just as Gwadar lies close to the Hormuz Strait at the entrance to the Persian Gulf. And Djibouti controls trade and information access to land-locked but formidable Ethiopia, with a hundred times Djibouti's population. Hambantota, on the southern coast of Sri Lanka, lies in the shadow of the Indian Ocean's principal shipping lane. Nearby Colombo is a principal transshipment port for south India, which lacks well-developed ports of its own. And Port Said lies astride the Suez Canal where it meets the Mediterranean, just as Algeciras, which received major new Chinese investment in 2018, is literally in the shadow of Gibraltar.

None of these locations, save Djibouti, currently houses a formal Chinese base. Yet all have strategic locations, complemented by versatile Chinese-operated port terminals, along the main maritime route—"China's Maritime Lifeline"—that links the rim nations of the Eurasian industrialized world. These strongpoints are geo-economically central to trade and political-economic connectivity in the twenty-first century, just as surely as were the "five keys" held by First Sea Lord John Fisher in the early twentieth century.

In Conclusion

For two centuries, geo-strategists have recognized the fragile rimland sea lanes between Europe and Northeast Asia as a linchpin of worldwide cohesion, assuring the dominance of the West. For a century and more those sea lanes served as the All Red Line, assuring British imperial dominance. Even as Britain's global role declined from the 1950s into the twenty-first century, those sea lanes remained a crucial, if often neglected, dimension of the *Pax Anglo-Americana*.

China's challenge as the twenty-first century proceeds is subtle and diffident, as we have seen. It is by no means preeminently military, except around the periphery of Taiwan, which Beijing sees as an integral part of China. Often, China's role builds on local host-nation aspirations. Yet Beijing's approach is nevertheless strategic and increasingly political-military at the margin.

China's sea-lane challenge, operating mainly through economic incentives but involving larger and more capable naval forces as well, has been building quietly and incrementally on the deepening twenty-first-century synergies between sea and land, born of the Digital Age, and intensely concentrated on the coastlines. Like China's overland expansion across Eurasia, this new hybrid rimland challenge strikes at the core of American global dominance in fundamental ways. It poses an even more direct challenge for the United States' allies, who use the Eurasian sea lanes much more extensively and compete with Chinese shipping and shipbuilding firms more directly, as the following chapter will explore.

6

The Stem of Victory
Infrastructure and the Sea Lanes

Victory is the beautiful, bright-colored flower. Transport is the stem, without
which it never could have blossomed.

—Winston Churchill, *The River War*[1]

AS WORLD WAR II DREW to its turbulent close, the United States had become decisively dominant on the international sea lanes. It had not only the world's most
powerful navy but also versatile strengths on the civilian side. In 1945, the US
Navy was unmatched in size, with 28 fleet carriers and 250 submarines. It had
enough amphibious lift to transport more than 400,000 troops at a time worldwide.[2] To field a navy of more than 6,700 ships—the most powerful fleet in
world history—between 1940 and 1945 the United States built 6,000 vessels,
with new government institutions strongly supporting the private sector.[3] It
poured up to 1.5 million workers into the task, laboring at eight US Navy shipyards and sixty-four private shipyards by war's end in 1945.[4] Construction crews
produced carriers, battleships, cruisers, destroyers, frigates, PT boats, submarines,
and landing craft, along with large numbers of commercially usable "Liberty"
and "Victory" ships.[5] In shipping, as in shipbuilding, the United States waxed
supreme. All the major commercial sea-transport lines were American, as wartime losses and financial constraints had debilitated their British counterparts.[6]
The shipping fleets of Germany and Japan—other erstwhile maritime powers—
had been decimated by Anglo-American submarine and bombing attacks in the
waning days of World War II.

Today, America's role in the Eurasian and Indo-Pacific sea lanes is vastly different, in both civilian and military dimensions, from that of 1945. So are the roles
of China, the Europeans, and America's Asian allies. Cross-national comparison,
over time, can give us deeper insights into those important changes and their
broader geopolitical significance.

America's Sea Power in Comparative and Historical Perspective

Sea lane transformation is multidimensional, proceeding at different rates in different sectors. To understand American sea power, it is important first to disaggregate the comparative political economy of the sea lanes into relevant dimensions, and then to reflect on how national roles are changing separately in each sector.

The US Navy and Its Infrastructure

The first dimension to consider is the explicitly military. The US Navy is a globally preeminent force, with a particular strength in sophisticated offensive weaponry such as aircraft carriers and attack submarines. It is supported by an extensive, far-flung basing network and advanced intelligence capabilities. The US shipbuilding and shipping sectors, however, are much weaker in comparative perspective, and American port infrastructure is much less developed, especially relative to Chinese ports and shipping. Despite the United States' enduring overall technological strengths and the global scope of its capacities, Chinese marine undersea cables, ASW ships and aircraft, UUVs, and hydrosonic devices appear to be making inroads in the undersea balance close to China's shores.[7]

The United States continues to be the only nation on earth with a credible aircraft-carrier fleet—eleven carriers, each with its own strike group.[8] Four other nations claim two, and three other countries one, but none have anything comparable to the US Navy's elaborate support infrastructure for carriers.[9] America also has a greater capability by far than any other nation to project its naval power globally. It enjoys the geopolitical advantage of extended coastlines on both the Atlantic and the Pacific, complemented by foreign bases in the Mediterranean; at the mouth of the Red Sea; in the midst of the Indian Ocean; and astride the Pacific's First Island Chain.[10] This dispersed global basing network strongly complements America's large, highly mobile aircraft-carrier fleet.

The United States also has noteworthy financial resources to support its navy and its military establishment more generally. For fiscal year (FY) 2024, the United States budgeted more than $202.5 billion for its Navy and $53.2 billion for its Marine Corps, out of a total defense budget of $841 billion that makes up 40 percent of the world's total defense spending.[11] China, with markedly lower input costs than the United States, budgeted almost $225 billion overall—second largest in the world, but less than one-third of the US level.[12] However, China's defense expenditures and deployment are concentrated within much narrower geographic and functional areas than those of the United States, which accounts for much of the discrepancy in outlays. US expenditures and operations are decidedly international; US bases are also worldwide in their scope of operations to meet global defense commitments. China is focused much more intensively than the United States on the East and South China Seas—east of the Strait of Malacca, inside the First Island Chain, and close to its own coasts. These asymmetries of focus are a source of leverage for both sides, with US leverage much stronger at distance from China's own shores.

Carrier Caveats

Despite Washington's relatively high levels of defense spending, the transformation in America's sea-lane role—and, in some troubling respects, its decline—are clear even in the crucially important military sphere. To be sure, the United States continues to maintain its aircraft carrier fleet, which together with its versatile base at Diego Garcia and formidable undersea capabilities gives it unassailable current military dominance over the blue waters of the Indian Ocean.[13] Yet as missile capabilities rise, a vigorous debate has broken out regarding the future utility of aircraft carriers, including those that currently play such a dominant role in the Indo-Pacific sea lanes.

Contrasts between the 1996 and 2022 Taiwan Strait crises illustrate the changing geopolitical role in the sea lanes of US carriers. In December 1995, as US-China tensions intensified, the United States sent the aircraft carrier *Nimitz*, escorted by four battleships, through the Strait to demonstrate resolve in the face of Chinese pressure, albeit under the pretext of inclement weather.[14] It followed up by dispatching two carrier groups to the vicinity of the Strait three months later in March 1996, just before Taiwan held sensitive presidential and legislative elections.[15] Under analogous circumstances in 2022, however, the US Navy was less forceful. It kept a major carrier, the USS *Ronald Reagan*, in the area, but in waters well to the east of Taiwan, though it indicated an intent to continue future passages through the Taiwan Strait.[16]

The traditional argument for carriers—still championed by politicians, retired admirals, and older members of the uniformed military—is that these "mobile, floating airfields, with evolving and new aircraft, future combat systems and weapons, coupled with creative and innovative operative operational concepts" are both versatile and highly adaptable to new missions.[17] They are capable of supporting humanitarian relief missions, as they proved in responding ably to the 2004 Indian Ocean tsunami and the 2011 Tohoku earthquake and tsunami in Japan. Carriers also have been critically important in Persian Gulf combat operations against terrorists and middle-range nation-state opponents such as

Saddam Hussein's Iraq, from the 1991 GulfWar and the enforcement of a no-fly zone over Kurdistan in the 1990s, to actual wars in Afghanistan from 2001 to 2021 and in Iraq from 2003 to 2015.[18]

Some analysts, however, have voiced skepticism about the future role of aircraft carriers. Many critics point to the growing costs of producing and maintaining them, caused both by the increasing sophistication of their weapons systems and the quasi-monopolistic nature of weapons production. The United States has only a single builder of aircraft carriers—Newport News Shipbuilding in Virginia. Over the years, Newport News has demonstrated its capabilities in carrier construction, having designed and built more than thirty carriers, including the Navy's newest *Ford*-class carriers.[19] Yet the ships produced are extremely expensive, with the USS *Gerald Ford* costing $13 billion by the time of its actual delivery. The Center for a New American Security has calculated that 1,227 anticarrier missiles could be deployed for the cost of one single such carrier.[20]

A second recent objection to carriers—compounded, of course, by their rising cost—is their vulnerability to a growing number of modern weapons systems. For instance, China's Dong Feng–21D antiship missile, nicknamed an "aircraftcarrier killer," has a range of 1,335 miles and carries a single warhead that can be equipped with a 250- or 500-kiloton-yield nuclear device.[21] Chinese and Russian submarines also have been fitted lately with precision-guided cruise missiles that potentially can overwhelm carrier-fleet missile defense systems. These carrier drawbacks would not be as much of a problem in conflicts with terrorists and less-sophisticated adversaries, but carriers could be highly vulnerable to peer competitors such as Russia and China, or proxies supplied by them.[22]

Statistical and geographical caveats notwithstanding, however, the United States in the narrowly military realm largely has held its own in relation to other major naval powers such as China, particularly in the subsea realm, even as the Europeans, including the British and the Russians, have declined markedly. It is on the civilian rather than the military side of the global sea-lane ledger that the equation has changed most markedly. In shipbuilding, shipping, port construction, and marine cable networks, America's capabilities have eroded while those of China and other Northeast Asian nations have risen.

Military Shipbuilding Capabilities

The deepening challenges to long-term US preeminence in the Indo-Pacific sea lanes—even the blue waters of the Indian Ocean—include the foregoing debate over aircraft carriers. Those challenges extend, however, to much broader political-economic questions beyond the military sphere. One of the most serious is the steady decline of the US shipbuilding industry, including its military dimension. That strategic industrial sector is intensely concentrated and devoid of substantial interfirm competition.

Today, 70 percent of all US naval surface ships are produced by a single firm: Huntington Ingalls. That company in turn has only two major subsidiaries: Newport News Shipbuilding, discussed above, which is the sole builder of aircraft carriers as well as one of only two builders of nuclear submarines; and Ingalls Shipbuilding, which builds Aegis DDG 51-class guided missile cruisers and amphibious assault ships.[23] The only other major contractors for the US Navy, which itself has much broader aerospace than maritime concerns, are General Dynamics and Lockheed Martin. General Dynamics' Electric Boat subsidiary is the premier builder of US nuclear submarines. Lockheed Martin, the top contractor for the US Navy and the Department of Defense more generally, provides the Navy with the Aegis system, aerospace contracts for naval aviation, and littoral combat ships.[24] Apart from the four main contractors, the US Navy works with a few other smaller companies, some of whom also produce specialized maritime equipment for the private sector. Among US-owned firms, Bollinger Shipyards produces patrol boats and *Sentinel*-class cutters. Edison Chouest Offshore mainly provides supply vessels for the offshore oil industry.[25]

There is also a small yet cosmopolitan group of foreign firms that build ships in the United States for both military and civilian clients. The Australian firm Austal, through its US subsidiary, produces littoral combat ships and expeditionary fast transport. The Fincantieri Marinette Marine Group, Italian-owned since 2009, provides guided missile frigates. Also, in 2024, the United States began a dialogue with Japanese and Korean shipbuilders about US naval contracting, to begin with maintenance and repair of US warships.[26]

The Decline of American Commercial Shipbuilding

From the early 1980s, the US commercial shipbuilders that might have bid for and filled significant defense contracts went into steady decline for three related reasons. First, construction differential subsidies provided by the US government to encourage private-sector bidding expired in 1981. Second, other national authorities continued to provide such support, putting US commercial shipbuilding at a distinct competitive disadvantage. Finally, naval construction demand soared during the 1980s with the advent of the Reagan administration's "600-ship Navy" plans, which diverted resources from civilian to military production. As a consequence of these complex pressures, between

1987 and 1993 the US shipbuilding industry sold only eight commercial ships of more than 1,000 gross tons for the entire period, compared to the seventy seven ships it built in 1975 alone.[27] Employment trends naturally followed those in production. In 1980, there were approximately 180,000 jobs in private American shipyards, but by 2023 that number had fallen by more than 40 percent, with only 105,652 private-sector shipbuilding jobs remaining.[28]

The story of the Philadelphia Naval Shipyard, once a pillar of the industry, epitomizes the decline of American shipbuilding and the foreign inroads made against it. The shipyard was founded in 1801 as the first federal naval shipbuilding facility. In World War I, it built minesweepers and a hospital ship, while the eastern end of the island in the Delaware River where the shipyard lay served as a seaplane manufacturing facility. During the war, employment at the yard grew to 12,000, and in the following decades bigger cranes and additional drydocks paved the way for construction of more and larger vessels, including the heavy cruiser *Wichita* and the 36,000-ton battleship *Washington* during the 1930s. Both of these vessels rushed across the Atlantic to reinforce Britain's Home Fleet after the Japanese surprise attack on Pearl Harbor in December 1941. World War II was the peak of activity at the yard, when employment hit 47,000 as the United States rapidly expanded its navy. At the height of the war, Philadelphia was the world's largest naval shipyard. Among its most famous products during the war were the battleships USS *Wisconsin* and USS *New Jersey*, two of the largest battleships ever produced in the United States. In 1995, however, the Philadelphia Naval Shipyard closed its doors.[29] Its commercial successor on the site, Philly Shipyard, is now owned by Norwegians and produces large container vessels for global shipping.[30] Two Singaporean firms, Keppel and ST Engineering, also build various specialized marine vessels in the United States, from oil rigs and dredges to icebreakers.[31] Yet both American and international firms actively building commercial vessels in the United States itself are now few and far between. In 2023, the United States ranked only nineteenth globally in commercial shipbuilding, accounting for less than 0.2 percent of new private ship orders.[32]

Contrasts with Northeast Asia

The contrast to the state of Northeast Asian shipbuilding, led recently by China, could not be more striking. By a substantial margin, China is the largest shipbuilder in the world, with 45 percent of the entire global order book by deadweight tonnage.[33] Recently, a significant proportion of that production has been military. At the end of 2023, China had 370 battle-force ships, compared with

TABLE 6.1

Northeast Asia's dominance in global shipbuilding

Rank	Shipyard	Order (million CGT)	Headquarters
1	China State Shipbuilding Corporation	19.7	Shanghai, China
2	HD Hyundai Heavy Industries	17.9	Ulsan, South Korea
3	Samsung Heavy Industries	9.7	Seoul, South Korea
4	Hanwha Ocean	7.9	Geoje, Gyeongsangnam-do, South Korea
5	Yangzijinag Shipbuilding	6.9	Taizhou, Jiangsu Province, China
6	Nihon Shipyard	6.7	Tokyo, Japan
7	COSCO Shipping Heavy Industry	6.0	Shanghai, China
8	New Times Shipbuilding	3.1	Jingjiang, Jiangsu Province, China
9	Tsuneishi Shipbuilding	2.3	Fukuyama, Hiroshima Prefecture, Japan
10	Nantong CIMC Sinopacific Offshore & Engineering	1.9	Nantong, Jiangsu Province, China

SOURCE: Tomas Kristiansen, "Five of the World's Ten Biggest Shipyards Are Now Chinese," *ShippingWatch*, January 10, 2024, https://shippingwatch.com/suppliers/article16740947.ece.

NOTE: (1) China Shipbuilding Industry Corporation (CSIC) was merged into China State Shipbuilding Corporation (CSSC) in November 2019. (2) Daewoo Shipbuilding & Marine Engineering (DSME) was acquired by Hanwha Group in December 2022.

280 for the US Navy.[34] The US Office of Naval Intelligence projects that by 2025, China will have 400 battle-force ships, and 425 by 2030.[35] South Korea was a distant second to China in shipbuilding, at 28 percent, and Japan ranked third at 22 percent. The rest of the world combined, including the entire European Union and the United States, accounted for less than 5 percent of global shipbuilding.[36]

Northeast Asia, led by China, looms equally large at the firm level. The world's largest shipbuilder today is the state-owned China State Shipbuilding Corporation (CSSC), with 2020 revenue of more than $54 billion, or more than five times its 2010 order book. CSSC makes around 80 percent of the Chinese navy's main equipment and ranks as one of China's top ten military suppliers.[37] Its signature products include conventional and nuclear submarines, warships, and torpedoes, as well as the *Liaoning*, China's first domestically produced aircraft carrier. The firm maintains a formidable civilian shipbuilding program in addition to supplying the PLA-N. CSSC's civilian work includes the production of oil and chemical tankers, container ships, bulk carriers, and engineering ships.[38] Four of the other top ten shipbuilding firms in the world are also Chinese. Three on that select list, however, are Korean, while two are Japanese, as indicated in Table 6.1. East Asian shipbuilders in 2023 thus monopolized the list of the ten largest shipbuilding firms on earth.

The Transformation in Shipping: Containerization's Rising Role

The global pattern and trends in shipping are broadly similar to those in ship-building. Northeast Asia, led by China, has assumed a prominent and growing position, while the once dominant American role is now generally minimal. The three largest categories of shipping by deadweight tonnage (bulk carriers, oil tankers, and container ships), together comprised 85 percent of global shipping as a whole in 2023. The United States ranked only eleventh in deadweight carry-ing capacity in these areas. Only in two niche markets tangentially related to shipping—offshore vessels such as drilling rigs, and ferries and passenger ships— was the US presence significant.[39] By contrast, Northeast Asia has a large role in the most significant shipping categories. Japan is ranked second and China third in bulk carriers by tonnage, following Greece, with Korea in sixth place. In oil tankers, China is ranked third, Japan fourth, and Korea eighth. In container ships, which carry the vast proportion of manufactured goods, the highest value-added items moving in international trade, China is in first place and Japan is in second.

The dynamic emergence since the 1960s of container shipping, in which Northeast Asia is dominant owing to aggressive capital investment, is a central reason for Northeast Asia's current prominence in this category.[40] Its powerful and rising role in manufacturing is another, as containers are especially important in the shipment of manufactured goods. East Asia also has been adept at building the massive ports that are optimal for container shipping. The importance of con-tainerization in global trade, and in international shipping itself, is suggested by the enormous recent growth in the use of containers themselves. In early 1991, fewer than 7 million TEUs (the standard container unit) were in use for seaborne trade. Two decades later, in January 2011, this figure had grown over fourfold, to 29 million TEUs.[41] By 2021, the figure had risen to 39.4 million TEUs. The United Nations Economic and Social Commission for Asia and the Pacific esti-mates that container trade will continue to grow at 7.6 percent annually, com-pounded, through 2025. That would be 20 percent faster than comparable growth for air freight.[42]

Container trade to and from Asia, especially China, has paralleled the explosive growth of international trade between Asia, the world's manufacturing center, and the broader world. China's overall global trade has expanded roughly tenfold since 2000, and container trade has grown even more rapidly. Macroeconomic supply-demand pressures have been important, of course, but the revolution in shipping logistics, inspired by the advent of container trade, has played a crucial role in directing transactions to the Eurasian sea lanes in particular. That revolu-tion has had three central dimensions.

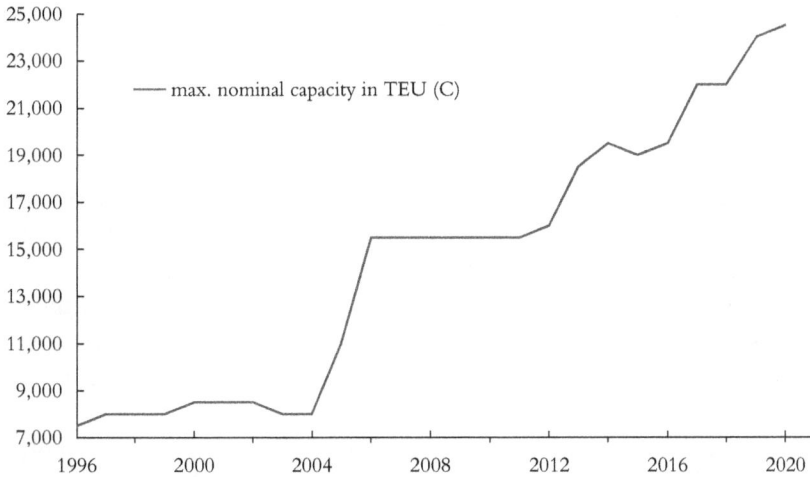

FIGURE 6.1 The steady expansion of global container ship capacity (1996–2020)

SOURCE: Hendrik Jungen et al., "The Rise of Ultra Large Container Vessels: Implications for Seaport Systems and Environmental Considerations," in *Dynamics in Logistics: Twenty-Five Years of Interdisciplinary Logistics Research in Bremen, Germany*, edited by Michael Freitag, Herbert Kotzab, and Nicole Megow (Hamburg: Springer, 2021), https://doi.org/10.1007/978-3-030-88662-2_12.

NOTE: Development of container ship sizes by nominal capacity, LOA and Beam, based on the largest ship in the respective year by nominal capacity.

A key driver has been the steady expansion of optimal port scale, driven by the increasing ease of handling standardized containers through computerized technology and robotics. For more than three decades, Asia has had the strongest incentives to undertake such expansion, owing to its strong manufacturing orientation, rapidly expanding exports, availability of capital investment, and relatively weak resistance to innovation from shipping unions. Since 1990, the largest port in the world consistently has been one of three cities in the Sinic economic world: first Hong Kong (1993–1995 and 1999–2004); then Singapore (2005–2008, as well as 1990 and 1998); and now Shanghai (2010–present).[43] Over those years, the scale of that largest port has risen from 5 million TEU throughput—the maximum annual scale for the Panama Canal—to 47 million TEU, or nearly ten times that volume.[44]

A second dimension of the container revolution has been a related expansion in the optimal scale of container ships. In 1988, as noted in Figure 6.1, the largest container ship in the world could carry around 6,000 TEU.[45] Two decades later, that capacity had more than doubled. By 2022, the largest container ship in the world, the *Ever Alot* of Taiwan's Evergreen Lines, had a capacity of more than 24,000 TEU, greater than three times the scale prevailing a quarter-century previously.[46]

Taken together, the changing scale economies of container shipping and of container ports over the past two decades have had important geo-economic implications for the Eurasian sea lanes. As suggested above, they have facilitated trade with China's massive container ports. However, they also encourage the routing of commerce in massive container ships, which are most efficiently handled in large-scale ports. The container revolution has thus discouraged trade through smaller ports, and through chokepoints such as the Panama Canal, that are too small to handle optimal-scale "super ships." It also has increased the dangers of catastrophic accidents in suboptimal ports, as so dramatically shown in the March 2024 disaster in which a container ship struck the Francis Scott Key Bridge in Baltimore, Maryland, killing several people and crippling the flow of traffic on a major US highway and waterway.[47]

The container revolution thus today privileges trade among the "super ports" of greater China, and those constructed to meet its standards elsewhere in the world. It encourages the creation of optimal-scale regional shipping hubs interacting preferentially with China, such as Piraeus, Colombo, and Algeciras, which are often developed by Chinese firms, and receive Chinese BRI assistance.[48] Changing scale economies in shipping also inhibits trans-Pacific trade to America's Atlantic ports, in light of the constraints on shipping through the Panama Canal and the danger of accidents, all while putting strong logistic pressure on US West Coast ports. The revolution also handicaps ports that do not innovate and expand, such as those of the Indian subcontinent and the United States, which lose competitively to the China-supported regional hubs.

The final implication of the container revolution is that it gives an advantage to firms that exploit the competitive opportunities that the revolution creates. East Asian firms, led by China's COSCO, have been among the greatest beneficiaries in recent years. As is evident in Figure 6.2, a few European firms do remain prominent in international container shipping, capitalizing on commercial stills honed over centuries, imperial trading traditions, and sophisticated global contacts. Extensive intraregional commerce within Europe and its periphery—around the Mediterranean and the Baltic Seas, for example—also magnifies Europe's share of global shipping. Unquestionably, however, the shadow of East Asia is rising in global shipping, especially in the Eurasian sea lanes between Shanghai and the Mediterranean.

Northeast Asia's Dominant Global Shipping Role

China's COSCO, in particular, looms large globally as the fourth-largest container-shipping line in the world. It also owns the world's largest bulk-carrier and oil-

TEU (twenty-foot equivalent)

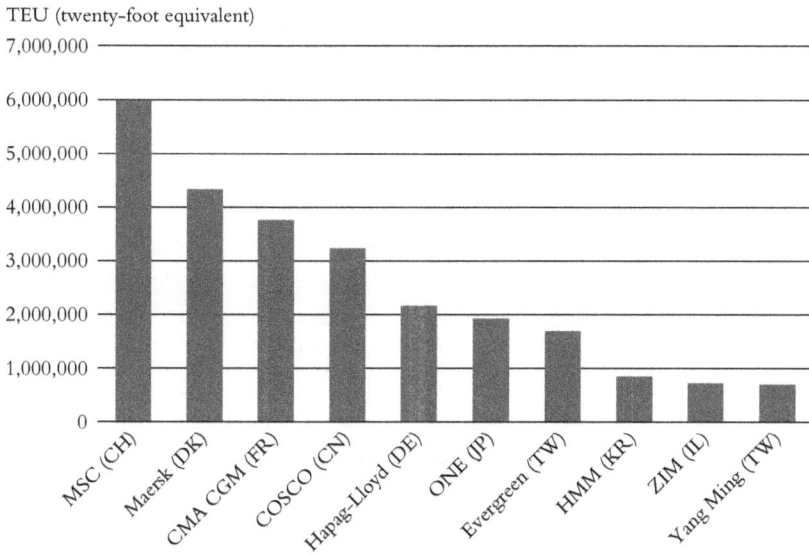

FIGURE 6.2 Northeast Asia's key role in global container shipping
SOURCE: "Alphaliner TOP 100," accessed June 29, 2024, https://alphaliner.axsmarine.com/PublicTop100/.

tanker fleets, and its LNG carrier fleet is significant in China's import market, covering routes from Australia, Papua New Guinea, and Russia.[49] In addition to its central role in shipping, COSCO is simultaneously the world's largest port operator, with investments in 51 major container terminals throughout the world.[50] It thus holds considerable leverage over ports in negotiating favorable terms of access, since it has the market power to redirect trade flows among nearby rival ports, leveraged by the massive scale of the Chinese economy. Other Asian lines, although smaller than COSCO, with a narrower range of operations, also cast a long shadow in global shipping. Ocean Network Express, a Japanese joint venture founded in 2017, is ranked sixth. It is accompanied in the top ten rankings by two Taiwanese firms—Evergreen (ranked seventh) and Yang Ming (ranked tenth), as well as one Korean firm (HMM at #8), as Figure 6.2 suggests.

American shipping capabilities, like those in shipbuilding, have declined from the global preeminence they enjoyed at the end of World War II.[51] In the middle of 1946, the United States had by far the world's largest merchant fleet, with nearly 5,000 ships and 50 percent of global tonnage. In 1960, the American merchant fleet still included almost 17 percent of all merchant ships in the world. That figure fell to 7.9 percent in 1970, 3.5 percent in 1980, 2.7 percent in 1990, 1 percent in 2000, and only 0.4 percent in 2015.[52] Today, the largest US shipping firm—Matson, Inc., which operates exclusively in the Pacific, ranks only twenty-seventh globally in container shipping, compared to COSCO's fourth place. The second-largest US shipping firm after Matson, Seaboard Marine, is ranked only forty-fifth globally.[53]

Why US Shipping is Weak

One key reason for the lamentable global standing of the US merchant marine is political: the Jones Act of 1920. That legislation requires that shipping between US ports be carried in ships that are at least 75 percent US owned, 75 percent US crewed, and assembled entirely in the United States, with all major components of hulls and superstructures manufactured domestically. Propellers, rudders, and engines often are imported, but to meet Jones Act requirements most of the rest of the ships operating between US ports must be produced in the United States. US domestic production, even in the limited form legally required, normally can be done only at exorbitant cost, compared particularly to levels in highly competitive Asian nations such as Japan, South Korea, and recently China. These Asian nations boast by far the world's most competitive shipbuilding and shipping sectors.

The profiles of America's two largest shipping companies, Matson Navigation and Seaboard Marine, ironically show how the Jones Act has limited the horizons of US shipping, even as it has provided these firms and their workers with comfortable, relatively lucrative, niche businesses and employment. Matson, which began operations in 1882 carrying plantation stores from the US West Coast to the Hawaiian Islands, continues to specialize in trade between the continental US and various US territories in the Pacific, such as Hawai'i, Guam, and American Samoa, as well as in servicing US government contracts worldwide. Virtually all of Matson's activities are covered by the Jones Act, insulating these transactions from foreign competition.[54] Similarly, Seaboard Marine, based in Miami, Florida, deals heavily with US possessions in the Caribbean, such as Puerto Rico and the Virgin Islands, and also handles government contracts with other parts of the Caribbean.[55] Neither of these top two American shipping lines ventures into the Eurasian sea lanes westward from Northeast Asia at all, where they would now face daunting East Asian competition.

Global Port Transformation: The Ironic Consequence of America's Shipping Logistics Revolution

Shipping logistics are a key reason why the global competitive dynamic in shipping has steadily and dramatically shifted against the United States and in favor of East Asia. During the 1960s, the advent of container shipping—

invented, ironically, in the United States, by Malcom Maclean, the founder of Sea-Land Service, revolutionized shipping logistics.[56] Standardized TEU containers, which could be flexibly loaded and transferred from ship to train and road transport, became the packaging norm for international shipping, as the standardization dramatically reduced shipping costs.[57] The container revolution facilitated the massive American military buildup in Vietnam itself, making it both quick and easy to transport huge volumes of goods across the Pacific. Yet that paradigm shift had remarkably little impact on US domestic shipping infrastructure, or on the long-term fortunes of American shipping lines, which were not globally oriented.

Capitalizing on this US-inspired logistics revolution naturally required massive capital investment. The Chinese, with their large domestic market, explosive growth, and soaring manufactured exports, were able and inclined to undertake such investments much more rapidly than the United States, following advent of the Reform and Opening Policy in 1978, just as Deng Xiaoping's Four Modernizations began. Throughout China's port-transformation process over the ensuing decades, the role of government financial support and state-owned operating institutions was central. Chinese government strategists recognized the synergies between shipping and port management, promoting the rise of shipping national champions such as COSCO that held stakes in both shipping and ports. As a result of these strategic efforts, involving major Chinese government support, COSCO is now the world's largest port operator and fourth-largest container shipping firm.[58]

COSCO enjoys government support at a variety of levels. This support was manifest in the construction of Shanghai's Yangshan, the world's largest port, which was built at a cost of close to $12 billion, invested over two decades.[59] COSCO operates the port in cooperation with SIPG, a state-owned port-management firm.[60] Shanghai's municipal government, with strong ties to the administration, served as indirect catalyst for Yangshan's construction, paying for the thirty-kilometer bridge connecting Shanghai to the port during the early 2000s. Prime Minister Zhu Rongji, previously the mayor of Shanghai, was supportive personally throughout the development process. At the national trade-policy level, China's 2001 entry into the World Trade Organization was likewise a catalyst, both in Shanghai and in Beijing.[61]

Seven of the top ten container ports in the world are now located in China, as indicated in Table 6.2.[62] Most, like Shanghai's Yangshan, are vertically integrated with Chinese state-owned shipping firms. Such arrangements allow operating-cost advantages that Chinese ports possess, due to their operating scale and

TABLE 6.2

China features the world's largest container ports (2021)

Rank	Port	2017 Volume	2021 Volume	Change (%)
1	Shanghai, China	40.23	47.03	16.9
2	Singapore	33.67	37.49	11.34
3	Ningbo, China	24.61	31.07	26.25
4	Shenzhen, China	25.21	28.77	14.12
5	Guangzhou, China	20.37	24.18	18.7
6	Busan, South Korea	20.49	22.71	10.83
7	Qingdao, China	18.3	23.71	29.56
8	Hong Kong, China	20.76	17.8	−14.26
9	Tianjin, China	15.07	20.27	34.5
10	Rotterdam, the Netherlands	13.73	15.3	11.43

SOURCE: World Shipping Council, "Top 50 Ports," accessed June 24, 2024, https://www.worldshipping.org/top-50-ports.
NOTES: (1) Volume expressed in terms of million TEU. (2) US container ports: Los Angeles (#17); Long Beach (#22); New York–New Jersey (#24); Savannah (#40); and Seattle-Tacoma (#54).

efficient design, to be translated into competitive commercial advantages downstream for shipping-sector owners such as COSCO.

COSCO holds major shares in large domestic Chinese ports like Yangshan, exploiting their scale economies both within China and in ports across the Eurasian sea lanes, from Shanghai, through Singapore to Port Said to Piraeus.[63] Other government-related Chinese firms, such as CCCC (Colombo) and China State Construction Engineering (Gwadar), likewise play important port-construction and port-operating roles. Those roles provide such firms with similar cost advantages in major container-shipping ports along the same sea lanes, often synergistic with those enjoyed by COSCO. And China's commercial role in the maritime nations stretching from Shanghai to Singapore, Suez, and beyond, generates a convenient customer base. Over the long Indo-Pacific route westward to Europe, across South Asia, the Middle East, and the Mediterranean, these rapidly modernizing, government-connected Chinese firms thus face remarkably little competition, especially in local port construction and management.

The American Ports Bottleneck

US ports, relative to the foregoing, are comparatively miniscule in size, and their users generally are unrelated institutionally to the ports themselves. The US national government also historically has played only a sporadic role in port development, analogous to its uneven role in both shipping and shipbuilding.

As a consequence of the foregoing, US container ports and their support infrastructure are remarkably underdeveloped in comparison with analogous facilities in China. America's two largest container ports, Los Angeles and Long

Beach, rank only seventeenth and twenty-second worldwide.[64] The vaunted New York Port Authority, which combines both New York and New Jersey ports in the New York City metropolitan area, holds only the twenty-fourth spot globally. Shanghai, by contrast, is first in the world, while seven of the global top ten are also within China. And these Chinese ports are growing faster than most other major international ports, as indicated in Table 6.2 above.

Many US container ports also have antiquated construction, giving them crucial safety and security defects. Recent studies suggest, for example, that at least eight major and many smaller bridges in the United States are vulnerable to collisions with supersized container ships, such as the one that caused Baltimore's March 2024 port catastrophe.[65] Large US port cranes imported from China to improve efficiency could also prove vulnerable from a security perspective.[66]

Over the past five years, technological change in the port sector has begun to give China a further advantage relative to the United States. Artificial intelligence, image recognition, 5G, and Internet of Things technology are beginning to reduce port-operating costs, creating new opportunities and challenges, in an international economy with increasingly global competition.[67] Once again, however, static trade volume and lack of incentives to introduce the latest technology are disadvantaging US ports from a global standpoint, and aiding their competitors in China, Singapore, and elsewhere along the Eurasian sea lanes.

China's smart-port automation remains at an early stage of development, though it is proceeding more rapidly there than elsewhere. Only eighteen automated container terminals were in operation in China during January 2024, but this was the largest national concentration on earth.[68] Singapore's Tuas Port is now the world's largest automated container terminal, unique in that tiny nation.[69] China will soon have more automated container ports, with at least twenty-seven such ports under construction or being upgraded.[70] The Chinese Ministry of Transportation already has selected several additional locations at which to build smart-port demonstration projects. These could jumpstart port automatization for the country as a whole and further lengthen China's lead in commercial mastery of the Eurasian sea lanes.[71] However, the imported Chinese technology may also come with related security risks, as noted above, making autonomous development an urgent priority.

The Undersea Transformation

The world's sea lanes are quietly yet steadily changing—beneath as well as above the waves. Technology in UUVs and hydro-sonar devices has been evolving worldwide, accelerated by advances in artificial intelligence as well as 5G communications. Many of these applications are strategically relevant along the Eurasian sea lanes, especially in the South China Sea and at assorted chokepoints through which large numbers of ships must pass, as in the Strait of Malacca and amid the nearby Andaman Islands.

Another important sea-lane transformation is in submarine communications—so strategically relevant even during British imperial days that the Crown mandated all government-related cables to be run exclusively between British territories around the world.[72] Since the mid-1980s, the advent of optical-fiber transmission, coupled with the Information Revolution, has massively increased both the speed and the volume of undersea internet communication, which now comprises more than 95 percent of total internet communications worldwide (space, overland, and undersea). Large and wealthy American technology firms such as Microsoft, Facebook, and Google have been global leaders in laying state-of-the-art submarine cable systems, so US geopolitical advantage is to some degree thereby embedded. China has targeted the optical-fiber realm, however, and its feverish infrastructure building has prioritized submarine optical-fiber network construction, often based on aggressive pricing.

China was, no doubt, a late-comer to this aspect of the Information Revolution. In 2004, half of all internet traffic worldwide flowed through the United States, and China had only a marginal role. That US global share declined by half during the ensuing two decades, however, to just under one-quarter of global traffic.[73] Explosive growth in Asian internet use was a major aspect of that transformation, with the continent becoming home to more than half of all internet users in the world by 2018.[74] Internet use has also been rising rapidly across Africa and South Asia.[75] Not surprisingly, China has seen this Information Revolution in the developing world as a tempting opportunity, remarkably neglected by sophisticated Western multinationals.

Just as it earlier capitalized on US innovations in container shipping, China has been moving rapidly, in particular, into subsea cables—traditionally an Anglo-American preserve. Huawei's 2009 joint venture with Cable and Wireless, the classic cable provider to the British Empire, enabled it to complete more than 100 projects, initially collaborative. The collaboration also propelled Huawei into position as the fourth-largest supplier of subsea cables worldwide.[76] Huawei chose to focus on the Global South, winning a contract in 2017 for the first submarine fiber-optic cable connection across the South Atlantic between Brazil and Cameroon, as well as numerous other projects throughout the Indo-Pacific, Africa, and Latin America.[77]

In 2020, the Hengtong Group, a private firm with previous ties to the Chinese military, acquired Huawei Marine Networks, renaming it HMN Technologies.

Hengtong itself is also one of China's largest producers of advanced submarine-grade fiber.[78] Through projects such as the PEACE Cable linking Pakistan and East Africa with the Mediterranean, Hengtong is continuing to target the Eurasian sea lanes as a priority area of activity.[79] It is also active in a variety of projects across the Indo-Pacific more broadly. It is, for example, currently completing a project in Papua New Guinea that will connect fourteen of the country's most densely populated coastal cities and cover more than 55 percent of the country's population.[80] It is also planning submarine cable projects to connect Japan, Hong Kong, Southeast Asia, Sri Lanka, and Africa—provided that politics does not intervene—as well as a land cable venture connecting the PEACE marine cable overland from Gwadar across Pakistan to Xinjiang, and ultimately to Hong Kong. Hengtong works not only on optical cable network projects around the world, but also on power-cable ventures.[81] It also recently has moved more explicitly into defense applications, partnering with the PLA Naval University of Engineering.[82]

In Conclusion

In 1945, the United States reigned supreme across the global sea lanes along both military and civilian dimensions. On the military side, it continues to retain a formidable and in many sectors hegemonic presence, with a defense-spending budget that remains a quarter of the entire world's total. US defense spending is orders of magnitude larger than that of China, the runner-up, although China's may be more cost-effective. America's fleet of eleven aircraft-carrier battle groups, and a basing network commanding important strongpoints such as Diego Garcia, provide a powerful foundation for that global sea-lane presence, although changing technology is calling the long-term strategic value of aircraft carriers in potential conflicts with peer competitors into serious question.

China's challenge to US military primacy in Asia lies partially in its focus on asymmetric warfare and A2/AD capabilities, as well as its defensive concentration of resources within the First Island Chain along its own coastline. In the longer run, however, Beijing's threat lies equally or even more decisively in growing, closely related dual-use capabilities—in shipbuilding, shipping, port construction, and undersea cable construction, as well as potentially related emerging technologies such as artificial intelligence. In all of these areas, China is capitalizing on rapidly increasing and interrelated scale economies that offer significant cost-competitive advantages to new physical and digital infrastructure that the country is building and situating geopolitically, to create strategic advantage over rivals such as the United States and Western Europe.

Across all these areas, China is fundamentally transforming the Eurasian sea lanes under its Maritime Silk Road program by finessing the "Strait of Malacca dilemma" through overland shortcuts across Pakistan and Myanmar and by developing new dual-use shipping and port-management capabilities. These new capabilities neutralize the traditional embedded advantages of European, Japanese, and Korean competitors while also fostering new regional infrastructural hubs under Chinese control. These increasingly integrated Chinese logistical networks, largely run by state-owned enterprises, and oriented toward "China's Maritime Lifeline" from Shanghai to Europe, enhance both commercial competitiveness and political-military power-projection capabilities for the future.

7

The Changing Chessboard of Sea-Lane Geopolitics

THE UNITED STATES AND CHINA are by no means the only players in Eurasian sea-lane geopolitics. To be sure, they play the classic central roles of guardian and challenger today, as the two largest political economies in the world, with the most formidable militaries of the Indo-Pacific. Yet a panoply of other actors, including nongovernmental organizations (NGOs), transnational corporations, mini-lateral coalitions of the willing, minimally recognized proto-states, national militaries, coast guards, and local governments also feature significantly on the Indo-Pacific chessboard. Naturally, nation states such as Japan, India, Australia, South Korea, and even European and Middle Eastern national governments have vested interests as well.

It is instructive to compare today's Indo-Pacific chessboard to that prevailing at the beginning of the twentieth century, in the days of what was fashionably called the "Great Game."[1] This exotic and byzantine imperial nation-state struggle featured Britain and Russia as central protagonists. The Great Game also had myriad subnational actors, such as minor princes and potentates, but there were far fewer transnational actors and far less fluid economic and financial interactions. Eurasia in recent years has gained a critical mass of new middle-range local actors, both public and private, that have increasing stakes in regional stability. Those actors include varied groups such as multinational corporations and NGOs, as well as cities and city-states.

Along the sea lanes themselves, the Eurasian maritime chessboard historically has featured a large number of small principalities interspersed with a few large maritime kingdoms, such as Srivijaya (based in what is now Sumatra) between the seventh and eleventh centuries CE. Yet Maritime Eurasia seldom has had indigenous rulers with the dominating capacity to shape regionwide outcomes. The limits of communications, transportation, resources, and weaponry made it difficult for large political units to form and sustain themselves, while NGOs in the modern sense did not exist. And from the sixteenth century, local non-Western aspirants to a regional role were preempted by the European empires, which have only in the past half-century finally disappeared.

With the coming of the Europeans to Asian shores at the beginning of the sixteenth century, it became more common to see periodic clashes of non-Asian empires within Asia itself. The first battles pitted the Portuguese against the Dutch, and then the Dutch against the French, with the English, Russians, Germans, Danes, Spanish, Americans, and finally Japanese joining in various permutations. Only since the 1960s have newly independent Asian nation states become major players on their own Eurasian maritime chessboard. In this post-colonial period, the smaller nations of Eurasia became much more prominent, especially in the economic arena. Several, including Japan, South Korea, and Singapore, grew explosively through increased prowess in manufacturing and services. Others, such as Australia and the GCC states, prospered by supplying the newly industrialized economies of Asia with raw materials. Decolonization ended the sway of longstanding empires, giving smaller Asia-Pacific countries more room to maneuver, even as the Russians—a second-tier player in all but the nuclear realm—sporadically intervened.

European players, together with multinationals and NGOs, have returned to the Eurasian sea lanes in nonimperial capacities. The Mediterranean Shipping Company of Geneva, for example, is now the largest container-shipping company in the Eurasian sea lanes, as throughout the world, although China's COSCO has been rising fast.[2] These players have advantages in the fluid, competitive world of maritime affairs that they cannot exercise so easily on land, where government regulation holds more sway.

Animating the changing role of individual nations across the Indo-Pacific has been the changing configuration of economic growth. Per-capita GDP expansion has accelerated rapidly since the Korean War—first in Japan, then in Korea and the other Little Dragons (1960s/1970s), and for the past four decades in mainland China.

The accelerating growth in Southeast and South Asia over the past decade is introducing a new dimension. Such rapid growth in densely populated nations like China and India has triggered both sharply rising local consumption and a related explosion in maritime trade. Though China is a more continentalist nation, its consumer class is still twice as large as India's—roughly 900 million to 500 million.[3] India, however, now has a larger population with a demographic tailwind at its back, and its maritime orientation is prospectively stronger than China. That situation will drive a substantial expansion of Indian maritime commodity trade, with India's share of emerging-market oil demand, to cite just one important sector, doubling to 24 percent over the coming decade.[4] That, plus rising Indian domestic consumer demand for a broad range of imports, and expanding Indian service and manufactured-export capacity, will drive substantial growth in Indian trade—which geography ordains to be primarily maritime.

Key Players in the Changing Eurasian Maritime Geopolitical Game

This chapter will focus on the evolving Eurasian sea-lane role of several nations, apart from the United States and China, that have in their interaction with like-minded powers been most influential in giving Maritime Eurasia its current political-economic configuration. Those intermediate powers include Japan, India, Korea, and Australia. The chapter will also consider the recent involvement of European and Middle Eastern nations. And it will examine nongovernmental actors, especially multinational firms and NGOs, that have helped make the Indo-Pacific a much more plural, diverse, fluid, and potentially resilient regional system than was true even a decade ago. What we ultimately seek is a comprehensive picture of the Eurasian maritime regime within which the United States and China must interact, and the potential of third parties to moderate and transform the deepening Sino-American confrontation.

Even though the United States and China are the crucial duo in the political economy of Eurasia's sea lanes, there are several important reasons to consider other players that have at least the potential to modify China's rising preeminence. Several of these countries, unlike the United States, are Eurasian maritime countries themselves, active in seaborne trade across the Eurasian sea lanes, stretching from the Mediterranean eastward to the Strait of Malacca and beyond. These countries have the most basic existential need to compete with China—to the extent that competition is involved—for supplies and political-military protection along the sea lanes. And on issues of cooperative security, ranging from piracy, refugee relief, and counterterrorism to financial stabilization, both America and China need the cooperation of actors throughout the region, including smaller national players and NGOs.

As China projects its political-economic presence more intensely beyond its immediate neighborhood, a distinct new Eurasian geopolitics is emerging.[5] Powers beyond the region, notably in Europe and to some degree in the Middle East and Latin America, are being drawn into Eurasian struggles. For Europe in particular, this shift has provoked increasing diplomatic and political-military attention to the Indo-Pacific sea lanes, with implications that deserve further attention. Smaller actors, often highly mobile, may be able to disrupt and complicate the relationships of larger powers, including the United States and China, anywhere in the world, including at sea. As Stephen Walt has pointed out, smaller powers often have distinctive fears of abandonment that may incentivize them to manipulate larger nations, including allies. In a related dynamic, small players also typically have incentives, as well as the ability, to entrap larger powers.[6] These pronounced incentives may cause smaller powers to be highly manipulative, and the flexible, ambiguous environment that the seas provide—devoid of clearcut national boundaries—gives them an important arena in which to practice these manipulative skills.

The interests of smaller powers along the Eurasian sea lanes frequently diverge from US and Chinese central concerns. The United States, after all, is located on the other side of the world and trades relatively little in the Eurasian sea lanes. China, for its part, is broadly feared as a potential hegemon, with impulses to dominate that diverge from the desires of others. The following list sets out twelve of the most clear-cut and strategically important instances of divergent interest across Maritime Eurasia in recent years:

(1) *Taiwan*. Japan has a strong national interest in Taiwan's autonomy, which Taiwan itself shares. China, of course, has directly contradictory opinions. The unambiguous American concerns, shared with regional actors at many levels, are regional stability, alliance cohesion, and strategic dominance of the First Island Chain in the Pacific.

(2) *Sino-Indian geopolitical rivalry*. Although much of this rivalry, including border clashes in the Himalayas and Ladakh, is continental, it has important maritime dimensions in the Indian Ocean, the Bay of Bengal, and amidst the rimland states of Maritime Eurasia, such as Sri Lanka, the Maldives, and Bangladesh.

(3) *The ten-dash line*. China's South China Sea claims clash with those of Vietnam, the Philippines, and Malaysia. Overriding American, Japanese, and South Korean interests focus on regional stability, alliance relations, and freedom of navigation, rather than the particulars of specific national boundaries.

(4) *North Korea and its neighbors.* Given its growing chemical, biological, nuclear, and power-projection capabilities, Pyongyang poses a deepening threat to Japan and South Korea, in particular. This threat is intensified by deepening cooperation with Russia since the outbreak of the Ukraine War. Important maritime dimensions include instabilities along the Northern Limit Line, the DMZ water boundary; as well as expanding North Korean submarine and missile development programs.

(5) *Indo-Pakistani disputes, including Kashmir.* Since partition in 1947, India and Pakistan, both now nuclear powers, have fought four wars with one another and continue to engage in periodic deadly skirmishes along the Line of Control in Kashmir.

(6) *Senkaku Islands (Diaoyudao/Diaoyutai) disputed claims.*[7] Japan has strong territorial and strategic interests in these islands. Neither China nor Taiwan share these interests, but they nevertheless attach symbolic importance to the islands, for nationalistic historical reasons.

(7) *Takeshima/Tokdo disputed claims.* South Korea has interests contradictory to those of Japan with respect to territory, fishing, and resource extraction.

(8) *Piracy along the sea lanes.* Despite the preeminent role of the US Navy, periodic piracy incidents occur. Nation-state interests generally coincide and cooperative security prevails.

(9) *Terrorism.* A cooperative-security problem for nation states, though at times terrorism is intertwined with interstate conflict, as in Baluchistan and Kashmir.

(10) *Ethnic and religious violence.* Periodic violent attacks against minority groups, such as those against the ethnic Chinese in Indonesia (1965–1968), or against the Rohingya in Myanmar since the late 1970s, have flowed from domestic schisms within individual nations. These outbursts of targeted violence must be understood in their own terms.

(11) *Refugee flows.* The flow of Rohingya from Myanmar into Bangladesh during 1977 and 1978, as well as 2017, needs to be understood much more in terms of local factors than from the perspective of US-China relations, or even international relations more generally. Understanding requires a more fine-grained inquiry into domestic politics and regional dynamics far beyond great-power rivalry.

(12) *Red Sea.* The waterway between Djibouti and the Suez Canal is a vital artery for energy trade between Europe and the Gulf, as well as for container trade between Europe and Asia. During the early 2020s, especially from the Gaza conflict since 2023, it became the site of confrontation

between Iranian proxy (Houthi) forces in Yemen and a varied coalition of US, European, and GCC actors. Instability in Sudan, Ethiopia, and Somalia has added further complications.

Maritime Eurasia's Middle-Range System Builders

Although the United States and China figure most prominently in the headlines, the key systemic architects of today's rimland Eurasia arguably reside far from both Washington and Beijing. They are the middle-range powers, from Northeast Asia to the Arabian Peninsula, that cannot readily configure political-economic regimes alone but nevertheless are profoundly affected by the consequences. They are the actors with the strongest incentives to hedge China's rise and America's possible decline through collective action by creating more durable multilateral structures. Their impulse for stability is intensified, in an era of deepening interdependence and connectivity, by the transnational character of the production networks and value chains initiated by their subnational enterprises and proliferating across the region. These middle-range powers along the Eurasian sea-lane littoral are almost exclusively "trading states" with powerful stakes in stable mutual interdependence, and little inclination to destabilizing security behavior.[8]

The system builders of Maritime Eurasia include seven dynamic political economies of the Indo-Pacific, and two additional catalysts in the Middle East. They vary in political persuasion and regime type. Yet all feature market-oriented political economies, with stakes in interdependence, that flow in substantial measure from their common proximity to the sea. Their principal features of these system builders are enumerated in Table 7.1.

As is clear from Table 7.1, Eurasia's key maritime-rimland system builders are all nations of substance in some dimension, albeit of diverse specializations. One (Japan) is an economic powerhouse—the third-largest economy in the world, with formidable manufacturing capabilities. Next door, South Korea is also a sizeable manufacturing power with strong defense capabilities, hardened from eight decades of confrontation with its smaller yet heavily militarized ethnic twin to the north. Two of the group, India and Indonesia, have huge populations (second and fourth largest in the world, respectively) and underlying strengths in services (India) and raw materials (Indonesia). Australia, a diverse resource power in its own right, in a region generally deficient of energy and other resources, including food, has unique cultural and geo-political ties outside the region, especially to the United States. Indeed, it has

TABLE 7.1
Potential system builders of maritime Eurasia

Country	Population (million)	GDP (billion USD)	Economic Orientation		
			Manufacturing	Resources	Services
Indo-Pacific					
Japan	124.52	4,212.95	X		X
India	1,428.63	3,549.92			X
South Korea	51.71	1,712.79	X		X
Australia	26.64	1,723.83		X	
Indonesia	277.53	1,371.17		X	
Singapore	5.92	501.43			X
Vietnam	98.86	429.72	X	X	
Arabian/Persian Gulf					
Saudi Arabia	36.95	1,067.58		X	
UAE	9.52	504.72		X	X

SOURCE: World Bank, "Population, total" and "GDP (current US$)," World Development Indicators (2023), accessed June 29, 2024.

NOTE: Although "Persian Gulf" is traditional in Western usage, "Arabian Gulf" is standard in the Arab world.

stood with the United States in every conflict America has waged for well over a century.

Several of these influential middle powers are increasingly bound by trade relations. India, Australia, and Indonesia, in particular, have experienced growing trade interdependence across the Indian Ocean over the past decade, with prospects for substantially deepening ties in future. Large populations and rapid economic growth are driving an expansion of economic interdependence, encouraging greater policy coordination as well.[9]

Apart from a critical mass of stabilizing middle powers, Maritime Eurasia includes three other important catalysts for a resilient regional system, capable of protecting the region's autonomy and encouraging innovation within its ranks. These are Singapore, the UAE, and Saudi Arabia. Singapore and the UAE, to be sure, are smaller—what might be called "virtual states."[10] Yet Singapore in particular enjoys deep, innovative capital markets, an efficient port, and a dense network of human ties throughout Asia, especially within ASEAN, that play an integrative regional role.[11] Saudi Arabia and the UAE, which recently have begun to actively "look east," possess deep energy and financial reserves that could support influential roles within Maritime Eurasia. Their Islamic legitimacy and large discretionary resources may be especially helpful in dealing with majority Muslim states such as Indonesia, Malaysia, and Bangladesh.

System-Building Initiatives

Japan, as the first non-Western industrial nation in world history, surprisingly has not been a forerunner in regional institution-building. Its early efforts, such as the Greater East Asia Co-Prosperity Sphere of World War II, have been almost universally discredited. Their perversity was felt especially keenly in Northeast Asia, and among ethnic Chinese groups across the region, who suffered immensely under Japanese rule. However, Japan's pre–World War II experience as a rising, independent non-Western power arguably did stimulate nationalist aspirations in nations ranging from Indonesia to India that ultimately helped demolish Western colonialist empires. [12]

Japanese foreign policies since World War II basically have been reactive, largely for structural reasons, especially toward the United States.[13] That said, Tokyo has taken a number of diplomatic initiatives toward Asia-Pacific system building consistent with its pro-US orientation, particularly in cooperation with Australia.[14] In 1967, for example, Foreign Minister Miki Takeo unveiled a formal Asia-Pacific Policy, in consultation with Australia; though this approach did not make much progress, Prime Minister Ohira Masayoshi's followed it with the Pacific Rim Cooperation Concept in 1979.[15] The two countries also worked together to establish the APEC Forum in 1989, even before the United States became actively involved. Their connections were especially close during the governments of Koizumi Junichiro (2001–2006) in Tokyo and John Howard (1996–2007) in Canberra. Japan strongly advocated the concept of ASEAN Plus Six to expand the East Asian region, giving scope for Japan and Australia to serve as core members of such groups as the East Asia Summit, and the Regional Comparative Economic Partnership, which continue up to the present day. Australia has also consistently supported Japan in the Comparative and Progressive Agreement for Trans-Pacific Partnership—a trans-Pacific partnership without the United States.[16]

Japan and Australia also have cooperated extensively on a bilateral basis on maritime issues of mutual concern. In 2007, they signed their first agreement on bilateral security cooperation, with a strong maritime dimension. They followed this with a bilateral information-security agreement in 2012 and a defense-technology transfer understanding in 2014.[17] In November 2020, they also reached broad agreement on a defense pact that would allow their forces to train in the other country's territory.[18] Overseas development issues have been another point of Japan-Australia cooperation. They both, for example, provide extensive development assistance to South Pacific states such as Papua New Guinea and the Solomon Islands, in an effort to inhibit Chinese inroads. These areas are of special strategic importance, lying as they do right at the edge of the Second Island Chain and along vital sea lanes linking the United States and Australia.

The further the twenty-first century proceeds, the higher expectations become for a catalytic Indian role in Maritime Eurasia. The country's massive population of 1.4 billion—which became the largest on earth in 2023—and its strategic location astride the Indian Ocean's sea lanes naturally give it a head start. Burgeoning commodities-fueled Indian Ocean trade creates strong economic incentives for proactive involvement.

India's possession of the Andaman and Nicobar Islands (ANI) is highly strategic, complementing Australia's important presence on the Cocos Islands and Christmas Island (as seen in Chapter 1) makes clear. ANI lies at the northern entrance to the Strait of Malacca, through which the bulk of Japanese, Chinese, and Korean energy flows from the Persian Gulf. Australia's island possessions to the south lie adjacent to the Lombok Strait—a deep-water passageway into the Indian Ocean, extremely important for nuclear submarines. Two Quad member states thus have crucially geostrategic positioning at the Indian Ocean entrances that complements the formidable undersea capabilities of the US Navy in the region and the nearby US island strong point at Diego Garcia.

India's rising military capabilities reinforce broader expectations of its future strategic role in balancing China, with the United States amplifying that role as an "offshore balancer."[19] Both India and Pakistan are nuclear powers, but the former has more sophisticated delivery systems, including nuclear subs, which present an increasing deterrent threat to China.[20] India historically has focused on its land borders with Pakistan and China, and spent relatively little on its navy.[21] Yet over the past decade, India's foreign trade has grown and third-country Indian Ocean transit trade has risen. As China has become more active in both surrounding waters and neighboring countries such as Bangladesh, Sri Lanka, and the Maldives, India's hegemonic role in the Indian Ocean, the Bay of Bengal, and littoral states, has eroded, necessitating new tactics.[22] Today, New Delhi operates the world's seventh-largest navy, including two small operational aircraft carriers as well as a large fleet of submarines.[23] Despite the 1,200-kilometer distance of the ANI from the Indian mainland, New Delhi is reinforcing its presence there. It also is building a major new base on the Bay of Bengal, INS Varsha, to house its nuclear-submarine deterrent.[24]

India has multiple strategic reasons for its emerging emphasis on the seas to its east, even apart from China's naval activism.[25] Pressure from China in the Himalayas, as well as broadening Chinese use of multiple access points into the Indian Ocean, increase India's incentives to strengthen its presence in the ANI, with an emphasis on surveillance over critical chokepoints.[26] New Delhi's military expansion on ANI includes plans for the basing of missile batteries, infantry, and aircraft, as well as the construction of additional warship docking facilities. The islands' three naval air stations are being upgraded into full-fledged air force bases, with critical assets such as P–8I aircraft and larger planes being deployed. A large-scale, ten-year, $670 million infrastructure development "roll-on" plan, valued at more than $670 million, also is being fast-tracked. Extended access for friendly foreign navies likewise is being considered.[27] Given the shallow waters and heavy traffic density of Malacca, which forces submarines to surface, it is likely that the Sunda, Lombok, and Ombai Straits will become major alternate routes for military vessels entering the Indian Ocean. Indeed, China is already using the Lombok Straits as a routine entry point for its vessels.[28]

Despite some formidable strengths, including size and population, India also has troubling short-term weaknesses as a potential strategic partner and system builder in the Indo-Pacific, especially as a balancer against China. Its economy is less than one-fifth the size of China's, and the gap is widening. Its domestic infrastructure, particularly its highways and electric-power grid, is substandard, and it is experiencing continuing internal societal tensions. Indian inflation is also soaring at six times China's rate, with superior Chinese productivity and capital formation in contrast to Indian reliance on monetary stimulus.[29] It will thus be many years before India rivals China in economic scale, even if the long-term demographics are in New Delhi's favor.

India also has major infrastructural shortcomings in the maritime realm, which are especially troubling in view of its central location on the Indo-Pacific sea lanes. Owing to the pervasive, embedded heritage of socialism, colonial bureaucracy, and caste-based social structure, together with autarkic trade policies, the country's ports and support infrastructure are in lamentably poor condition.[30] As a result, India remains reliant on transshipment ports like Colombo in Sri Lanka, where Chinese influence is growing.[31] Confirming its bias to autarky in trade, India in 2020 rejected membership in the Regional Comparative Economic Partnership Asian regional trade agreement, alone among the major nations of the region.[32]

Western interlocutors with India have long been frustrated by its strident neutralism and unwillingness to accommodate external security and economic concerns. Influenced by their nation's colonial legacy, Indians are sensitive to foreign troops and to the questions of absolute sovereignty. The country does not accommodate foreign bases, status of forces agreements, or other formal alliance relationships, and foreign investment has faced persistent obstacles. Since the mid-1950s to early 1960s, when the socialist Krishna Menon served as defense minister, India also has maintained defense procurement relations with Russia that continue to complicate parallel ties with the United States and other NATO members.

Indian domestic politics likewise can impede foreign-policy responses that would be optimal from a broader regional perspective. India was slow, for example, in responding to the protracted Sri Lanka civil war (1983–2009), in part because of ambivalence in Tamil Nadu about Indian central government involvement. India's hesitation, despite a 1987 bilateral agreement to help assure stability, gave China an opening in 2009 that it has been aggressively exploiting, and generating political dividends with the Sinhalese within Sri Lanka.[33] Yet despite complex domestic headwinds, India has responded intermittently to regional overtures to balance China. In 2007, Manmohan Singh hosted Japanese Prime Minister Abe Shinzo's historic "Confluence of the Two Seas" address to the Lok Sabha in New Delhi, marking the beginning of Japan's Indo-Pacific initiative.[34] In June 2020, following border clashes with China in the Himalayas, Narendra Modi met virtually with Australian Prime Minister Scott Morrison to conclude a far-reaching agreement on bilateral security cooperation, including joint naval exercises and basing arrangements in the Keeling and Cocos Islands, giving Indian ASW aircraft effective access to the South China Sea.

The Quad: Balancing against China

Japan's Abe Shinzo (2006–2007, 2012–2020), a confirmed political realist and a grandson of the hawkish Prime Minister Kishi Nobusuke (1957–1960), harbored distrust of China's rise throughout his political career. Balancing China through a coalition of like-minded democratic nations came naturally to him. Abe therefore was glad, following his 2007 bilateral summit in New Delhi with Manmohan Singh, to participate in a Quad side-session at the ASEAN Regional Forum in Manila a few months later with Australia's John Howard, India's Manmohan Singh, and US Vice President Dick Cheney.[35] Responding to the Shanghai Cooperation Organization's first joint military exercise, the four, together with Singapore, collaborated in the ninth Malabar Naval Exercises in the Bay of Bengal during September 2007.[36]

The evolution of the Quad has been profoundly shaped by domestic political forces in each of the four partner nations. Abe abruptly resigned as Japanese prime minister for health reasons in late 2007; the Quad thereafter lapsed, especially once George W. Bush had also left office, in January 2009. The concept thereafter floundered until Abe returned to power in December 2012. His "Asia's Democratic Security Diamond," presented in a December 2012 Project Syndicate piece, clearly expressed Abe's strategic views.[37]

At first there was little resonance elsewhere in the Quad. Australia, under Labour Party China specialist Kevin Rudd (2007–2010) and his successor Julia Gillard (2010–2013) was unresponsive. Tony Abbott (2013–2015) of the Liberal/National Coalition that followed Labour signed a free trade agreement with China.[38] Meanwhile, the Obama administration and Manmohan Singh's Congress Party in India were deepening their own bilateral ties.[39] Yet they also, for diverse reasons, pursued detente with China.

China's BRI, enunciated by Xi Jinping in the fall of 2013, laid out a collective challenge to the disunited erstwhile Quad members. Some considered bandwagoning. All major Indo-Pacific nations except Japan, for example, joined the China-initiated Asian Infrastructure Investment Bank (AIIB) after its inception in 2014. Even India joined the so-called BRICs Bank (later renamed the New Development Bank), headquartered in Shanghai, which was founded in July 2014, and also joined the AIIB in 2016.

Japan's Abe was the first to respond competitively to China, and to craft a comprehensive strategic vision for responding to Beijing's new overtures. In 2016, he unveiled his Free and Open Indo-Pacific concept at the opening session of the Tokyo International Conference on African Development VI Japan-Africa conference in Nairobi, Kenya.[40] Yet broadbased Quad cooperation did not immediately emerge.

The Trump administration, not generally known for its interest in broader alliance building, improbably served as catalyst for deepening the Quad. In October 2017, US Secretary of State Rex Tillerson visited New Delhi to discuss the concept. A month later, President Donald Trump visited Japan and expressed strong support for the Free and Open Indo-Pacific notion.

Meanwhile, in Australia, Prime Minister Malcolm Turnbull had started his term (2015–2018) with relatively amicable ties to China.[41] Technology, security, and espionage concerns, however, together with the shift in Washington's orientation due to the transition from Obama to Trump, propelled Canberra toward a more confrontational stance with Beijing.[42] A deepening sense of domestic vulnerability to Chinese inroads was also a factor. By 2017, Australia had more than 1 million ethnic Chinese residents, making up 5.6 percent of the population, or roughly the share of the entire Asian-American community in the United States.[43] China was Australia's largest trading partner, absorbing nearly 36 percent of Australian exports, and Chinese students contributed over $10 billion annually in tuition and fees to the Australian university system.[44]

Driven by domestic politics and, from the spring of 2020, the COVID 19 pandemic, Turnbull's successor Scott Morrison (2018–2022) was even more confrontational against China than was Turnbull, and more committed to the Quad. He confirmed and strengthened Turnbull's restrictions on the use of Huawei and ZTE communications equipment over national security considerations, and called for an investigation into the purported Chinese origins of the coronavirus—which, as will be discussed later, triggered retaliatory Chinese sanctions. In July 2020, Morrison further angered Beijing by approving preferential visa arrangements on human-rights grounds for Hong Kong passport holders to remain in Australia, with pathways to permanent residence.[45] In regional affairs, Morrison offered expanded basing rights to Indian forces in the Keeling and Cocos Islands, within range of the South China Sea, with India in return offering Australia permanent membership, alongside the United States, Japan, and India, in the annual Malabar Naval Exercises.[46]

The United States conclusively affirmed the Quad concept through the US Strategic Framework for the Indo-Pacific, issued in summary form during February 2018 and further declassified in January 2021.[47] This document emphasized the need to deny China air and sea dominance inside the First Island Chain in a conflict; to defend First Island Chain territories; and to dominate territory beyond the First Island Chain. Reflecting this new priority in strategic relations between the Pacific and Indian Oceans, the US Pacific Command was renamed INDOPACOM in May 2018, with operating responsibilities stretching westward from the US West Coast across the Pacific and Indian Oceans to the west coast of India. US INDOPACOM became responsible for military operations in an area of more than 100 million square miles, or roughly 52 percent of the earth's surface.[48] Figure 7.1 indicates its enormous scale.

Efforts to operationalize the Quad concept accelerated in 2020 as the Chinese challenge grew more intense following the onset of the COVID-19 crisis. China came out of the initial stage of the crisis more rapidly than any other major country and grew more assertive throughout the Indo-Pacific, including unprecedented economic sanctions against Australia.[49] China also took broadly coercive steps in areas ranging from the South China Sea and

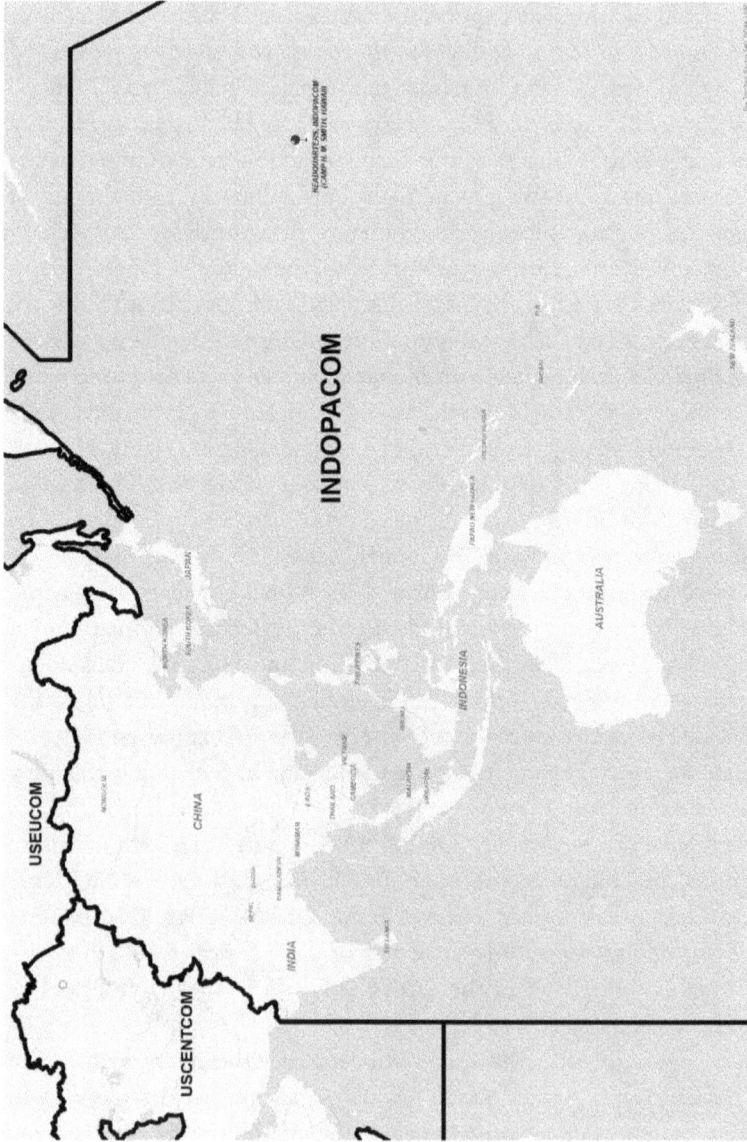

FIGURE 7.1 The geographic sweep of America's Indo–Pacific Command

SOURCE: US INDOPACOM, "USPACOM Area of Responsibility," September 2023, https://www.pacom.mil/About-USINDOPACOM/USPACOM-Area-of-Responsibility/.

Hong Kong to the Himalayas.[50] The Quad responded with regular virtual high-level meetings, as well as actual in-person meetings in Tokyo and New Delhi. This intensified cooperation continued seamlessly into the Biden administration.

Achievements and Challenges of the Quad

Since its revival in 2017, Quad 2.0 has already achieved substantially more than did Quad 1.0, during the brief interlude before Chinese opposition and the departure of key leaders (particularly Abe) led to its predecessor's demise. The Malabar Naval Exercises series, previously an Indo-American bilateral, has been broadened into a permanent event involving each of the Quad partners.[51] The Blue Dot Network coalition among the US, Japanese, and Australian national development banks has been established, with India, an aid recipient, as a priority long-term partner.[52] Japan, Australia, and India have launched a mini-lateral supply chain initiative to move away from China through such measures as digitalization of trade procedures and support for reshoring related capital expenditures—with formal support from the foreign ministers of all four nations.[53]

The Quad has no secretariat or institutional mechanism for coordinating defense planning. Enthusiasm for such steps remains limited among policy elites in all four countries, most conspicuously India.[54] Yet some additional progress toward a tighter quadrilateral relationship, including stronger defense ties, has been made, exploiting inherent geographic synergies within the Indo-Pacific. For instance, Australia has agreed to joint use of its strategically located Indian Ocean island base on the Cocos (Keeling) Islands, within range of both the Strait of Malacca and the South China Sea. It is also cooperating with Japan and the United States on base-related economic development projects in the South Pacific, close to Australia's northern shores.[55]

India has also agreed to enhanced mini-lateral naval cooperation. In addition to the annual Malabar exercises, regularly involving Australia, India, Japan, and the United States, in April 2021 India also hosted La Perouse, a Quad-plus exercise initiated by France. Warships from the United States, Japan, Australia, India and France sailed together during a three-day naval exercise in the Bay of Bengal. Germany and the United Kingdom also sent warships to the region during 2021.[56]

Support within the Quad appears strongest for regular summit meetings, and for cooperation in strategic foreign assistance, as manifest in recent South Pacific initiatives just within the Second Island Chain.[57] Other options recently pursued include vaccine partnerships, academic cooperation ("Quad Scholars"), and planning for cooperative action on natural-disaster relief, as well as action against piracy, illegal fishing, and global warming related threats to coastal zones.[58] Many observers envision the creation of a "Quad Plus" with a hybrid hard-security and "human-security" character, also involving other major Indo-Pacific players such as Korea and Singapore, or even actors as far afield as Europe.[59] Others see hard-security arrangements like AUKUS, involving longstanding allies outside the Indo-Pacific but with tacit Quad-partner cooperation, as more fundamental. Quad 2.0, in some incarnation, seems destined to be an enduring and substantive feature of the Indo-Pacific strategic landscape, in contrast to its predecessor a little more than a decade ago.

Challenges, of course, remain, rendering other formulations optimal for many policy purposes.[60] India, as noted, is hesitant to abandon its traditional detached, autarkic approach to regional affairs, based on a firm commitment to strategic autonomy and "multi-alignment."[61] Some other potential system builders, such as Indonesia, appear more tempted to bandwagon with China for economic reasons, rather than to balance it through "Quad Plus" arrangements. Similarly, some potential participants in loose balancing arrangements, such as France, have been alienated by stronger political-military steps, such as AUKUS, taken by the more determined antagonists of China.[62]

The "In-Between World": Virtual and Pariah States as Pivot Players

The Asiatic Great Game of the nineteenth century was dominated by powerful nations—even empires, which Britain and tsarist Russia effectively were. Yet the geo-economic chessboard of Maritime Eurasia a century and more later is much more complex. On a separate yet substantive level—intermediate between the abovementioned middle-power system builders and the local governments that also play meaningful roles—the virtual states and pariah regimes maneuver feverishly among the larger nations for advantage, and at times for survival.

Singapore, like the UAE in the Middle East, is one such virtual state. Located on an island just four times the size of Washington, D.C., with a population of only 6 million citizens, Singapore is hardly a nation in the conventional sense. Yet it is a political-economic powerhouse, with the most active options, derivatives, and commodities markets in Asia; a larger defense budget than Vietnam; and an ability to convene the most consequential diplomatic forums of the entire continent, from the annual Shangri La Dialogue on regional security to high-profile international summits.[63] Singapore is unquestionably the most influential diplomatic player in Southeast Asia, and arguably the most subtle global agenda-setter in all of Asia.

Taiwan, by contrast, has an ambiguous standing on the global political stage and a declining cast of formal diplomatic interlocutors.[64] Nevertheless, "Island China" arguably is of increasing importance on Maritime Eurasia's geo-economic chess-board, particularly since the COVID-19 pandemic broke out in early 2020.[65] It occupies a highly strategic location at the heart of the First Island Chain, giving it a notable degree of geopolitical clout. It also has a formidably com-petitive semiconductor industry. and did a remarkably good job in handling the virus. In 2020, its real economic growth exceeded that of mainland China for the first time in two decades, at 3.1 percent to 2.3 percent, respectively.[66] And, thanks to its booming semiconductor industry, Taiwan sustained growth nearly comparable to that of mainland China in the years that followed.[67]

Although the United States recognized the People's Republic of China at the beginning of 1979, it has retained strong nondiplomatic ties to Taiwan through the Taiwan Relations Act of 1979 and the Six Assurances of 1982, which affirmed that the United States would not limit arms sales to Taiwan. The US Congress later passed the Taiwan Travel Act of 2018, allowing high-level governmental visits. In 2020, it likewise enacted the Taiwan Allies International Protection and Enhancement Initiative (TAIPEI) Act, providing American support for Taiwanese efforts to retain international diplomatic standing.

Based on this new legislation, as well as concern about Beijing's rising geo-political clout, the United States has collaborated informally with Japan, Australia, and other allies in such small Pacific nations as the Marshall Islands, Tuvalu, and Palau to shore up Taiwan's diplomatic standing. The US Navy has conducted regular freedom-of-navigation operations in the Taiwan Strait and the South China Sea, under both the Trump and Biden administrations.[68] And the United States has continued to sell high-performance weaponry to Taiwan, including Patriot missile-defense upgrades, to enhance its deterrence capabilities in the face of perceived security threats from the mainland.[69]

Taiwan's importance in the Indo-Pacific has been further enhanced by nearby geopolitical developments, especially mainland China's increased political-economic confidence and assertiveness. China's introduction of a new National Security Law in June 2020, for example, led to a doubling in the number of Hong Kong residents seeking Taiwanese residence permits during the year.[70] China's pressure on India and Australia also has led to deepening Taiwanese political-economic relationships with those two Quad members, as the Quad itself grows more active in Indo-Pacific affairs.[71]

Europe's New Indo–Pacific Fascination

For more than four centuries, throughout an Age of Empire extending until World War II, Europe dominated most of Maritime Eurasia. Yet for half a century from the 1950s, remarkably little of that presence remained. The last major European military presence, that of Britain's Royal Navy, eroded east of Suez during the 1970s, amidst a more general decline of European naval power around the globe.[72]

The Europeans, to be sure, have retained a significant economic presence in ASEAN, much of it the residue of colonial days. In 2020, total European Union foreign direct investment stock in the ten nations of ASEAN reached over €350 billion—the second-largest investor in the region.[73] Between 8 and 12 percent of all the trade conducted by Britain, France, and Germany passes through the South China Sea.[74] It was French President Emmanuel Macron who revived European diplomatic involvement in the Indo-Pacific, to supplement this residual economic presence. He made "Indo-Pacific" a concept of French foreign policy for the first time during his May 2018 visit to Australia. France, he stressed, is a "resident power" in the Indo-Pacific, with overseas French territories spread broadly across the region, from Réunion to New Caledonia, French Polynesia, and beyond. The exclusive economic zones surrounding these small territories collectively make France's EEZs the second most extensive in the world.[75] More than 1.8 million French citizens live in those Maritime Eurasian dependencies. Building on this underlying French presence, Macron called in Australia for a Canberra-Delhi-Paris axis of cooperation to supplement and balance the Washington-centric Quad.

France followed up Macron's initiative by sending Defense Minister Florence Parly to deliver a high-profile address at the 2019 Shangri La Dialogue, as the French aircraft carrier *Charles de Gaulle* lay berthed nearby at Changi Naval Base.[76] Paris also concluded a reciprocal basing agreement with India, opening the use of French Indian Ocean facilities at Réunion to the Indian Navy. In December 2020, France was admitted to the Indian Ocean Rim Association as a resident member—the first country to attain that standing whose metropole itself did not front on the Indian Ocean. The September 2021 "AUKUS Shock" may have marginally constrained the French Eurasian maritime role, but Paris has rebounded by completing a new Indo-Pacific base-sharing agreement with Canberra in 2023.[77]

Several other European nations, following France, have shown deepening interest in the Indo-Pacific through policy steps and political-military gestures, reaffirming the currency of the "Maritime Eurasia" concept. Britain, already a Five Power participant, sent its aircraft carrier *Queen Elizabeth II* across the Indo-Pacific to Japan, even as it confirmed its long-term Indo-Pacific role through participation in AUKUS.[78] Germany also sent a frigate to Japan in the summer of 2021, while the European Union as a whole announced an Indo-Pacific strategy, prepared by France, Germany, and the Netherlands jointly, in September 2021.[79]

That being said, European approaches to the Indo-Pacific, apart from those of Britain, contrast significantly to those of the United States. Europe's proposals have less of a political-military focus, despite recent symbolic deployments, and pointedly avoid an anti-China cast. They stress "free and open" in their characterization of the desirable state of Indo-Pacific affairs. Some, such as those made by France's Macron, position their countries as "balancing powers," avoiding confrontation with either the United States or China. The Europeans also raise issues such as preventive diplomacy, women's rights, and environmental protection, including threats posed by global warming to island nations, that are less frequently raised by the United States.[80] European involvement with Maritime Eurasia thus appears to broaden the agenda of policy issues debated on the regional chessboard, as well as the heuristic value of alternative approaches to regional membership.

The Gulf Looks East

The Persian Gulf has been linked significantly in energy terms to the Indo-Pacific ever since the Korean War, as noted in Chapter 2. Since the 1960s, East Asia has become the principal customer for Gulf oil; today close to three-quarters of its overall exports, including gas and oil, flow eastward across the sea lanes to Asia. China, in turn, is the Gulf's principal source of light manufacturers and Japan of automobiles, with Korea supplying construction services and the Indian subcontinent as well as the Philippines providing a substantial fraction of the Gulf's labor force. Yet despite this deep economic interdependence stretching back decades, only recently have the Gulf nations begun to "look east" diplomatically to a degree even remotely approaching Asia's economic importance to them as both customer and supplier. Given the severity of China's challenge to traditional American preeminence along the sea lanes, and the substantial Muslim populations inhabiting such Asian maritime nations as Indonesia, Malaysia, Bangladesh, and Pakistan, Gulf involvement with the Indo-Pacific promises to have ever broader geopolitical consequences.

Three Gulf nations have become particularly consequential on the Indo-Pacific geo-economic chessboard: Saudi Arabia, the UAE, and recently Qatar.

Saudi Arabia looms large across Asia as the world's largest oil exporter, and the home of the Islamic religion. It also dominates the Red Sea, which is vital to maritime trade northwest from Maritime Asia toward Europe. The UAE is a large oil and gas exporter with well-developed transport and financial hubs and a robust, cosmopolitan foreign policy.[81] Qatar is the largest LNG exporter, and an active interlocutor with dissident groups across the region, including Afghanistan's Taliban.

Saudi Arabia, the largest of the Arab Gulf states, was also the first to reach out systematically to Maritime Asia. King Saud made the first formal step, undertaking a state visit to India in 1955, but the substantive watershed was King Abdullah's twin 2006 state visits to China and then to New Delhi, the latter as a principal state guest for Republic Day in January 2006.[82] Thereafter, Saudi relations progressed significantly with both Asian giants, especially since Prince Mohammed Bin Salman began to assume significant leadership roles in 2014. Both countries are massive and increasingly important customers for Saudi oil, sites for Saudi downstream investment, and significant participants in Saudi Arabia's Vision 2030 and Future Investment Initiative programs.[83] There are, however, significant contrasts in the evolution of the two bilateral trajectories, which in turn affect the prognosis and the strategic challenges confronting US-China relations in the Eurasian sea lanes.

Saudi Arabia was among the last major nations in the world to recognize the People's Republic of China, doing so only in 1990. Taiwan, heavily dependent on Saudi oil, tried hard to keep Saudi Arabia as a partner, appointing a colorful and well-connected Hui Muslim Kuomintang general, Ma Bufang, as its first ambassador.[84] Its operatives performed a variety of useful services for the Saudis, including piloting Yemeni F–5s and manning air-defense batteries on Saudi Arabia's behalf during its proxy war against Cuban and Soviet personnel in Yemen during the late 1980s.[85] Ultimately, however, the geo-economic logic of Saudi ties with Beijing grew inexorable, and Riyadh sent its trusted ambassador to Washington, Prince Bandar, to Beijing to negotiate the establishment of diplomatic relations. In 1999, President Jiang Zemin became the first Chinese head of state to visit Saudi Arabia, where he signed an important strategic oil cooperation agreement.

Going forward, Saudi relations with China are likely to enjoy a surprising tailwind, the long history of strong ties with Taiwan notwithstanding. Nuclear energy is one unexpected driver: Saudi Arabia is determined to hedge with China, both on the future of hydrocarbons and on Iran's nuclear weapons program, with not only China but also South Korea supplying reactors on the civilian side. Information and communications technology is another area where the Saudis are hedging; Huawei received a Saudi investment license in 2016, and has been cooperating with Saudi Arabia actively in 5G communications and broader telecommunications network development since then. Crown Prince Mohammed bin Salman has made numerous trips to China since assuming significant policy responsibilities in 2014, and his personal support for deepened China ties has created further momentum for relations with Beijing.

Saudi relations with India, while strong, are more complex. Most importantly, the Modi government in India is seen to be systematically discriminating against India's substantial Muslim minority of more than 200 million—the world's third-largest Muslim population—through policies and legislation such as the December 2019 Citizenship Amendment Act.[86] Coupled with the government's push for a nationwide citizenship verification process, the new law also aims at identifying "illegal migrants."[87] There is also the intractable issue of Kashmir, an irritant to Saudi-Indian relations across the decades. In recent years, Saudi foreign policy has had a pronounced realist streak, but domestic pressures and the predilections of the crown prince create a deepening preference for China over India. The December 2022 visit of Xi Jinping to Saudi Arabia epitomized this shift in the Sino-Saudi relationship.[88]

India appears to have a strong interest in the Gulf, but prefers to deal with the more secular UAE and Oman. One consideration is that nearly one-third of the 13.6 million Indians residing abroad live in the UAE—which is over 38 percent Indian—with a substantial contingent in Oman as well and 9 million in the Gulf as a whole.[89] During Prime Minister Narendra Modi's first nine years in office (2014–2023), he undertook thirteen visits to the Gulf, including seven to the UAE and Oman.[90] For both countries, the relationship with India has major strategic and economic dimensions. The UAE Air Force, for example, has been mid-air refueling Indian Rafale jets en route from France to India.[91] The Indian Navy also has begun using Oman's strategically located Duqm port, outside the Strait of Hormuz, for berthing and refueling.[92]

The Catalytic Chessboard Role of NGOs

On the increasingly complex geo-economic chessboard of twenty-first-century Maritime Eurasia, the range of policy challenges is increasing for all parties involved. Issues have arisen that policymakers in the days of the classical Great Game could not remotely have considered, ranging from ecotourism and business travel to oil-spill management. Even on more timeless geopolitical questions, the very complexity of the emerging chessboard makes human networks to navigate its multiple levels more important than ever before. For a variety of reasons, it therefore is vital to consider the systemic role in Maritime Eurasia of the NGOs, semigovernmental organizations, and IGOs that stabilize the region and moderate deepening US-China tensions. Three such bodies, active in the Indo-Pacific, yield useful insights into the stabilizing role that such bodies can play:

(1) *The Indian Ocean Rim Association.* This association of twenty-three nation states and nine dialogue partners, founded in 1997, includes government, business, and academic members from each participant nation. With Singapore, the UAE, Australia, and India serving as especially active participants, but also including France (via its overseas territory of Réunion), the Indian Ocean Rim Association deliberates and proposes policy solutions to challenges relating to ecotourism, bioresources, disaster management, business travel, and trade liberalization.[93] The organization's headquarters is in Mauritius.

(2) *The Organization of Islamic Cooperation.* Founded in 1972, the Organization of Islamic Cooperation deliberates on human rights, cultural, and political questions of collective importance to the worldwide Muslim community. The body has fifty-seven members from countries with a total of 1.8 billion people, many of whom inhabit Maritime Eurasia. Indonesia, Bangladesh, Pakistan, India, the UAE, and Saudi Arabia are among the active members. The war in Yemen, and the plight of Muslims in Kashmir, are some of the major issues the body has considered, though its members often come to ambiguous conclusions. The organization does, however, perform important networking and legitimation functions, especially because it hosts a top-level Leaders' Summit every three years.[94]

(3) *The Pacific Environmental Security Forum.* This multilateral body, founded in 2010, is affiliated with INDOPACOM in Honolulu. Although not formally a branch of the US government, it considers at a realistic technical level emerging challenges to the Indo-Pacific natural environment requiring international cooperation and potential military support.[95] Issues recently considered by the forum include oil spills and water security in the Maldives, and in South Asia more generally; ocean waste management; and coastal-zone environmental management. Although

the forum's concerns are specific to the Pacific Ocean, its membership includes countries such as France that have Pacific territories but whose metropoles may lie outside the region.[96]

In Conclusion

The United States and China may well be the protagonists in a deepening struggle for preeminence along the Eurasian sea lanes, as suggested in previous chapters. They are, however, by no means the only significant actors in the region's emerging geo-economic equation. A variety of additional national, subnational, and transnational actors, animated by Indo-Pacific trade flows, are also shaping the future of the sea lanes, with potentially critical consequences for their ultimate geopolitical profile and the stability of Maritime Eurasia itself.

The most influential "third parties" are the middle-range system builders, beginning with Japan, that combine the economic scale and technical capacity to meaningfully contribute to the stability of a "free and open" regional order. Other actors with this capacity include India, Australia, ASEAN, South Korea, and certain key Persian Gulf states, such as Saudi Arabia and the UAE. Since 2017, Japan, India, and Australia have joined in an increasingly dynamic mini-lateral configuration whose cohesion appears stronger today than when "Quad 1.0" emerged in 2007 and soon sunk into irrelevance. Korea is also developing an increasingly dynamic "Southward Diplomacy" with an important maritime dimension.

Some of the pivotal middle powers with the capacity to help stabilize the existing open Maritime Eurasian geo-economic order may well bandwagon with China rather than support the Quad, or a "Quad Plus" variant. Four large Islamic nations, Indonesia, Pakistan, Bangladesh, and Saudi Arabia, may well fall into this category. India also has cross-cutting interests, and appears unwilling to see informal Quad-type arrangements evolve into formal alliances.

However, major nations outside the Indo-Pacific yet within Eurasia, notably in the states of Western Europe, have begun to play a balancing role along the Eurasian sea lanes, against the prospect of unilateral hegemony. Their naval power has atrophied from a peak in previous centuries, but France, Britain, Germany, and the Netherlands in particular have significant investments in Southeast Asia, many dating from their colonial days. The operations of Shell Oil, Nestlé, Philips, and Société Générale are cases in point. The Europeans also have begun to reassert an Indo-Pacific geo-economic role at the national level, dramatized most recently by naval ship visits and British participation in the important AUKUS maritime-defense initiative, also including the United States and Australia. A more substantial European Community role at the supranational level may well emerge, although it is not unambiguously pro-American.

Nation states are by no means the only significant players on the Maritime Eurasian chessboard. Regional organizations and financial institutions also are liable to play important roles in stabilization, especially on technical questions where cooperative action is needed such as ocean-waste and fisheries management. The combined efforts of NGOs and middle-range powers throughout East, South, and Southeast Asia; the Gulf; and Europe as well will be crucial to the stability of the region in coming years, despite lingering uncertainties about the ultimate configuration of the region as a whole.

8

Shadows and Critical Uncertainties

DESPITE PERSISTENT FEARS TO THE CONTRARY, dating back to the Korean War and even before, the Washington-centric political-economic order of Maritime Eurasia has proven remarkably durable. Formidable challengers such as the Soviet Union have collapsed, and maritime connectivity has steadily grown, to match and substantially exceed that over land. Energy interdependence, engineering progress, and the Information Revolution have all given the Eurasian sea lanes important new functional roles in the global political economy undreamed of a generation, or even a decade, ago.

The Eurasian sea lanes are assuming greater importance in the global political economy. There are clear reasons to hope that their role will continue to support economic growth and intellectual progress. Yet troubling shadows remain over both the future political-economic profile of those sea lanes and their global functional role. To understand these issues, this chapter employs two dichotomous concepts frequently used in scenario planning: (1) the predictable elements of the future and (2) critical uncertainties.[1] The former includes durable patterns that likely will persist well into the future, while the latter denotes contingencies with potential to significantly alter future trajectories, such as a major leadership transition, whose consequences are inherently more difficult to predict.[2] This chapter focuses on three prevailing critical uncertainties complicating the future of the Eurasian sea lanes: (1) the profile of China in global affairs, (2) the evolution of the Eurasian continent, and (3) the global political economy as a whole.

Shadows on China's Transformation

China has four times the population of the United States; and is the second-largest economy on earth in nominal GDP terms.[3] Over the past three decades, it has experienced unprecedented economic growth, as well as sustained increases in defense spending. Its per-capita levels of GDP, food, and natural-resource consumption are still considerably below those of advanced industrial nations. China will doubtless loom still larger in future years on the global stage than it does today, given its huge population and rising individual affluence.

Yet much about the profile that China will ultimately project—both domestically and internationally—remains unsettlingly unclear. Most developing nations over the past two decades have grown increasingly pluralistic politically as per-capita incomes pass $2,000/year.[4] That shift has not transpired in China, where concern for political stability and economic performance run deep. At the same time, China's political-economic order, while remaining emphatically Leninist, has allowed more room for market forces than did the former Soviet Russia or other Warsaw Pact countries of the 1980s.[5] Still, since around 2015, the role of state-owned enterprises in the Chinese political economy has begun to expand once again.[6] And since late 2020, the Chinese state has begun to apply pressure to private high-tech enterprises as well.[7]

Chinese society harbors troubling uncertainties, including employment, income inequality, and a developing real-estate bubble. The last of these has become a significant recent danger, as evidenced in recent years by the bankruptcy of some major property developers.[8] China Evergrande, for example, was dismantled in early 2024, sending the country's housing market into a tailspin. Seeking to slow an unsustainable real-estate boom, the Chinese government slapped restrictions on borrowers, leading to a wave of defaults by real-estate firms, the largest of these being Evergrande with more than $300 billion in debt. Likewise, income inequality, especially between coastal regions and the landlocked interior, has widened in recent years. Real estate has been both a source of inequality and one of the few potential means for less-affluent citizens to redress it. Tightening state controls in finance and politics have intensified dissatisfaction while leaving little room for healthy dissent and precious little space for a vibrant civil society.

Meanwhile, rapid demographic change is unfolding. Between 2020 and 2035, for example, China's aging workforce will shrink by almost 7 percent.[9] Such change implies that China may well grow old before it grows rich. Persistent ethnocentrism also discourages the entry of the imported talent, including service workers, that a graying China will need.[10] Immigration from South Asia, with its young, growing population, into China as it ages may well be politically difficult. As these social challenges deepen, environmental pollution—although less of an immediately dire concern than in previous years—has risen to socially disruptive and economically dysfunctional levels that threaten future basic industrial growth.

Another potential uncertainty is leadership succession. For the past two decades, power succession in contemporary China has demonstrated a high degree of stability. Under the leadership of Xi Jinping, however, foundational succession procedures have grown more ambiguous. This political hardening of the arteries could, in the long run, provoke serious divisions among Chinese elites and ultimately threaten political stability.[11]

Chinese foreign policy, buffeted by multiple domestic and international pressures, has oscillated in ways that render its likely future approach to the Eurasian sea lanes unclear. Beijing has declared a willingness to conclude codes of conduct regarding maritime issues with ASEAN neighbors, and yet it also is actively building and fortifying artificial islands in the South China Sea, encouraging jingoistic Wolf Warrior diplomacy, and setting constraints on political activity in Hong Kong that directly contradict explicit previous international commitments.[12] Although China has taken on increased international responsibilities at IGOs and in international peacekeeping, some pessimistically argue that a "Peak China" consciousness of impending relative decline could inspire aggressive near-term Chinese political-military behavior.[13] Given China's scale and rising political-military capabilities, the Middle Kingdom casts an ambiguous shadow over the future of the Eurasian sea lanes, with a profile and future prospects that need to be better understood.

Shadows on the Future of Maritime Eurasia

In *Super Continent,* I considered prospects for the evolution of overland political-economic ties across continental Eurasia. I concluded that the continent as a whole, while far from achieving political, economic, or military cohesion, was nevertheless moving toward an unprecedented level of interdependence in at least two respects. China and Russia, I argued, were moving closer. China was also deepening political-economic linkages with Eastern and Central Europe.[14]

These findings raise the unsettling question of whether developments in the maritime rimlands of Eurasia, as in offshore Southeast Asia, can counterbalance the rising continentalist influence of China itself. The most populous nations of Maritime Eurasia, including India and Indonesia, are neither as large nor as rapidly growing as China, but collectively they have clear potential to shape the continent's future, particularly by countervailing continentalist trends. India in particular already exceeds China in population and is competitive economically in some important sectors, such as software and pharmaceuticals. New Delhi is also steadily expanding its military, including the navy. Nevertheless, India and several other large developing countries of Maritime Eurasia, including Indonesia, Pakistan, and Myanmar, also suffer serious infrastructural deficiencies—ports, airports, and railways among them. In contrast to China, none of them has a heavy industrial base, foundational technologies, or robust overall research and development expenditure levels. In the military sphere, they continue to import their core hardware, mainly from Russia, and lack cutting-edge weapons and effective doctrines for pursuing policy objectives. Bottlenecks to trade could easily stifle their growth. Many of these nations are also corrupt, and suffer from unstable (if often democratic) politics.

The maritime region's overarching capacity to counterbalance dynamic authoritarianism on the continent, including both a rising China and a potential Sino-Russian entente, are uncertain, particularly given the scale and momentum of China's recent naval buildup.[15] Domestic institutional weaknesses in Maritime Eurasia, broadly co-terminus with the Indo-Pacific, thus cast shadows across the future of Eurasia as a whole.

Shadows on Global Political Economic Transformation

Fueled by the Information Revolution, the techno-economic parameters of daily lives in the major urban centers of the industrialized world are evolving at warp speed.[16] Yet major segments of the world's population are being excluded, exacerbating the global digital divide. For a variety of reasons, many of them transcending information access, global political-economic inequities are also deepening.

These disturbing trends are, contrary to general public understanding, deeply related to the evolution of the sea lanes themselves. The overwhelming share of worldwide information flows move, after all, beneath the oceans, through submarine cables, just as the bulk of world commodity trade, including indispensable hydrocarbons and other raw materials, moves predominantly on the waters above. So the ability of major nations to concur on conventions for stable maritime transit, and on rules for submarine information flow, will be crucial in shaping the global future, just as the profile of great-power conflict will be. We desperately need more trenchant analysis of the global political-economic regimes regulating the world of the Eurasian sea lanes, in both their predictable dimensions and the critical uncertainties surrounding them.

Predictable Elements of the Future

Anticipating the future is always an exercise in probability, yet one can foresee some elements with relative confidence. In this assessment of the uncertainties within Maritime Eurasia and its surrounding sea lanes, it would be appropriate to start with the most predictable elements.

Demography

Regardless of political-economic developments, the likely population structure of nations and their subunits can be derived from detailed actuarial data. Across Maritime Eurasia, Japan and Korea are aging rapidly. China likely will follow them in little more than a decade, as a consequence of its longstanding one-child policy from 1979 to 2015 and the delayed effect on its national birth rate. Just as demography is generating headwinds for the three large Northeast Asian nations over the coming decades, it will provide a economic tailwind for South Asia as well as several Southeast Asian, Middle Eastern, and African sea-lane rimland nations, as the labor forces and populations of those countries continue to expand. Over the coming century, Eurasia and Africa could face dramatic demographic transitions. India, Pakistan, Bangladesh, Ethiopia, and Egypt, among nations along the Eurasian sea lanes, likely will rise in relative global population scale. Meanwhile, the populations of China and Japan could well both fall by half, according to United Nations projections.[17]

Although anticipating demographic trends is quite straightforward, assessing the political, economic, and strategic implications of such transformations is more complex and subjective. Large youth cohorts in maritime developing nations, from Indonesia and Bangladesh to Sri Lanka, Yemen, and Egypt, coupled with rising unemployment and income inequality, suggest the likelihood of increased domestic political instability and possibly more nationalistic and aggressive tendencies at sea.[18] In China, the long-term prospect of aging, across the 2030s and beyond, may stimulate short-term activism in Beijing's sea-lane policies, including its approach to Taiwan and the South China Sea. Foreseeing deepening long-term resource shortages and social adjustment difficulties, Chinese leaders could be tempted to prioritize cherished political goals, such as national reunification, before demographically dictated constraints render those goals infeasible.[19] Demography thus could compound the importance and the urgency of critical political-military uncertainties regarding Taiwan, which will be discussed later in this chapter.

Growing Connectivity

Since the early twentieth century, global connectivity has risen steadily across a multitude of socioeconomic dimensions, driven by the falling costs of that connectivity. Marine transport charges in 1960, for example, were only a third of their 1920 levels.[20] A three-minute phone call that cost $293 in 1931 could be made for less than a nickel today. Since the 1950s, air fares have been declining rapidly as well. Cross-border data flow has been an area of particularly rapid, sustained, and consequential increases in connectivity. Between 2005 and 2014, for example, cross-border data flows increased by 4,500 percent.[21] By 2022, traffic is expected to reach 150,000 gigabytes (GB) of traffic *per second*, a thousand-fold increase compared to the 156 GB two decades earlier, in 2002.[22] Digital trade today is a $1 trillion business.[23] As such flows have expanded, mobile communications have spawned a new era of social media across a variety of platforms.[24] This development has allowed mass publics to reflect on global issues in real time, accelerating the rise of global debates on matters ranging from the environment and human rights to geopolitical crises.

Like demographic change, rising connectivity is a predictable result of advances in communications technology and the resultant reduction in transaction costs. Political frictions can constrain the socioeconomic effects to some degree, but technological pressures nevertheless are inexorable. Connectivity has major, predictable implications for sea-lane rimland states, rendering their domestic politics at once both more volatile and more interdependent.

The unbounded character of the sea lanes themselves also facilitate connectivity. More than 95 percent of internet communications, increasingly vital to the smooth functioning of the global economy, flow through fiber-optic cables beneath the seas. According to the US Federal Communications Commission, such submarine cables carry well over $10 trillion in transactions daily—greater than the GDP of Japan, Germany, and Australia combined.[25]

Ethnic and Religious Conflict

Rising connectivity may help bring increased intercultural understanding. It also, however, may be a recipe for ethnic conflict in a diverse world marked by deepening economic inequality. Not surprisingly, as cross-border information flows have risen, transnational and transcultural tensions have also increased. Within Islam, for example, Sunni-Shia socioeconomic and political tensions have risen within and among the nations of Maritime Eurasia in recent decades, from Malaysia and Pakistan to Saudi Arabia, Iran, Yemen, and Lebanon.[26] Endemic tensions between Muslims and Christians, dating back nearly a thousand years to the time of the Crusades, have been exacerbated by the social connectivity provided for the works of culturally controversial authors like Salman Rushdie or publications like the French satirical weekly *Charlie Hebdo* by advances in social media. Jewish-Islamic frictions also challenge geopolitical and security calculations in the Middle East, with profound implications beyond the region. And the Rohingya crisis casts a diplomatic and humanitarian shadow over the Bay of Bengal.

Weapons of Mass Destruction

As if the tensions generated by social connectivity, leveraged by advanced technology, were not enough, weapons of mass destruction, together with their delivery systems, are growing more powerful and sophisticated as their potential sphere of operations broadens, both beneath the seas and into outer space. This tendency is proceeding along the sea-lane rimland countries as well as inland, and it has maritime and continentalist dimensions, in the wake of the AUKUS agreement and a potential Chinese response.

The specter of potential nuclear conflict, of course, lies behind the deadly rivalry between Israel and Iran in the Middle East. Israel perceives its survival is at stake in the shadow of Iranian nuclear advances and progress in delivery systems. Saudi Arabia and the other Gulf states likewise view Iran with a wary eye, given the Sunni-Shia historical sectarian rivalry. India and Pakistan are geopolitical rivals and nuclear powers that have fought four major wars over the past seventy years. The extension of their nuclear rivalry to the sea lanes raises a multitude of dangerous imponderables, including the proliferation of ready-to-fire warheads in nontransparent locations and their potential to fall into the hands of terrorists. The deepening linkage of South Asian and Sino-American strategic rivalries is another potentially destabilizing factor.[27] Yet the most predictable dangers of conflict, related to weapons of mass destruction, appear to lie in the East China Sea, on the Korean Peninsula, and across the Taiwan Strait.

Until recently, few contemplated serious armed conflict in the Taiwan Strait. Yet the geopolitical stakes are so high, political-military imbalances are building so inexorably, and the domestic pressures for resolution are so great that cross-strait issues—especially since the Russian invasion of Ukraine—raise urgent issues of global war and peace. For China, such issues represent fundamental "core interests." For the United States, and nearby Asian allies such as Japan, they raise vital questions of maintaining the status quo, including the integrity of the First Island Chain defense line against Chinese and Russian expansion. The related integrity of Japan's energy sea lanes to the Persian Gulf, and of commercial routes further beyond to Europe, also are matters of deepening concern to Washington, Tokyo, and Seoul.

The political-military balance across the Taiwan Strait has shifted steadily in favor of China over the past decade. Ten years ago, China had four times as many warships as Taiwan; today, it has six times as many. It now has six times the number of warplanes and eight times as many tanks. China's defense budget, merely double Taiwan's at the end of the 1990s, is now more than twelve times greater.[28] Indeed, China accounts for close to half of the defense spending of Asia as a whole.[29] The massive and steadily increasing political-military asymmetries across the Taiwan Strait have given Beijing an increasingly credible A2/AD capability and a corresponding ability to threaten Taiwan. Consequently, deterrence of actual Chinese coercive action has rested on American strategic ambiguity. Beijing is consequently unsure, yet nevertheless fearful, of US commitment to Taiwan. Since 1972, the United States has pursued a One China policy that acknowledges the official contentions of both Beijing and Taipei that there is only one China. Yet the deliberate ambiguity in the application of this policy has given Washington diplomatic cover to continue to supply Taipei with high-quality defensive weapons. The United States has strongly stressed the importance of maintaining stability in the Taiwan Strait without specifying how it would respond to efforts by either side to change the status quo.[30]

To credibly maintain deterrence across the Strait in the face of rising Chinese A2/AD capabilities, US strategists around 2010 began propounding the concept of "air-sea battle." This concept involves deep, potentially preemptive strikes by US forces against Chinese command and control capabilities—on land, in space, and in cyberspace—as a means of preserving US power-projection capabilities in a crisis.[31] Any US involvement in a Taiwan crisis, of course, would be a matter of pure speculation. Yet the deepening asymmetries across the Strait, the strategic importance of Taiwan itself, and the escalatory strategies being developed for US response to China's growing strength—involving the potential to finesse local Chinese capabilities along the country's coastline—suggest that Taiwan contingencies are relevant to broader US-China strategic issues related to weapons of mass destruction.

Quest for Resources

Global economic growth for the four decades starting in the 1960s meant an increased demand for raw materials, especially in East Asia. The consequent resource trade significantly increased the strategic importance of sea lanes between Northeast Asia and the Persian Gulf.[32] To be sure, Asian growth has grown less-resource intensive over the past decade or two, as knowledge-intensive sectors have expanded. Yet Asia's overall resource dependence on the broader world via the sea lanes nevertheless continues to deepen, in highly predictable fashion, enhancing the strategic significance of those sea lanes themselves. In 2017, China surpassed the United States to become the world's largest importer of crude oil. And by 2023, China's crude oil imports exceeded 11 million bbl/day—over 30 percent more than those of the United States.[33]

Chinese hydrocarbon dependence on the Persian Gulf could well continue to deepen until after 2030. IEA projections released just before the COVID-19 pandemic suggest that Chinese oil imports from the Middle East would double by 2035.[34] The Sino-Russian Power of Siberia pipeline projects, given increased urgency for Russia by the war in Ukraine, could reduce this projected dependence on the Gulf, but their actual implementation schedule remains uncertain.[35] China's overall imports of natural gas are also expected to double, reaching around 553 billion cubic meters (bcm) by 2030, and 688 bcm by 2050, accounting for more than half of Asia's overall gas demand.[36]

As a result of this growing external energy dependency, China will become far more exposed to the risks of global supply disruptions. Its primary sea routes from the Middle East—transiting the Indian Ocean, the Strait of Malacca, and the South China Sea—thus could play an increasing role in shaping its national energy security.[37] China's Malacca Dilemma, in short, is unlikely to disappear, despite continuing efforts to neutralize the problem.

Environmental Degradation

Persistent economic growth, a predictable hallmark of the East Asian political economy for six decades and more, has led and continues to lead to environmental deterioration. Widespread Chinese and Indian coal usage has been a particular offender, with China for the past decade being the world's largest contributor to global warming by a considerable margin. In 2022, China was the largest annual global carbon dioxide (CO_2) emitter, at 15.68 thousand metric tons, followed by the United States at 6.02, India at 3.94, Russia at 2.58, and Brazil at 1.30.[38] Since Asia's contribution to global warming has been rooted in coal usage, with coal being by far the most inexpensive fuel source for both households and for industry, present trends are likely to persist, even though China in particular is taking steps to reduce CO_2 usage, as through its active promotion of electric vehicles.[39]

Together with its troubling socioeconomic implications, global warming would have predictably disruptive consequences for the Eurasian sea lanes. In particular, it would increase the viability of the Arctic as an alternate transportation route between Europe and Northeast Asia. If moving at comparable speeds, a ship traversing the Northern Sea Route across the Arctic between major ports such as Hamburg and Shanghai could complete the journey in around twenty-three days, compared to thirty-four days if headed to a similar destination using the Suez Canal route, or forty-six days by circumnavigating the Cape of Good Hope.[40] The most rapidly clearing Arctic sea routes are overwhelmingly on the Russian side, which comprises more than one-third of the entire shore of the Arctic Ocean.

The Arctic is also said to house one of the largest storehouses of unexploited raw materials on earth—around a quarter of global oil and gas reserves, to begin with.[41] Predictably, global warming will render those resources easier to exploit. Opportunities like trans-Arctic transportation could prove especially strategic for Russia. Indeed, Russia's Arctic already produces around 95 percent of the country's gas and an estimated 70 percent of its oil, not to mention 99 percent of its diamonds, 96 percent of its platinum, and 90 percent of its nickel.[42]

Deepening Continental Eurasian Interdependence

The continent of Eurasia is in no sense becoming comprehensively unified in any geopolitically meaningful way. Yet important sections of the continent—most notably China, Russia, Central Asia, and major portions of Eastern and Mediterranean Europe—are developing deeply symbiotic geo-economic ties. These ties are beginning to assume broad, predictable international significance in light of China's active BRI connectivity program.[43]

Most important, for the future of Maritime Eurasia and the surrounding sea lanes, are the deepening ties between China and Russia, facilitated by a series of historic critical junctures (see Chapter 3). China's Four Modernizations, the collapse of the Soviet Union in 1991, the 2008 global financial crisis, the 2014 Crimean crisis, and the 2022 war in Ukraine all have accelerated the deepening of Sino-Russian partnership, simultaneously transforming those bilateral ties into an increasingly asymmetric arrangement with Beijing assuming a dominant role. Although the partnership does yield synergies attractive to both parties, such as that between Russian energy abundance and Chinese energy demand, Chinese bilateral leverage is continuing to rise.

The deepening Sino-Russian partnership, although consummated overland, already has had concrete implications in the sea lanes in East Asia and around the world. To begin with, the militaries of the two nations are beginning to coordinate more closely on maritime issues. In 2015, for example the Chinese and the Russians conducted their first joint naval exercise in the eastern Mediterranean. In 2017 the PLA-N returned to the Mediterranean for a live-fire drill with targets, proceeding thereafter to a joint exercise with the Russian Navy in the Baltic Sea.[44] In July 2019, the Chinese People's Liberation Army–Air Force (PLA-AF) and the Russian Air Force jointly conducted a long-range aerial patrol over the East China Sea and the Sea of Japan, and in December 2020 Russian and Chinese bombers conducted a similar joint patrol over the same waters.[45] Then, in May 2022, six Chinese and Russian strategic bombers flew near the Japanese archipelago in an apparent bid to warn Japan against the Quad summit, then underway.[46] In July 2023, they redoubled pressure on Japan, through joint air and naval exercises in the Sea of Japan itself.[47]

Russia and China also have begun to collaborate more closely on matters of military technology with maritime implications. In April 2015, for example, Russia sold its advanced S–400 air-defense system to China in a $3 billion arms deal. With a range of more than 400 kilometers, this system puts all of Taiwan's air space within the range of mainland-based surface-to-air missile batteries.[48] The first unit was delivered in May 2018. Moscow also contracted to supply advanced Sukhoi–35 (Flanker E) fighters to Beijing, which could help expand China's air superiority over the Taiwan Strait, and also aid China in enhancing the capabilities of its J–20 stealth fighter close to those of the US F–22 and F–35. These Su–35 fighters have been serially delivered since December 2016, and China has continued work on carrier-based fifth-generation fighters as well.[49] Russia has also been instrumental in enhancing China's A2/AD efforts against US aircraft carriers, presumptive deterrents to Chinese Taiwan Strait activism, by providing Sunburn and other high-performance antiship missiles to the Chinese, as well as upgrades to Chinese SU–30 fighters.[50]

Steadily deepening Chinese economic interdependence with Mediterranean nations such as Greece, Italy, and Spain on the north shore, as well as Egypt and Algeria on the south, has also quietly transformed the geopolitics of the Eurasian sea lanes. Capitalizing on both China's massive trade volume and expanding economies of scale in ship tonnage and port capacity, COSCO has assumed a commanding presence in both Mediterranean shipping and port ownership. Chinese firms have also built industrial parks at Port Suez and elsewhere, while financing railways inland from port facilities. Such initiatives are allowing them a powerful presence in European continental distribution, based on their port and shipping dominance. In all these activities, BRI funding has provided strategic support.

Deepening American Debt

In 1978, American dependence on foreign credit and public debt, made possible by the dollar's reserve-currency role, was around 20 percent of GDP. By early 2021 that dependence had risen to exceed the size of the entire US economy, rivaling levels at the peak of World War II as the highest in American history. The Congressional Budget Office forecasts that that US national debt will continue to rise relative to the size of the economy—to 107 percent of GDP in FY 2031, and to as much as 202 percent by FY 2050.[51]

Multiple factors have been at work in the steady deterioration of US government finances. Supply-side economic policies pursued by Republican administrations during the Reagan years and beyond, including the aggressive tax cuts during the Trump presidency, were one dimension. Two decades of overseas military commitment in Afghanistan and Iraq following the September 11th attacks, at a cost of around $2 trillion for each of the two conflicts, were a second catalyst.[52] A third important driver has been the COVID shock of 2020–2021, which entailed $3.1 trillion in economic stimulus and humanitarian assistance in FY 2020 alone.[53] This massive deficit was more than triple the scale of its FY 2019 counterpart, and surpassed the largest previous annual deficit of $1.4 trillion generated during the 2009 Great Recession. Following the passage in March 2021 of the American Rescue Act, a $1.9 trillion stimulus bill, the US federal deficit was destined to expand still further during the FYs 2021–2023 period, contributing to the deteriorating long-term trajectory outlined above. By the spring of 2024, the national debt had risen to over $34.6 trillion and was increasing at a rate of around $1 trillion every 100 days.[54]

The Congressional Budget Office suggests that America's growing federal debt could have serious and predictable consequences. "A growing debt burden," in its words, "could increase the risk of a fiscal crisis and higher inflation, as well as undermine confidence in the U.S. dollar, making it more costly to finance public and private activity in international markets."[55] Larry Summers, former treasury secretary under Bill Clinton and economic advisor to Barack Obama, indicated clear concern, as the United States was emerging from the COVID pandemic, that aggressive COVID-related stimulus measures, while arguably necessary in humanitarian and even macroeconomic terms, could over time have "consequences for the dollar and for financial stability".[56] Summers also expressed concerns about the continuing inflationary implications of US economic policies after the pandemic which proved to be prescient as well.[57]

The increase in US fiscal deficits, responding to health and macroeconomic crises as well as national security commitments, are of special geopolitical concern

$ Billion

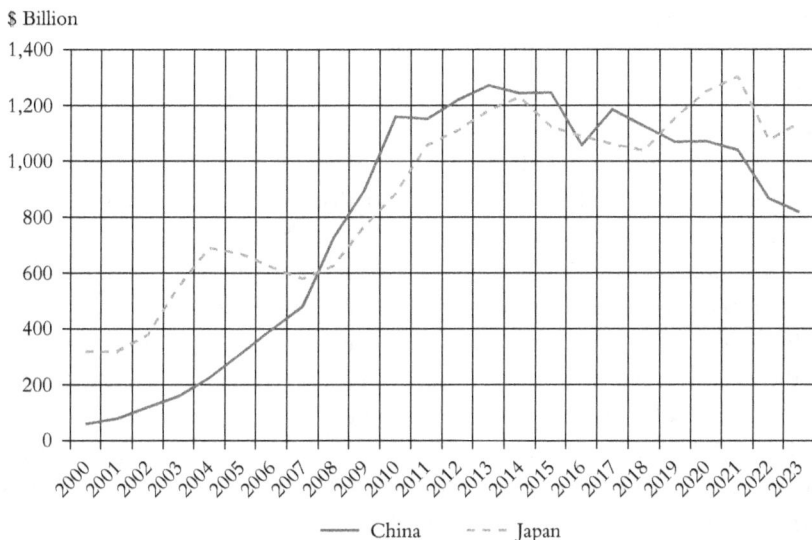

FIGURE 8.1 Top foreign holders of US debt: China vs. Japan
SOURCE: Department of the Treasury/Federal Reserve Board, "Major Foreign Holders of Treasury Securities,"
updated June 18, 2024, https://ticdata.treasury.gov/Publish/mfhhis01.txt.
NOTE: Figures reflect holdings at end of period.

to the United States because of its heavy reliance on foreign debt and the source
of that reliance. As indicated in Figure 8.1, China was the largest foreign holder
of US debt throughout most of the decade and more following the global
financial crisis of 2008–2009, and remains the second-largest holder with well
over $1 trillion outstanding. Meanwhile, China required much smaller fiscal
outlays in response to the COVID crisis: its total fiscal spending, in that connection over the first year of the crisis, was 6 percent of 2020 GDP, versus
26 percent for the United States, according to the International Monetary Fund.[58]
China retains the largest foreign-exchange reserves in the world, exceeding
$3.4 trillion, followed by Japan at over $1.2 trillion.[59] Since 2014, however, Beijing
has begun to shift away from reliance on US dollar securities in its foreign-
exchange portfolio, with potentially significant long-term implications.

To some extent, the massive Japanese purchases of US debt, which have
continued at over $1 trillion annually for more than a decade and recently
accelerated as China's purchases began to decline, have mitigated the perverse
geo-economic and geopolitical implications for the United States of financial
reliance on China. The support of major allies such as Japan is certainly helpful.
Yet that support cannot fully offset a deepening, predictable long-term challenge
to America's maritime as well as global roles. That challenge would become

much more serious if the international key-currency status of the US dollar were to erode.

Predictable long-term trends, including but transcending the issue of US debt, point to potential future challenges to the dollar. Since 2013, China has been the world's largest trading country.[60] By 2018, more than two-thirds of the world's nations traded more with China than with the United States, contrasting to an 80:20 ratio in favor of the United States as recently as 2001.[61] In 2020, China overtook the United States as the largest merchandise trading partner of the European Union, although it still lags in service trade.

In trade-finance settlements, there has been a distinct shift from the dollar to the Chinese yuan among nations such as Russia and Iran that are close politically to China but estranged from the United States. The war in Ukraine has accelerated this trend markedly.[62] Reflecting the scale of the Chinese economy, the yuan's share of International Monetary Fund Special Drawing Rights, currently over 12 percent, is also rising.[63]

The dollar remains dominant in most areas of international finance, with the transparency, openness, depth, and sophistication of American financial markets providing formidable advantages. Some marginal shifts in global trade finance appear to be underway. Currency-swap agreements and some central-bank accumulation of Chinese renminbi by BRI and BRICS (Brazil, Russia, India, China, South Africa, Iran, Egypt, Ethiopia, and the UAE) member countries are becoming more prominent. Digital transformations—increasing flows of data and information, as well as new digital infrastructure—are also important.

The advent of central-bank digital currency may provide China with yet another important opportunity to expand its international financial role. So too could a new strategic alliance with SWIFT, the international payment-clearance system.[64] In February 2021, China's central bank set up a joint venture with SWIFT to facilitate global use of a digital yuan. This decision follows the establishment of a SWIFT subsidiary that opened in China early in 2020 to support China's renminbi internationalization efforts. Despite such promising initiatives, data from SWIFT reveal that 38 percent of transactions on its platform are still denominated in dollars. The yuan's share remained at a much lower 4.7 percent as of March, 2024, but this share had doubled in little more than two years.[65] This share represents its peak since January 2016.[66] G-7 financial sanctions on Russia, following its invasion of Ukraine, appear to be contributing to the increased global use of the yuan since early 2022.

What is clear is that the long-term pressures for an erosion of dollar hegemony in global finance are rising, with two early indications being Beijing's recent efforts to pay yuan for oil and to develop a digital yuan.[67] This trend is especially pronounced in the less-developed economies of Asia, Africa, and even Latin America that have strong economic ties with China or Russia. The war in Ukraine, as noted above, triggered broader financial and trade sanctions that have encouraged Russia, Belarus, and numerous developing nations to pursue work-around arrangements, many of which use the yuan.[68] This gradual shift away from dollar hegemony is magnifying the importance of critical uncertainties, analogous to the 2008 global financial crisis, that could be the catalyst for more definitive shifts in the role of the dollar in future years.

Critical Uncertainties

A variety of predictable long-term trends, including rising global connectivity, a relentless quest for natural resources, and deepening American indebtedness, suggest the possibility of future geo-economic volatility along the Eurasian sea lanes and a gradual erosion of US global hegemony. However, the question of whether long-term pressures result in concrete and meaningful changes in political-economic structure or in consequential policies is subject to a different calculus. To understand the shadows most likely to seriously impinge upon the future, it is important to consider the critical uncertainties that loom over Maritime Eurasia and the sea lanes that traverse it.

Fragile States

The rimland states of Maritime Eurasia stretch from the Pillars of Hercules on Spain's southern coast to Japan and China, more than 6,000 miles away. Those states vary enormously in their political-economic configuration, but to a surprising degree share a common political fragility. Many of them are young nations, trapped in the throes of social transition, where the support of a major outside power—any power—is vital to local stability.

As suggested in Table 8.1, twenty-two rimland nations border the Eurasian sea lanes. They fall into five geographically defined groups: Mediterranean, Red Sea, South Asian, Southeast Asian, and Northeast Asia. With the exception of Spain, Turkey, Egypt, China, Korea, and Japan, these rimland states are not nations with long, coherent histories. Relatively few are well-established democracies. And virtually all, as the table also suggests, face powerful domestic social pressures such as rapidly growing populations, rapid urbanization, and high rates of youth unemployment. All of these challenging factors place governments perpetually on the defensive in relation to local civil societies.

TABLE 8.1

Socioeconomic parameters of fragile Eurasian littoral states

	Population Growth (annual %)	Youth Unemployment (% of total labor force ages 15–24)	Poverty Rate (headcount ratio at $2.15 a day, 2017 PPP)	GDP Growth (annual %)	Urbanization Rate (annual %)
Mediterranean					
Spain	1.2	28.7	0.6 (2021)	2.5	1.5
Italy	−0.3	22.7	0.8 (2021)	0.9	0.1
Greece	−0.6	26.6	0.6 (2021)	2.0	−0.2
Turkey	0.4	17.6	0.4 (2021)	4.5	1.0
Egypt	1.5	19.0	1.5 (2019)	3.8	1.9
Red Sea					
Saudi Arabia	1.5	16.3	N/A	−0.8	1.7
Yemen	2.2	32.7	19.8 (2014)	0.8 (2018)	3.8
Eritrea	1.7	10.0	N/A	8.7 (2011)	3.2
Djibouti	1.4	76.5	19.1 (2017)	6.7	1.6
South Asia					
Pakistan	2.0	9.7	5.1 (2015)	0.0	2.8
India	0.8	15.8	18.1 (2016)	7.6	2.2
Sri Lanka	−0.7	25.3	1.3 (2016)	−2.3	0.3
Bangladesh	1.0	15.7	13.5 (2016)	5.8	2.9
Southeast Asia					
Myanmar	0.7	9.7	6.2 (2015)	1.0	1.8
Malaysia	1.1	12.5	0.0 (2015)	3.7	1.7
Singapore	4.9	8.3	N/A	1.1	4.9
Indonesia	0.7	13.9	8.3 (2015)	5.0	1.8
Vietnam	0.7	6.2	1.3 (2016)	5.0	2.5
Philippines	1.5	6.9	6.5 (2015)	5.5	2.2
Northeast Asia					
China	−0.1	15.7	2.1 (2014)	5.2	1.5
Japan	−0.5	4.1	0.7 (2013)	1.9	−0.4
South Korea	0.1	5.4	0.2 (2014)	1.4	0.1

SOURCES: World Bank, "Population growth (annual %)," "Unemployment, youth total (% of total labor force ages 15-24) (modeled ILO estimate)," "Poverty headcount ratio at $2.15 a day (2017 PPP) (% of population)," "GDP growth (annual %)," and "Urban population growth (annual %)," World Development Indicators (latest data available), accessed July 25, 2024.

NOTES: (1) All figures as of 2023, unless otherwise noted. (2) "N/A" indicates no data available for the past twenty years.

Social Challenges to Political Stability: A Cross-National Comparison

As suggested in Table 8.1 above, there are multiple serious challenges to socio-political stability across the rimlands of Maritime Eurasia. Rapid urbanization, especially pronounced in the volatile transit regions between the Mediterranean and the East China Sea, creates social disruption that often translates into political instability.[69] High youth unemployment, also endemic to the same regions, intensifies this bias toward volatility. Both absolute poverty and the myriad forms of relative deprivation accompanying growth generate their own sociopolitical uncertainties and frustrations.

India's Maritime Orientation

Some of the most strategically important nations along the sea lanes fail to accord consistent policy priority to maritime matters, making their strategic orientation on such questions critical uncertainties. The most important case in point is India. As a vast peninsula jutting deep into the Indian Ocean, India has major potential influence over the Eurasian sea lanes between the Persian Gulf and the Strait of Malacca, and a pivotal role in international coalitions to counterbalance the rise of China. India itself, however, has a strong historically and institutionally rooted orientation toward land power, giving strategic priority to its continuous conflict with Pakistan (against whom it has fought four major wars) and its continuing confrontation with China in the Himalayas.[70]

To the extent that India deploys naval power at all, its orientation is toward the west, against Pakistan in the Arabian Sea, rather than to the east, against China in the Bay of Bengal. The extent to which India would exercise leverage against China in crises important to its Quad partners in the East and South China Seas is an uncertainty of some strategic importance, as that is where the greatest challenges ultimately lie. Also in question is India's willingness to take determined action against destabilizing Russian strategic moves, as evidenced by its passivity during the latest Ukraine war.

Russian Efforts to Revive the Soviet Union

As noted earlier, Russia under Vladimir Putin has made determined efforts, for well over a decade, to revive a moribund Soviet empire that collapsed in 1991. In 2008, it occupied part of Georgia, following the West-oriented Rose Revolution there. In 2014–2015, following the collapse of the Moscow-oriented administration of Viktor Yanukovich, Russia annexed Ukraine's southeastern Crimea region and abetted pro-Russia Ukrainian separatists in the eastern

Donbas region. These incursions culminated in February 2022 when Russia launched a wholesale armed invasion of Ukraine.

Despite major initial military setbacks and unprecedented Western sanctions, as well as massive Western military aid to Ukraine, the Putin regime persisted in its efforts to forcefully reintegrate Ukraine into an expanded Russian sphere of influence. At the onset of the Ukraine war, Russia successfully linked its 2014–2015 acquisitions in Donbas and Crimea, while threatening Ukraine's access to the Black Sea coastline. Even as the conflict settled into an extended war of attrition during 2023–2024, and as NATO resistance to Russian expansion hardened, the Putin administration's aspirations for dominance over a resistant Ukraine remained unchanged.

The momentous potential geo-economic implications of the war, both for the Eurasian sea lanes and for the world more generally, were evident from the earliest months of the war. Most immediately, Russia's invasion led to a swift redefinition of energy relations between Russia and the Western world. The United States and Britain banned imports of Russian oil and gas, Germany terminated the two Nord Stream pipeline projects from Russia, and the European Union made plans to phase out Russian hydrocarbon imports entirely. Major Western firms such as BP, Shell, and Exxon withdrew from multibillion-dollar Russian investments as well.

The termination of overland Western pipeline links with Russia naturally led to greater European reliance on global sea lanes for energy. Although LNG imports from the United States began to rise, the most immediate and readily accessible source was the Persian Gulf. Qatar in particular rapidly began expanding exports to Germany and other key European nations, helping those countries to reduce the European Union's 38 percent dependence during 2020 on Russian gas.[71] The alternative to overland piped Russian gas was clearly LNG via the sea lanes, although the permanence and scale of such flows remained uncertain.[72] Some Russian energy, of course, seemed likely to continue flowing by land, especially to smaller Central European states like Hungary. India was emerging as a significant low-cost, sanctions-breaking customer for Russia, but geographic reasons dictated that these shipments were best made by sea. Only China would remain, in the wake of the Russia-Ukraine war, as a major overland client for Russian gas.

The Ukraine conflict also created major uncertainties for future foodstuff flows. In 2020, Ukraine provided more than 10 percent of the world's feedstuff grain exports.[73] Russia and Ukraine together generated 28 percent of the world's wheat exports; 26 percent of global barley exports; and 16 percent of world corn exports.[74] The conflict threw all these flows into uncertainty, with initially calamitous implications for developing nations—especially across the Middle East and North Africa.[75] Although Black Sea food export shortages were eased by a July 2022 compromise agreement among the warring parties, mediated by Turkey, and later by rising Ukrainian drone capacity at sea, chronic uncertainties persisted.[76]

Prospects are dim for any easy resolution to the Russia-Ukraine conflict. That reality will in turn create political uncertainties for energy prices, food supplies, and ultimately for political-economic stability over a swath of the Middle East, North Africa, and the Eurasian sea lanes. Populous Middle Eastern, South Asian, and Southeast Asian nations without extensive energy reserves easily could be hard hit by higher inflation and interest rates, as well as rising commodity prices. Political-economic instability in Sri Lanka during the spring and summer of 2022 was just one early harbinger of dangers to come.

Taiwan

Without question, the most important critical uncertainty casting shadows over the geo-economic stability of Maritime Eurasia and the surrounding sea lanes is the ambiguous standing of Taiwan. Lying at the very heart of the First Island Chain, between Japan and the Philippines, Taiwan stands geographically between mainland China and the blue waters of the Pacific, as indicated in Figure 8.2. Were Beijing to occupy Taiwan, the rugged harbors of its east coast, fronting directly on one of the deepest maritime trenches in the Pacific Ocean, would give the PLA-N some of the most strategic submarine bases in the world.[77] From the ports of Hualien and Keelung on Taiwan's east coast, the PLA-N would be roughly 140 nautical miles from ports in Ishigaki, part of the Ryukyu Islands in Japan's Okinawa Prefecture. Even more importantly, China's PLA-N would gain direct access from Taiwan to the Philippine Sea, and hence the broad Pacific, without having to circumnavigate the US-dominated First Island Chain.

Control of Taiwan is particularly strategic from a geopolitical standpoint because of its profound impact on submarine monitoring.[78] ASW essentially is a search problem—finding and tracking small but adversarial submarines in the vastness of the ocean. Sophisticated twenty-first-century ASW typically employs two types of tracking sensors: deep sound channel sensors, capable of crudely monitoring from long distances; and reliable acoustic path (RAP) sensors, or hydrophones that can track passing submarines with precision in close proximity.

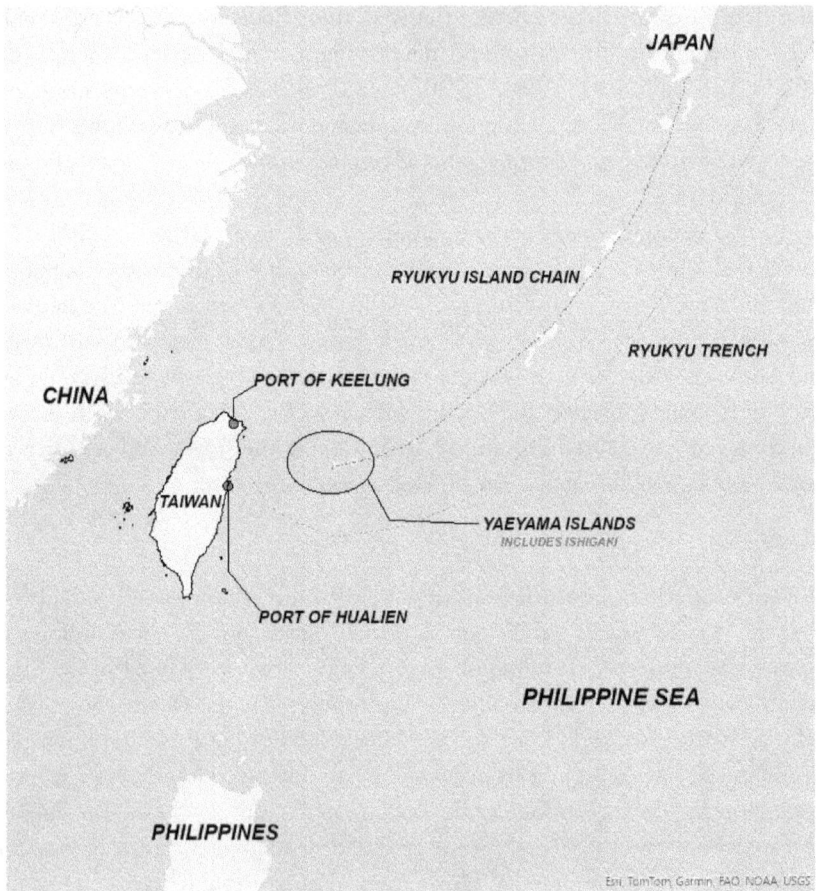

FIGURE 8.2 Taiwan's strategic location
SOURCES: Esri, HERE, Garmin, FAO, NOAA, USGS, © OpenStreetMap contributors, and the GIS User Community.

Under current conditions, with Taiwan autonomous and positively inclined toward the United States and its allies, the United States can activate both varieties of hydrophone sensors to track the Chinese submarines constrained within the First Island Chain that borders Asia's eastern coastline. Were Taiwan controlled in political-military terms by the People's Republic of China, the United States likely could not operate a precise RAP sensor network based on the First Island Chain. Additionally, Chinese submarines would have direct basing access themselves to the Philippine Sea and the broader Pacific from Taiwanese east-coast bases. The United States could still engage in deep sound channel monitoring from the Second Island Chain (primarily from Guam), but such monitoring would be much less precise than the RAP plus deep-channel combination. Japan and Korea would thus face a grave submarine threat to their shipping, especially in the energy sea lanes leading toward Southeast Asia and the Persian Gulf. And if China developed quieter submarines capable of evading US Navy surveillance, the US military would confront a dangerously expanded nuclear threat to the continental United States.

What would be the prospect for Taiwan's successful defense, and the regional implications thereof? Taiwan is by far the largest component, geographically speaking, of the First Island Chain. It has thirty times the land area of Okinawa, and rugged mountains that afford much more space for concealment and maneuver than any of the other islands to its north or south.[79] Politically, Taiwan remains de facto autonomous and heavily armed, even though virtually all major nations of the world, including the United States and Japan, diplomatically recognize Taipei's bitter opponent in Beijing, whose military strength far exceeds that of Taiwan.[80] China's defense budget totals around twelve times that of Taiwan and is growing much faster in quantitative terms, implying that the substantial cross-Strait capabilities gap is likely to widen in coming years.

Taiwan is important strategically and economically not only to the United States, but also to its Northeast Asian allies and many countries in Southeast Asia and Europe. Japan, for instance, imports 99 percent of its oil supply, and more than 85 percent of that imported oil comes over sea lanes southward from Japan that pass directly by Taiwan. Those sea lanes would be gravely threatened if adversarial submarines could move freely in the waters east of Taiwan, as suggested above. South Korea likewise imports virtually all its oil and LNG over East China Sea sea lanes passing by Taiwan—in closer proximity even than those passing Japan. Taiwan also is home to 63 percent of the world's foundry semiconductor capacity, with that production strategically crucial across broad industrial sectors, from automobiles and consumer electronics to defense. Taiwan's largest firm, Taiwan Semiconductor, with 2023 sales of $69.67 billion, is also the largest semiconductor manufacturer on earth, with 56 percent of global production. UMC, also a Taiwanese firm, ranks third, with 7 percent of global production. Mainland China's largest producer, SMIC, ranks only fifth, producing just 5 percent of the world's semiconductors.

Taiwan is also a major force in global shipping. Its largest firm, Evergreen Marine, ranks seventh in the world, with a global market share of around 5.6 percent, as noted in Chapter 6. Yang Ming, Taiwan's second-largest shipper, ranks tenth internationally. Both are many times larger than America's largest carrier, Matson, Inc., which ranks twenty-eighth.[81] And both large Taiwanese shipping firms engage heavily with market economies elsewhere in Asia.

Taiwan likewise has made important recent strides in strengthening its local manufacturing base, both by incentivizing reshoring from the mainland and by attracting Western multinationals. In 2018, Tsai Ing-wen's administration launched a three-year reshoring incentive program, running through 2021.[82] The program targeted high-end industrial sectors such as technology, communications, and energy, offering loans and tax breaks to Taiwanese companies. The reshoring program has generated $42 billion of in-bound investment since 2019, with more than two-thirds of that total attributed to Taiwanese firms returning from the Chinese mainland. One of the most prominent Taiwanese firms to reshore has been Quanta Computer, the assembler of MacBooks and Apple Watches, as well as a supplier of data-center servers to Facebook and Google. Quanta is investing NT$15 billion to build a new factory in Taoyuan that will take over some of the company's China production.[83] Taiwan's New Kimpo Group, a Taiwan-based world leader in electronic manufacturing services, also has been shifting its manufacturing operations out of China.[84] Giant is another high-tech manufacturer that since late 2018 has moved bicycle and e-bike production back from the Shanghai area to its central Taiwan plant.[85]

Although Hong Kong has long served as the critical hub for Asian data centers, many US tech companies are looking to other viable locations, like Taiwan, following the June 2019 passage of restrictive Chinese national-security laws constraining Hong Kong and further tightening in 2024.[86] In September 2020, for example, Google announced that it would build its third data transfer hub in Taiwan's Yunlin County, at a cost of $681 million.[87] In a separate project, Microsoft in October, 2020 announced that it would build its first Azure cloud data center in Taiwan, generating over 30,000 jobs by 2024 in the digital infrastructure realm.[88]

Taiwan has a remarkably broad global prominence, even outside the economic and security spheres. It was remarkably effective in confronting the COVID-19 virus during its early stages, suffering less than 900 deaths across the first two years of the pandemic, compared to well over 800,000 in the United States alone.[89] Taiwan's healthcare system is ranked among the ten most efficient healthcare systems in the world.[90]

"Island China," as Taiwan is sometimes called, shares a broad range of sociopolitical values with the democratic world, which has given it increasing legitimacy and political weight in Washington over the past three decades even as its diplomatic representation abroad has contracted.[91] Although an autocratic regime until the 1990s, Taiwan has held regular democratic elections since 1996, and experienced three party-to-party transitions in political power. It also has been environmentally conscious, rejecting both hydrocarbons and nuclear power while vigorously pursuing alternate energy. Despite the continuing confrontation with Beijing across the Taiwan Strait, Taiwan's ruling party has been remarkably liberal on a range of human-rights questions, including LGBTQ rights and gender prerogatives. From 2016 to 2024, Taiwan was led by a resolute, forceful female president, Tsai Ing-wen, who was reelected with 57 percent of the vote in 2020, and succeeded by fellow Democratic Progressive Party leader Lai Ching-te in May 2024.

As noted above, Taiwan also has developed a strong health policy record, which was evident in the early stages of the COVID-19 pandemic. Responding rapidly to the pandemic after its emergence in nearby Wuhan, Taiwan scrupulously followed scientific guidance, with Vice President Chen Chien-jen, a noted epidemiologist, taking particular initiative.[92] During 2020–2021 Taiwan incurred the smallest number of coronavirus infections and COVID-related fatalities of any major regime in the world, with only twelve confirmed deaths and fewer than 1,200 cases during the first three months of the pandemic.[93]

To reinforce its political position in Washington, D.C., Taipei has developed strong ties with the US Congress, with the previously mentioned Taiwan Relations Act as a point of departure.[94] This standing was reinforced by the TAIPEI (Taiwan Allies International Protection and Enhancement Initiative) Act, which became public law in March 2020 and was crafted to help Taiwan maintain its precarious international diplomatic position.[95] Washington and Taipei have concluded various executive understandings, facilitating continued weapons sales. Taiwan likewise has retained strong ties with the 600,000 Taiwanese Americans, which retain active lobbying capabilities on Capitol Hill through the Formosan Association for Public Affairs.[96] Several Taiwanese Americans have attained prominence in recent US presidential administrations, helping to sustain the island's strong informal elite-support network.[97]

Taiwan's recent representative to the United States, Hsiao Bi-khim (2020–2023) attended college in the United States at Oberlin and later Columbia University, having spent extensive time in Japan as well. She maintained active liaison with the US Congress, as her predecessor Stanley Kao (2016–2020) also did.[98] Hsiao, who arrived in Washington in July 2020, attended the inauguration of US President Joe Biden in January 2021, in a notable intensification of the US-Taiwan relationship. In May 2024, she gained even more influence over US-Taiwan relations when she became vice president of Taiwan.

Taiwan has become influential both because of the democratic example it sets and the strength of its grassroots political networks in US congressional districts. Its considerable standing in Washington was symbolized in the visit of House of Representatives Speaker Nancy Pelosi to Taipei in August 2022, and the positive response on Capitol Hill.[99] Its political future remains radically uncertain, however, in light of determined reunification efforts from Beijing, rendering Taiwan's situation an equally critical uncertainty for the security of the sea lanes and global geopolitics, as a whole.

China's military capacity and economic power are rising even as Taiwan's diplomatic standing is eroding. Beijing's deepening network of global ties, especially with Europe and Russia, also constrain Taiwan. And Chinese leadership is apparently determined, with the approaching 100th anniversaries of the PLA in 2027 and the People's Republic of China in 2049, to intensify pressures on the current status quo. This stark reality is especially disturbing to US allies like Japan, who make extensive use of the sea lanes to the Strait of Malacca and beyond.

Taiwan contingencies are of course a major concern of government policy in Washington, Beijing, Tokyo, and other major national capitals, and the subject of considerable academic and policy literature.[100] Scenarios for the future broadly divide into three categories: nonmilitary political transitions, incremental encroachment, and military conflict. All of these view the shift of the status quo in the direction of greater Chinese suasion over Taiwan, reflecting the rising differentials in economic and military capacity between Beijing and Taipei.

The political transition model was the paradigm behind Deng Xiaoping's "one country, two systems" proposal touted during the handover of Hong Kong in 1997, and lay behind the positive cross-Strait relations during Taiwanese President Ma Ying-jeou's administration (2008–2016). During that era, cross-Strait relations were so conciliatory that Ma and Chinese President Xi Jinping actually met personally in Singapore. The plausibility of this transition scenario, however, waned sharply following Beijing's promulgation of the restrictive Hong Kong National Security Law and the effective demolition of the "one-country, two-systems" model in Hong Kong during the summer of 2020, as Taiwan grew highly skeptical of voluntary reunification scenarios. As of late-2023, less than 1 percent of Taiwanese reportedly favored immediate unification with mainland China. Conversely, there is strong support, especially among young people, for closer economic and even security relations with the United States.[101]

Prospects for the incremental coercion paradigm have risen since mid-2020 as the plausibility of the political transition model has waned. Taiwan appears increasingly unlikely to drift toward the mainland of its own accord, regardless of economic attractions. And the approaching centenary of the PLA (2027) gives Beijing incentives to intensify pressure on Taiwan as well. Taiwan's geography makes this "soft" military-coercion alternative plausible to many Chinese for three related reasons: (1) Taiwan itself is an island, and thus relatively vulnerable to milder forms of coercion than direct attack, such as quarantine or blockade. As Corbett always maintained, the sea is not susceptible of ownership; conversely, however, it is a realm where gray tactics are relatively easy to deploy. Mainland China can use this geopolitical reality to its advantage, legitimating such measures through its claims of national sovereignty, broadly recognized worldwide, at least formalistically. (2) Taiwan has multiple outlying territories, such as the Pratas, Quemoy, Matsu, and the Pescadore Islands, that China could opt to occupy as evidence of the seriousness of its intent.[102] (3) These milder and relatively ambiguous forms of coercion would be less costly for Beijing than frontal military assault, and more plausible politically as a coercion strategy.

Such symbolic moves, or other forms of relatively costless coercion from a Chinese standpoint such as air defense identification zone encroachments; soft marine blockades; "gray" trade quarantines by domestic coastguards; offshore missile tests; and anonymous cyberattacks, could have a similar coercive yet incrementalist character. Measures like these would obviate the need to immediately tackle the daunting challenges of direct invasion while still exerting pressure on Taiwan. Collectively, they are tactically plausible, if politically contingent, critical uncertainties, whose likelihood was suggested by the configuration of China's response to the August 2022 Pelosi visit to Taiwan, and to subsequent US political moves affirming Taiwan's international standing.[103]

A final option would be direct military action. This, too, could have multiple forms and gradations. Yet all would be highly provocative compared with the status quo, and could well trigger broader conflict beyond Taiwan itself, including retaliatory strikes against the Chinese mainland.[104] The extreme case would be full-scale invasion across the 100-mile-wide Taiwan Strait—an event that specialists believe would be most likely to occur during the month of April, a season of heavy fog in the Strait; just before high tide; and supported by large numbers of submarines.[105] A full-scale frontal attack of this nature could require an invasion force of up to 1 million troops, although preparatory airborne assaults, missile barrage, or local domestic support could reduce military requirements significantly.

Military and diplomatic specialists consider three broad plausible scenarios for a Chinese military takeover of Taiwan.[106] The simplest, though arguably the least likely because of the prospective military cost, would be direct invasion either through a swift operation attacking centers of power, harbors, and airfields; or a full-scale siege beginning with an amphibious landing. Both options have the counterproductive demerits, from the Chinese standpoint, of deepening anti-mainland sentiment in Taiwan and mobilizing global political and military support for the embattled regime.

Under a second scenario, the PLA-N could impose a naval blockade or a broader sea-air quarantine, possibly under the pretext of response to some allegedly provocative foreign action.[107] This prospectively would involve controlling all international access to Taiwan and diverting incoming shipments for clearance on the mainland. Such a blockade could be explicitly military, or center on more deniable "gray-zone" tactics by nominally nongovernmental fishing boats, drones, or periodic crossing of established median lines by sea and air.[108] China's new coast guard law, passed in January 2021, empowers the Chinese Coast Guard to manage foreign vessels in its "waters," making such a "gray-zone" scenario increasingly plausible.[109]

A third possibility would be more indirect. The PLA potentially could invade some or all of Taiwan's peripheral territories, such as the Pescadore or Pratas Islands, through "gray-zone" intimidation tactics. Alternatively, it could disrupt vital undersea fiber-optic communications with Taiwan itself, or impose a blockade. China could also simultaneously strengthen and perhaps arm Taiwan's pro-Chinese forces to create clear anarchy and division among Taiwanese. Many specialists consider this third scenario of pressure on the offshore islands, with an important but ambiguous "gray warfare" dimension; or alternatively the second Taiwan blockade scenario triggered by a foreign "provocation," as the most plausible options for an attempted mainland takeover of Taiwan.[110]

In Conclusion

The oceans have been the preserve of Anglo-American naval power for more than two centuries, with free and open passage across them a pillar for the global market-capitalist political-economic order. Major geopolitical turbulence has broken out on land, including two major world wars and the collapse of global empires, while the high seas until recently have remained remarkably unaffected. As seen in previous chapters, that durable and remarkably pacific maritime order quietly has begun to change, mainly driven by a gradual transformation in the relationship of China and the United States to their maritime environments.

Previous chapters have chronicled the structural changes in the maritime world since World War II across various sectors—shipbuilding, shipping, and submarine communications, to name a few. They have surveyed changes in government policies, not only of the United States and China, the major protagonists, but also of other relevant actors, especially those of the Indo-Pacific. Together, the analysis so far has produced a schematic view of the structural and human biases likely to shape the future of Maritime Eurasia and its surrounding sea lanes. Yet this book has yet to formulate a probabilistic notion of that potential future, which it will do in the remaining pages.

In assessing the future, it is important to distinguish between predictable elements and the critical uncertainties that exert outsized impact on ultimate outcomes. Through such a bifurcated analytical approach, it should be possible to craft a conditional but high-probability general paradigm of the future, and at the same time identify the crucial developments with the highest likelihood of configuring alternative variants of that future. This assessment will help focus analytical attention on the determinants of the future that most matter. On the issue of probability and uncertainty with respect to the Eurasian sea lanes at three levels—developments within China; transformations across Eurasia; and global changes—the following are the salient points:

(a) **Predictable elements of the future:** Demography, growing connectivity, ethnic conflict, weapons of mass destruction, the quest for resources, deepening Eurasian continental interdependence, environmental degradation, political polarization, and deepening American debt. This combination suggests a deepening short-term challenge to American preeminence, albeit potentially limited over time by demographic change in China.

To be sure, the United States has enduring strengths to meet these challenges.[111] Prominent among them is the rapid pace of technological innovation, rooted in flexible capital markets congenial to entrepreneurs; world-class higher education; and global sourcing of both labor and capital. Compared to virtually all Eurasian nations, the United States has favorable land and resource to population ratios, as well as geographical location.[112] These all, however, are long-term advantages, suggesting a predictable shorter-term interval of prospective challenge, especially from China, with the sea lanes being a central arena of possible contention.

(b) **Critical uncertainties:** Fragile states, maritime orientation of key national actors, and the future of Taiwan. Over the short to intermediate term, at least, grave challenges could arise from the foreseeable uncertainties. Compared to the 1950s and 1960s, or even more recent years, America's unilateral political-economic ability to meet these challenges is distinctly limited. Washington will need to rely increasingly on both formal allies, especially in Northeast Asia, and also more subjective ententes of convenience. That said, the potential limitations of such arrangements with some key nations, such as India, must be recognized.

Taken together, predictable elements and critical uncertainties suggest an emerging world in which the industrial democracies, led by the United States, face serious albeit potentially short-lived challenges along the Eurasian sea lanes. China's naval strength, gray-zone capabilities, and dual-use infrastructure are all steadily improving, tempting Beijing to press at dangerous points of vulnerability like Taiwan. The United States, however, retains powerful leverage owing to China's deepening energy dependence on the Gulf, and this leverage is reinforced by Anglo-American strongpoints like Diego Garcia and formidable subsurface maritime capabilities augmented by AUKUS.

The emerging reality of Eurasia's maritime transformation presents both challenges and opportunities. It is a call for policy activism—particularly the strengthening of America's Indo-Pacific alliances, based on a realistic appreciation of what others can and cannot do. That is the task to which we now turn.

9

Prospects and Policy Implications

AN ENDURING FASCINATION FOR ME over the years has been the role of geography in international affairs. In two previous books, I have explored that issue, focusing on Eurasia's continental configuration and the ways in which its political trans-formation has reshaped its functional role in the global political-economic system.[1] The research in this volume centers on a complementary issue: the role of sea lanes as a pivotal theater in US-China strategic competition.

More than 71 percent of the Earth's entire surface is water.[2] Yet the great majority of geopolitical studies concern not those maritime spaces, including vast oceans like the Pacific and the Indian, but rather land areas that cover a much smaller share of the whole. The spatial location, political-economic role, and security structure of water bodies—as well as the relationships of rimland nations along their shores and of islands within them—can shape international affairs in fateful ways.[3] However, the only coverage these issues have received has been highly exploratory studies at most.[4]

Over the past two decades, a veritable cottage industry in policy-oriented analytical work has emerged with the names of major oceans, particularly "Asia-Pacific" and more recently "Indo-Pacific," featured prominently in their titles. Few of these studies, however, spend much time considering the physical or even political-economic traits of the maritime bodies that appear in these titles. Their authors often use the terms loosely to denote relations of all varieties among nations in a particular part of the world. Such vagueness also obscures the concrete geopolitical role of the water bodies themselves, and the ways in which both the economic and the strategic significance of those maritime spaces and their contingent rimlands might be changing.

Key Findings in Review

Across the past eight chapters, we have sought to correct these biases of previous geopolitical work, and to understand just how the Eurasian sea lanes themselves influence the functioning of the global political economy and security structure today. We also have devoted considerable attention to how the political-economic functions of those sea lanes have evolved over time, and how their profound transformation since the 1990s has in turn begun to reshape global affairs.

Because of their pivotal geopolitical character, we chose the sea lanes between Europe and Asia, rather than those across the Atlantic or the Pacific, as a subject of study. Those sea lanes and the rimland nations adjoining them, as Nicholas Spykman realized, have for 600 years and more been the one vibrant link between the east and the west of the Eurasian continent, following the demise of the medieval Silk Road. Without the sea lanes stretching from Southampton to Shanghai and beyond, the Eurasian continent as a whole had no vehicle for systematic transcontinental political or economic exchange until around the 1980s. And in the wake of the disruptions caused by the war in Ukraine, the overland connections via Russia that emerged following the 1991 Soviet collapse have been disrupted as well.

During the days of European empire, the Eurasian sea lanes reinforced the global preeminence of those empires. In the more recent era of American hegemony, control of the Eurasian sea lanes helped sustain US global dominance, complemented by heavy capital flows from East Asia. Yet as overland connections across the continent improve and Chinese cooperation with Russia and parts of Eastern Europe intensifies, new patterns could emerge, eroding American global dominance. Whether and how the sea lanes affect relationships and grand strategy, both within the Eurasian continent and beyond, are destined to become major questions for world affairs in coming years.

We have devoted special attention to understanding the quiet changes in the global political-economic role of Eurasia's sea lanes over the past three post–Cold War decades because this transformation is altering the dynamics of the international political economy. Key changes have included the rising scale of intra-Asian energy trade, growing Northeast Asian energy dependence on the Middle East, the shifting naval balances above and beneath the ocean surface; the changing political orientation of key rimland nations, and the profound undersea maritime transformations wrought by the Information and Robotics

Revolutions. Multilateral maritime cooperation has also deepened along both civilian and military dimensions.[5]

All these changes are reconnecting parts of the world that for generations have been at best loosely tied together, even as they finesse and counterbalance shifting political-economic equations on land. Our research has indicated that these geo-economic changes transforming Eurasia's sea lanes are historic, and may well have long-term effects even greater than those we can now foresee. Four of the five most populous nations on earth lie along the waters between Shanghai and Suez. Their per capita energy, food, and raw-material consumption levels are still far lower than typical G-7 norms, but these inevitably will rise over time. And the nations of Maritime Eurasia rely heavily on those sea lanes to supply their growing demands for both commodities and manufactures.

True to this book's focus on geography and its economic correlates as an elemental point of departure, it begins with a political, military, and geo-economic review of the diverse maritime bodies that comprise the Eurasian sea lanes, stressing their contrasting characters and the subtle obstacles that diversity poses to stable interdependence. Obscure corners of the massive oceans, especially the Pacific and the Indian, hold special importance in the nuclear age as the preserve of underwater deterrent forces. The strategic island chains of Maritime Eurasia, like the Ryukyus and the Indonesian and Philippine archipelagoes, have gained geopolitical importance as the sea-lane dependence and military capabilities of resurgent powers both continue to rise. Various important bays and smaller maritime indentations, ranging from the Arabian Sea to the East China Sea, by way of the Bay of Bengal, have changing strategic functions. The chokepoints—at the Strait of Malacca, near the Andaman Islands, at the Strait of Hormuz and the Bab al-Mandab, and at the Suez Canal—have the potential to constrict maritime flows. And the ports themselves, eastward from Piraeus to Djibouti, Gwadar, Hambantota, Shanghai, and Yokohama, all route commercial traffic and serve as logistical connections to inland points. It is important to look beyond generalizations about nation-state strategy and to understand the nuanced contours of actual bodies of water and their secure linkages to the land. Such detailed, geographically embedded insights are vital to accurately grasp how sea lanes influence world affairs, and how maritime influence evolves over time.

In looking concretely at the varied functional role of the water bodies along the Eurasian sea lanes, we have discovered sobering potential for conflict along waterways as their economic importance grows. At present, there is a built-in Anglo-American geopolitical advantage within the sea lanes. With its multiple aircraft carriers; powerful submarine fleet; and far-flung basing network, including the strategic Diego Garcia bastion in the depths of the Indian Ocean, the United States enjoys a strong degree of leverage on and under the blue waters over which an increasing volume of "south-south" commerce—much of it to and from China—inevitably must ply. This structural advantage for Washington in the Indo-Pacific geopolitical calculus faces challenges both from the rise of Chinese naval power and from the increasing technical vulnerability of some weaponry, such as aircraft carriers, on which US security architecture traditionally has relied. Yet America's current capabilities are fortuitously embedded and require remarkably low-cost current maintenance. Its formidable strongpoints, such as Diego Garcia, would be immensely difficult for rivals to offset in the short term.

US allies also have complementary strengths that can efficiently support their American counterparts within a broader multilateral structure of federated defense, involving decentralized initiatives capitalizing on local capabilities, coupled with unitary oversight, as in federated government. On the military side, such federated defense can involve common force planning, collaborative servicing, cooperative scheduling of deployments, interoperability, and coordinated procurement, as well as collaborative weapons development that includes components and subassemblies.[6] On the economic and humanitarian side, hospital ships, construction projects, and diplomatic support against illegal fishing, as well as efforts to combat climate change and natural disasters, are all plausible options for collaboration.[7] Among the most potent prospective examples of federated defense is the AUKUS agreement of September 2021. This agreement capitalizes on distinctive American technological strength, together with the diverse locations and capabilities of allied nations beneath the seas, to balance and offset rising Chinese power. The resulting deterrent impact promises to be palpably greater than any of the three parties—even America—could achieve alone.

After reviewing the geographic profile of the Eurasian sea lanes as a whole, the challenges they pose to stable interdependence, and the geostrategic advantages these structures and challenges accord to the United States, the book considers how major powers have viewed these sea lanes in classical strategic terms. For the Europeans, especially the British, these Eurasian sea lanes were once vital to national security as lifelines to their lucrative Asian empires. After World War II, with the loss of empire, the importance of those sea lanes waned for the Europeans, only to revive in the recent past. Postcolonial European trade with Asia has expanded, and the rise of China has provoked balancing behavior for Europeans in the Indo-Pacific, generally in cooperation with other G-7 nations. The rising role of Europeans in the Indo-Pacific naturally enhances the analytic value of the Eurasian maritime geopolitics concept.

For Asian nations, including even China, the importance of Eurasia's sea lanes long has been primarily economic. That importance has continued to rise as sea-lane traffic has increased in volume and global interdependence has become more pronounced. Over the past three decades, those sea lanes have become ever more important as conduits for oil from the Persian Gulf, as well as for manufactured trade. Asian countries have hoped first and foremost for political stability among rimland nations, with corresponding stable trade flows and economic prosperity. Their concerns have in that sense been defensive. The central fear—common to China, Japan, and Korea for different reasons—has been regional instability and interrupted trade.

American dominance in the blue waters of the Indo-Pacific has been at once a reassurance to the oil-supply fears of allies, such as Japan and Korea, and a deterrent to Russian and Chinese actions east of Malacca. As American preeminence wanes, however, and Asian technological capabilities grow more sophisticated, intra-Asian political-military competition in the Eurasian sea lanes, as well as overt challenge to the status quo, has become more prominent. China's rise as both an economic and a military power risks upsetting the current finely balanced strategic equation in the sea lanes, with broader potential consequences.[8]

For much of its history, the United States focused its involvement in the Eurasian sea lanes to the east of the Strait of Malacca. Until remarkably late— the early 1960s, to be precise—Washington had virtually no direct political-military involvement in the Indian Ocean. To the extent that its interests were engaged, the US government operated through proxies, ranging from the British Empire to the Shah of Iran. Even today, America's economic stakes between Suez and Singapore remain surprisingly low. Moreover, as the United States itself has grown more self-sufficient in energy production, its reduced dependence on the Persian Gulf actually has lowered these parochial stakes to some degree.

American involvement in the Indian Ocean, in short, reflects US attitudes toward globalism, particularly of Cold War strategic competition with the Soviet Union. That rivalry intensified following India's acquisition of Soviet nuclear submarines in 1964 and the ensuing deepening of Soviet-Indian diplomatic and military ties. Reflecting Washington's traditionally limited stakes in South Asia and the weakness of related domestic political interests in the United States, members of Congress expressed considerable resistance in the mid-1970s to establishment of a military base complex at Diego Garcia.[9] Since then, however, Diego has become one of the most strategically important US bases on earth, and the AUKUS agreement could even strengthen its operational role.

In contrast to a paucity of parochial American economic stakes in the Indian Ocean, all three major Northeast Asian states—China, Japan, and Korea—have become deeply dependent on the Eurasian waterways since the end of the Cold War. South and Southeast Asia have similar dependencies. All center on the flow of oil: more than three-quarters of Japan and Korea's entire oil supply now comes from the Persian Gulf, and nearly the same share of China's supply comes from either the Gulf or Africa, across the Indian Ocean and through the Strait of Malacca.

The empirical focus of this research, and the bulk of our policy-relevant findings, concern the contrasting roles of the United States and China in the Eurasian sea lanes and the rimland countries of Maritime Eurasia. Broadly speaking, the United States has been globalist and reactive to the interests of its Asian and European partners in its Indo-Pacific policies, even though its domestic economic interests in the sea lanes and their rimland are much less compelling than those of its Asian allies. Driven by global strategic concerns, originally versus the Soviet Union and now in relation to China, the United States has retained its dominance in the high-performance naval sphere, particularly beneath the seas. It is also sustaining a much more extensive and strategically located military basing network than Beijing, not to mention a much more robust network of alliances.

Since Xi Jinping became the paramount leader of China in 2012, China has been strikingly proactive, however, in expanding its presence across Maritime Eurasia, including the Eurasian sea lanes. Beijing is rapidly gaining on Washington in the dual civil-military use emerging technology sphere; in raw numbers of naval vessels; and in militarily relevant infrastructure, including ports, shipping, and logistics. China is also building an array of strategic physical and digital infrastructural networks across the rimland under the banner of BRI, connecting systematically to its homeland.

These infrastructural ties include undersea telecommunications networks and cables with rimland developing nations, from Myanmar to Djibouti, Egypt, and beyond. These systems offer Beijing critical access to maritime and coastal areas with strategic significance. At the same time, China also has taken pains to develop dual-use strongpoints, with comprehensive communications and operational capabilities, that it could use for military purposes in the future. And its economic statecraft is quietly but deftly stimulating the interest of maritime Indo-Pacific nations in trade and financial interdependence with China, ultimately with geopolitical implications.

China's capabilities are thus far concentrated geographically in sea lanes close to its own shores in the East and South China Seas. These littorals, however, also are important access routes to the Persian Gulf and beyond for the United States' Northeast Asian allies. The most dangerous flashpoint is Taiwan—claimed by mainland China as a renegade province, but strategically and economically important to both Japan and the United States.[10] Nevertheless, American leverage with China at key chokepoints, as well as west of Malacca in the Indian Ocean, has inhibited Chinese efforts to revise the status quo militarily to date.

Recent Japanese signaling regarding the importance of Taiwanese autonomy may also be giving China pause.[11] Yet longer-term vulnerabilities on the Chinese side give Beijing deeper incentives to seek early reunification, possibly exploiting a critical window of US strategic vulnerability. Opinions vary on how rapidly China's incentives to redress the status quo will intensify.[12] The combination of perverse Chinese and US incentives, however, is creating in the Taiwan Strait the most troubling shadow for the future of political-military stability in the Eurasian sea lanes.

The East and South China Seas are not the only parts of the Eurasian sea lanes where the balance of power is shifting away from US hegemony. In the Arctic Ocean, China and Russia are playing ever more dominant roles even in the face of Western sanctions. Notably, Russia lies next to two-thirds of the span of littoral land area astride the Arctic sea lane from Europe to Northeast Asia that is most likely to open as climate change reduces ice coverage around the pole. Moscow also has developed by far the largest fleet of Arctic icebreakers and has prioritized Arctic development. Chinese capital supplies and geopolitical leverage with Russia may create the conditions in which the Sino-Russian axis, and not the United States, could dominate economic development and transportation in the Far North—although this pattern could take many years to materialize.

Internet development is a final dimension of Eurasian sea lane evolution where China's influence has become more prevalent, with broader global consequences. More than 95 percent of global Internet communication flows through fiber-optic cables beneath the sea lanes. Across the Atlantic and the Pacific Ocean expanses, well-capitalized American IT firms such as Microsoft, Facebook, and Google have dominated Internet capital construction, operation, and ownership. Yet the less developed areas of South Asia, Southeast Asia, the Pacific Island region, and Africa have little commercial logic for such infrastructure, even where its presence or the lack thereof is geopolitically sig-nificant.[13] Private firms based in the G-7 industrialized nations thus have few incentives to devote commercial resources to filling these gaps. Instead, China is doing so through its BRI program. Chinese state-owned enterprises like Huawei, COSCO, and Hengtong are providing the infrastructure for the Digital Silk Road, driven by strategic impulses foreign to profit-oriented Western multinationals. Beijing's efforts are steadily linking China, beneath the increas-ingly dynamic Eurasian sea lanes, to Europe and the Middle East. At the same time, they are building "south-south" bridges to populous and growing parts of the developing world such as Africa, with which the West, and the United States in particular, has only limited postcolonial ties.

Future Prospects

The United States has enduring strengths in technology, energy, and food supply that ultimately could confer formidable long-term advantages over China and other potential rivals in the Eurasian sea lanes. There is consider-able doubt, however, as to whether the US government will respond to—or has even fully grasped—the issues at hand. These emerging issues have both political-military and economic dimensions.

Recent Chinese advances in fields such as artificial intelligence, 5G com-munications, robotics, and space-related activities—coupled with the United States' high levels of welfare spending and its two-decade-long preoccupation with conflicts in areas of peripheral strategic importance—have led to a "Davidson window" of US vulnerability and Chinese incentive to escalate military pressure against Taiwan (2021–2027). Gaps in US strategic-weapons procurement schedules, compounded by Chinese infrastructural and logistic strengths along the sea lanes outlined above, also could ignite dangerous US-China tensions in the Eurasian sea lanes east of Malacca.[14] Over the coming half-decade, China's military capabilities could well be increasing at rates faster than those of the United States, at least until its faces the intense new demographic pressures anticipated to arise during the late 2020s. Conversely, the US military will be retiring some of its most important current strategic assets—including *Ohio*-class SSBNs, B–1 and B–2 bombers, and *Ticonderoga*-class cruisers—before it can constitute a next-generation fleet and aerospace capabilities to meet the Chinese threat.[15]

It is in this context that the AUKUS project and related forms of federated defense among allies loom so large. China is both exerting its influence over and increasingly dependent on the Eurasian sea lanes, whereas Anglo-American strengths have long been—and continue to be—maritime, particularly beneath the sea.

Issues for Future Research

Previous chapters have suggested a deepening pattern of US-Chinese competition in the Eurasian sea lanes and adjacent rimlands, from the Arabian Peninsula to Southeast Asia and beyond. They also have revealed contrasting profiles of Chinese and US capabilities and weaknesses in dealing with the emerging political, economic, and miliary challenges along the Shanghai to Southampton seaways. Broadly speaking, China has a formidable and rising advantage in shipbuilding, port development, shipping, and development finance, as well as local military strength around its immediate periphery. The United States, by contrast, has a powerful blue-water navy, strategic basing locations, and advanced civilian and military technical capabilities on surface ships and beneath the sea. The pronounced asymmetries in Sino-American capabilities along the Eurasian sea lanes suggest numerous areas to explore in future policy research, including the following:

(1) *What implications do ambitious Chinese Maritime Silk Road policies in the Eurasian sea lanes, including port development and fiber-optic cable construction, have for international affairs?*

China's active maritime-infrastructure building program includes not just ports and related logistic facilities but also a massive network of undersea fiber-optic cables and landing stations. This network is connecting China with nations throughout the world, particularly with the Global South. Especially striking has been China's focus on developing fiber-optic communication ties with Asian and African nations that do not have extensive internet access, and on laterally connecting parts of the developing world that have lacked mutual communications access in the past. Both the PEACE Cable, connecting much of Africa and the Red Sea with China through Pakistan, and the Brazil-Cameroon undersea cable, constructed by Huawei between Africa and South America, are cases in point.

China's fiber-optic cable development programs beneath the seas appear to give Beijing newfound information autonomy from US-based communications systems, with potential defense applications. These projects also may give China preferential rights of information access in rimland developing nations that have underdeveloped digital infrastructure. Key examples of such countries include Myanmar, Eritrea, Ethiopia, and Sudan, all of which are newly dependent on Chinese cable systems.[16]

(2) *How might information societies in such rimland nations evolve, and what implications will this evolution have for Eurasian sea-lane geopolitics?*

Maritime Silk Road infrastructure initiatives are occurring at formative stages in the information-society development of such key developing nations as Pakistan, Myanmar, Saudi Arabia, and Ethiopia. Those initiatives also are deepening South-South information-sector ties among Africa, South Asia, and Latin America, and connecting them directly with China. Such emerging infrastructural ties bypass the traditional informatics hubs in the Western industrial world.

(3) *What is the nature of the new global regimes that Chinese maritime activism is now provoking into existence?*

One dimension of such new global regimes could be the development of alternate internet protocols that conform to Chinese standards, owing to their extensive use of Chinese cables and landing stations. A second could be the development of marine-resource extraction regimes. Expanded Chinese intelligence gathering is provoking more proactive regime-building efforts by Beijing. The rapid increases in Chinese port construction along the sea lanes, even as a revolution in port logistics technology generates large new efficiency gains for greenfield ports, are giving Beijing a de facto ability to set operational trade conditions in ports across the rimlands.

(4) *How might the United States offset rising Chinese capabilities in economic sectors with defense implications, such as shipping, shipbuilding, and port development? What role might "federated defense" and "coalitions of the willing" play in merging the capabilities of like-minded nations to counter this potential threat?*

The AUKUS agreement, capitalizing on the complementary capabilities and geographic location of the United States, Great Britain, and Australia, presents one paradigm of response. The March 2021 Quad summit collaborative effort to combat the COVID-19 pandemic provides a second, nonmilitary paradigm, which evolved productively in later years.[17] Other alternative applications, as well as options for improving implementation, deserve serious policy study.

(5) *What sort of new institutions will the United States, allied nations, and the world in general need to create as part of an optimal response to emerging challenges?*

As observed in Chapter 6, shipping, shipbuilding, and port development are areas in which US capabilities are notably weak in comparison with China, even as the related capabilities of its Japanese and Korean allies are particularly strong. What sort of institutions are needed to strengthen the defense-industrial base, and how might they be nurtured? Can cross-national borrowing, such as between the United States and Japan, be effective? Can effective institutions in one nation—the Japan Bank for International Cooperation (JBIC), for example—be harnessed to support development in another?

One emerging paradigm that deserves support and further elaboration is the US Defense Industrial Cooperation, Acquisition, and Sustainment Forum, inaugurated in June 2024. This initiative is designed precisely to mobilize US-Japan cooperation to invigorate the trans-Pacific defense-industrial base through codevelopment, coproduction, and cosustainment.[18] Initial steps include working groups to identify opportunities for sustaining forward-deployed US Navy ships and opportunities for missile co-production.

Such new forms of trans-Pacific cooperation, involving possible Northeast Asian investment in US shipyards or collaboration on dual military-civilian use technologies, may well be needed. The most effective and sensitive way to handle the politics of this transnational cooperation is an important subject for future policy research.

(6) *How should the United States and its Indo-Pacific allies most effectively gather intelligence to cope with the lengthening shadows of uncertainty along the Eurasian sea lanes?*

To formulate a concrete response, the United States and like-minded Indo-Pacific nations need to reorganize their public and private analytical capabilities to better understand the predictable elements and critical uncertainties that challenge regional stability. Demography and geographical location, for instance, are relatively predictable, whereas the future of the South China Sea as a whole is more nebulous. How might these tasks most effectively be accomplished?

Policy Implications and Recommendations

Chinese maritime construction programs in the ports and transportation systems of the world and in the underwater fiber-optic infrastructure have major global economic and national-security implications for the industrial democracies. Industrial-base support programs in areas ranging from shipbuilding and shipping to fiber-optic cable construction likewise demand a coherent response. It is not helpful to condemn such projects indiscriminately as "debt traps," especially as they often prove attractive—at least in the short run—to developing nations that may not share US security concerns.

Industrial democracies must respond directly to the expressed and unexpressed needs of the countries in question. They must come together and put up the financing to provide innovative and creative alternatives to China, or otherwise lose influence in key parts of the world. As the democracies vary in their comparative advantages, the aforementioned "federated security" approach, capitalizing on those differing strengths in a decentralized yet coordinated fashion, as federated government ideally does, has much to recommend it. In the maritime area, the sophisticated manufacturing capabilities of the United States' Northeast Asian allies in shipbuilding and electronics, for example, are synergistic with American strengths in software and systems integration, suggesting the rising potential importance of "friend-shoring."[19]

Countering the vast scale of China's building program, as well as Beijing's financial firepower, will require a coordinated, multilateral response from the United States and its allies. A few multilateral institutions such as the Asian Development Bank doubtless will play a significant role. The bulk of the Western response, however, will need to be mini-lateral, mobilizing groups of like-minded nations such as the G-7 and the Quad, as well as civil society.[20]

JBIC and the US International Development Finance Corporation (DFC) both play significant roles in linking private investment to support economic development in emerging Indo-Pacific economies, and also around the world. In 2019, the United States, Japan, and Australia announced the "Blue Dot Network" to help operationalize the G-20 commitments to quality infrastructure by bringing together government and civil society. In January 2021, JBIC and the DFC signed a memorandum of understanding to further deepen cooperation in such areas as infrastructure, energy, natural resource development, supply-chain resilience, and digital connectivity.[21] And in the summer of 2021, the United States and Japan combined with G-7 partners to launch the Build Back Better World Initiative.[22] Following the 2023 New Delhi G-20 summit, the innovative India–Middle East–Europe Economic Corridor (IMEC) infrastructure initiative, involving the United States, India, the European Union, and the GCC, was unveiled as well.[23]

Western democracies should respond to China's aggressive infrastructure investment push in Eurasia by supplying their own quality infrastructure at prices that the developing world along the sea lanes can afford.[24] Investment in the digital infrastructure area in particular will have an outsized impact on how the sectoral and geopolitical orientation of developing nations evolves over time. China's approach is to embed closed architecture, such as Beidou communications systems, that link developing nations mechanically to its own infrastructure, thereby narrowing their margin of self-reliance and compromising their integrity. In response, the G-7 democracies should make serious efforts to embed open technical architecture, such as connections to the Global Positioning System, that will connect the nations in question to an open-world system.

Even in the face of persistent geopolitical tensions and outright military conflict, Eurasia is steadily growing more integrated on both land and sea. The rising connectivity does tend to advantage China, as it is both centrally located within the continent and growing rapidly. China almost inevitably will have a prominent role across major swaths of the continent, precisely because of its scale and increasing economic sophistication. If China promotes stable growth, and if pluralism across the continent can be maintained, that role is not necessarily a bad thing. It does underline, however, the importance of maintaining pluralism, in which the traditionally cosmopolitan rimland sea lane nations play a vital role. It also emphasizes the importance of multilateral cooperation among allies to draw on differing but complementary strengths.

The active involvement of the United States and likeminded democratic nations—preeminently Japan, the second-largest capitalist economy in the world, will be a crucial prerequisite to maintaining such continental pluralism. Cooperation with Japan is especially vital for four reasons. First, among US partners in Asia, Japan has the largest economy and is the most technologically advanced. Second, Japan is situated in highly strategic geographic proximity to the Eurasian sea lanes. It commands geographic chokepoints controlling both Russian and Chinese access to the Pacific Ocean and the East China Sea, including the Soya, Tsugaru, and Miyako Straits. It also has high-quality maritime defense capabilities, including advanced diesel-electric submarines and mining/demining technology, to help control those chokepoints. Third, Japan is geographically and culturally detached from mainland Asia, and so it has more strategic autonomy than continental nations like Korea and stronger incentives to cooperate with the United States. Finally, Japan has complementary socioeconomic incentives and capabilities to those of the United States, as it is especially good at organization and quality control and has a long-term strategic orientation.

The United States and Japan can pool their respective strengths to counter Chinese advances along the sea lanes in five specific ways. First, they need to engage in more intensive and systematic contingency planning, including updating the 2015 US-Japan Defense Cooperation Guidelines and reviewing possibilities for collaborative development and interoperability of defense-related components and subassemblies. Second, they need to align their operational abilities to cooperate with respect to science and technology, including precompetitive research and development in dual-use areas such as cybersecurity and artificial intelligence.[25] Third, they should expand their cooperation in policy finance, competing with China in providing quality infrastructure for sectors where their products have comparative advantage, such as LNG and precision machinery.[26] Fourth, the United States and Japan should promote a new division of labor in industrial production, through such steps as more Japanese involvement on policy grounds in US shipbuilding, as well as related policy finance and training. Finally, both countries need to informally coordinate their public diplomacy more closely, capitalizing on comparative advantages that each ally has in third nations of common interest.

As the two largest free-market economies and most sophisticated technological powers in the Indo-Pacific—and also as strong bilateral allies—one might suppose that the United States and Japan would be natural partners in every dimension of a common federated defense. This supposition, however, might not necessarily be true. In some dimensions, their partnership is more potent for both sides through extended deterrence than through mechanical joint participation in all dimensions. An AUKUS partnership without Japan's direct initial involvement, for example, could be more credible in deterring Beijing than one involving Tokyo directly, owing to Japan's close proximity to China.[27] Similarly, a non-nuclear Japan under the umbrella of US extended deterrence likely would be more stabilizing than alternative defense configurations, as it would undercut the potential for future arms races and inhibit further proliferation.

Although US-Japan bilateral cooperation has a vital role in the Eurasian/Indo-Pacific sea lanes, a broader federated approach also should be central to future considerations. Trilateral cooperation among the United States, Japan, and Korea has a vital role, especially in defense-industrial cooperation, as in shipbuilding.[28] Eurasian transcontinental "AP-4" cooperation among NATO plus four likeminded Asia-Pacific democracies (Japan, Korea, Australia, and New Zealand) also may be appropriate, especially on digital issues with relaxed linkages to geography, such as cybersecurity.[29] For the United States and all likeminded parties concerned with preserving an open international maritime order, attention to coast guard development and other means of countering gray-zone tactics like arbitrary quarantines and blockades will be a continuing concern.

India and Australia have particular sway over specific subregions of Maritime Eurasia, especially in Southeast Asia and parts of the Indian Ocean, as they dominate important chokepoints around the Strait of Malacca. However, both have operational limitations that do not constrain the United States or Japan. India, most notably, has significant infrastructure deficiencies and a relatively weak manufacturing base compared to several other Asian democracies, except in the important pharmaceutical sector. It also historically has found intimate alliance-style cooperation difficult, as evidenced by its decision to rebuff G-7 energy and commodity sanctions on Russia over the war in Ukraine. Nonetheless, India has taken incremental steps to deepen mini-lateral defense cooperation with Quad members in such important areas as sonar monitoring around the Strait of Malacca.

Although Australia is much smaller than the other three, it has been an effective, loyal ally of the United States, capable of difficult and sensitive security roles, for more than a century. With Indian and Pacific Ocean coastlines, it is well-placed geographically for intense naval cooperation. Its distance from alliance partners actually can be an advantage in the Space Age, where the speed of advanced communications profoundly outpaces much slower naval mobility. Furthermore, it has advanced service and repair capabilities for accommodating US naval vessels, including strategic submarines. In the diplomatic sphere, Australia is deepening its support for a rule-based maritime order, especially in Melanesia, Indonesia, and the Pacific islands. Together with Japan, it can be an important partner in development assistance and humanitarian activities there, owing to a combination of geographical propinquity and funding capacity.[30] The 2021 AUKUS agreement, one of the most important recent developments in Indo-Pacific relations, capitalizes on the considerable underlying political-military strengths of Australia. Indeed, considering the strategic advantages that Australia's geographical location still provides in a world of increasingly advanced technology, AUKUS could facilitate a broader role for Australia in the military dimensions of response to the Eurasian sea-lane challenge.

In Conclusion

We have shown throughout these pages the enduring importance of geography across the Eurasian sea lanes, and the powerful ways in which high-speed economic growth in the most populous nations of the world have magnified this importance. China's Malacca Dilemma has deepened over the two decades since Hu Jintao first articulated it, and parallel concerns are shared in varying ways across the continent. Economic growth and the ensuing demand for commodities have given the Eurasian sea lanes, together with their chokepoints and rimlands, unprecedented significance for both Eurasia and the broader world.

For Northeast Asia, of course, one resolution to a Malacca Dilemma has long been alliance with the United States. That is the path that Japan and South Korea—both heavily dependent on the Persian Gulf for their total oil supply—have taken. There is no guarantee of that pattern persisting, but it has driven both countries' strategic thinking for more than six decades, and increasingly it has animated the United States' own Indo-Pacific strategy as well.

There is little question, as we have documented in previous work, that the role of China within the Eurasian continent is rising, at least on land and over the short run. Western analysts optimistically have assumed that even if such dynamics prevail on land, the seas will be an equalizer. They assume that American maritime dominance effectively offsets China's influence on land, and assures the autonomy of Maritime Eurasia's rimland states and the adjoining sea lanes.

The analysis in this volume suggests that the potential for equalization through the sea lanes—so important to Maritime Eurasia—is not a foregone conclusion, especially above the ocean surface. In some dimensions, such as Arctic transport and development, Chinese dominance continues to intensify through their cooperation with Russia. The undersea dimension, by contrast, is highly complex and dynamic, but it provides particular advantages to the United States and its allies, and the recent AUKUS agreement presciently capitalizes on these beneficial aspects.

In the end, the Eurasian sea lanes, especially those west of Malacca, provide a crucial opportunity for Western and Asian democracies to arrest Super Continent dynamics that point to rising Sino-Russian influence and deepening threats of instability in the Taiwan Strait, the South China Sea, and elsewhere along the Eurasian littoral. Exploiting that opportunity to reverse Sino-Russian advances, however, will require creativity and courage, as well as deepened involvement with able allies like Japan and in many cases Korea. It will involve multifaceted economic, humanitarian, and political-military efforts. Only a pluralistic Maritime Eurasia, after all, with a continuing US-Japan alliance at its core, can reliably assure real stability for the broader world.

Notes

PREFACE

1. Plato quoted Heraclitus as saying: "You could not step twice into the same river." See "Heraclitus," *Stanford Encyclopedia of Philosophy*, September 3, 2019, https://plato.stanford.edu/entries/heraclitus/.

2. Kent E. Calder, "Asia's Empty Tank," *Foreign Affairs* 75, no. 2 (March/April 1996): 55–68; and Kent E. Calder, *Pacific Defense: Arms, Energy, and America's Future in Asia* (New York: William Morrow, 1996).

3. Kent E. Calder, *The New Continentalism: Energy and Twenty-First Century Eurasian Geopolitics* (New Haven, CT: Yale University Press, 2012).

4. Xi Jinping, "President Xi Jinping Delivers Important Speech and Proposes to Build a Silk Road Economic Belt with Central Asian Countries," Ministry of Foreign Affairs of the People's Republic of China, September 7, 2013, https://www.mfa.gov.cn/mfa_eng/topics_665678/3755_666062/2013zt/xjpfwzysiesgjtfhshzzfh_665686/201309/t20130913_707056.html; and Xi Jinping, "President Xi Gives Speech to Indonesia's Parliament," *China Daily*, October 2, 2013, http://www.chinadaily.com.cn/china/2013xiapec/2013=10/02/content_17007915.htm.

5. Kent E. Calder, *Super Continent: The Logic of Eurasian Integration* (Stanford, CA: Stanford University Press, 2019).

6. See, for example, Calder, *Super Continent*, 133.

INTRODUCTION

1. On details and sources, see Kent E. Calder, *Super Continent: The Logic of Eurasian Integration* (Stanford, CA: Stanford University Press, 2019), 7–8. The term "Eurasia," as we shall see, is also more central in classical geopolitical literature than "Indo-Pacific," allowing us to draw on those classics as well.

2. Halford John Mackinder, "The Geographical Pivot Point of History," *Geographical Journal* 23, no. 4 (2004): 421–37.

3. Alfred Thayer Mahan, *The Problem of Asia: Its Effect upon International Politics* (Boston: Little, Brown, 1900), 98.

4. Mahan, *The Problem of Asia*, 22–25.

5. Christian W. Spang, "Karl Haushofer Re-Examined," in *Japanese-German Relations, 1895–1945: War, Diplomacy, and Public Opinion*, edited by Christian W. Spang and Rolf-Harald Wippich (London: Routledge, 2006).

6. See Risaburo Asano, *Nichidokuso tairiku burokku ron: Sono chiseigakuteki kosatsu* [On the Japanese-German-Soviet continental bloc: Geopolitical observations] (Tokyo: Tokaido, 1941), 297. For a modern assessment, see Mark R. Peattie, *Ishiwara Kanji and Japan's Confrontation with the West* (Princeton, NJ: Princeton University Press, 1975).

7. See, for example, Sergey Karaganov, "The Promise of Eurasia," *Publikatsii*, October 26, 2015, http://www.karaganov.ru/publications/preview/378. Karaganov, director of the Council on Foreign and Defense Policy in Moscow, has served as a presidential advisor to Vladimir Putin. On the emergence of Russian geopolitical thinking in the Mackinder tradition, see William C. Wohlforth, "Heartland Dreams: Russian Geopolitics and Foreign Policy," in *Perspectives on the Russian State in Transition*, edited by Wolfgang Danspeckgruber (Princeton, NJ: Liechtenstein Institute on Self-Determination, 2006), 266.

8. For Spykman, beyond the coastland regions (the rimland) lay an "outer crescent" of offshore islands and continents, including Britain and Japan, that also were of some strategic significance. See Nicholas John Spykman, *The Geography of the Peace* (New York: Harcourt, Brace, and Co., 1944), 37–38.

9. Spykman, *Geography of the Peace*, 41. Supportive of Spykman's analysis, post–World War II regional conflicts have occurred in Korea, Vietnam, and Iraq/Syria.

10. Zbigniew Brzezinski, *The Grand Chessboard: American Primacy and Its Geostrategic Imperatives* (New York: Basic Books, 1997).

11. On hegemonic-stability theory and systems transformation, see, for example, A. F. K. Organski, *World Politics* (New York: Knopf, 1958); Charles P. Kindleberger, *The World in Depression, 1929–1939* (Berkeley: University of California Press, 1973); Charles F. Doran, "Modes, Mechanisms, and Turning Points: Perspectives on the Transformation of the International System," *International Political Science Review* 1, no. 1 (1980): 35–61; Robert Gilpin, *The Political Economy of International Relations* (Princeton, NJ: Princeton University Press, 1987); Michael C. Webb and Stephen D. Krasner, "Hegemonic Stability Theory: An Empirical Assessment," *Review of International Studies* 15, no. 2 (April 1989): 183–98; Andrew Walter, "The United States and Western Europe: The Theory of Hegemonic Stability," in *Explaining International Relations Since 1945*, edited by Ngaire Woods (Oxford, UK: Oxford University Press, 1996), 126–54; G. John Ikenberry, *After Victory: Institutions, Strategic Restraint, and the Rebuilding of Order After Major Wars* (Princeton, NJ: Princeton University Press, 2000); and Robert O. Keohane, *After Hegemony* (Princeton, NJ: Princeton University Press, 2005).

12. See, for example, Edward Gibbon, *The Decline and Fall of the Roman Empire*, 6 vols. (New York: Alfred A. Knopf, 1993); and Paul Kennedy, *The Rise and Fall of Great Powers: Economic Change and Military Conflict from 1500 to 2000* (New York: Random House, 1987).

13. Robert Gilpin, *War and Change in International Politics* (Cambridge, UK: Cambridge University Press, 1981).

14. Robert O. Keohane, *After Hegemony: Cooperation and Discord in the World Political Economy* (Princeton, NJ: Princeton University Press, 1984), 9. Keohane also notes that

institutions, broadly defined, can significantly affect the actual patterns—not just the possibility— of cooperation.

15. Charles P. Kindleberger, *The World in Depression, 1929–1939* (Berkeley: University of California Press, 1973).

16. See Graham Allison, *Destined for War: Can America and China Escape Thucydides's Trap?* (Boston: Houghton Mifflin Harcourt, 2017).

17. See, for example, Melvyn P. Leffler, *Safeguarding Democratic Capitalism: U.S. Foreign Policy and National Security, 1920–2015* (Princeton, NJ: Princeton University Press, 2017); Odd Arne Westad, *The Cold War: A World History* (New York: Basic Books, 2017); as well as Campbell Craig and Frederik Logevall, *America's Cold War: The Politics of Insecurity*, 2nd ed. (Cambridge, MA: Harvard University Press, 2020).

18. Leffler, *Safeguarding Democratic Capitalism,* 15.

19. The US share of global population declined from 4.6 percent in 2000 to 4.2 percent in 2020, while its share of global GDP in purchasing power parity (PPP) terms declined from 20.3 percent to 15.8 percent over the same period. See World Bank, "Population, Total," Total https://data.worldbank.org/indicator/SP.POP.TOTL; and International Monetary Fund, "GDP Based on PPP, Share Of World," https://www.imf.org/external/datamapper/PPPSH@WEO/OEMDC/ADVEC/WEOWORLD.

20. Brzezinski, *Grand Chessboard,* 31.

21. President of Russia, "Joint Statement of the Russian Federation and the People's Republic of China on the International Relations Entering a New Era and the Global Sustainable Development," February 4, 2022, https://en.kremlin.ru/supplement/5770.

22. Calder, *New Continentalism*; and Calder, *Super Continent.*

23. Julian S. Corbett, *Some Principles of Maritime Strategy: A Theory of War on the High Seas; Naval Warfare and the Command of Fleets* (Middletown, DE: Adasonia Press, 2018), 16.

24. Mahan, *Problem of Asia,* 1–45.

25. John J. Mearsheimer, *The Tragedy of Great Power Politics* (New York: W.W. Norton, 2001), 87–96.

26. Spykman, *Geography of the Peace,* 41.

27. Mearsheimer, for example, regards the oceans only as moats, and therefore only obstacles to land-based developments. See Mearsheimer, *Tragedy of Great Power Politics,* 87–88.

28. International Energy Agency (IEA), *Global EV Outlook 2023,* April 2023, https://www.iea.org/reports/global-ev-outlook-2023.

29. "Total Population by Country, 2024," *World Population Review,* https://world populationreview.com/countries; and Energy Institute, *Statistical Review of World Energy* (2024). The other top energy consumers, apart from the US, are China, India, Russia, Japan, and Canada.

30. Mahan, *Problem of Asia,* 75.

31. On the economic significance of transactional profiles, see Oliver E. Williamson, *The Economic Institutions of Capitalism* (New York: The Free Press, 1985), especially 15–42.

32. Trefor Moss, "Coronavirus Has Been a Boom for China's Railways," *Wall Street Journal,* May 13, 2020, https://www.wsj.com/articles/coronavirus-has-been-a-boon-for-chinas-railways-11589364002.

33. See Freightos, "Freightos Baltic Index (FBX): Global Container Pricing Index," accessed June 24, 2024, https://terminal.freightos.com/freightos-baltic-index-global-container-pricing-index/.

34. On the details, see Marc Levinson, *The Box: How the Shipping Container Made the World Smaller and the World Economy Bigger* (Princeton, NJ: Princeton University Press, 2006); Edna Bonacich and Jake B. Wilson, *Getting the Goods: Ports, Labor, and the Logistics Revolution* (Ithaca, NY: Cornell University Press, 2008), 14–15; and Calder, *Super Continent*, 84–93.

35. See Moss, "Coronavirus Has Been a Boom for China's Railways."

36. On the optimal scale of commodity transport and the impact of recent changes in transport economics, see Jean-Paul Rodrigue, *The Geography of Transport Systems*, 5th ed. (London: Routledge, 2020).

37. For details, see Kent Calder and Min-Jung Paik, "Quiet Crisis Beneath the Waves: Fiber-Optic Cables, Internet Revolution, and International Order," *Korean Journal of Defense Analysis* 36, no. 1 (March 2024), 103–20.

38. Bonacich and Wilson, *Getting the Goods*, 3–22.

39. Calder and Paik, "Fiber-Optic Cables, Internet Revolution, and International Order."

40. During 2022–2024 alone, for example, cables cut offshore Matsu Island in the Taiwan Strait by Chinese fishing vessels; potential Russian sabotage of Baltic cables; and Houthi sabotage of Red Sea cables linking Europe and the Middle East, surreptitiously cut by Houthi forces in Yemen, were all in the headlines. See Huizhong Wu and Johnson Lai, "Taiwan Suspects Chinese Ships Cut Islands' Internet Cables," Associated Press, April 18, 2023, https://apnews.com/article/matsu-taiwan-internet-cables-cut-china-65f10f5f73a346fa788 436366d7a7c70, and Jon Gambrell, "3 Red Sea Data Cables Cut as Houthis Launch More Attacks in the Vital Waterway," Associated Press, March 4, 2024, https://apnews.com/article/red-sea-undersea-cables-yemen-houthi-rebels-attacksb53051f61a41bd6b357860bbf0b0860a.

41. On the details of Spykman's view, see Nicholas J. Spykman, *America's Strategy in World Politics: The United States and the Balance of Power* (New York: Harcourt Brace and Co., 1942); and Spykman, *Geography of the Peace*.

42. A third, the *Fujian*, was christened in June 2022 but will not be operational until 2025–2026. See Brad Lendon, "China's Newest Aircraft Carrier Heads to Sea for First Time," CNN World, May 1, 2024, https://www.cnn.com/2024/05/01/china/china-navy-newsts-aircraft-carrier-fujian-sea-trial-intl-hnk-ml/index.html.

43. The PLA-N and the Russian navy, for example, jointly circumnavigated Japan in November 2021, and are cooperating more intensively in the sphere of military technology. See "China, Russia Ships Needle through Japan's Southern Checkpoint," *Nikkei Asia*, October 24, 2021, https://asia.nikkei.com/Politics/International-relations/China-Russia-ships-needle-through-Japan-s-southern-chokepoint; and Samuel Bendett and Elsa Kania, "The Resilience of Sino-Russian High-Tech Cooperation," *War on the Rocks*, August 12, 2020, https://warontherocks.com/2020/08/the-resilience-of-sino-russian-high-tech-cooperation/.

44. On the details, see Kent E. Calder, *Embattled Garrisons: Comparative Base Politics and American Globalism* (Princeton, NJ: Princeton University Press, 2007); as well as US Department of Defense, *Worldwide Manpower Distribution by Geographical Area* (Washington, DC: US Government Printing Office, annual); and US Department of Defense, *Base Structure Report* (Washington, DC: US Government Printing Office, annual).

45. The USS *George Washington* replaces the USS *Ronald Reagan*, which left in May 2024 after being homeported there since 2015.

46. The US Navy currently has in service fourteen *Ohio*-class SSBNs and four SSGNs. Each *Ohio*-class boat displaces 18,750 tons submerged; these boats are the largest submarines ever built for the US Navy. The *Ohio* class gradually will be replaced by the *Columbia*-class

SSBNs becoming operational in 2031. *Virginia*-class fast-attack submarines, which have the latest stealth, intelligence gathering, and weapons systems technology, are designed to seek and destroy enemy submarines and surface ships; project power ashore with Tomahawk cruise missiles and special operation forces; conduct intelligence, surveillance and reconnaissance missions; support battle-group operations; and engage in mine warfare. For details, see Vice Admiral Daryl Caudle, *Sustaining the Submarine Force's Competitive Edge* (Annapolis, MD: US Naval Institute, October 2020), https://www.usni.org/magazines/proceedings/2020/october/sustaining-submarine-forces-competitive-edge.

47. The US *Ohio*-class submarines, for example, reportedly carry up to fifty-four cruise missiles each—26 percent more than America's best-armed surface ship. See "Gunboat, Diplomacy," *The Economist*, January 13, 2024, 49.

48. AUKUS is a trilateral security pact among Australia, the United Kingdom, and the United States, announced on September 15, 2021 for the Indo-Pacific region. Under the pact, the United States and the United Kingdom will help Australia to acquire nuclear-powered submarines. This agreement also includes cooperation on cyber capabilities, artificial intelligence, quantum technologies, and additional undersea capabilities. Under the pact, Australia also will acquire new long-range strike capabilities for its air force, navy, and army. See Prime Minister of Australia, "Joint Leaders Statement on AUKUS," March 14, 2023, https://www.pm.gov.au/media/joint-leaders-statement-aukus.

49. In 2023 the defense budgets of China, Saudi Arabia, India, the United Kingdom, France, Germany, Russia, Japan, South Korea, and Ukraine came to $757 billion, while the US defense budget totaled over $929 billion. See International Institute for Strategic Studies, *The Military Balance*, 2024 ed. (London: Routledge, 2024), 542–44.

50. Half of all US Navy vessels, for example, are now more than twenty years old. See Heritage Foundation, 2023 *Index of U.S. Military Strength*, 2023, https://www.heritage.org/sites/default/files/2022-10/2023_IndexOfUSMilitaryStrength.pdf.

51. Energy Institute, *Statistical Review of World Energy* 2024, https://www.energyinst.org.

52. Japanese, South Korean, and Chinese customs-clearance figures for 2023. Actual Gulf imports are likely higher than official data, especially for China, due to unrecorded imports from Iran. These figures are derived from customs data for the three countries, as follows: (a) China: People's Republic of China General Administration of Customs, at http://stats.customs.gov.cn/indexEN; (b) South Korea: Republic of Korea Customs Service, at https://tradedata.go.kr/cts/index_eng.do; and (c) Japan: Ministry of Finance, at https://www.customs.go.jp/toukei/srch/indexe.htm.

53. Energy Institute, *Statistical Review of World Energy 2024*.

54. Andrew Hayley and Chen Aizhu, "China's 2023 Crude Oil Imports Hit Record as Fuel Demand Recovers," Reuters, January 11, 2024, https://www.reuters.com/business/energy/chinas-2023-crude-oil-imports-hit-record-fuel-demand-recovers-2024-01-12/.

55. IEA, "Data and Statistics," https://www.iea.org.

56. Cyril Ip, "About Half of China's 6,000 Citizens in Ukraine Evacuated as Safety Concerns Grow," *South China Morning Post*, March 3, 2022, https://www.scmp.com/news/china/diplomacy/article/3169135/about-half-chinas-6000-citizens-ukraine-evacuated-safety.

57. Xi Jinping has been personally stressing the importance of these issues in recent years. See, for example, Liu Zhen, "Xi Jinping Orders China's Military to Be Ready for War 'At Any Second,' " *South China Morning Post*, January 5, 2021, https://www.scmp.com/news/china/military/article/3116436/xi-jinping-orders-chinas-military-be-ready-war-

any-second. For a more recent statement from the 20th Party Congress, see Yew Lun Tian and Ben Blanchard, "China Will Never Renounce Right to Use Force over Taiwan, Xi Says," Reuters, October 16, 2022, https://www.reuters.com/world/china/xi-china-will-never-renounce-right-use-force-over-taiwan-2022-10-16/.

58. "Dual circulation" has been defined in the initial Chinese academic study on the topic, at Nanjing University, as "the domestic consumption-driven economic rebalancing to achieve sustainable economic development." See Hung Tran, "Decoupling/Reshoring versus Dual Circulation: Competing Strategies for Security and Influence," Issue Brief, Geoeconomics Center, Atlantic Council, April 2021, https://www.atlanticcouncil.org/in-depth-research-reports/issue-brief/decoupling-reshoring-versus-dual-circulation-competing-strategies-for-security-and-influences/.

59. Thomas C. Schelling, *The Strategy of Conflict* (Cambridge, MA: Harvard University Press, 1960), 21–52.

CHAPTER 1

1. Nicholas J. Spykman, *The Geography of the Peace* (New York: Harcourt, Brace, 1944), 41.

2. On the sociopolitical meaning of place, see Harm de Blij, *The Power of Place: Geography, Destiny, and Globalization's Rough Landscape* (New York: Oxford University Press, 2009).

3. In total surface area, the Pacific Ocean covers 44.7 percent of global bodies of water; the Atlantic Ocean 23.5 percent; the Indian Ocean 19.5 percent; the Southern Ocean 6.1 percent; the Arctic Ocean 4.3 percent; and the South China Sea 1.9 percent. See B. W. Eakins and G. F. Sharman, *Volumes of the World's Oceans from ETOPO1* (Boulder, CO: NOAA National Geophysical Data Center, 2010), https://www.ngdc.noaa.gov/mgg/global/etopo1_ocean_volumes.html.

4. The All Red Line was a globe-spanning British telegraph network constructed entirely on British imperial territory, created to link the British Empire together. It was referred to as "red" owing to the traditional practice of coloring British possessions red on maps.

5. White House Indo-Pacific coordinator Kurt Campbell, for example, personally visited the Solomon Islands in April 2022 to dissuade local leaders from allowing China to establish an in-country naval base. See Stephen Wright, "At Start of Pacific Tour, Senior American Official Underscores Solomon Islands-China Concerns," *Benar News*, March 18, 2023, https://www.benarnews.org/english/news/pacific/kurt-campbell-pacific-tour-03182023230538.html.

6. Literally, Australia, New Zealand, and the United States, bound by the ANZUS security treaty of 1951.

7. The island of New Guinea is divided politically into West Irian, the Indonesian-ruled western part of New Guinea; and Papua New Guinea to the east—formerly an Australian trust territory, and now an independent nation.

8. Fiji is the only Melanesian country with a significant population of ethnic Indians. Between 1879 and 1916, the British brought 60,000 Indians to Fiji to work in the local sugarcane fields. Today, their descendants make up around 32 percent of Fiji's population. See Grant Wyeth, "Indo-Fijians and Fiji's Coup Culture," *The Diplomat*, March 28, 2017, https://thediplomat.com/2017/03/indo-fijians-and-fijis-coup-culture/.

9. See, for example, White House "Readout of Senior Administration Official Travel to the Indo-Pacific Region," March 28, 2023, https://www.whitehouse.gov/briefing-room/statements-releases/2023/03/28/readout-of-senior-administration-official-travel-to-the-indo-pacific-region/.

10. Michael J. Green, *By More than Providence: Grand Strategy and American Power in the Asia Pacific since 1783* (New York: Columbia University Press, 2017).

11. John Foster Dulles, "Security in the Pacific," *Foreign Affairs* 30, no. 2 (January 1952), https://www.foreignaffairs.com/articles/united-states/1952-01-01/security-pacific; and Andrew Erickson and Joel Wuthow, "Barriers, Springboards, and Benchmarks: China Conceptualizes the Pacific 'Island Chains,'" *China Quarterly* 225 (January 2016): 1–22, doi:10.1017/S0305741016000011. See also Andrew S. Erickson and Joel Wuthnow, "Why Islands Still Matter in Asia: The Enduring Significance of the Pacific 'Island Chains,'" *The National Interest*, February 5, 2016. Dulles also mentioned island chains in his farewell address to Congress in 1951.

12. On these Chinese fears, see Toshi Yoshihara, "China's Vision of Its Seascape: The First Island Chain and Chinese Sea Power," *Asian Politics and Policy* 4, no. 3 (2012), 293–314.

13. For an authoritative scholarly estimate, see Rana Mitter, *China's War with Japan, 1937–1945: The Struggle for Survival* (London: Allen Lane, 2013); and R. J. Rummel, "Statistics of Japanese Democide: Estimates, Calculations, and Sources," *Statistics of Democide*, https://www.hawaii.edu/powerkills/SOD.CHAP3.HTM.

14. In 2010, for example, tensions escalated markedly following Japanese nationalization of several of the disputed Senkaku (Diaoyutai) islands, with the Japanese Coast Guard detaining at length a Chinese trawler captain. As a result, Chinese maritime activity increased considerably, and China suspended talks with Japan on joint exploration of gas and oil resources in the East China Sea. In November, 2013, China also declared an Air Defense Identification Zone (ADIZ) over most of the East China Sea, although other national governments in the area did not recognize that ADIZ. Since then, China continuously has intruded into the territorial airspace of its neighbors, including Japan and Taiwan, in unprecedented numbers. See Japanese Ministry of Defense, *Defense of Japan 2023* (2023), 4–5 (digest version), https://www.mod.go.jp/en/publ/w_paper/wp2023/DOJ2023_Digest_EN.pdf; and Keoni Everington, "China's September Incursions into Taiwan ADIZ Up by 42% from August," *Taiwan News*, October 2, 2023, https://www.taiwannews.com.tw/news/5011824.

15. Ma Zhiping, "Miracle Campaign: The Liberation of Hainan Island," *China Daily*, March 17, 2021, http://www.chinadaily.com.cn/a/202103/17/WS6051a949a31024ad0baafc70_2.html.

16. Roughly one-quarter of US-China trade, for example, flows through the Osumi Strait, a narrow passage from the East China Sea into the Pacific, just south of Kyushu. This passage, which offers the most direct access to the Great Circle Route across the Pacific from China to the United States, cuts transit distances across the Pacific by more than 1,000 kilometers. See Toshi Yoshihara and James R. Holmes, *Red Star Over the Pacific: China's Rise and the Challenge to U.S. Maritime Strategy*, 2nd ed. (Annapolis, MD: Naval Institute Press, 2018), 88–89.

17. See Robert D. Kaplan, *Asia's Cauldron: The South China Sea and the End of a Stable Pacific* (New York: Random House, 2014), 32–50.

18. More than 64 percent of Chinese maritime trade, including almost 80 percent of oil imports, for example, transits the South China Sea, compared with 42 percent for Japan and only 14 percent for the United States. These figures are based on International Monetary Fund (IMF) data, drawn from the Center for Strategic and International Studies (CSIS) China Power Project, "How Much Trade Transits the South China Sea?," CSIS, January 25, 2021, https://chinapower.csis.org/much-trade-transits-south-china-sea.

19. Zhanjiang, in Kwangsi Province, is the home port of China's Southern Fleet. China's most advanced submarines are homeported at Yulin in Hainan, which also houses extensive intelligence and communication facilities. See Kaplan, *Asia's Cauldron*, 43. Also Stavridis, *Sea Power*, 170. Half of the world's liquefied natural gas (LNG) and roughly a third of the world's seaborne crude oil also pass through the South China Sea.

20. In 2016, 64 percent of China's own maritime trade, including almost 80 percent of its oil imports, transited the South China Sea. Nearly 42 percent of Japan's trade, including 90 percent of its oil imports, passed that way as well as well.

21. See CSIS China Power Project, "How Much Trade Transits the South China Sea?"

22. IMF, *Direction of Trade Statistics* (Washington, DC: IMF, 2024) 49, https://data.imf.org/?sk=85b51b5a-b74f-473a-be16-49f1786949b3.

23. Kaplan, *Asia's Cauldron*.

24. The prerevolutionary Nationalist Chinese regime also asserted an eleven-dash line claim in 1947. Two dashes in the Gulf of Tonkin were removed in 1953 by agreement with Vietnam, making nine. This convention continued until August 2023, when an additional dash was added to reiterate Taiwan-related claims. See David Shambaugh, *Where the Great Powers Meet: America and China in Southeast Asia* (New York: Oxford University Press, 2021), 152; and Colin Clark, "New Chinese 10-Dash Map Sparks Furor across Indo-Pacific: Vietnam, India, Philippines, Malaysia," *Breaking Defense Indo-Pacific*, September 1, 2023, https://www.breakingdefense.com/2023/09/new-chinese-10-dash-map-sparks-furor-across-indo-pacific-vietnam-india-philippines/Malaysia/.

25. Kaplan, *Asia's Cauldron*, 42.

26. Thomas Shugart, "China's Artificial Islands Are Bigger (and a Bigger Deal) Than You Think," *War on the Rocks*, September 21, 2016, https://warontherocks.com/2016/09/chinas-artificial-islands-are-bigger-and-a-bigger-deal-than-you-think/; see also the CSIS Asia Maritime Transparency Initiative's China Island Tracker at https://amti.csis.org/island-tracker/china/.

27. Michael Dahm, "Undersea Fiber-Optic Cable and Satellite Communications," Johns Hopkins University Applied Physics Laboratory, December 2022, 2, https://www.jhuapl.edu/sites/default/files/2022-12/UnderseaFiber-OpticCableandSATCOM.pdf.

28. "Exploring China's Unmanned Ocean Network," CSIS Asia Maritime Transparency Initiative, June 16, 2020, https://amti.csis.org/exploring-chinas-unmanned-ocean-network/.

29. Hillary Rodham Clinton, "Remarks at Press Availability," National Convention Center, Hanoi, Vietnam, July 23, 2010, https://2009-2017.state.gov/secretary/20092013clinton/rm/2010/07/145095.htm.

30. The Philippines initiated the arbitration under the dispute settlement procedures of Annex VII to the 1982 United Nations Convention on the Law of the Sea. See Robert D. Williams, "Tribunal Issues Landmark Ruling in South China Sea Arbitration," *Lawfare* (blog), July 12, 2016, https://www.lawfaremedia.org/article/tribunal-issues-landmark-ruling-south-china-sea-arbitration. For the ruling, see "The South China Sea Arbitration (The Republic of Philippines v. The People's Republic of China)," Permanent Court of Arbitration, July 12, 2016, https://pca-cpa.org/en/cases/7/.

31. China has been expanding its undersea observation system in the South China Sea since around 2010. See David Hambling, "China's Quantum Submarine Detector Could Seal South China Sea," *New Scientist*, August 22, 2017, https://www.newscientist.com/article/2144721-chinas-quantum-submarine-detector-could-seal-south-china-sea/; and Lyle J.

Goldstein, "China Is Building an 'Undersea Great Wall' to Take on America in a War," *The National Interest*, October 27, 2019, https://nationalinterest.org/blog/buzz/china-building-undersea-great-wall-take-america-war-90601

32. "Exploring China's Unmanned Ocean Network." The goals for the Blue Ocean Information network are as expressed by the China Electronics Technology Group Corporation (CETC), which has been doing the network's strategic planning.

33. Around $124 billion of British trade flows through the South China Sea, making up 11.8 percent of all Britain's trade in goods; for France the comparable figures are $83.5 billion (7.77 percent of national trade); for Japan $240 billion (19.1 percent of national trade); and for China $208 billion (39.5 percent of national trade). See CSIS China Power Project, "How Much Trade Transits the South China Sea?"

34. The South China Sea covers around 3.5 million square kilometers, as opposed to 1.249 million for the East China Sea.

35. Exact figures are difficult to calculate, since they depend in part on one's definition of "vessel." According to *Sea Trade Maritime News*, there were an average of 231 vessel reports daily in 2017 transiting the Strait of Malacca, with a "vessel" defined as having a displacement of over 300 gross tons. Thousands of smaller vessels also passed through the Strait. See Marcus Hand, "Malacca Straits VLCC Traffic Doubles in a Decade as Shipping Traffic Hits All-Time High in 2017," *Sea Trade Maritime News*, February 19, 2018, https://www.seatrade-maritime.com/asia/exclusive-malacca-straits-vlcc-traffic-doubles-decade-shipping-traffic-hits-all-time-high-2017.

36. In 2016, 26 percent of the world's maritime oil trade passed through the Strait of Malacca. See US Energy Information Administration (EIA), "World Oil Transit Chokepoints," accessed September 28, 2024, https://www.eia.gov/international/analysis/special-topics/World_Oil_Transit_Chokepoints. This rose to 30 percent, in EIA calculations, by 2023.

37. EIA, "Almost 40% of Global Liquefied Natural Gas Trade Moves through the South China Sea," November 2, 2017, https://www.eia.gov/todayinenergy/detail.php?id=33592.

38. See Spencer Feingold and Andrea Willige, "These Are the World's Most Vital Waterways for Global Trade," World Economic Forum, February 15, 2024, https://www.weforum.org/agenda/2024/02/worlds-busiest-ocean-shipping-routes-trade/.

39. Fisher is quoted in Arthur Marder, *The Anatomy of British Sea Power: A History of British Naval Policy in the Pre-Dreadnought Era, 1880–1905* (Hamden, CT: Archon Books, 1964), 473.

40. Daniel Yergin, *The Prize: The Epic Quest for Oil, Money, and Power* (New York: Simon and Schuster, 1991), 305–27.

41. Kent E. Calder, *Singapore: Smart City, Smart State* (Washington, DC: Brookings Institution Press, 2016), 98–101. The expression "poisonous shrimp" describes Singapore's defense posture, intended to allow it to coexist with much larger powers without being "eaten."

42. On the connection, see Kalyan Parbat, "PM Modi to Inaugurate Chennai-Andaman and Nicobar Submarine Cable Project on Monday," *The Economic Times*, August 7, 2020, https://economictimes.indiatimes.com/industry/telecom/telecom-news/pm-modi-to-inaugurate-chennai-andaman-nicobar-submarine-cable-project-on-monday/articleshow/77415072.cms?from=mdr.

43. Jeff Smith, "Andaman and Nicobar Islands: India's Strategic Outpost," *The Diplomat*, March 2014, https://thediplomat.com/2014/03/andaman-and-nicobar-islands-indias-strategic-outpost/.

44. The Azad Hind was a short-lived Japanese supported provisional government of India, established in Japanese-occupied Singapore on October 21, 1943. It proclaimed authority over Indian civilian and military personnel in Southeast Asian British colonial territory and prospective authority over Indian territory as it fell to the Japanese and their Indian National Army allies.

45. Smith, "Andaman and Nicobar Islands."

46. See Australian Government Department of Foreign Affairs and Trade, "India: Country and Trade Information," accessed June 9, 2024, https://www.dfat.gov.au/geo/india.

47. "India Bids to Rule the Waves: From the Bay of Bengal to the Malacca Strait," *Japan Focus*, July 16, 2012, https://apjjf.org/-Ramtanu-Maitra/1610.

48. See Harsh V. Pant, "China's Naval Expansion in the Indian Ocean and India-China Rivalry," *Asia-Pacific Journal* 8, no. 18 (May 3, 2010), https://apjjf.org/harsh-v-pant/3353/article.

49. "India, Australia Could Sign Pact For a Military Base in Andaman's and Cocos Islands," *Eurasian Times*, May 23, 2020, https://www.eurasiantimes.com/india-australia-could-sign-pact-for-a-military-base-in-andamans-and-cocos-islands-experts/.

50. See Pradeep Chahan, "India and Japan—A Yen for Closer Maritime Engagement," Center for International Maritime Security, November 7, 2017, https://cimsec.org/india-japan-yen-closer-maritime-engagement/; and Levina, "Indian Submarine Surveillance Network Ready to Catch Chinese Submarines, Japan and America Are Partners," *Resonant News,* July 3, 2020, https://resonantnews.com/2020/07/03/indian-submarine-surveillance-network-ready-to-catch-chinese-submarines-japan-and-america-are-partners/.

51. Rajat Pandit, "Amid LAC Faceoff, US Military Aircraft Refuels at Port Blair," *Times of India*, October 3, 2020, https://timesofindia.indiatimes.com/india/amid-lac-faceoff-us-military-aircraft-refuels-at-port-blair/articleshow/78455745.cms.

52. "China and Myanmar to Proceed with $7.3 Billion Deep-Sea Port Project," *Marine Insight*, January 2, 2024, https://www.marineinsight.com/shipping-news/china-and-myanmar-to-proceed-with-7-3-billion-deep-sea-port-project/.

53. Sunil S. Amrith, *Crossing the Bay of Bengal: The Furies of Nature and the Fortunes of Migrants* (Cambridge, MA: Harvard University Press, 2013), 9.

54. Bangladesh's capital of Dacca, at the head of the bay, is, for example, only 700 air miles from Kunming, less than 1,500 miles from Guangzhou, and under 2,000 miles from Shanghai.

55. Amrith, *Crossing the Bay of Bengal*, 10.

56. Amrith, *Crossing the Bay of Bengal*, 11.

57. Vedika Sud and Prema Rajaram, "Cyclone Amphan Caused an Estimated $13.2 Billion in Damage in India's West Bengal: Government Source," CNN, May 22, 2020, https://www.cnn.com/2020/05/22/weather/cyclone-amphan-damage-intl-hnk/index.html.

58. "Sri Lanka Civil War: Rajapaksa Says Thousands Missing Are Dead," BBC, January 20, 2020, https://www.bbc.com/news/world-asia-51184085.

59. See "Sri Lanka Attacks: What We Know About the Easter Bombings," BBC, April 8, 2019, https://www.bbc.com/news/world-asia-48010697.

60. On the geopolitics of the Bay of Bengal, see Kent E. Calder, *The Bay of Bengal: Political-Economic Transition and Strategic Implications* (Tokyo: Sasakawa Peace Foundation, 2018).

61. Robert D. Kaplan, *Monsoon: The Indian Ocean and the Future of American Power* (New York: Random House, 2010), 15.

62. Stavridis, *Sea Power*, 94.

63. Stavridis, *Sea Power*, 93. Geography and the complex interplay of geopolitics and economics have contributed to this result.

64. Under Zheng He, as is well known, the Chinese fleet conducted several different ocean expeditionary trips. These continued from 1405 to 1433, spanning areas from the east coast of Africa to Southeast Asia and India, traversing the Strait of Malacca, the Persian Gulf, and the Indian Ocean, with both commercial and diplomatic objectives. See Tansen Sen, "The Impact of Zheng He's Expeditions on Indian Ocean Interactions," *Bulletin of the School of Oriental and African Studies* 79, no. 3 (October 2016): 610–11.

65. Magellan's fleet left Spain in 1519 with five ships. Magellan himself was killed in the Philippines during 1521, but one of his initial fleet of five did return to Spain successfully in 1522. "Ferdinand Magellan," Oxford Reference, accessed March 2021, https://www.oxfordreference.com/view/10.1093/oi/authority.20110803100125489.

66. On the geophysics of the annual monsoons, see "Monsoon," *National Geographic*, accessed May 3, 2024, https://www.nationalgeographic.org/encyclopedia/monsoon/; and T. N. Krishnamurti, "Indian Monsoon," *Encyclopedia Britannica*, accessed May 3, 2024, https://www.britannica.com/science/indian-monsoon#ref284694.

67. Mathew Koll Roxy et al., "The Curious Case of Indian Ocean Warming," *Journal of Climate* 27, no. 22 (November 5, 2014): 8501–9, https://journals.ametsoe.org/view/journals/clim/27/22/jcli-d-14-0047.1.xml.

68. Alan Villiers, *Monsoon Seas: The Story of the Indian Ocean* (New York: McGraw-Hill, 1952), 5.

69. Kent E. Calder, *Embattled Garrisons: Comparative Base Politics and American Globalism* (Princeton, NJ: Princeton University Press, 2007), 183–87.

70. For example, in May 1975—one month after the fall of Saigon—US Senate Majority Leader Mike Mansfield proposed that the expansion of US military facilities at Diego Garcia be disapproved. See Calder, *Embattled Garrisons*, 186.

71. In 2017, China imported 8.4 million bbl/day, compared to 7.9 million bbl/day for the United States. This gap has widened: in 2019, China' crude-oil imports exceeded 10 million bbl/day, compared with the US crude oil imports on average of 7 million bbl/day. See EIA, "China's Crude Oil Imports Surpassed 10 Million Barrels Per Day in 2019," March 23, 2020, https://www.eia.gov/todayinenergy/detail.php?id=43216.

72. EIA, "China's Crude Oil Imports Surpassed 10 Million Barrels Per Day in 2019."

73. The Persian Gulf was China's largest LNG supplier, after Australia. See EIA, "Natural Gas Weekly Update," December 16, 2021, https://www.eia.gov/naturalgas/weekly/archivenew_ngwu/2021/12_16/.

74. Stavridis, *Sea Power*, 119.

75. In October 2023, India announced it will acquire a third aircraft carrier. Adithya Krishna Menon, "India Closer to Procuring Third Aircraft Carrier, More MPA," *Naval News*, October 9, 2023, https://www.navalnews.com/naval-news/2023/10/india-closer-to-procuring-third-aircraft-carrier-more-mpa/.

76. In 2018, an average of 21 million barrels of oil transited the Strait of Hormuz every day. See EIA, "The Strait of Hormuz Is the World's Most Important Oil Transit Chokepoint," June 20, 2019, https://www.eia.gov/todayinenergy/detail.php?id=39932.

77. EIA, "Strait of Hormuz."

78. See EIA, "Oil and Petroleum Products Explained—Oil Imports and Exports," 2024, https://www.eia.gov/energyexplained/oil-and-petroleum-products/imports-and-exports.php. Only 11 percent of total US petroleum imports and 13 percent of US crude oil imports

were from Persian Gulf countries in 2019, compared with around 89 percent of Japan's and 81 percent of South Korea's crude oil imports.

79. Japan received 95 percent of its crude oil imports from the Persian Gulf in 2023, while South Korea received 74 percent from that source, and Taiwan 74 percent (2021). Around 33 percent of Korea's LNG, 25 percent of Taiwan's, and 9 percent of Japan's also came from the Gulf. For Japan and Korea, see country-specific customs-clearance data from the following national sources: (a) Japan: Ministry of Finance trade statistics for 2023 at https://www.customs.go.jp/toukei/srch/indexe.htm; and (b) Korea: Korea Customs Service data for 2023 at https://tradedata.go.kr/cts/index_eng.do. For Taiwan, see EIA, "Taiwan Analysis Overview," December 2016, https://www.eia.gov/international/analysis/country/TWN.

80. China gets around half of its imported crude from the Persian Gulf (including a significant but ambiguous amount from Iran), together with 15 percent of its crude from West Africa. Over a quarter of China's LNG imports come from Qatar, Oman, and the United Arab Emirates. See People's Republic of China General Administration of Customs customs-clearance data for 2023 at http://stats.customs.gov.cn/indexEn.

81. Robert J. Schneller Jr., *Anchor of Resolve: A History of U.S. Naval Forces Central Command/Fifth Fleet* (Washington, DC: Naval History and Heritage Command, 2007), 22.

82. In 2016, 18.5 million barrels of crude oil and petroleum products flowed through the Strait of Hormuz daily, compared to 4.8 million through the Bab al-Mandab. See EIA, "Red Sea Chokepoints Are Critical for International Oil and Natural Gas Flows," December 4, 2023, https://www.eia.gov/todayinenergy/detail.php?id=61025.

83. In 2020, Saudi Arabia struck a deal with Djibouti to build a base there, although it has not yet been constructed. India is also reportedly trying to reach an agreement with Djibouti to build a base there. See De Facto Intelligence Research Observatory, "Open Source Backgrounder: Djibouti, Foreign Military Bases on the Horn of Africa - Who Is There? What Are They Up To?," *Small Wars Journal*, February 3, 2019, https://smallwarsjournal.com/jrnl/art/open-source-backgrounder-djibouti-foreign-military-bases-horn-africa-who-there-what-are.

84. Camp Lemonnier was leased to the United States following the terrorist attacks on September 11, 2001, and the Horn of Africa Task Force was deployed there in 2003, although the base facility was not fully operationalized until 2007. See Zach Vertin, "Red Sea Rivalries: The Gulf, the Horn, and the New Geopolitics of the Red Sea," Brookings Doha Center, August 8, 2019, https://www.brookings.edu/articles/red-sea-rivalries-the-gulf-the-horn-and-the-new-geopolitics-of-the-red-sea/.

85. Around 12 percent of the world's trade volume, as well as 8 percent of seaborne-traded petroleum and LNG passes from the Red Sea through the Suez Canal and Sumed Pipeline. See "The New Geopolitics of the Red Sea," in *Strategic Survey, 2020*, edited by the International Institute for Strategic Studies (London: Routledge, 2020), 277–87. The United States (2002), Japan (2011), Italy (2012), and China (2017) have established bases in Djibouti, while the United Arab Emirates has done the same in nearby Assab, Eritrea (2015), and Russia in Port Sudan (Sudan, 2019). The Peace Cable, initiated by China, has been built under the Red Sea, from Gwadar in Pakistan to Marseilles in France, and was completed in August 2022. See Winston Qiu, "PEACE Cable System Goes Live," *Submarine Networks*, December 24, 2022, https://www.submarinenetworks.com/en/systems/asia-europe-africa/peace/peace-cable-system-goes-live.

86. BBC News Middle East Section, "Egypt Launches Suez Canal Expansion," BBC, August 6, 2015, https://www.bbc.com/news/world-middle-east-33800076.

87. Shin Watanabe, "China's COSCO Raises Stake in Top Greek Port Piraeus to 67 Percent," *Nikkei Asia*, October 26, 2021, https://asia.nikkei.com/Business/Transportation/China-s-COSCO-raises-stake-in-top-Greek-port-Piraeus-to-67.

88. Hamburg and Shanghai are roughly 15,000 kilometers apart via the Northern Sea Route, but 21,000 kilometers apart via the Southern Sea Route. See Cargo Partners, "A Shortcut through the Arctic?," Trend Letter 13, accessed May 2, 2024, https://www.cargo-partner.com/trendletter/issue-13/northern-sea-route-shortcut.

89. Geoffrey F. Gresh, *To Rule Eurasia's Waves: The New Great Power Competition at Sea* (New Haven, CT: Yale University Press, 2020), 250.

90. "The Northeast Passage," University of Cambridge St. Johns College, accessed May 2, 2024, https://www.joh.cam.ac.uk/northeast-passage.

91. George Kish, "Discovery of the Northeast Passage: The Voyage of the VEGA, 1878–1879," *GeoJournal* 3, no. 4 (1979): 387–94.

92. Sandra Cassotta et al., "Polar Regions," in *IPCC Special Report on the Ocean and Cryosphere in a Changing Climate* (Geneva: Intergovernmental Panel on Climate Change, 2019), https://www.ipec.ch/srocc/chapter/chapter-3-2/.

93. Eric Post et al., "The Polar Region in a 2°C Warmer World," *Science Advances* 5, no. 12 (December 14, 2019), https://www.science.org/doi/10.1126/sciadv.aaw9883.

94. US Geological Survey, "Huge Amount of Fossil Fuels in Arctic: 90 Billion Barrels of Oil and 1,670 Trillion Cubic Feet of Natural Gas," *Science Daily*, July 24, 2008, https://www.sciencedaily.com/releases/2008/07/080724115043.htm.

95. US Geological Survey, "Huge Amount of Fossil Fuels in Arctic."

96. Nearly 53 percent of the Arctic coastline fronts on Russia. See Rebecca Hersman, Eric Brewer, and Maxwell Simon, "Deep Dive Debrief: Strategic Stability and Competition in the Arctic," CSIS, January 2021, https://csis-website-prod.s3.amazonaws.com/s3fs-public/publication/210106_Hersman_Strategic_Stability.pdf.

97. See Karin Kneissl, "Russia and Its National Arctic Passage: Pushing Trade Frontiers Eastward," *The Cradle.co*, January 12, 2023, https://thecradle.co/articles-id/1653.

98. C.J. Chivers, "Russians Plant Flag on the Arctic Seabed," *New York Times*, August 2, 2007, https://www.nytimes.com/2007/08/03/world/europe/03arctic.html.

99. Russia has claimed rights to more than half the floor of the Arctic Ocean, together with the potentially massive natural resources situated there. However, the other nations with Arctic coastlines—the United States, Canada, Denmark, Norway, Sweden, Iceland, and Finland—also have rights to economic zones within 200 miles of their shores on the Arctic Ocean. This complicates Russia's claims. See Chivers, "Russians Plant Flag on the Arctic Seabed."

100. Russia has reopened fifty Soviet era military posts, including thirteen air bases, ten radar stations, twenty border outposts, and ten integrated rescue stations. New bases have been established on strategic Arctic islands, including Novaya Zemlya, Alexandra Land, and Kotelny Island. See Heather A. Conley, Matthew Melino, and Jon B. Alterman, "The Ice Curtain: Russia's Arctic Military Presence," CSIS, March 26, 2020, https://www.csis.org/features/ice-curtain-russias-arctic-military-presence.

101. US Coast Guard, "Major Icebreakers of the World," May 2017, https://www.dco.uscg.mil/Portals/9/DCO%20Documents/Office%20of%20Waterways%20and%20Ocean%20Policy/20170501%20major%20icebreaker%20chart.pdf?ver=2017-06-08-091723-907.

102. Arctic LNG 2 is Novatek's $21 billion project on the Gyda Peninsula, seventy kilometers from the Yamal facility. It consists of three production trains: despite Western sanctions, the first became operational in December 2023, with the second slated for 2024 and the third in 2026. On details, see Malte Humpert, "Novatek Confident It Will Complete Arctic LNG2 on Schedule Despite Western Sanctions," *High North News*, December 16, 2022, https://www.highnorthnews.com/en/novatek-confident-it-will-complete-arctic-lng-2-schedule-despite-western-sanctions.

103. See Arctic Council, "Arctic States," accessed May 2, 2024, https://arctic-council.org/about/states/.

CHAPTER 2

1. Calder, *Super Continent*.

2. Janet L. Abu-Lughod, *Before European Hegemony: The World System A.D. 1250–1350* (New York: Oxford University Press, 1989), 3.

3. Abu-Lughod, *Before European Hegemony*, 3.

4. Abu-Lughod, *Before European Hegemony*, 251–60.

5. Abu-Lughod, *Before European Hegemony*, 359–62.

6. Abu-Lughod, *Before European Hegemony*, 252.

7. See Marco Polo, *The Travels* (London: Penguin Books, 1958), 241–312.

8. See Li Qingxin, *Maritime Silk Road*, trans. William W. Wang (Beijing: China Intercontinental Press, 2006), 111–14.

9. Li, *Maritime Silk Road*, 111–12. Zheng He's expeditions included as many as 27,000 people in up to 200 vessels.

10. Li, *Maritime Silk Road*, 116.

11. Peter Frankopan, *The Silk Roads: A New History of the World* (New York: Alfred A. Knopf, 2015), 215–26.

12. In the case of Guangdong, Jorge Alvares, a private Portuguese merchant, visited under the kingdom's auspices in that year. The first official visit by Portugal to China, at Canton (Guangzhou), was in 1517 by Fernão Pires de Andrade, as ambassador. See John E. Wills, Denis C. Twitchett, and Frederick W. Mote, "Relations with Maritime Europeans, 1514–1662," in *The Cambridge History of China*, vol. 8, *The Ming Dynasty, 1368–1644, Part 2* (Cambridge, UK: Cambridge University Press, 1998), 333–75.

13. Charles R. Boxer, *The Portuguese Seaborne Empire, 1415–1825* (New York: Alfred A. Knopf, 1969).

14. Warren I. Cohen, *East Asia at the Center: Four Thousand Years of Engagement with the World* (New York: Columbia University Press, 2000), 204–10.

15. Owing to these exchange rate anomalies, which the isolated Japanese did not clearly perceive, annual profits of Dutch traders in Japan (709,603 guilders in 1649) were much higher than in Formosa (467,538 guilders), Persia (326,842), or Malabar on the west coast of India (42,964). See Albert Hyma, *The Dutch in the Far East: A History of the Dutch Commercial and Colonial Empire* (Ann Arbor, MI: G. Wahr, 1942), 155 and 159; as well as Frankopan, *Silk Roads*, 233–34.

16. Limited demand for conventional British exports, competition from other European nations in the mercantilistic world of China trade, and tight Chinese restrictions until the

1840s on East India Company opium exports all limited the profitability of British trade with China. See S. Chaudhury, *Merchants, Companies, and Trade: Europe and Asia in the Early Modern Era* (Cambridge, UK: Cambridge University Press, 1999).

17. The British began their dominance of Malaya by acquiring Penang in 1786, and then by taking over Malacca from the Dutch in 1824. The British Colonial Office then took direct control of the three major ports (Penang, Malacca, and Singapore), known as the Strait Settlements, in 1867. Britain gained control of Burma as a result of three conflicts: 1824–1826; 1852 (the Second Anglo-Burmese War), through which the British colonized Lower Burma; and 1885 (the Third Anglo-Burmese War), through which the whole country was made a province of India on January 1, 1886.

18. Paul M. Kennedy, *The Rise and Fall of British Naval Mastery* (London: Allen Lane, 1976), 149–75.

19. Among the other German South Pacific possessions held between the mid-1880s and 1919 were the Northern Solomon Islands, Bougainville, Nauru, the Marshall Islands, the Northern Mariana Islands, the Caroline Islands, and Samoa.

20. For the British, India alone supplied 1.5 million military recruits in World War I—more than the 1.3 million that the Dominions, including Canada, Australia, New Zealand, and South Africa, supplied to the conflict. For the French, the colonies, many of them in Asia, supplied nearly 500,000 troops. More than 1.5 million Africans also served as military laborers, while 140,000 Chinese contract workers were also hired at close to subsistence wages by the British and French governments. See Santanu Das, "Experiences of Colonial Troops," under the theme of "Race, empire, and colonial troops" in the World War One digital collection of the British Library, published on January 29, 2014. See the archived British Museum website on the Internet Archive Wayback Machine at https://web.archive.org/web/20150117111825/http://www.bl.uk:80/world-war-one/articles/colonial-troops.

21. Cohen, *East Asia at the Center.*

22. The so-called Asian Tigers or Asian Dragons included South Korea, Taiwan, Hong Kong, and Singapore. See Kent E. Calder and Roy Hofheinz Jr., *The Eastasia Edge* (New York: Basic Books, 1982); and Ezra F. Vogel, *The Four Little Dragons: The Spread of Industrialization in East Asia* (Cambridge, MA: Harvard University Press, 1991).

23. Calder and Hofheinz, *Eastasia Edge*, 158–70.

24. According to the World Bank, energy use in the Asia-Pacific region increased from 658 kilograms of oil equivalent per capita in 1971 to 2,135 kilograms per capita in 2014, a more than threefold increase. See World Bank, "Energy Use (kg of Oil Equivalent per Capita) - East Asia & Pacific," accessed May 2, 2024, https://data.worldbank.org/indicator/EG.USE.PCAP.KG.OE?locations=Z4.

25. Robert Bryce, "Gas Pains," *The Atlantic* (May 2005), https://www.theatlantic.com/magazine/archive/2005/05/gas-pains/303897/.

26. Asian Development Bank, "Energy Outlook for Asia and the Pacific," October 2009, https://www.adb.org/publications/energy-outlook-asia-and-pacific#.

27. Michael A. Palmer, *Guardians of the Gulf: A History of America's Expanding Role in the Persian Gulf, 1833–1992* (New York: Simon & Schuster, 1992), 45.

28. James A. Field, *History of United States Naval Operations in Korea* (Washington, DC: US Government Printing Office, 1962), 383–84.

29. Kent E. Calder, *Pacific Defense: Arms, Energy, and America's Future in Asia* (New York: William Morrow, 1996), 43–61.

30. Closure of Japanese nuclear plants following the March 2011 Fukushima nuclear disaster also stimulated additional LNG demand in Japan, although aggregate energy demand also fell owing to tepid economic growth.

31. Calder, *Pacific Defense*.

32. Calder, *New Continentalism*, 106. US, Indian, and Australian naval forces also dominate approaches to the Malacca, Lombok, and Sunda Straits—key chokepoints also used extensively by China between the Indian Ocean and the South China Sea.

33. In 2019, around 89 percent of Japanese, 70 percent of Korean, 60 percent of Indian, and 41 percent of Chinese crude-oil imports flowed from the Middle East, overwhelmingly from the Gulf. See "Asia-Middle East Oil Factbox," Reuters, January 8, 2020, https://www.reuters.com/article/asia-mideast-oil-idUKL4N29D17R/.

34. Recent IEA projections suggest that Asia-Pacific aggregate oil demand will rise until around 2040, led by increases in India and Southeast Asia. Japanese demand peaked around 2010, and Chinese demand will peak in the latter half of the 2020s. Asian dependence on the Gulf, however, is likely to rise. See IEA, *World Energy Outlook 2020* (Paris: IEA, 2020), https://www.iea.org/reports/world-energy-outlook-2020.

35. In 2023, Qatar supplied 14 percent of Europe's LNG, while Russia provided 13 percent and the United States 48 percent. See EIA, "The United States Remained the Largest LNG Supplier to Europe in 2023," February 29, 2024, https://www.eia.gov/todayinenergy/detail.php?id=61483.

36. US Department of Energy, "DOE to Update Public Interest Analysis to Enhance National Security, Achieve Clean Energy Goals and Continue Support for Global Allies," January 26, 2024, https://www.energy.gov/articles/does-update-public-interest-analysis-enhance-national-security-achiev-clean-energy-goals.

37. CNPC, for example, received three of the first Iraqi oil concessions granted after the end of the Iraq War in 2003: Al-Adhab (August 2008), Rumaila (2009, joint with BP), and Halfaya (2009, joint with Total and Petronas). By 2014, China was the largest foreign investor in Iraq, and was buying half of all the oil that Iraq produced. See John Calabrese, "China-Iraq Relations: Poised for a Quantum Leap," Middle East Institute, February 1, 2022, https://www.mei.edu/publications/china-iraq-relations-poised-quantum-leap.

38. For a case study on Hyundai's Middle East construction operations, see Calder and Hofheinz, *Eastasia Edge*, 166–70.

39. On the Yanbu project, see "Saudi Aramco Yanbu Refinery," *Hydrocarbons Technology*, accessed June 24, 2024, https://www.hydrocarbons-technology.com/projects/aramco-yanbu.

40. Haider Hamood Radhi Ai-Shafiy, "CNPC, CNOOC, and SINOPEC in Iraq: Successful Start and Ambitious Cooperation Plan," *Journal of Middle Eastern and Islamic Studies* 9, no. 1 (2015): 78–98.

41. Simon Watkins, "China Awarded Major Contract by Iraq for Supergiant Oil and Gas Field," Oilprice.com, January 16, 2024, https://oilprice.com/Energy/Energy-General/China-Awarded-Major-Contract-By-Iraq-For-Supergiant-Oil-And-Gas-Field.html.

42. McKinsey and Company LNG Flow Dashboard, "Oil and Gas," accessed June 24, 2024, https://www.mckinsey.com/industries/oil-and-gas/contact-us/lngflow-dashboard-download; and BP, *Statistical Review of World Energy, 2022*, June 2022, https://www.bp.com/content/dam/bp/business-sites/en/global/corporate/pdfs/energy-economics/statistical-review/bp-stats-review-2022-full-report.pdf.

43. *TeleGeography*, "Submarine Cable Map," 2023, https://www2.telegeography.com/submarine-cable-faqs-frequently-asked-questions.

44. NATO Cooperative Cyber Defense Centre of Excellence, "Strategic Importance of, and Dependence on, Undersea Cables," November 2019, https://ccdcoe.org/library/publications/strategic-importance-of-and-dependence-on-undersea-cables.

45. Nicole Starosielski, *The Undersea Network* (Durham, NC: Duke University Press, 2015), 31–37. The British went to great lengths, even well into the twentieth century, for example, to avoid Hawai'i in their Pacific cable network, running cables instead through Fanning Island in the Gilbert Islands of the South Pacific.

46. Google, Facebook, Amazon, and Microsoft dramatically expanded their presence in undersea cables. Indeed, these four now own or lease nearly half of the world's undersea bandwidth. See Nadia Schadlow and Brayden Helwig, "Protecting Undersea Cables Must Be Made a National Security Priority," *Defense News*, July 1, 2020, https://www.defensenews.com/opinion/commentary/wowo/07/01/protecting-undersea-cables-must-be-made-a-national-security-priority.

47. Jonathan E. Hillman, *The Digital Silk Road: China's Quest to Wire the World and Win the Future* (New York: HarperCollins, 2021), 141–52; and, on the Saudi case, "Saudi Telecom Company (STC) and Huawei Signed a Memorandum of Understanding towards the 5.5 G Era to Build an All-Optical Strategic Partnership," Huawei, March 3, 2023, https://www.huawei.com/en/news/2023/3/mwc2023-stc-huawei-f5-point-5g-mou. In the spring of 2023, Saudi Arabia announced that China's Huawei would provide central technological assistance for development of its domestic informatics system, including cloud computing and the construction of high-tech complexes in Saudi cities.

48. See Calder and Paik, "Quiet Crisis Beneath the Waves," 103–20.

49. Hillman, *Digital Silk Road*.

50. Keith Bradsher, "New Fiber-Optic Cable Will Expand Calls Abroad, and Defy Sharks," *New York Times*, August 15, 1990, https://www.nytimes.com/1990/08/15/business/business-technology-new-fiber-optic-cable-will-expand-calls-abroad-defy-sharks.html.

51. Scadlow and Helwig, "Protecting Undersea Cables Must Be Made a National Security Priority."

52. Anna Gross et al., "How the US Is Pushing China Out of the Internet's Plumbing," *Financial Times*, June 13, 2023, https://ig.ft.com/subsea-cables/.

53. As of 2019, China's share of undersea cables (landing stations, cable ownership, or supplier for undersea cables) was 11.4 percent, and could possibly grow to 20 percent by 2030. See Richard Ghiasy and Rajeshwari Krishnamurthy, *China's Digital Silk Road: Strategic Implications for the EU and India* (Leiden, Netherlands: Leiden Asia Centre, August 2020), https://leidenasiacentre.nl/wp-content/uploads/2021/01/LAC-IPCS-DSR-Report-Aug-2020.pdf.

54. *TeleGeography*, "Submarine Cable Map."

55. "The Digital Side of the Belt and Road Initiative Is Growing," *The Economist*, February 6, 2020, https://www.economist.com/special-report/2020/02/06/the-digital-side-of-the-belt-and-road-initiative-is-growing.

56. Rates of internet connectivity for 2019, in percent, were: Bangladesh (12.9); Pakistan (15.5); Myanmar (30.7); and Sri Lanka (34.1). India was around 45 percent for 2021. See *Statista* country-specific figures at www.statista.com/statistics/792074/india-internet-penetration-rate/.

57. Thomas Pfeiffer and Ilya Khrennikov, "Melting Arctic Means New Undersea Cables for High-Speed Traders," Bloomberg, September 12, 2019, https://www.bloomberg.com/

news/articles/2019-09-12/global-warming-gives-traders-and-google-an-arctic-speed-lane?sref=oHj5uY85.

58. Valerie Zhu, "Envisioning China's Digital Silk Road," *The Gate*, January 25, 2020, http://uchicagogate.com/articles/2020/1/25/envisioning-chinas-digital-silk-road/.

59. See the Huawei Marine website at https://www.huaweimarine.com/cn/Experience.

60. Paran Balakrishnan, "China's Digital Route to Dominance," *The Hindu Business Line*, October 15, 2019, https://www.thehindubusinessline.com/opinion/chinas-digital-route-to-dominance/article29692762.ece.

61. "Peace Singapore Segment Launches Cable Installation," *PEACE Cable*, December 15, 2023, http://www.peacecable.net/News/Detail/616638934.

62. Huawei Marine has taken part in around 100 global projects, and as of 2019 had laid 59,000 kilometers of undersea cable. It is the fourth-largest cable construction firm in the world, following SubCom (United States); Alcatel Submarine Networks (France/Finland); and NEC (Japan). See Balakrishnan, "China's Digital Route to Dominance"; and Jeremy Page, Kate O'Keeffe, and Rob Taylor, "America's Undersea Battle with China for Control of the Global Internet Grid," *Wall Street Journal*, March 2, 2019, https://www.wsj.com/articles/u-s-takes-on-chinas-huawei-in-undersea-battle-over-the-global-internet-grid-11552407466.

63. See the PEACE Cable website at www.peacecable.net#about.

64. The spur to South Africa is still in the works, but the cable linked Singapore to the Maldives in 2024. See Winston Qiu, "Ooredoo Maldives Lands PEACE Cable in Kulhudhuffushi City," *Submarine Networks*, February 22, 2024, https://www.submarinenetworks.com/en/systems/asia-europe-africa/peace/ooredoo-maldives-lands-peace-cable-in-kulhudhuffushi-city.

65. "Submarine Cable Networks: SEA-ME-E-6," *Submarine Networks*, January 2024, https://www.submarinenetworks.com/en/systems/asia-europe-africa/smw6.

66. Joe Brock, "Exclusive: China Plans $500 Million Subsea Internet Cable to Rival US-Backed Project," Reuters, April 6, 2023, https://www.reuters.com/world/china/china-plans-500-mln-subsea-internet-cable-rival-us-backed-project-2023-04-06/.

67. Jessica Aldred, "The Future of Deep Seabed Mining," *China Dialogue Ocean*, February 25, 2019, https://dialogue.earth/en/ocean/6682-future-deep-seabed-mining/.

68. Aldred, "The Future of Deep Seabed Mining"; and Todd Woody, "China Extends Domain with Fifth Deep Sea Mining Contract," *China Dialogue Ocean*, August 15, 2019, https://dialogue.earth/en/ocean/9771-china-deep-sea-mining-contract/.

69. "Japan Successfully Undertakes Large-Scale Deep-Sea Mineral Extraction," *Japan Times*, September 26, 2017, https://www.japantimes.co.jp/news/2017/09/26/national/japan-successfully-undertakes-large-scale-deep-sea-mineral-extraction/.

70. David Rogers, "China to Build World's First Subsea 'Space Station,'" *Global Construction Review*, June 16, 2013, https://www.globalconstructionreview.com/china-build-worlds-first-subsea-space-station/.

71. Aldred, "The Future of Deep Seabed Mining."

72. Woody, "China Extends Domain with Fifth Deep Sea Mining Contract."

73. Todd Woody, "Governments Turn Against Deep-Sea Mining as EV Boom Drives Demand for Metals," Bloomberg, July 18, 2022, https://www.bloomberg.com/news/articles/2022-07-18/deep-sea-mining-gains-critics-as-ev-boom-drives-minerals-demand; Todd Woody, "Seabed Mining Regulator Meets as Critical Minerals Drive Heats Up," Bloomberg, March 22, 2024, https://www.bloomberg.com/news/articles/2024-03-22/the-us-sees-seabed-mining-as-its-next-flashpoint-with-china; and Elizabeth Claire Alberts, "Deep-Sea Mining's

Future Still Murky as Negotiations End on Mixed Note," *Mongabay Environmental News*, April 2, 2024, https://news.mongabay.com/2024/04/deep-sea-minings-future-still-murky-as-negotiations-end-on-mixed-note/.

CHAPTER 3

1. Spykman, *Geography of the Peace*, 43.

2. See, for example, Joe Brock, "US and China Wage War Beneath the Waves—Over Internet Cables," Reuters, March 24, 2023, https://www.reuters.com/investigates/special-report/us-china-tech-cables/.

3. Spykman, *Geography of the Peace*, 37.

4. Spykman, *Geography of the Peace*, 43–44. Spykman considered the rimlands plural because he occasionally separated them into two major groupings based on centers of power: the European peninsula (within the context of the Eurasian landmass) and East Asia.

5. In the twenty-first-century geopolitical equation, the expansive definition of rimlands here—slightly broader than that of Spykman—includes both coastal areas of continents and also peripheral islands close to and economically integrated with the continental rim, such as Sri Lanka, Singapore, and the Indonesian archipelago.

6. A critical juncture is defined here, as in *Super Continent* and in *The New Continentalism* before it, as "a historical decision point at which there are distinct alternative paths to the future." For a particular decision point to qualify as a critical juncture, three conditions are both necessary and sufficient: (1) A *crisis* exists, that calls the legitimacy of existing arrangements into serious question. (2) Crisis breeds *stimulus for change;* and (3) The parties involved confront *intense time pressure.* See Calder, *New Continentalism*, 53–54.

7. For a concise description of these critical junctures, and their broader significance to the structural transformation of the Eurasian political economy, see Calder, *Super Continent*, 49–79.

8. Alan Keenan, "Sri Lanka's Economic Meltdown Triggers Popular Uprising and Political Turmoil," International Crisis Group, April 18, 2022, https://www.crisisgroup.org/asia/south-asia/sri-lanka/sri-lankas-economic-meltdown-triggers-popular-uprising-and-political-turmoil; and Emily Schmall and Mujib Mashal, "Embattled Leaders in Hiding, Sri Lankans Ask: What's Next?," *New York Times*, July 10, 2022, https://www.nytimes.com/2022/07/10/world/asia/sri-lanka-crisis-rajapaksa-ranil-wickremesinghe.html.

9. On the origins of container shipping in the United States, see Levinson, *The Box*.

10. See "China Shipping Profits Surge," *American Shipper*, March 11, 2005, http://www.freightwaves.com. Those profits continued at high levels until the global financial crisis of 2008.

11. See the COSCO website at http://en.coscoshipping.com/col/col6918/index.html.

12. China COSCO Shipping Corporation Limited, "Group Profile," accessed May 17, 2024, https://en.coscoshipping.com/col6918/art/2016/art_6918_45339.html.

13. COSCO manages and operates 357 terminals in 36 ports around the world, owning 96 of these facilities outright. See the COSCO website at http://en.coscoshipping.com.

14. COSCO's Chancay megaport will shorten shipping time between Peru and China by one third, stimulating trade in copper, lithium, soybeans, and electric vehicles, among other products. See "Why China Is Building Its First Megaport in Peru," *Wall Street Journal*, August 26, 2024, at https://www.wsj.com/video/series/breaking-ground/why-china-is-building-its-first-megaport-in-peru/AA7EAE52-9FB5-483E-82C0-10915E6DCF2A.

15. Another smaller, more specialized COSCO support firm is Sinotrans, which focuses on the logistics of marine transport. See "Sinotrans Ltd. Company Overview and News," *Forbes*, accessed June 24, 2024, https://www.forbes.com/companies/sinotrans/?sh=1e880bd05e0b.

16. "China Merchants Port Holdings Co.," *Nikkei Asia*, accessed May 17, 2024, https://asia.nikkei.com/Companies/China-Merchants-Port-Holdings-Co.-Ltd2.

17. Isaac B. Kardon and Wendy Leutert, "Pier Competitor: China's Power Position in Global Ports," *International Security* 46, no. 4 (Spring 2022): 9–47.

18. The Soviet Navy in 1990 included 657 ships, but the Russians listed only 172 in 2015. Soviet/Russian ballistic missile nuclear submarines, a classic indicator of strategic capabilities, fell from fifty-nine to thirteen. For relevant statistics, see, Jeremy Bender, "This Graphic Shows How Tiny the Russian Navy Is Compared to the Former Soviet Fleet," *Business Insider*, March 2, 2016, https://www.businessinsider.com/size-of-russian-navy-compared-to-soviet-fleet-2016-3.

19. Consistently Vietnam's top donor, Japan accounted for around 30 percent of total overseas development assistance commitments from the international community to Vietnam over the past three decades. See Japan International Cooperation Agency, "Vietnam: Where We Work," accessed January 1, 2024, https://www.jica.go.jp/english/overseas/vietnam/index.html.

20. "Japan and Vietnam Ink First Maritime Patrol Ship Deal as South China Sea Row Heats Up," *Japan Times*, August 1, 2020, https://www.japantimes.co.jp/news/2020/08/11/national/Japan-vietnam-patrol-ships-south-china-sea/.

21. For example: the amount of assistance in 2001 was only $25 million. In 2020, it reached a high of $260 million. See "US Foreign Assistance by Country: Vietnam," ForeignAssistance.gov, April 25, 2024, https://www.foreignassistance.gov/cd/vietnam/.

22. David Barboza, "China Unveils $586 Billion Stimulus Plan," *New York Times*, November 10, 2008, https://www.nytimes.com/2008/11/10/world/asia/10iht-10china.17673270.html.

23. The Western Development Strategy, initiated by Jiang Zemin in 1999, aimed to reduce interregional socioeconomic differentials through infrastructural projects and paired relationships between affluent and less-developed regions. On this domestic precursor to BRI, and the political-economic roots of Chinese infrastructure spending, see Calder, *Super Continent*, 100–121, as well as David M. Lampton, Selina Ho, and Cheng-Chwee Kuik, *Rivers of Iron: Railroads and Chinese Power in Southeast Asia* (Berkeley: University of California Press, 2020).

24. Wu Jiao, "President Xi Jinping Gives Speech to Indonesian Parliament," *China Daily*, October 2, 2013, https://www.chinadaily.com.cn/china/2013xiapec/2013-10/02/content_17007915.htm; and Xi Jinping, "Speech by Chinese President Xi Jinping to the Indonesian Parliament," ASEAN-China Centre, October 3, 2013, http://www.asean-china-center.org/english/2013-10/03/c_133062675.htm.

25. On the Maritime Silk Road and its broader implications, see Richard T. Griffiths, *The Maritime Silk Road: China's Belt and Road at Sea* (Leiden, Netherlands: International Institute for Asian Studies, 2014).

26. "Hainan FTZ to Establish China's Biggest Free Trade Port by 2035," *China Briefing News*, June 5, 2020, https://www.china-briefing.com/news/hainan-ftz-masterplan-released-establish-chinas-biggest-free-trade-port-2035/.

27. "Hainan to Invest $35 Billion in the Development of Transport Infrastructure," TASS, June 11, 2021, https://tass.com/economy/1301731.

28. Damen Cook, "China's Most Important South China Sea Military Base," *The Diplomat*, March 9, 2017, https://thediplomat.com/2017/03/chinas-most-important-south-china-sea-military-base/; and Mike Yeo, "Satellite Images Reveal Chinese Expansion of Submarine Base," *Defense News*, September 21, 2022, https://www.defensenews.com/naval/2022/09/21/satellite-images-reveal-chinese-expansion-of-submarine-base/.

29. Richard Maslen, "New Mattala Rajapaksa International Airport Opens in Sri Lanka," *Routes*, March 18, 2013, https://www.routesonline.com/news/29/breaking-news/189186/mew-mattala-rajapaksa-international-airport-opens-in-sri-lanka/.

30. Emily Schmall, Skandha Guasekara, and Mujib Marshal, "Sri Lanka's President Resigns After Months of Protest," *New York Times*, July 14, 2022, https://www.nytimes.com/2022/07/14/world/asia/sri-lanka-president-rajapaksa-resigns-protests.html.

31. Declan Walsh and Vivian Yee, "A New Capital Worthy of the Pharaohs Rises in Egypt, But at What Price?," *New York Times*, June 21, 2023, https://www.nytimes.com/2022/10/08/world/middleeast/egypt-new-administrative-capital.html.

32. Soroush Aliasgary and Ekstrom Marin, "Chabahar Port and Iran's Strategic Balancing with China and India," *The Diplomat*, October 21, 2021, https://thediplomat.com/2021/10/chabahar-port-and-irans-strategic-balancing-with-china-and-india/.

33. China did not recognize Bangladesh until 1976, five years after its independence, but bilateral relations have deepened substantially over the past decade. Bangladesh joined BRI and the Maritime Silk Road during President Xi Jinping's visit to Dhaka in 2016. At that time, the two countries signed investment and loan agreements totaling $24 billion for bridges, a deep-sea port, and a power plant. See Anu Anwar, "How Bangladesh Is Benefiting from the China-India Rivalry," *The Diplomat*, July 12, 2019, https://thediplomat.com/2019/07/how-bangladesh-is-benefiting-from-the-china-india-rivalry/; and J. Mohan Malik, "Myanmar's Role in China's Maritime Silk Road Initiative," *Journal of Contemporary China* 27, no. 111 (2018): 362–78, https://doi.org/10.1080/10670564.2018.1410969.

34. See C. Textor, "China: Share of Global Gross Domestic Product 2029," *Statista*, April 17, 2024, https://www.statista.com/statistics/270439/chinas-share-of-global-gross-domestic-product-gdp/; and World Bank, "Country Specific Data: China," accessed May 17, 2024, https://data.worldbank.org/country/china.

35. Spykman, *Geography of the Peace*, 43–44.

36. "President Xi Jinping Delivers Important Speech and Proposes to Build a Silk Road Economic Belt with Central Asian Countries," Consulate General of the People's Republic of China in Toronto, September 7, 2013, http://toronto.china-consulate.gov.cn/eng/zgxw/201309/t20130913_7095490.htm

37. "Speech by Chinese President Xi Jinping to Indonesian Parliament."

38. Jeff Merritt, "Even as the War Persists, Ukraine Is Rebuilding—Here's How," World Economic Forum, February 6, 2024, https://www.weforum.org/agenda/2024/02/even-as-the-war-persists-ukraine-is-rebuilding-heres-how/.

39. World Bank, "Updated Ukraine Recovery and Reconstruction Needs Assessment," March 23, 2023, https://www.worldbank.org/en/news/press-release/2023/03/23/updated-ukraine-recovery-and-reconstruction-needs-assessment; and Merritt, "Even as the War Persists, Ukraine Is Rebuilding."

40. Merritt, "Even as the War Persists, Ukraine Is Rebuilding."

41. "Inflation Forces Desperate Leaders to Try and Soften the Blow," Bloomberg, May 24, 2022, https://www.bloomberg.com/news/articles/2022-05-25/inflation-what-desperate-governments-are-doing-to-soften-the-blow.

42. On the strategic importance of Odessa and Russia's longstanding relationship with that Black Sea port, see Kent E. Calder, "Odessa and Putin's Imperial Dream," *Japan Times*, April 22, 2022, https://www.japantimes.co.jp/opinion/2022/04/22/commentary/world-commentary/putin-wants-odessa/. On the subsequent Ukrainian naval offensive, see Graham Allison, "Ukraine's Black Sea Counter-offensive Has Been a Triumph," *Telegraph,* December 6, 2023, https://www.telegraph.co.uk/news/2023/12/06/ukraine-war-counteroffensive-success-black-sea-fleet-navy/.

43. Jan Strupczwski, "Europe to Phase Out Russian Oil, Gas, Coal Imports—Leaders Draft," Reuters, March 7, 2022, https://www.reuters.com/markets/rates-bonds/eu-phase-out-russian-gas-oil-coal-imports-leaders-draft-2022-03-07/.

44. EIA, "Petroleum and Other Data," May 13, 2024, https://www.eia.gov/dnav/pet/hist/LeafHandler.ashx?n=pet&s=emm_epm0_pte_nus_dpg&f=m; and World Bank, "Food and Energy Price Shocks from Ukraine War Could Last for Years," April 26, 2022, https://www.worldbank.org/en/news/press-release/2022/04/26/food-and-energy-price-shocks-from-ukraine-war.

45. Calder, "Odesa and Putin's Imperial Dream."

46. Sri Lanka in 2022 owed more than $50 billion in foreign debt, with $7 billion in overseas debt and interest payments coming due during that year. Russia and Ukraine were its first- and third-largest tourist markets. Russia was also its second-largest market for tea, the country's main goods export. To make matters worse, the country is populous (22 million people) and a heavy energy importer. For details, see Mark Malloch-Brown, "Sri Lanka Is an Omen," *Foreign Policy*, May 25, 2022, https://foreignpolicy.com/2022/05/25/sri-lanka-economic-crisis-rajapaksa/; and Benjamin Parkin, "Ukraine Crisis Batters Sri Lanka's Tea and Tourism Recovery Strategy," *Financial Times*, March 6, 2022, https://www.ft.com/content/3a6d3822-7c7a-4c62-9a0e-dcff37e2a175.

47. Jonathan M. Winer, Krzysztof Sfrachola, and Mahmood Sariolghalancy, "The Russia-Ukraine War Has Turned Egypt's Food Crisis into an Existential Threat to the Economy," Middle East Institute, November 28, 2023, https://www.mei.edu/publications/russia-ukraine-war-has-turned-egypts-food-crisis-existential-threat-economy.

48. Sal Gilbertie, "World's Largest Wheat Producer Now World's Largest Wheat Importer Too," *Forbes*, April 17, 2023, https://www.forbes.com/sites/salgilbertie/2023/04/14/worlds-largest-wheat-producer-now-worlds-largest-wheat-importer-too/?sh=3d71329b3b97

49. Winer, Sfrachola, and Sariolghalancy, "The Russia-Ukraine War Has Turned Egypt's Food Crisis into an Existential Threat to the Economy."

50. Tehseen Ahmed Quireshi and Abdul Wajid Rana, "Pakistan: Impacts of the Ukraine and Global Crises on the Economy and Poverty," International Food Policy Research Institute, October 2022, https://doi.org/10.2499/p15738coll2.136406.

CHAPTER 4

1. A. T. Mahan, *The Influence of Sea Power upon History, 1660–1783* (Boston: Little, Brown, 1949), 91.

2. Figures for the twenty-nine countries with direct sea-lane access, from Northeast Asia to the eastern Mediterranean, excepting China. In 2023, more than 40 percent of the global population lived in this area, and they produced more than 20 percent of global GDP.

See World Bank, "Data Bank," accessed February 15, 2024, https://databank.worldbank.org/home.

3. Calder, *Super Continent*, especially 49–69.

4. Calder, *Super Continent*, 70–99 and 140–59.

5. Calder, *Super Continent*, 160–84. Ties between China and western Balkan states like Serbia, as well as Hungary, have enjoyed particular improvement. See the Johns Hopkins University SAIS doctoral dissertation research of Yun Han on this point: "Varieties of China Policy in the EU: A Case for Neo-classical Realism" (forthcoming May 2025).

6. Michael A. Palmer, *Guardians of the Gulf: A History of America's Expanding Role in the Persian Gulf, 1833–1992* (New York: The Free Press, 1992), 2.

7. Palmer, *Guardians of the Gulf*, 5.

8. Stephen Fox, *Wolf of the Deep: Raphael Semmes and the Notorious Confederate Raider CSS Alabama* (New York: Alfred A. Knopf, 2007), 179–83.

9. Shufeldt landed in Busan on May 4, 1880, following his visit to Japan, to deliver a letter to the king of Korea. He later returned to the country in 1882 to complete the negotiations and signing of the so-called Shufeldt Treaty. See Charles Oscar Paullin, *Diplomatic Negotiations of American Naval Officers, 1778–1883* (Baltimore, MD: Johns Hopkins University Press, 1912), 296–97, 319–22.

10. East Asia Company ships arrived at Surat in Gujarat (1608), and the firm established its first Indian factory in 1613. See Margot Finn and Kate Smith, eds., *The East Asia Company at Home, 1757–1857* (London: University College of London Press, 2018); and Pedro Nobre, "The East India Company and the Portuguese Loss of the Província do Norte," *Tempo* 21, no. 37 (2015): 134–50, https://doi.org/10.1590/TEM-1980-542X2015v213702.

11. Andrew Porter, William Roger Louis, and Alaine Low, *The Oxford History of the British Empire*, vol. 2 (Oxford: Oxford University Press, 1999).

12. Prabir Bhattacharya, "India in the Rise of Britain and Europe: A Contribution to the Convergence and Great Divergence Debates," *Journal of Interdisciplinary Economics* 33, no. 1 (2021): 24–53, https://doi.org/10.1177/0260107920907196.

13. J. R. Seeley, *The Expansion of England: Two Courses of Lectures* (London: Macmillan, 1883).

14. See Nicolas Mansergh, *The Commonwealth Experience* (New York: Frederick A. Praeger, 1969), 256. On Curzon's career in India, as well as his tenure as British foreign secretary, see David Gilmour, *Curzon: Imperial Statesman* (New York: Farar, Straus and Giroux, 1994).

15. P. K. Kemp, *The Papers of Admiral Sir John Fisher* (London: Ballantyne for the Navy Records Society, 1960), 161.

16. Kennedy, *Rise and Fall of British Naval Mastery*, 212–13.

17. Because British possessions failed to provide logistic support, the Russian Baltic Fleet was forced to sail around the Cape of Good Hope, rather than transiting the Suez Canal, and forage desperately for supplies along the way. They arrived exhausted in East Asian waters to be decisively defeated by Admiral Heihachiro Togo at Tsushima. On the fateful voyage of the Baltic Fleet, see Constantine Pleshakov, *The Tsar's Last Armada: The Epic Voyage to the Battle of Tsushima* (New York: Basic Books, 2002).

18. Charles Nelson Spinks, "The Termination of the Anglo-Japanese Alliance," *Pacific Historical Review* 6, no. 4 (1937): 321–40.

19. Saki Dockrill, *Britain's Retreat from East of Suez: The Choice between Europe and the World?* (Basingstoke, UK: Palgrave Macmillan, 2002).

20. H. W. Brands, *Bound to Empire: The United States and the Philippines* (New York: Oxford University Press, 1992), especially 3–226; and Calder, *Embattled Garrisons*, 2007, 147–48.

21. In 1998, the United States and the Philippines signed a Visiting Forces Agreement, and have held joint military exercises periodically ever since. In 2014, they signed an additional Enhanced Defense Cooperation Agreement, in the wake of new Chinese activities in the South China Sea near the Philippines. See Sebastian Strangio, "Former US Bases in the Philippines Prompt Mixed Feelings," *The Diplomat*, September 17, 2020, https://thediplomat.com/2020/09/former-us-bases-in-the-philippines-prompt-mixed-feelings/.

22. Office of the Historian, "Secretary of State John Hay and the Open Door in China, 1899–1900," US Department of State, https://history.state.gov/milestones/1899-1913/hay-and-china.

23. Mahan, *Problem of Asia*; and Green, *By More than Providence*, 79–108.

24. Winston Churchill personally spearheaded this oil-driven geo-economic transition in Britain during his tenure as First Lord of the Admiralty on the eve of World War I. See Daniel Yergin, *The Prize: The Epic Quest for Oil, Money, and Power* (New York: Simon and Schuster, 1991), 11–12 and 151–164.

25. On this strategically important economic transition, see Yergin, *The Prize*, 167–83; and Adam Tooze, *The Wages of Destruction: The Making and Breaking of the Nazi Economy* (New York: Penguin Books, 2007), 203–43.

26. Palmer, *Guardians of the Gulf*, 14.

27. Palmer, *Guardians of the Gulf*, 13; and BP, "Our History," n.d., accessed March 4, 2024, https://www.bp.com/en/global/corporate/who-we-are/our-history.html. In 1901, British businessman William d'Arcy obtained the first concession in Iran, and the British government held shares in the Anglo-Persian Oil Company from 1914 until 1987. See also Yergin, *The Prize*, 184–206.

28. Palmer, *Guardians of the Gulf*, 18–19.

29. Stephen D. Krasner, *Defending the National Interest: Raw Materials Investments and U.S. Foreign Policy* (Princeton, NJ: Princeton University Press, 1978), 106–27.

30. Palmer, *Guardians of the Gulf*, 22.

31. Persian Gulf refinery capacity rose by 89 percent between 1938 and 1944, with high-octane aviation fuel increasingly available at Abadan, Bahrain, and Ras Tanura. See Palmer, *Guardians of the Gulf*, 23.

32. United Nations, *Statistical Yearbook, 1949–1950*, table 41, cited in Palmer, *Guardians of the Gulf*, 269.

33. Field, *History of United States Naval Operations in Korea*, 383–84.

34. Black oil is a type of heavy crude oil. See "Crude Oil," Energy Education, University of Calgary, December 20, 2021, https://energyeducation.ca/encyclopedia/Crude_oil. On the use of oil in Korea, see Field, *History of United States Naval Operations in Korea*.

35. See, for example, "George Kennan's 'Long Telegram,'" February 22, 1946, National Archives and Records Administration, Department of State Records (Record Group 59), Central Decimal File, 1945–1949, 861.00/2-2246; reprinted in US Department of State, ed., *Foreign Relations of the United States, 1946*, Vol. VI, *Eastern Europe and the Soviet Union* (Washington, DC: Government Printing Office, 1969), 696–709, History and Public Policy Program Digital Archive, Wilson Center, https://digitalarchive.wilsoncenter.org/document/116178; and George Frost Kennan, *Memoirs: 1925–1959* (New York: Pantheon Books, 1983).

36. "USC 68: United States Objectives and Programs for National Security (April 14, 1950): A Report to the President by the U.S. Department of State's Policy Planning Staff, led

by Paul Nitze, Washington, D.C., April 7, 1950," Intelligence Resource Program, Federation of American Scientists, https://fas.org/irp/offdocs/nsc-hst/nsc-68.htm.

37. On technological change and US naval capabilities during this period, especially in submarine warfare, see Thomas G. Mahnken, *Technology and the American Way of War since 1945* (New York: Columbia University Press, 2008), 45–46, 69–72.

38. The Polaris and Poseidon missiles had ranges of around 2,500 miles, while the Trident has a range of more than 6,000 miles. See James John Tritten, "The Trident System: Submarines, Missiles, and Strategic Documents," *Naval War College Review* 36, no. 1 (1983): 64–65.

39. See National Aeronautics and Space Administration, "Explorer I Overview," August 21, 2023, https://www.nasa.gov/mission_pages/explorer/explorer-overview.html.

40. SCORE referred to Signal Communications by Orbital Relay Equipment.

41. Gorshkov was commander in chief of the Soviet Navy from 1956 to 1985, during which time he transformed a largely obsolete coastal defense force into a blue-water navy that became the principal strategic challenger to US and NATO naval forces, with continual presence in all the major oceans of the world. See Normal Polmar, Thomas A. Brooks, and George E. Federoff, *Admiral Gorshkov: The Man Who Challenged the US Navy* (Annapolis, MD: US Naval Institute Press, 2019), https://www.usni.org/press/books/admiral-gorshkov.

42. The US-Navy RIMPAC (Rim of the Pacific) exercises are the largest recent maritime activities of their kind, with 38 surface warships, 4 subs, and 170 aircraft from 26 countries involved in 2022. OKEAN 1970, however, involved eighty-four surface warships and more than eighty submarines—a substantially larger configuration than RIMPAC, and largely drawn from the Soviet Navy. See Norman Polmar, "OKEAN: A Massive Soviet Exercise, 50 Years Later," *US Naval Institute Proceedings* 146, no. 4 (2020): 44–49; and Brad Lendon, "World's Largest Naval Exercises to Include All 4 Quad Countries," CNN, June 1, 2022, https://www.cnn.com/2022/05/31/politics/rimpac-navy-exercises-intl-hnk-ml/index.html.

43. Mark Barnes, *The Impact of the Cold War on the Creation of Bangladesh* (Munich: GRIN Verlag, 2015), https://www.grin.com/document/336248.

44. See, for example, Avinash Paliwal, "New Alignments, Old Battlefield: Revisiting India's Role in Afghanistan," Carnegie India, June 15, 2017, https://carnegieendowment.org/files/6152017_Paliwal_IndiasRoleinAfghanistan_Web.pdf; and Avinandan Choudhury, "India in Afghanistan after the Soviet Withdrawal," *The Diplomat*, May 14, 2019, https://thediplomat.com/2019/05/india-in-afghanistan-after-the-soviet-withdrawal/.

45. For early discussions of this phenomenon, see Kent E. Calder, "Asia's Empty Tank," *Foreign Affairs* 76, no. 2 (March/April 1996): 55–68, https://www.foreignaffairs.com/articles/asia/1996-03-01/asias-empty-tank; and Calder, *Pacific Defense*.

46. IEA, "World Oil Statistics," *IEA Oil Information Statistics*, 2022, https://stats.oecd.org.

47. In 2012, China imported less than 40,000 million cubic meters (mcm) of natural gas, but by 2020 that figure had more than tripled to over 130,000 mcm, or 65 percent more than the United States. See IEA, "World - Natural Gas Statistics," *IEA Natural Gas Information Statistics*, 2022, https://www.oecd-ilibrary.org/energy/data/iea-natural-gas-information-statistics/world-natural-gas-statistics-edition-2023_1bd510fd-en.

48. See Yergin, *The Prize*.

49. The US Navy first established its presence in Bahrain in 1941 at the invitation of the British, but it was in 1948 that the base formally became part of the US Middle East Force.

50. Diego and surrounding Chagos Archipelago islands lack local populations, which were deported by the British before the construction of the bases. Many inhabitants had

been only temporary workers, but some workers had lived on the islands for two generations. This situation led to extended legal proceedings in Britain between 2000 and 2004,
ending in British Government Orders in Council prohibiting access to all the Chagos Islands
without explicit government permission. On the details, see Calder, *Embattled Garrisons,*
186–87.

51. During the 1991 Gulf War, for example, more than 600 B–52 bombing missions were
carried out from Diego, while aircraft based at Diego's 12,000-foot airstrip dropped more
ordnance on Afghanistan in 2001 than from any other location in the world. See Calder,
Embattled Garrisons, 186.

52. On the "Twin Pillars" strategy of reliance in different ways on Iran and Saudi Arabia,
see Stephen Brannon, "Pillars, Petroleum, and Power: The United States in the Gulf," *Arab
Studies Journal* 2, no. 1 (Spring 1994), 4–10. Diego Garcia played an important role as leverage
for this "Twin Pillars strategy."

53. Palmer, *Guardians of the Gulf,* 87–88; and Henry Kissinger, *White House Years* (Boston:
Little, Brown, 1979), 1264.

54. In March 1987, the US Navy offered to provide military protection to foreign tankers
reflagged as American, under what in July 1987 became known as Operation Earnest Will.
This support, provided mainly for Kuwaiti ships, continued until September 1988, following the end of the Iran-Iraq War. On details of the reflagging, see Joe Stork, "Reagan
Reflags the Gulf," *Middle East Report* 148 (September/October 1987), https://www.merip.
org/1987/09/Reagan-Reflags-the-Gulf.

55. Paul Richter, "Markets React to Kuwait Crisis: Stocks: Invasion Rocks Market;
Dow Slides 34.66," *Los Angeles Times,* August 3, 1990, https://www.latimes.com/archives/
la-xpm-1990-08-03-fi-1121-story.html.

56. Jacob Knutson, "Where U.S. Troops Are Stationed in the Middle East," *Axios,*
October 31, 2023, https://www.axios.com/2023/10/31/american-troops-middle-east-israel-
palestine. The Defense Manpower Data Center indicated a US Middle East military presence of almost 45,000 troops in March, 2024, including temporary deployments.

57. Before the Ukraine war, the United States had about 80,000 troops forward deployed
in Europe. After the Russian invasion of Ukraine in February 2022, the United States deployed
an additional 20,000 troops to Europe. See US Department of Defense, "Fact Sheet—
U.S. Defense Contributions to Europe," June 29, 2022, https://www.defense.gov/News/
Releases/Release/Article/3078056/fact-sheet-us-defense-contributions-to-europe/.

58. The Al-Dhafra Air Base in the United Arab Emirates, like Al-Udeid in Qatar, also
provides important air support to US naval units.

59. This position was especially well represented under the leadership of Jawaharlal
Nehru, one of the most prominent leaders of the worldwide nonaligned movement. See
Sunil Khilnani, *The Idea of India* (London: Hamish Hamilton, 1997).

60. For India's fiscal 2023–24 year (April 2023 to March 2024), the United States was
India's largest market, with 17.7 percent of India's exports, including 35 percent of smart-
phone exports, and generating a trade surplus of over $36 million for India. See "India
in Trade Deficit with 9 of Top 10 Trading Partners in 2023–24: Data," *Business Standard,*
May 26, 2024, https://www.business-standard.com/economy/news/india-in-trade-deficit-
with-9-of-top-10-trading-partners-in-2023-24-data-124052600247_1.html.

61. China recorded $118.4 billion in highly unbalanced total trade with India in fiscal
2023, including a massive $85 billion Chinese bilateral surplus. See "India in Trade Deficit."

62. See Congressional Research Service, "India-US: Major Arms Transfers and Military
Exercises," CRS Report IF12438, May 30, 2024, https: crsreports.congress.gov/product/

pdf/IF/IF12438. Procurements from the United States in the maritime area have included MH–60R Seahawk helicopters, maritime drones, and Harpoon antiship missiles. In 2023 US arms made up 13 percent of India's imports.

63. In 2023 arms imports from Russia constituted 36 percent of India's total, or nearly three times the US share, but this dependence on Russia was down from 76 percent during the 2009–2013 period. See "SIPRI Act Sheet: Trends in International Arms Transfers, 2023," Stockholm International Peace Research Institute, March 2024, https://www.sipri.org/sites/deault/iles/2024-03/s_2403_at_2023.pdf.

64. Tom Waldwyn, "India's Defense Plans Fall Victim to Putin's War," *Foreign Policy*, April 3, 2023, http://foreignpolicy.com/2023/04/03/india-modi-defense-military-russia-putin-war-weapons-procurement/; and Krishn Kaushik, "India Pivots Away from Russian Arms, but Will Retain Strong Ties," Reuters, January 28, 2024, http://reuters.com/world/india/india-pivots-awayrussian-arms-will-retain-strong-ties-2024-01-28/.

65. International Institute for Strategic Studies, *The Military Balance 2023* (London: Routledge, 2023); Waldwyn, "India's Defense Plans"; and Kausik, "India Pivots Away from Russian Arms." Forty-four percent of the Indian Navy's subs and naval vessels continue to be Russian-made.

66. India's second carrier, INS *Vikrant*, was commissioned in September 2022, and its navy has plans for a third carrier. See Yukio Tajima and Satoshi Iwaki, "China and India Race to Expand Aircraft Carrier Fleets," *Nikkei Asia*, January 9, 2024, https://asia.nikkei.com/Politics/Defense/China-and-India-race-to-expand-aircraft-carrier-fleets.

67. India, for example, abstained on multiple United Nations resolutions condemning Russia's invasion of Ukraine, actively has increased purchases of Russian oil in the face of Western sanctions on Russia, and vetoed Japanese transit flights carrying arms for delivery to the Ukraine. See Manjari Chatterjee Miller, "India's Faltering Non-alignment," *Foreign Affairs*, February 22, 2022, https://www.foreignaffairs.com/articles/india/2022-02-22/indias-faltering-nonalignment.

68. Scot Paltrow, "Special Report: Aircraft Carriers: Championed by Trump, Are Vulnerable to Attack," Reuters, March 9, 2017, https://www.reuters.com/article/idUSKBN16G1CY/. The USS *Gerald Ford* does have tremendous versatility, as it can carry the US Navy's most advanced aircraft, including the F–35 Lightning; the E–2F Advanced Hawkeye, and MH–60 helicopters.

69. Paltrow, "Special Report: Aircraft Carriers." The Dong Feng–21 has a range of 1,100 miles and a top speed of Mach 10.

70. See Bert Chapman, *The AUKUS Nuclear Submarine Agreement: Potential Implications*, FORCES Initiative: Strategy, Security, and Social Systems Paper 4 (Purdue University, April 1, 2022), https://docs.lib.purdue.edu/forces/4/. The AUKUS agreement will substantially increase US and allied on-station nuclear submarine capacity in the Indo-Pacific, by giving the United States and United Kingdom new basing and surfacing options, while adding Australian capacity and service know-how.

71. See Calder, *Embattled Garrisons*.

CHAPTER 5

1. Sun Tzu, *The Art of War*, trans. Lionel Giles (New York: Race Point Publishing, 2017), 26.

2. World Bank, "Exports of Goods and Services (% of GDP)—China," World Bank National Accounts Data, accessed January 1, 2024, https://data.worldbank.org/indicator/NE.EXP.GNFS.ZS?locations=CN.

3. See David Shambaugh, *Modernizing China's Military: Progress, Problems and Prospects* (Berkeley, CA: University of California Press, 2003). Even the navy's appellation—PLA-N, or People's Liberation Army–Navy, symbolizes its subordination to the land forces.

4. Jennifer Rice and Erik Robb, *The Origins of "Near Seas Defense and Far Seas Protection,"* China Maritime Report No. 13 (Newport, RI: China Maritime Studies Institute, Naval War College, February 2021), https://digital-commons.usnwc.edu/cgi/viewcontent.cgi?article=1012&context=cmsi-maritime-reports.

5. See Chris Buckley, "China Appoints Naval Commander as Defense Minister," *New York Times*, December 29, 2023, https://www.nytimes.com/2023/12/29/world/asia/china-defense-minister.html. Admiral Dong has substantial previous command experience related to the South China Sea.

6. See, for example, Feng Liang, Do Bo, and Chen Suohua, "Chuangzaoxing kuozhan guoji gonggong haiyu liyi de zhanlue sikao" [Strategic consideration of the creative expansion of maritime interests on the high seas], *Taipingyang Xuebao* (*Pacific Journal*) 22, no. 6 (2024): 89–98. Cited in Kardon and Leutert, "Pier Competitor," 25.

7. Fully 90 percent of China's trade is seaborne, exceeding the global average of 80 percent. See Kardon and Leutert, "Pier Competitor," 11.

8. See Jung-pang Lo, *China as a Sea Power: 1127–1368* (Singapore: National University of Singapore Press, 2012); and Carla P. Freeman, "An Uncommon Approach to the Global Commons: Interpreting China's Divergent Positions on Maritime and Outer Space Governance," *China Quarterly* 241 (March 2020): 1–21, https://doi.org/10.1017/S0305741019000730.

9. Bill Hayton, *The South China Sea: The Struggle for Power in Asia* (New Haven, CT: Yale University Press, 2014), 11–16 and 19–24.

10. During the 4500–3000 BCE period, early Austronesian people used seagoing rafts and later "outrigger canoes" to migrate from China to Taiwan, and then onward to the Philippines and elsewhere. See Charlotte Minh-Hà L. Pham, *Asian Shipbuilding Technology* (Bangkok: UNESCO Asia and Pacific Regional Bureau for Education, 2012), https://archive.org/details/unit-14-unesco.

11. Mountainous southern China, after all, did not integrate with terrestrially-focused northern China until the Qin dynasty (only fifteen years), and then only again during and after the Han Dynasty (202 BCE to 220 CE). See Pham, *Asian Shipbuilding Technology*.

12. Shambaugh, *Where Great Powers Meet*, 115.

13. W.W. Rockhill, "Notes on the Relations and Trade of China with the Eastern Archipelago and the Coast of the Indian Ocean during the Fourteenth Century. Part II," *T'oung Pao* 16, no. 1 (1915): 61–159, http://www.jstor.org/stable/4526442.

14. Guangzhou began to prosper in the fifth century CE, while Quangzhou, another classical port, began to do so only in the tenth century. See Hayton, *The South China Sea*, 15 and 21.

15. Hayton, *South China Sea*, 15 and 21.

16. Yoshihara and Holmes, *Red Star over the Pacific*, 208.

17. In 1567, the modification of *haijin* (port closure) allowed one port and licensed private traders from two cities to conduct trading again with all nations except Japan. See Ivy Maria Lim, "From Haijin to Kaihai: The Jiajing Court's Search for a Modus Operandi along the Southeastern Coast (1522–1567)," *Journal of the British Association for Chinese Studies* 2 (July 2013), 20–21, http://bacsuk.org.uk/wp-content/uploads/2014/10/Lim_sep_fv.pdf.

18. Shi Zhihong, "China's Overseas Trade Policy and its Historical Results: 1522–1840," *Intra-Asian Trade and the World Market* (Abingdon, UK: Routledge, 2006), 4–23. The Qing also feared expatriates in Luzon, where a Ming pretender was rumored to be hiding.

19. Sterling Seagrave, *Lords of the Rim 2010: China's Renaissance* (London: Bowstring Books, 2010), 104.

20. This total included 2.8 million in the Dutch East Indies, 2.7 million in Siam (later Thailand), 1 million in Malaya, 134,000 in British Burma, and 83,000 in the Philippines. Cited in Tjio Kayloe, *The Unfinished Revolution: Sun Yat-sen and the Struggle for Modern China* (Tarrytown, NY: Marshall Cavendish, 2017), 143.

21. Australia's Department of Foreign Affairs and Trade estimated in 1995 that the collective GDP of Southeast Asian Overseas Chinese totaled around $450 billion, compared to $500 billion for the People's Republic of China. See East Asia Analytic Unit, *Overseas Chinese Business Networks in Asia* (Canberra: Department of Foreign Affairs and Trade, 1995), 1, cited in Sebastian Strangio, *In the Dragon's Shadow: Southeast Asia in the Chinese Century* (New Haven, CT: Yale University Press, 2020), 287.

22. See Min Ye, *Diasporas and Foreign Direct Investment in China and India* (Cambridge, UK: Cambridge University Press, 2014), 45–68.

23. People's Republic of China General Administration of Customs, "Customs Clearance Statistics for 2023," http://stats.customs.gov.cn/indexEn.

24. IEA, *World Energy Outlook 2020*, October, 2020, https://www.iea.org/reports/world-energy-outlook-2020. More recent sources from 2023 affirm this projection for 2030. See Charles Kennedy, "CNPC Sees China' Oil Demand Peaking in 2030," OilPrice.com, December 7, 2023, http://www.oilprice.com/Latest-Energy-News-World-News/CNPC-Sees-Chinas-Oil-Demand-Peaking-in-2030.html.

25. United Nations Food and Agriculture Organization (FAO), *The State of World Fisheries and Aquaculture, 2022* (Rome: FAO, 2022), https://doi.org/10.4060/cc0461en.

26. FAO, *The State of World Fisheries and Aquaculture, 2020* (Rome: FAO, 2022), 8, https://doi.org/10.4060/ca9229en.

27. In global fisheries export data from 2019, China (22.7 percent) was followed by Norway (11.9 percent), while in imports China (22.4 percent) followed the United States (22.4 percent), and was followed by Japan (15.5 percent). See FAO, *The State of World Fisheries and Aquaculture, 2020*, 8 and 80.

28. In 2015, there reportedly were 370,000 nonpowered fishing vessels and another 672,000 motor-powered. See FAO, "Fishery and Aquaculture Country Profile: China," December 2017, https://www.fao.org/fishery/en/facp/41/en.

29. *China Fisheries Statistical Yearbook*, 2022 ed. (Beijing: China Statistics Press, 2022), https://www.stats.gov.cn/sj/ndsj/2022/indexeh.htm.

30. Sally Yozell and Amanda Shaver, "Shining a Light: The Need for Transparency Across Distant Water Fishing," Stimson Center, November 1, 2019, https://www.stimson.org/2019/shining-light-need-transparency-across-distant-water-fishing/.

31. As the *China Youth Daily* of June 15, 2004, put it, interpreting Hu, "It is no exaggeration to say that whoever controls the Strait of Malacca will also have a stranglehold on the energy route of China." See Ian Storey, "China's 'Malacca Dilemma,'" *China Brief* 6, no. 8 (2006), 4–6, https://jamestown.org/program/chinas-malacca-dilemma/.

32. "Mass Rally in the Capital Welcoming the Romanian Party and Government Delegation," *People's Daily*, June 9, 1971, 2.

33. See, for example, Li Xiannian, "Speech by Comrade Li Xiannian at the Capital's Mass Rally Commemorating the 20th Anniversary of the Korean War," *People's Daily*, June 26, 1970, 2. Sato was the brother of former Prime Minister Kishi Nobusuke, who had served as a member of Tojo Hideki's wartime cabinet.

34. Ji Yangeng, "Sulian zai 'Yaling'diqu de kuozhan zhanlue" [The Soviet Union's expansion strategy in the "dumbbell area"], *People's Daily*, June 22, 1979, 6.

35. On the suspicions of such a prospect, see, for example, Brzezinski, *Grand Chessboard*.

36. On the Hainan incident, see Elizabeth Rosenthal with David E. Sanger, "US Plan in China after It Collides with Chinese Jet," *New York Times*, April 2, 2001, http://nytimes.com/200/04/02/world/us-plane-in-china-after-it-collides-with-chinese-jet.

37. Huang Zuquan and Huang Peizhao, "The Situation in the Middle East and Energy Security," *People's Daily*, August 5, 2002.

38. Zhang Yuncheng, "The Strait of Malacca and Global Oil Security," *Global Times*, December 5, 2003. Hu demanded that the Chinese state establish strategic oil reserves, build overseas energy production and supply bases, develop alternative oil products, and take "proactive measures" (presumably military) to ensure national energy security.

39. Zhang Qian, "Hu Jintao Reportedly Calls for the Formulation of an Energy Development Strategy," Central News Agency, Hong Kong, January 14, 2004.

40. Minnie Chan, "10 Things You Should Know about China's First Home-Built Aircraft Carrier," *South China Morning Post*, April 12, 2017, https://www.scmp.com/news/china/diplomacy-defence/article/2087064/10-things-you-should-know-about-chinas-first-home-built.

41. M. Taylor Fravel, *Active Defense: China's Military Strategy since 1949* (Princeton, NJ: Princeton University Press, 2019), 232.

42. US Naval Institute Staff, "Report to Congress on Chinese Naval Modernization," February 1, 2024, https://news.usni.org/2024/02/01/report-to-congress-on-chinese-naval-modernization-20.

43. The US Navy operates ten overseas bases/installations spanning the globe, from Cuba to Korea, including facilities in Europe, East Asia, and Africa. China's only formal overseas facility is currently in Djibouti. For a full list of the US Navy's current overseas bases, see the NavyAdvancement.com website at https://www.navyadvancement.com/navy-bases/navy-bases-overseas.php.

44. The *Liaoning*, a converted Ukrainian "heavy aircraft-carrying cruiser," was commissioned by the Soviet Navy but left unfinished when the Soviet Union collapsed in 1991. In 1998, a Chinese travel agency purchased its unfinished hull and towed to China from Ukraine in 2001. After extensive modifications to its hull, radar systems, and electronics, the *Liaoning* finally was commissioned in 2012 as a training ship. Two months after its commissioning, it was used for China's first carrier-based takeoffs and landings. In November 2016, it officially was reported to be "combat ready," and the next month participated in its first live-fire drills. The *Shandong*, commissioned in 2019, is China's first domestically produced carrier and is being used for operational military service, recently in the Yellow Sea. China's third carrier, the *Fujian*, is currently undergoing sea trials. See Dzirhan Mahadzir, "Chinese Aircraft Carrier Fujian Leaves for First Set of Sea Trials," *USNI News*, May 2024, https://news.usni.org/2024/05/0/chinese-aircraft-carrier-fujian-leaves-for-first-set-of-sea-trials.

45. China's fourth carrier also is reported likely to use advanced launching and landing systems, increasingly similar to US counterparts, making it possible to launch and recover more (and heavier) aircraft from a carrier's deck. See Peter Schweizer, "Dragon Ships: China's Naval Threat," Gatestone Institute, March 8, 2021, https://www.gatestoneinstitute.org/17159/china-naval-threat.

46. Kathrin Hille, "China Plans Hybrid Assault Vessel to Strengthen Overseas Power," *Financial Times*, July 24, 2020, https://www.ft.com/content/5f0e15d8-406a-47f1-9be3-1a9ace242830.

47. Ronald O'Rourke, *China Naval Modernization: Implications for U.S. Navy Capabilities—Background and Issues for Congress*, RL33153 (Washington, DC: Congressional Research Service, March 9, 2021), https://crsreports.congress.gov/product/pdf/RL/RL33153/250.

48. See the CSIS Missile Threat Project website at https://missilethreat.csis.org/missile.

49. On the Bay of Bengal's strategic importance, see Calder, *Bay of Bengal*.

50. On these conflictual elements, see Saurav Jha, "The Bay of Bengal Naval Arms Race," *The Diplomat*, December 30, 2016, https://thediplomat.com/2016/12/the-bay-of-bengal-naval-arms-race/.

51. Henry Boyd and Tom Waldwyn, "China's Submarine Force: An Overview," *Military Balance* (blog), International Institute for Strategic Studies, October 4, 2017, https://www.iiss.org/blogs/military-balance/2017/10/china-submarine-force.

52. China has both defensive and offensive advantages within the First Island Chain. See Erickson and Wuthnow, "Barriers, Springboards, and Benchmarks," 1–22.

53. The third carrier, the *Fujian*, has been launched but is not yet operational. China's carriers so far are conventionally powered rather than nuclear, giving them less operational flexibility than their US counterparts. See Matthew P. Funaiole, Joseph S. Bermudez Jr., and Brian Hart, "Signs Point to China's Third Aircraft Carrier Launching Soon," CSIS, November 9, 2021, https://www.csis.org/analysis/signs-point-chinas-third-aircraft-carrier-launching-soon.

54. Iskander Rehman, "The Subsurface Dimension of Sino-Indian Maritime Rivalry," *India and China at Sea: Competition for Naval Dominance in the Indian Ocean*, edited by David Brewster (New Delhi: Oxford University Press, 2018), 137–61.

55. Ryan Fedasiuk, "Leviathan Wakes: China's Growing Fleet of Autonomous Undersea Vehicles," CIMSEC, August 17, 2021, https://cimsec.org/leviathan-wakes-chinas-growing-fleet-of-autonomous-undersea-vehicles/.

56. International Institute for Strategic Studies, *The Military Balance 2024*, 36 and 254. The US Navy operates 14 *Ohio*-class SSBNs, with the remaining 4 *Ohio*-class submarines being cruise-missile submarines. The follow-on *Columbia*-class SSBNs are scheduled to enter service in 2031 to replace the *Ohio*-class boats.

57. Goldstein, "China Is Building an 'Undersea Great Wall'"; and Stephen Chen, "Surveillance under the Sea: How China Is Listening in Near Guam," *South China Morning Post*, January 23, 2018, https://www.scmp.com/news/china/society/article/2130058/surveillance-under-sea-how-china-listening-near-guam.

58. Ewen Levick, "China's Underwater Great Wall," *The Maritime Executive*, June 18, 2018, https://maritime-executive.com/editorials/china-s-underwater-great-wall.

59. On China's evolving submarine fleet, see Nuclear Threat Initiative, "China Submarine Capabilities," March 6, 2023, https://www.nti.org/analysis/articles/China-submarine-capabilities/.

60. For a general description, see Nuclear Threat Initiative, "China Submarine Capabilities."

61. Hainan has roughly 35,000 square kilometers of land, compared to only 728 for Singapore.

62. Drake Long, "China Works on Undersea Cables between Paracel Island Outposts," *Radio Free Asia*, October 11, 2020, https://www.rfa.org/english/news/china/undersea-paracels-06082020190921.html.

63. "Hainan to Invest $35 Billion in the Development of Transport Infrastructure."

64. See Frank Tang, "China's Expat Tax System: Who Pays and How Does It Work?" *South China Morning Post*, January 9, 2022, https://www.scmp.com/economy/china-economy/article/3162559/chinas-expat-tax-system-who-pays-and-how-does-it-work.

65. On the "string of pearls" concept, see Booz Allen Hamilton, *Energy Futures in Asia Seminar: After Action Report*, April 2007, https://www.esd.whs.mil/Portals/54/Documents/FOID/Reading%20Room/Other/15-F-0953_DOC_07_Energy_Futures_In_Asia.pdf; and Bertil Lintner, *The Costliest Pearl: China's Struggle for India's Ocean* (London: Hurst and Co., 2019).

66. Ports serve, in particular, militarily relevant logistics and intelligence-gathering functions. On the comprehensive civil-military functions of Chinese port projects along the Eurasian sea lanes, see Kardon and Leutert, "Pier Competitor," 14–15.

67. In 2011, China evacuated more than 35,000 of its citizens from Libya during the civil war; in 2015, it evacuated 225 foreign nationals (not just Chinese citizens) from Yemen. On these two important steps, see Shaio H. Zerba, "China's Libya Evacuation Operation: A New Diplomatic Imperative—Overseas Citizen Protection," *Journal of Contemporary China* 23, no. 90 (2014), 1093–112, https://doi.org/10.1080/10670564.2014.898900; and Megha Rajagopalan and Ben Blanchard, "China Evacuates Foreign Nationals from Yemen in Unprecedented Move," Reuters, April 3, 2015, https://www.reuters.com/article/idUSKBN0MU09M/.

68. Fravel, *Active Defense*, 232.

69. The United States, by contrast, has a twenty-year lease agreement at an annual fee of $63 million, and has been present since 2003. Japan established an independent Maritime Self-Defense Force base in Djibouti in 2011, and pays $30 million annually. See Eric Schmitt, "US Signs New Leave to Keep Strategic Military Instillation in the Horn of Africa," *New York Times*, May 6, 2014, https://www.nytimes.com/2014/05/06/world/africa/us-signs-new-lease-to-keep-strategic-military-installation-in-the-horn-of-africa.html.

70. Bonnie S. Glaser, "China's First Overseas Military Base: A Conversation with Erica Downs and Jeffrey Becker," CSIS China Power Project, Center for Strategic and International Studies, January 19, 2018, https://www.csis.org/podcasts/chinapower/chinas-first-overseas-military-base-conversation-erica-downs-and-jeffrey-becker.

71. David Pilling, "Djibouti Row with DP World Embodies Horn of Africa Power Struggle," *Financial Times*, October 30, 2018, https://www.ft.com/content/bcaf5452-4f0e-11e8-ac41-759eee1efb74; and Mercy A. Kuo, "China in Djibouti: The Power of Ports," *The Diplomat*, March 25, 2019, https://thediplomat.com/2019/03/china-in-djibouti-the-power-of-ports/.

72. Andrew Jacobs and Jane Perlez, "US Wary of Its New Neighbor in Djibouti: A Chinese Naval Base," *New York Times*, February 25, 2017, https://www.nytimes.com/2017/02/25/world/africa/us-djibouti-chinese-naval-base.html.

73. China owns or operates at least one terminal at ninety-six foreign ports, or 61 percent of the world's leading container-shipping ports. See Kardon and Leutert, "Pier Competitor," 12.

74. See, for example, Sun Mesa, "Golden Dragon Drills End in Triumph," *Khmer Times*, April 1, 2020, https://www.khmertimeskh.com/708147/golden-dragon-drills-end-in-triumph/.

75. "China Pledges Over $100 Million Military Aid to Cambodia," Reuters, June 19, 2018, https://www.reuters.com/article/us-cambodia-china/china-pledges-over-100-million-military-aid-to-cambodia-idUSKBN1JF0KQ.

76. Jeremy Page, Gordon Lubold, and Rob Taylor, "Deal for Naval Outpost in Cambodia Furthers China's Quest for Military Network," *Wall Street Journal*, July 22, 2019, https://www.wsj.com/articles/secret-deal-for-chinese-naval-outpost-in-cambodia-raises-u-s-fears-of-beijings-ambitions-11563732482.

77. See, for example, Sopheng Cheang, "Chinese Navy Ships Are First to Dock at New Pier at Cambodian Naval Base Linked to Beijing," Associated Press, December 7, 2023, https://apnews.com/article/cambodia-china-navy-base-thailand-gulf-25fd5ba4af472ec96c68108ea0371c11.

78. On Chinese gray-zone tactics and related policy implications, see Andrew S. Erickson and Ryan D. Martinson, eds., *Chinese Maritime Gray Zone Operations* (Annapolis, MD: Naval Institute Press, 2019).

79. On the details of this approach, see Isaac B. Kardon, *China's Law of the Sea: The New Rules of Maritime Order* (New Haven, CT: Yale University Press, 2023).

80. Gabriel Collins and Michael Grubb, *A Comprehensive Survey of China's Dynamic Shipbuilding Industry*, CMSI Red Books Study 1 (Newport, RI: US Naval War College, 2008), https://digital-commons.usnwc.edu/cgi/viewcontent.cgi?article=1000&context=cmsi-red-books.

81. In 1995, for example, Russia granted Chinese fishing boats preferential treatment in the Sea of Okhotsk, as did the Marshall Islands in the South Pacific. See Jinkai Yu and Qingchao Han. "Exploring the Management Policy of Distant Water Fisheries in China: Evolution, Challenges and Prospects," *Fisheries Research* 236, no. 1 (2021): 1–10, https://doi.org/10.1016/j.fishres.2020.105849.

82. On that transformation and its political-military implications, see Erickson and Martinson, *China's Maritime Gray Zone Operations*.

83. Erickson and Martinson, *China's Maritime Gray Zone Operations*, 12.

84. Erickson and Martinson, *China's Maritime Gray Zone Operations*, 15.

85. Lyle Morris, "Blunt Defenders of Sovereignty—The Rise of Coast Guards in East and Southeast Asia," *Naval War College Review* 70, no. 2 (Spring, 2017): 1–38, https://digital-commons.usnwc.edu/cgi/viewcontent.cgi?article=1016&context=nwc-review; and Tsukasa Hadano, "China Fires Opening Salvo at Biden, Making Coast Guard Quasi-Military," *Nikkei Asia*, January 23, 2021, https://asia.nikkei.com/Politics/China-fires-opening-salvo-at-Biden-making-coast-guard-quasi-military. In 2020, 1100 Chinese government ships entered the contiguous zone around Japan-China disputed islands.

86. Hadano, "China Fires Opening Salvo at Biden."

87. Katsuji Nakazawa, "Analysis: Xi Takes Over Coast Guard and Gives It a License to Fire," *Nikkei Asia*, February 4, 2021, https://asia.nikkei.com/Editor-s-Picks/China-up-close/Analysis-Xi-takes-over-Coast-Guard-and-gives-it-a-license-to-fire. Following his tenure there, Meng Hongwei became the first Chinese director of Interpol, but was purged on corruption charges when he returned to China in 2018. See Sophie Richardson, "China Disappeared Interpol's Chief. The World Can't Pretend It's Business as Usual," *Washington Post*, October 9, 2018, https://www.washingtonpost.com/opinions/china-disappeared-interpols-chief-the-world-cant-pretend-its-business-as-usual/2018/10/09/835bf628-cbf6-11e8-a3e6-44daa3d35ede_story.html.

88. Hadano, "China Fires Opening Salvo at Biden"; and Yew Lun Tian, "China Authorizes Coast Guard to Fire on Foreign Vessels If Needed," Reuters, January 22, 2021, https://www.reuters.com/article/idUSKBN29R1EQ/.

89. See Kent E. Calder, "Renaissance of the Rimlands: How Eurasia's Transformation at Sea Re-Shapes Geopolitics on Land," *Korean Journal of International Affairs* (December 2023): 31–58, http://dx.doi.org/10.18031/jip.2023.12.28.2.31.

90. Daniel S. Markey, *China's Western Horizon: Beijing and the New Geopolitics of Eurasia* (New York: Oxford University Press, 2020), especially vii–viii.

91. Kaplan, *Monsoon*, 69.

92. See Declan Walsh, "Chinese Firm Will Run Strategic Pakistani Port at Gwadar," *New York Times*, January 31, 2013, https://www.nytimes.com/2013/02/01/world/asia/chinese-firm-will-run-strategic-pakistani-port-at-gwadar-html.

93. Jalanzaib Haque and Qurat ul ain Siddiqui, "The CPEC Plan for Pakistan's Digital Future," *Dawn*, October 3, 2017, https://www.dawn.com/news/1361176. Completion of an overland optical-fiber link to China in 2018, and subsequent construction of the PEACE underwater cable to Europe gave Gwadar this new twenty-first century intermediary role in advanced communications, as the connecting point between land and sea.

94. See Lucas Mayers, "The China-Myanmar Economic Corridor and China's Determination to See It Through," *Asia Dispatches* (blog), Wilson Center, May 26, 2020, https://www.wilsoncenter.org/blog-post/china-myanmar-economic-corridor-and-chinas-determination-see-it-through.

95. Monica Wang, "China's Strategy in Djibouti: Mixing Commercial and Military Interests," *Asia Unbound* (blog), Council on Foreign Affairs, April 13, 2018, https://www.cfr.org/blog/chinas-strategy-djibouti-mixing-commercial-and-military-interests.

96. Two thirds of China's overseas port projects, for example, are within operational range of major chokepoints between Europe and China's eastern seaboard. See Kardon and Leutert, "Pier Competitor," 26.

97. The COVID crisis intensified the relative attractiveness of the Chinese market, as China was the one major nation to have emerged relatively unscathed by the crisis during 2020, and consequently the one major nation to sustain positive economic growth. In 2021, that dynamic continued, although China's Covid Zero policies inhibited growth in 2022. See Tom Hancock and Enda Curran, "China Set to Topple U.S. as Biggest Economy Sooner After Virus," Bloomberg, January 14, 2021, https://www.bloomberg.com/news/articles/2021-01-14/a-year-after-covid-began-china-s-economy-is-beating-the-world. For the economic slowdown, see Shi Jiangtao, "How the Economic Slowdown and Zero-Covid Threaten China's Global Ambitions," *South China Morning Post*, June 6, 2022, https://www.scmp.com/news/china/diplomacy/article/3180352/how-economic-slowdown-and-zero-covid-threaten-chinas-global.

98. Chinese Ambassador to Greece Zou Xiaoli used this terminology in 2016 to describe the developmental implications of Piraeus port development and BRI railway projects from Athens north to Budapest. See "Speech by Ambassador Zou Xiaoli at the Seminar 'The New Silk Road of China: One Belt, One Road (OBOR) and Greece,'" Embassy of the People's Republic of China in the Hellenic Republic, March 30, 2016, http://gr.china-embassy.gov.cn/eng/zxgx/201603/t20160330_3167607.htm.

99. For details, see Calder, *Embattled Garrisons*, 27.

100. Under the 2016 acquisition agreement, $400 million of mandatory investment was promised, and Chinese President Xi Jinping promised another $400 million during his 2019 visit. *The Economist*, however, claims that COSCO investments in Piraeus total over $5 billion. See "China Is Making Investment in Ports and Pipelines Worldwide," *The Economist*, February 6, 2020, https://www.economist.com/special-report/2020/02/06/china-is-making-substantial-investment-in-ports-and-pipelines-worldwide.

101. See page 10 of the "Presentation of P.P.A SA—April 2011," under "Presentations" of "Investor Relations" on the Piraeus Port Authority website: https://www.olp.gr/en/investor-relations/presentations.

102. The Piraeus port complex includes diverse services from container shipping and ship repairing to car terminals and cruise operations. See "Presentation of P.P.A. SA—May 2020" under "Presentations" of "Investor Relations" on the Piraeus Port Authority website: https://www.olp.gr/en/inveestor-relations/presentations.

103. Zhong Nan, "COSCO Raises Stake in Greek Port," *China Daily*, October 26, 2021, https://global.chinadaily.com.cn/a/202110/26/WS61775552a310cdd39bc7140a.html.

104. "A Decade of Transformation—The Rebirth of the Piraeus Port," *China Daily*, October 06, 2021, http://www.chinadaily.com.cn/a/202109/06/WS615e641da310cdd39bc6d4f8.html.

105. CCCC concluded deals with Italy to work in both Trieste and Genoa in March 2019, shortly after Italy joined the BRI. Ningbo Zhoushan Port Group has signed up to develop intermodal transport at Koper. The apparent intent in both cases is to increase trade volumes between China on the one hand and Central European countries on the other. China also has financed rail projects to the east, synergistic with its port development commitments. See "Port of Trieste and CCCC Signed a Cooperative Agreement," *Österreichische Verkehrszeitung*, March 26, 2019, https://oevz.com/en/port-of-trieste-and-cccc-signed-a-cooperation-agreement/.

106. See Francesca Ghiretti, "Demystifying China's Role in Italy's Port of Trieste," *The Diplomat*, October 15, 2020, https://thediplomat.com/2020/10/demystifying-chinas-role-in-italys-port-of-trieste.

107. See Robert D. Kaplan, *Adriatic: A Concert of Civilization at the End of the Modern Age* (New York: Random House, 2022).

108. In 2012, Hutchison Ports Holdings of Hong Kong purchased Barcelona's BEST terminal, which is now the most technically advanced port in Spain. In June 2017, COSCO acquired a 51 percent stake in Spanish port operator Noatum for $228 million. And in November 2018, China's Ningbo Zhoushan signed an agreement with the Algeciras Port Authority, directly adjacent to Gibraltar, establishing Algeciras and Ningbo in Zhejiang Province (near Shanghai) as global logistical centers for increased trade between southern Europe and East Asia. See Jem Newton, "HPH Extends Barcelona Concession, Pledges Full Automation," *Journal of Commerce Online*, September 25, 2015, https://www.joc.com/port-news/terminal-operators/hutchison-port-holdings/hph-extends-barcelona-concession-pledges-full-automation_20150925.html; "China's COSCO Shipping Buys $228 Million Stake in Spain's Noatum Port," Reuters, June 12, 2017, https://www.reuters.com/article/us-cosco-ship-hold-noatum-port/chinas-cosco-shipping-buys-228-million-stake-in-spains-noatum-port-idUSKBN19405I; and "China, Spain Sign Export Accord for Iberian Ham - Government Sources," Reuters, November 27, 2018, https://www.reuters.com/article/spain-china-ham/china-spain-sign-export-accord-for-iberian-ham-government-sources-idUKE8N1X3006.

109. Miriam Vázquez, "Las terminales chinas gestionan el 35% de los contenedores en España" [Chinese terminals manage 35 percent of containers in Spain], *El Mercantil*, May 20, 2019, https://elmercantil.com/2019/05/20/las-terminales-chinas-gestionan-el-35-de-los-contenedores-en-espana/.

110. "China Harbour Builds New Terminal in Egypt," Xinhua, August 30, 2018, http://www.china.org.cn/world/2018-08/30/content_61027233.htm.

111. Tahrir Institute for Middle East Policy, "TIMEP Brief: China's Role in Egypt's Economy," November 21, 2019, https://timep.org/reports-briefings/timep-brief-chinas-role-in-egypts-economy/.

112. The "Malacca Dilemma" was first expressed at the policy level by Chinese President Hu Jintao at a Chinese Communist Party economic work conference in November 2003. On details and strategic implications, see Marc Lanteigne, "China's Maritime Security and the 'Malacca Dilemma,'" *Asian Security* 4, no. 2 (Spring 2008): 143–61, https://doi.org/10.1080/14799850802006555.

113. "Pakistan Security Forces Kill Two After Attack on Chinese Convoy," Al Jazeera, August 23, 2023, https://www.aljazeera.com/news/2023/8/13/pakistan-security-forces-kill-two-after-attack-on-chinese-convoy-in-gwadar; and Ayaz Gul, "Insurgents Kill 14 Soldiers in Southwestern Pakistan," Voice of America News, November 3, 2023, https://www.voanews.com/a/insurgents-kill-14-soldiers-in-southwestern-pakistan/7340645.html.

114. Adnan Aamir, "Pakistan Vote Elevates Belt and Road Critic in Key Port of Gwadar," *Nikkei Asia*, February 18, 2024, https://asia.nikkei.com/Politics/Pakistan-elections/Pakistan-vote-elevates-Belt-and-Road-critic-in-key-port-of-Gwadar.

115. Joe Brock, "China Plans $500 Million Subsea Internet Cable to Rival US-Backed Project," Reuters, April 6, 2023, https://www.reuters.com/world/china/china-plans-500-mln-subsea-internet-cable-rival-us-backed-project-2023-04-06/. Gwadar is also completing a new international airport in 2024.

116. Dorothy Ellicott, *Our Gibraltar* (London: Gibraltar Museum Committee, 1975), 111.

117. On the rising global geo-economic importance of undersea fiber-optic cables, see Calder and Paik, "Quiet Crisis Beneath the Waves," 103–20.

118. Rudra P. Pradhan, Girijasankar Mallik, and Tapan P. Bagchi, "Information Communications Technology (ICT) Infrastructure and Economic Growth: A Causality Evinced by Cross-Country Panel Data," *IIMB Management Review* 30, no. 1 (March 2018): 91–103, https://doi.org/10.1016/j.iimb.2018.01.001.

119. Huawei's average annual sales growth in Greece (2015–2019) was 10.5 percent, and the firm supported 600 jobs there. See "China, Greece Have Vast Rooms for Cooperation in Improving Economy, Social Welfare and Mitigating Climate Change", *Global Times*, September 25, 2023. https://www.globaltimes.cn/page/202309/1298868.shtml.

120. Erik Brattberg, Philippe Le Corre, Paul Stronski, and Thomas de Waal, *China's Influence in Southeast, Central and Eastern Europe* (Washington, DC: Carnegie Endowment for International Peace, October 2021), https://carnegieendowment.org/files/202110-Brattberg_et_al_EuropeChina_final.pdf.

121. "China, Saudi Arabia Cement Ties with Deals Including Huawei," Al Jazeera, December 8, 2022, https://www.aljazeera.com/news/2022/12/8/saudi-crown-prince-meets-chinas-xi-in-push-to-deepen-ties.

122. Fahad Abduljadayel, "Huawei Looks to Move Middle East Headquarters to Saudi Arabia," Bloomberg, April 9, 2023 https://www.bloomberg.com/news/articles/2023-04-09/huawei-looks-to-move-middle-east-headquarters-to-saudi-arabia.

123. "Huawei Helps Unleash Saudi Arabia's Digital Capabilities at LEAP 2023," *Teletimes*, February 9, 2023, https://teletimesinternational.com/2023/huawei-helps-unleash-saudi-arabias-digital-capabilities-at-leap-2023/.

124. Qiu, "PEACE Cable System Goes Live"; and "PEACE Cable Project Enters into Cable and Material Manufacturing Stage," Huawei, October 22, 2018, https://www.huawei.com/en/news/2018/10/huawei-peace-cable-project.

125. Brock, "China Plans $500 Million Subsea Internet Cable." HMN Tech Company—which lost to SubCom on the SeaMeWe-6 cable bid—will manufacture and lay the Chinese cable.

126. Michael Safi, "Sri Lanka's 'New Dubai': Will Chinese-Built City Suck the Life Out of Colombo," *Guardian*, August 2, 2018, https://www.theguardian.com/cities/2018/aug/02/sri-lanka-new-dubai-chinese-city-colombo.

127. Stuart Heaver, "Sri Lanka's Chinese-Built Port City Stirs White Elephant Fears," Al Jazeera, February 17, 2023, https://www.aljazeera.com/economy/2023/2/17/sri-lankas-chinese-built-port-city-stirs-white-elephant-fears; and "US Plans to Build a $553 Million Terminal at Sri Lanka's Colombo Port in Rivalry with China," Associated Press, November 9, 2023, https://apnews.com/article/us-sri-lanka-port-china-bri-debt-d39cdd2446e8c5ab95f4181960f7958a.

128. Economist Impact, *Inclusive Internet Index 2022*, accessed September 28, 2024, https://impact.economist.com/projects/inclusive-internet-index/2022.

129. Mid-2021 Internet penetration in Bangladesh, for example, was 67 percent; the comparable figure in Myanmar was 52 percent, and in Cambodia 69 percent. Comparable figures for Pakistan and Sri Lanka, both recipients of major Chinese telecommunications investment, were 34 percent and 35 percent, respectively. Elsewhere along the PEACE undersea cable, Internet penetration ratios were 55 percent in Djibouti, 29 percent in Sudan, 26 percent in Yemen, 53 percent in Egypt, and 78 percent in Greece. In the United States, Internet penetration was 96 percent. For comparative statistics, see "Internet World Stats," accessed January 22, 2023, https://www.internetworldstats.com/stats1.htm.

130. "Chinese Naval Fleet Arrives in Greece for Friendly Visit," Xinhua, July 24, 2017, http://en.people.cn/n3/2017/0724/c90786-9245366.html.

131. Gresh, *To Rule Eurasia's Waves*, 120.

CHAPTER 6

1. Winston Churchill, *The River War*, vol. 1, 1st ed. (London: Longmans, Green, 1899), 413.

2. Michael M. McCrea, Karen N. Nornabyl, and Alexander F. Parker, "The Offensive Navy Since World War II: How Big and Why, A Brief Summary," Naval History and Heritage Command, July 1989, https://www.history.navy.mil/research/library/online-reading-room/title-list-alphabetically/o/the-offensive-navy-since-world-war-ii-how-big-and-why-a-brief-summary.html.

3. In 1936, the US Congress passed the Merchant Marine Act and created the Maritime Commission. That commission supervised an expansion of the US civilian maritime fleet in preparation for war. The War Shipping Administration, an emergency war agency established in 1942 under the War Powers Act of 1941, was responsible for purchasing and operating the civilian shipping tonnage that the United States needed to supply its war effort.

4. William D. Walters, "American Naval Shipbuilding, 1890–1989," *Geographical Review* 90, no. 3 (2000): 318–431; as well as Tim Colton and Lavar Huntzinger, "A Brief History of Shipbuilding in Recent Times," CNA, September 2002, https://www.cna.org/archive/CNA_Files/pdf/d0006988.a1.pdf.

5. "Liberty" and "Victory" ships were commercial vessels produced explicitly for the war effort.

6. Britain did lose substantial shipping during the war, but the losses were offset to some extent by increases in wartime production and Lend-Lease purchases from the

United States. By 1948, Britain's shipping fleet was back to 95 percent of its prewar tonnage. See S. G. Sturmey, *British Shipping and World Competition* (London: University of London Athlone Press, 1962), 138–59.

7. Bryan Clark, "Submarines Will Not Solve America's Eroding Undersea Advantage," *Washington Examiner*, December 5, 2022, https://www.washingtonexaminer.com/news/2877254/submarines-will-not-solve-americas-eroding-undersea-advantage/.

8. Loren Thompson, "In Brief: The Logic of Aircraft Carrier Strike Groups," The Lexington Institute, September 2019, https://www.lexingtoninstitute.org/wp-content/uploads/2019/10/Brief-The-Logic-of-Aircraft-Carrier-Strike-Groups2.pdf.

9. China, the United Kingdom, India, and Italy claim two aircraft carriers, while Russia, France, and Spain claim to possess one. See International Institute for Strategic Studies, *The Military Balance 2020*; and "Aircraft Carrier Fleet Strength by Country (2024)," Global Firepower, 2024, https://www.globalfirepower.com/navy-aircraft-carriers.php.

10. For details, see Calder, *Embattled Garrisons*. This naval network has declined from its pinnacle following the loss of Cam Ranh Bay in Vietnam, Subic Bay in the Philippines, and Piraeus in Greece, but it is still substantial.

11. Office of the Under Secretary of Defense (Comptroller), "Defense Budget Overview: United States Department of Defense Fiscal Year 2024 Budget Request," US Department of Defense, March 2023, https://comptroller.defense.gov/Budget-Materials/Budget2024/.

12. Amrita Jash, "China's 2023 Defense Spending: Figures, Intentions, and Concerns," *China Brief* 23, no. 7 (April 14, 2023), https://jamestown.org/program/chinas-2023-defense-spending-figures-intentions-and-concerns/.

13. The United States maintains eleven carrier battle groups, together with bases at Diego Garcia and Manama, Bahrain. China has only two carriers (the *Liaoning* and the *Shandong*) and a single base in the Indian Ocean region, at Djibouti, that is capable of servicing carriers, as well as amphibious assault ships. India has one carrier, INS *Vikramaditya*. See Tsukasa Hadano, "China Adds Carrier Piers to Djibouti Base, Extending Indian Ocean Reach," *Nikkei Asia*, April 27, 2021, https://asia.nikkei.com/Politics/International-relations/Indo-Pacific/China-adds-carrier-pier-to-Djibouti-base-extending-Indian-Ocean-reach.

14. John C. Roper, "U.S. Aircraft Carrier in Asia 'Routine,'" UPI, January 26, 1996, https://www.upi.com/Archives/1996/01/26/US-aircraft-carrier-in-Asia- routine/5535822632400/.

15. James Risen, "US Warns China on Taiwan, Sends Warships to Area," *Los Angeles Times*, March 11, 1996, https://www.latimes.com/archives/la-xpm-1996-03-11-mn-45722-story.html; and Dana Priest, "Second Group of US Ships Sent to Taiwan," *Washington Post*, March 11, 1996, https://www.washingtonpost.com/archive/politics/1996/03/11/second-group-of-us-ships-sent-to-taiwan/34280337-be79-4d6e-b859-8046682a37b3/.

16. White House, "On the Record Press Call by Kurt Campbell, Deputy Assistant to the President and Coordinator for the Indo-Pacific," August 12, 2022, https://www.whitehouse.gov/briefing-room/press-briefings/2022/08/12/on-the-record-press-call-by-kurt-campbell-deputy-assistant-to-the-president-and-coordinator-for-the-indo-pacific/.

17. Robert J. Natter and Samuel J. Locklear, "Former 4-Star Fleet Commanders: Don't Give Up on Carriers," *Defense News*, August 19, 2022, https://www.defensenews.com/naval/2019/11/22/former-4-star-fleet-commanders-dont-give-up-on-carriers/.

18. Benjamin S. Lambeth, ed., *American Carrier Air Power at the Dawn of a New Century* (Santa Monica, CA: RAND Corporation, 2005), 9–38; Thomas E. Ricks, "Operation Provide Comfort: A Forgotten Mission with Possible Implications for Syria," *Foreign Policy*, February 6,

2017, https://foreignpolicy.com/2017/02/06/operation-provide-comfort-a-forgotten-mission-with-possible-lessons-for-syria/; and David B. Larter, "What If the U.S. Stopped Sending Aircraft Carriers to the Arabian Gulf?," *Defense News*, May 2, 2018, https://www.defensenews.com/naval/2018/05/02/what-if-the-us-stopped-sending-aircraft-carriers-to-the-arabian-gulf/.

19. See Newport News Shipbuilding, "Fact Sheet," August 2020, https://www.huntingtoningalls.com/wp-content/uploads/2020/08/nn_facts05aug20.pdf.

20. Paltrow, "Special Report: Aircraft Carriers."

21. See CSIS Missile Threat Project, "DF-21 (CSS-5)," April 23, 2024, https://missilethreat.csis.org/missile/df-21/.

22. See Paltrow, "Special Report: Aircraft Carriers."

23. See the Ingalls Shipbuilding website at https://ingalls.huntingtoningalls.com.

24. Forecast International, "Meet the Top 3 Navy Contractors of 2021," December 9, 2022, https://dsm.forecastinternational.com/2022/12/09/meet-the-top-3-navy-contractors-of-2021. Raytheon, which produces Aegis SM-3 interceptors, is the third-largest Navy contractor following Lockheed Martin and General Dynamics.

25. See "Highly Specialized Vessels Designed for Job Specific Tasks," on the Edison Chouest Offshore website at http://www.chouest.com/vessels.html.

26. Ken Moriyasu, "Repairing US Ships in Japan 'Very Important': Defense Chief Kihara," *Nikkei Asia*, October 6, 2023; and Christy Lee, "U.S. Navy Looking to S. Korean, Japanese Shipbuilders to Revive American Shipyards," *Voice of America News*, March 7, 2024, https://voanews.com/a/us-navy-looking-to-s-korean-japanese-shipbuilders-to-revive-american-shipyards/7518826.html.

27. Industrial College of the Armed Forces, "In Touch with Industry: ICAF Industry Studies 1998: Shipbuilding," Homeland Security Digital Library, 1998, https://www.hsdl.org/c/abstract/?docid=1759.

28. On the employment statistics for 2023, see "Shipbuilding in the US—Employment Statistics, 2005–2030," IBISWorld, March 21, 2024, https://www.ibisworld.com/industry-statistics/employment/ship-building-united-states/.

29. Philadelphia Naval Shipyard produced a diverse range of vessels, from aircraft carriers to cruisers and landing craft. See Colin Woodward, "The Coolest Shipyard in America," *Politico Magazine*, July 21, 2016, https://www.politico.com/magazine/story/2016/07/philadelphia-what-works-navy-yard-214072.

30. Kvaener, the fourth-largest shipyard group in the world at the time, concluded a public-private partnership agreement with the city of Philadelphia and the state of Pennsylvania in 1997 to save the yard. In 2005, control of the yard passed to Aker, another Norwegian company, and Aker American Shipping ASA was formed. In 2007, Aker American Shipping was split into two companies: the shipbuilding company, Aker Philadelphia Shipyard, and the ship-owning company, Aker American Shipping (known as American Shipping Company today). See Michael Kleiner, "'Vikings' Rescue Philadelphia Shipyard Twice," *The Norwegian American*, April 21, 2021, https://www.norwegianamerican.com/vikings-rescue-philadelphia-shipyard-twice/.

31. Keppel AmFELS, based in Brownsville, Texas, produces primarily oil rigs and other specialized vessels for private industry. In October 2020, it was awarded a contract to build the largest dredge in US history for Manson Construction Company of Seattle, Washington. ST Engineering received a $1.9 billion contract in 2019 from the US Navy, through its VT

Halter Marine affiliate in Mississippi, to build polar security cutters (icebreakers). On these transactions, see Steve Clark, "Keppel AmFELS Wins Contract: Port-Based Company Will Build Nation's Largest Dredge," *Brownsville Herald*, October 22, 2020; and "ST Engineering Wins Up to $1.9 Billion Contract to Build Icebreakers for U.S. Navy," Reuters, April 23, 2019, https://www.reuters.com/article/us-st-engineering-contract/st-engineering-wins-up-to-1-9-billion-contract-to-build-icebreakers-for-u-s-navu-idUSKCN1S007E.

32. John Frittelli, "U.S. Commercial Shipbuilding in a Global Context," IF12534 (Washington, DC: Congressional Research Service, November 15, 2023), https://crsreports.congress.gov/product/pdf/IF/IF12534.

33. In 2019, China not only was the largest shipbuilder, but also possessed the largest navy in number of ships at the end of 2020—360, vs. 297 for the United States. See Ronald O'Rourke, *Chinese Naval Modernization: Implications for U.S. Navy Capabilities: Background and Issues for Congress*, RL33153 (Washington, DC: Congressional Research Service, March 2021), https://fas.org/sgp/crs/row/RL33153.pdf; and BRS Brokers, *Shipbuilding Market Review 2020* (Neuilly-sur-Seine, France: BRS Brokers, 2020), https://cdn.brsshipbrokers.skreycloud.com/annualreview2020_ec15c629b3.html.

34. US Department of Defense, *Military and Security Developments Involving the People's Republic of China 2023: Annual Report to Congress*, October 19, 2023, https://media.defense.gov/2023/Oct/19/2003323409/-1/-1/1/2023-MILITARY-AND-SECURITY-DEVELOPMENTS-INVOLVING-THE-PEOPLES-REPUBLIC-OF-CHINA.PDF.

35. O'Rourke, *Chinese Naval Modernization*.

36. See BRS Brokers, *Shipbuilding Market Review 2020*.

37. See "China Shipbuilding Industry Corporation (CSIC): Company Background," *Nikkei Asia*, accessed June 17, 2024. https://asia.nikkei.com/Companies/China-Shipbuilding-Industry-Co.-Ltd.

38. Defense Universities China Tracker, "China Shipbuilding Industry Corporation," International Cyber Policy Centre, Australian Strategic Policy Institute, May 5, 2021, https://unitracker.aspi.org.au/universities/china-shipbuilding-industry-corporation.

39. Bulk carriers in 2023 accounted for 43 percent of global shipping tonnage, oil tankers for 29 percent, and container ships for 13 percent. The United States was the largest owner of ferries and passenger ships, a category covering less than 1 percent of global shipping tonnage, and second in offshore vessels, with 4 percent of global tonnage. See United Nations Conference on Trade and Development, *Review of Maritime Transport 2023*, November 12, 2023, 30, https://unctad.org/webflyer/review-maritime-transport-2023.

40. On the transition to container shipping, which ironically originated in the United States, see Levinson, *The Box*, especially 1–15.

41. Arbia Hlali and Sami Hammami, "The Evolution of Containerization and Its Impact on the Maghreb Ports," *Analysis of Marine Science*, February 16, 2019, https://dx.doi.org/10.17352/ams.000012.

42. "Annual Facts and Figures Card," The Port of Los Angeles, accessed June 17, 2024, https://www.portoflosangeles.org/business/statistics/facts-and-figures.

43. See World Shipping Council, "The Top 50 Container Ports," accessed June 17, 2024, https://www.worldshipping.org/top-50-ports.

44. Linton Nightingale, "One Hundred Ports: The Numbers Tell the Story," Lloyd's List, August 18, 2022, https://lloydslist.com/LL1141949/One-Hundred-Ports-The-numbers-tell-the-story.

45. For 1968–2012 statistics, see the Container Transportation website: https://www.containertransportation.com.

46. Michele Labrut, "World's Largest Boxship *Ever Alot* Flagged with Panama," *Sea Trade Maritime News*, July 12, 2022, https://www.seatrade-maritime.com/containers/worlds-largest-boxship-ever-alot-flagged-panama.

47. Sapna Ramaswamy and Paul Davidson, "The Devastating Baltimore Bridge Collapse Will Have Sweeping Economic Impacts," *USA Today*, March 28, 2024, https://www.usatoday.com/story/news/politics/2024/03/28/baltimore-bridge-collapse-economic-cost/73117309007/.

48. The holistic Chinese approach typically involves provision of optimal-scale Chinese-made port equipment; construction services; oversight for cargo movements, transshipment, and storage; as well as container leasing, finance, and maritime insurance. Comprehensive services of this sort tent to lock provider and customer into ongoing ties where Chinese parties enjoy strong leverage. See Kardon and Leutert, "Pier Competitor," 28.

49. See the COSCO website at http://en.coscoshipping.com.

50. China COSCO SHIPPING Corporation Limited, "Group Profile," accessed January 2, 2024, https://en.coscoshipping.com/col6918/art/2016/art_6918_45339.html.

51. Division of Ship Statistics, Office of Subsidy and Government Aid, *Merchant Fleets of the World: September 1939–December 31, 1951* (Washington, DC: US Department of Transportation, Maritime Administration November 1952), 3.

52. Bureau of Transportation Statistics, "Table 1-24: Number and Size of the U.S. Flag Merchant Fleet and Its Share of the World Fleet," US Department of Transportation, October 21, 2016, https://www.bts.gov/archive/publications/national_transportation_statistics/table_01_24.

53. "Alphaliner Top 100," Alphaliner, March 31, 2024, https://alphaliner.axmarine.com/PublicTop100/.

54. On Matson's operations, which include personal automobile shipments and other consumer services that no Northeast Asian line would consider, see the Matson website at https://www.matson.com.

55. On Seaboard Marine, America's number-two shipping line, see the Seaboard website at https://www.seaboardmarine.com.

56. On Maclean's key role in the development of containerized shipping, especially during the Vietnam War, see Levinson, *The Box*, 36–52.

57. See Levinson. *The Box*, 150–70.

58. China COSCO SHIPPING Corporation Limited, "Group Profile." It was second largest globally in 2020, but fell back during the COVID pandemic, which inhibited Chinese trade and economic growth.

59. In 2000–2001, the decision was made to begin construction on the first of four phases. The fourth phase began operation in December 2017. Overall, the port has thirty berths, capable of handling 15 million TEUs annually. See "PSA, China Shipping Hold Share," *China Daily*, January 26, 2007, http://www.chinadaily.com.cn/bizchina/2007-01/26/content_793875.htm.

60. In Shanghai, COSCO owns 15 percent of the shares of SIPG. It also owns minority stakes in two companies that utilize container berths within the port. See the "Terminals" section of the COSCO SHIPPING Ports website at https://ports.coscoshipping.com/en/Businesses/Portfolio/#GreaterChinaTerminals.

61. See the memoir of Chinese Commerce Ministry official Zhang Guobao, "The demonstration and decision-making process of the construction of Shanghai Yangshan Deepwater Port in which I participated" [in Chinese], Guancha, November 1, 2018, https://www.guancha.cn/ZhangGuoBao/2018_11_02_477931_2.shtml.

62. Lloyd's List, "One Hundred Container Ports 2023," accessed June 20, 2024, https://lloydslist.com/one-hundred-container-ports-2023.

63. COSCO owns 49 percent of a joint venture with PSA in Singapore, 20 percent of an operating company at Port Said; and a controlling interest in Piraeus. Among these ports along the Eurasian sea lanes in which COSCO holds major shares, Piraeus ranked thirtieth worldwide; and Algeciras was thirty-first. Between 2014 and 2018, the TEU volume of Piraeus rose 36.8 percent, whereas the volume at Los Angeles' largest port only rose by 13.6 percent during the same period. See the World Shipping Council website at https://www.worldshipping.org.

64. If combined, Los Angeles and Long Beach would rank ninth globally, but they are logistically separate and do not enjoy the scale economies of a consolidated port. See the World Shipping Council, "The Top 50 Container Ports," accessed June 20, 2024, http://worldshipping.org/top-50-ports. Figures are for 2021 volumes. For 2022, New York ranked seventeenth, but comparative figures are not fully complete.

65. Jo Craven McGinty and Paul Overberg, "These Eight US Bridges Are Vulnerable to a Repeat of the Baltimore Crash," *Wall Street Journal*, March 29, 2024, https://www.wsj.com/us-news/these-eight-u-s-bridges-are-vulnerable-to-a-repeat-of-the-baltimore-crash-f2a2a057.

66. Dustin Volz, "Espionage Probe Finds Communication Device on Chinese Cranes at US Ports," *Wall Street Journal*, March 7, 2024, https://www.wsj.com/politics/national-security/espionage-probe-finds-communications-device-on-chinese-cargo-cranes-867d32c0.

67. At Shanghai's Yangshan Deep Water Port, for example, introduction of state-of-the-art technology has boosted the average crane capacity of the port to 36.1 containers per hour—50 percent above the global average. See "The Future of Automation at Terminals and Ports," *Containers*, October 9, 2018, https://www.icontainers.com/us/2018/10/09/the-future-of-automation-at-terminals-and-ports/.

68. "China Leads World's Automated Container Terminals amid Smart Technology Boom," *CGTN*, January 29, 2024, https://news.cgtn.com/news/2024-01-29/China-leads-world-s-automated-container-terminals-amid-smart-tech-boom-1qLvtCaraog/p.html.

69. "World's Largest Automated Terminal," *Sea Trade Maritime News,* June 20, 2024, https://www.seatrade-maritime.com/ports/worlds-largest-automated-terminal-psa-tuas-port-pioneering-automation-transformation-event.

70. "World's Largest Automated Terminal."

71. "World's Largest Automated Terminal."

72. Nicole Starosielski, *The Undersea Network* (Durham, NC: Duke University Press, 2015), 31–37.

73. Tim Stronge, "Does 70 Percent of the World's Internet Traffic Flow through Virginia?," *TeleGeography* (blog), May 30, 2019, https://blog.telegeography.com/does-70-of-the-worlds-internet-traffic-flow-through-virginia.

74. In December 2020, more than 53 percent of global internet users were in Asia. See "Internet Users in the World by Regions," Internet World Statistics, December 31, 2018, https://www.internetworldstats.com/stats.htm.

75. In India, for example, the number of internet users more than tripled during 2012–2016 from 92 million to 390 million; in Nigeria, it more than doubled from 18 million to 48 million. See International Telecommunications Union, "Internet Users by Region and Country, 2010–2016," 2024, https://www.itu.int/en/ITU-D/Statistics/Pages/stat/Treemap.aspx.

76. Page, O'Keeffe, and Taylor, "America's Undersea Battle." This was unchanged in 2021. Hiroyuki Akita, "Undersea Cables — Huawei's Ace in the Hole," *Nikkei Asia*, May 28, 2019, https://asia.nikkei.com/Spotlight/Comment/Undersea-cables-Huawei-s-ace-in-the-hole

77. Huawei's Brazil-Cameroon undersea cable project is known as the South Atlantic Inter Link (SAIL) project, a government-to-government affair funded heavily by the Export-Import Bank of China. See Tom McGregor, "China Breakthroughs: SAIL Ahead on South Atlantic Cable Network," CCTV, July 5, 2017, https://english.cctv.com/2017/07/05/ARTITioQntQhXqvZoN4dwobj170705.shtml; and Hillman, *Digital Silk Road*, 145–46.

78. In 2020, Hengtong had the third-largest global market share in fiber-optic cable, while YOFC, also a Chinese firm, was number two, and the US firm Corning was number one. See Network Telecom Information Institute. "The Top 10 Competitiveness Enterprises in the Optical Communications Industry of China & Global Market in 2019," accessed June 17, 2024, http://www.networktelecom.cn/dianxin/2020/baogao/en/index.html

79. "Made in China 2025," with which major Chinese firms like Hengtong are involved, is also targeting a 60 percent global Chinese share for fiber-optic communications equipment as a national goal. See the unofficial US-China Business Council chart of localization target by sector, set in the MIIT Made in China 2025 Key Technical Road Map, in Nick Marro, "Navigating the 'Made in China 2025' Roadmap and China's Market Share Goals," US-China Business Council, February 3, 2016, https://www.uschina.org/navigating-%E2%80%98made-china-2025%E2%80%99-roadmap-and-china%E2%80%99s-market-share-goals.

80. BRI Monitor, "Case Study: Kumul Submarine Cable Network Project," Institute for National Affairs Papua New Guinea, 2021, https://www.brimonitor.org/case-studies/kumul-submarine-cable-network-project-kscnp/#16146558966y6-2d/fad11-0659.

81. HT GD, "Products," June 24, 2024, http://www.hengtonggroup.com/en/home/products/index.html.

82. "Hengtong Optic-Electrical Unit to Jointly Set Up Underwater Optical Network Joint Laboratory," Reuters, November 1, 2016, https://www.reuters.com/article/idUSL4N1D22TU/.

CHAPTER 7

1. Peter Hopkirk, *The Great Game: The Struggle for Empire in Central Asia* (New York: Kodansha America, 1994).

2. The top three global shipping companies in 2023 were European, with COSCO ranking fourth. For details, see the Alphaliner Top 100 listings, https://alphaliner.axsmarine.com/PublicTop100/.

3. Juan Caballero and Marco Fengler, "China and India: The Future of the Global Consumer Market," Brookings, April 14, 2023, https://www.brookings.edu/articles/china-and-india-the-future-of-the-global-consumer-market/.

4. Yongchang China and Rakesh Sharma, "India Set to Surpass China in Need for Oil as Growth Paths Diverge," Bloomberg, March 23, 2023, https://www.bloomberg.com/

news/articles/2023-03-23/new-demand-engine-for-crude-oil-tilt-to-India-foreshadows-china-s-green-shift/.

5. On this dynamic, and its global systemic implications, see Calder, *Super Continent*.

6. Stephen M. Walt, *The Origin of Alliances* (Ithaca, NY: Cornell University Press, 1987), 10, 17–49.

7. Beijing and Taipei have different names for the Senkakus—Diaoyudao and Diaoyutai, respectively.

8. On the concept of "trading state," and the inclination of such states to seek stable interdependence, see Richard Rosecrance, *The Rise of the Trading State: Commerce and Conquest in the Modern World* (New York: Basic Books, 1986); Etel Solingen, *Nuclear Logics: Contrasting Patterns in East Asia and the Middle East* (Princeton, NJ: Princeton University Press, 2007); and Etel Solingen, *Comparative Regionalism: Economics and Security* (New York: Routledge, 2015).

9. See Darshana M. Baruah, Nitya Labh, and Jessica Greely, "Mapping the Indian Ocean Region," Carnegie Endowment for International Peace, June 15, 2023, https://carnegie endowment.org/2023/06/15/mapping-indian-ocean-region-pub-89971.

10. Richard Rosecrance, *The Rise of the Virtual State: Wealth and Power in the Coming Century* (New York: Basic Books, 1999). Such states provide a variety of important financial, technical, and research services, despite their small scale.

11. See Calder, *Singapore*, especially 16–27.

12. See, for example, Joyce C. Lebra, *Japanese-Trained Armies in Southeast Asia* (Singapore: Institute of Southeast Asian Studies, 2010); Joyce C. Lebra, *The Indian National Army and Japan* (Kuala Lumpur: ISEAS Yusof Ishak Institute, 2008); and Niall Ferguson, *Civilization: The West and the Rest* (London, Allen Lane, 2011).

13. See Kent E. Calder, "Japanese Foreign Economic Policy Formation: Explaining the Reactive State," *World Politics* 40, no. 4 (July 1988): 517–41. Japan's parliamentary system, lack of a powerful chief executive, and factionalism inside the ruling Liberal Democratic Party have contributed to this pattern, as has an asymmetrical US-Japan relationship.

14. Peter J. Katzenstein and Takashi Shiraishi, eds., *Network Power: Japan and Asia* (Ithaca, NY: Cornell University Press, 1997); and Mireya Solis, *Japan's Quiet Leadership: Reshaping the Indo-Pacific* (Washington, DC: Brookings Institution Press, 2023).

15. Takashi Terada, "Australia and Japan's Alliance Can Beat China's Interdependence Trap," *Japan Times*, February 20, 2021, https://www.japantimes.co.jp/opinion/2021/02/20/commentary/world-commentary/api-australia-china/.

16. The six included a Northeast Asian triad of Japan, South Korea, and China, augmented by Australia, New Zealand, and India.

17. K.V. Kesavan, "The Expanding Japan-Australia Security Cooperation," Observer Research Foundation, December 4, 2020, https://www.orfonline.org/expert-speak/the-expanding-japan-australia-security-cooperation/.

18. Danie Hurst and Justin McCurry, "Australia and Japan Agree in Principle to Defense Pact That Will Increase Military Ties," *Guardian*, November 17, 2020, https://www.theguardian.com/australia-news/2020/nov/17/australia-and-japan-agree-in-principle-to-defence-pact-that-will-increase-military-ties.

19. On this concept, see John J. Mearsheimer and Stephen M. Walt, "The Case for Off-shore Balancing," *Foreign Affairs*, June 13, 2016, https://www.foreignaffairs.com/articles/united-states/2016-06-13/case-offshore-balancing.

20. Aqeel Akhtar, "Nuclear Submarines Shift Strategic Balance of Indian Ocean," International Institute for Strategic Studies, January 19, 2019, https://www.iiss.org/online-analysis/online-analysis//2019/01/nuclear-submarines-indian-ocean.

21. In 2018–2019, 55 percent of the Indian defense budget went to the army, 23 percent to the air force, and only 15 percent to the navy. Since independence, troubles along India's continental borders, including a devastating war with China and a number of wars with Pakistan, have kept the country's defense focused on its northern frontiers. A placid maritime environment—primarily owing to weaker littoral states and a strong navy inherited from the British—has allowed India to establish a prominent maritime role in the Indian Ocean region without much effort. See Laxman Kumar Behera, *Defense Budget 2018–19: The Imperative of Controlling Manpower Cost* (New Delhi: Institute of Defense Studies and Analysis, February 2, 2018), https://idsa.in/issuebrief/defence-budget-2018-19-controlling-manpower-cost-lkbehera-020218.

22. Yaroslav Trafimov, "India Seeks Naval Edge as China Penetrates Indian Ocean," *Wall Street Journal*, September 24, 2020, https://www.wsj.com/articles/india-seeks-naval-edge-as-china-penetrates-indian-ocean-11600945203. Also, Roygit, "Chinese Submarines and Indian ASW in the Indian Ocean," Fahamu Networks for Social Justice, December 11, 2014, https://www.fahamu.org/ep_articles/chinese-submarines-and-indian-asw-in-the-indian-ocean/.

23. International Institute for Strategic Studies, *The Military Balance 2024*, 267.

24. H. I. Sutton, "India's Submarines Make Strategic Move to Dominate Indian Ocean," *Forbes*, June 20, 2020, https://www.forbes.com/sites/hisutton/2020/06/20/indias-submarines-make-strategic-move-to-dominate-in-indian-ocean/?sh=57508e3d604f. That activism has included the commissioning of more than eighty naval vessels in the past five years, and establishment of new bases at Djibouti and elsewhere.

25. See James Kynge, Chris Campbell, Amy Kazmin, and Farhan Bokhari, "Beijing's Global Power Play: How China Rules the Waves," *Financial Times*, January 12, 2017, https://ig.ft.com/sites/china-ports/.

26. See Ankit Panda, "Chinese Naval Exercise in Eastern Indian Ocean Sends Mixed Signals," *The Diplomat*, February 07, 2014, https://thediplomat.com/2014/02/chinese-naval-exercise-in-eastern-indian-ocean-sends-mixed-signals/

27. Abhijit Singh, "Militarizing Andamans: The Costs and the Benefits," *Hindustan Times*, July 29, 2020, https://www.hindustantimes.com/analysis/militarising-andamans-the-costs-and-the-benefits/story-J3mGWFQS3NgLUiPYwIVb2N.html.

28. Panda, "Chinese Naval Exercise In Eastern Indian Ocean Sends Mixed Signals."

29. India's GDP was around $3.2 trillion in 2021, compared to $17.7 trillion for China. The coronavirus pandemic hurt India's growth much more than China. India will, to be sure, experience a long-term demographic dividend, contrasting to China's demographic time bomb. Owing to the huge gap in current economic scale, however, it will be many years before India even comes close to China's economic scale. On this issue, see "India vs. China: Is There Even a Comparison?," Management Study Guide, February 14, 2021, https://www.managementstudyguide.com/india-vs-china.htm. On statistics, see the World Bank's 2021 data at https://data.worldbank.org/indicator/NY.GDP.MKTP.CD.

30. In terms of logistics capability, India consistently is being outperformed by many of its Asian neighbors. On the World Bank's logistics performance index, India ranked 38th, beaten out by Japan (14th), Singapore (1st), Hong Kong (7th); and China (19th). Though in

Singapore, average ship turnaround time was 1.2 days, compared to 1.1 days in India. See the 2023 World Bank Logistics Performance Index at https://lpi.worldbank.org/international/global.

31. More than 70 percent of Sri Lanka's transshipments are linked to India. See Harry G. Broadman, "India's Ossified Ports Are Ceding Indo-Pacific Trade to China," *Forbes*, July 14, 2021, https://www.forbes.com/sites/harrybroadman/2021/03/26/indias-ossified-ports-are-ceding-indo-pacific-trade-to-china/.

32. Surupa Gupta and Sumit Ganguly, "Why India Refused to Join the World's Biggest Trading Bloc," *Foreign Policy*, November 23, 2020, https://foreignpolicy.com/2020/11/23/why-india-refused-to-join-rcep-worlds-biggest-trading-bloc/.

33. See Calder, *The Bay of Bengal*, 72.

34. Shinzo Abe, "Confluence of the Two Seas" (speech before the Parliament of the Republic of India, August 22, 2007), Japanese Ministry of Foreign Affairs, https://www.mofa.go.jp/region/asia-paci/pmv0708/speech-2.html.

35. For a succinct history of the Quad, see Tanvi Madan, "The Rise, Fall, and Rebirth of the 'Quad,'" *War on the Rocks*, November 16, 2017, https://warontherocks.com/2017/11/rise-rebirth-quad/.

36. Gurpreet Khurana, "India–US MALABAR Naval Exercises: Trends and Tribulations," National Maritime Foundation, October 2023, https://www.academia.edu/7879273/India_US_MALABAR_Naval_Exercises_Trends_and_Tribulations.

37. See Shinzo Abe, "Asia's Democratic Security Diamond," *Project Syndicate*, December 27, 2012, https://www.project-syndicate.org/magazine/a-strategic-alliance-for-japan-and-india-by-shinzo-abe.

38. The Liberal National Coalition, a center-right agglomeration consisting of libertarian, business, and rural interests, was in power after 2013.

39. Obama was Singh's principal guest at the January 2015 Republic Day celebrations. "Obama Becomes First US President to Be Chief Guest at Republic Day Parade," *India Today*, January 26, 2015, https://www.indiatoday.in/obama-in-india/story/obama-first-us-president-to-be-chief-guest-at-republic-day-celebrations-237410-2015-01-26.

40. "Address of Prime Minister Shinzo Abe at the Opening Session of TICAD VI," August 27, 2016, Japanese Ministry of Foreign Affairs, https://www.mofa.go.jp/afr/af2/page4e_000496.html.

41. John Garnaut, "Is Malcolm Turnbull 'Soft' on China Because of His Family Connections?," *Sydney Morning Herald*, September 15, 2015, https://www.smh.com.au/national/is-malcolm-turnbull-soft-on-china-because-of-his-family-connections-20150915-gjnbz8.html.

42. Bruce Vaughn, *Australia, China, and the Indo-Pacific*, CRS IN10888 (Washington, DC: Congressional Research Service, April 23, 2018), 1, https://crsreports.congress.gov/product/pdf/IN/IN10888/5.

43. Australian Bureau of Statistics, "2021 Australia, Census All Persons QuickStats," June 28, 2021, https://www.abs.gov.au/census/find-census-data/quickstats/2021/AUS.

44. International education contributed A$37.6 billion (US$25 billion) to the Australian economy during the 2018–2019 financial year, and Chinese students made up over 38 percent of all international enrollments. See Hazel Ferguson and Henry Sherrell, "Overseas Students in Australian Higher Education: A Quick Guide," Social Policy Section, Parliament of Australia, 2019, https://www.aph.gov.au/About_Parliament/Parliamentary_Departments/Parliamentary_Library/pubs/rp/rp2021/Quick_Guides/OverseasStudents.

45. "Joint Statement with the Honorable Scott Morrison MP, Prime Minister—Hong Kong," Home Affairs Portfolio, Parliament of Australia, July 9, 2020, https://minister.homeaffairs.gov.au/alantudge/Pages/hong-kong-visa-arrangement-20200709.aspx.

46. Sahil Pandey and Joymala Bagchi, "Modi-Morrison Virtual Summit Elevated India-Australia Ties: Indian High Commissioner," ANI News, July 10, 2020, https://www.aninews.in/news/national/general-news/modi-morrison-virtual-summit-elevated-india-australia-ties-indian-high-commissioner20200710112534/.

47. See National Security Council, "U.S. Strategic Framework for the Indo-Pacific," Trump White House Archives, US National Archives and Records Administration (declassified January 15, 2021), https://trumpwhitehouse.archives.gov/wp-content/uploads/2021/01/IPS-Final-Declass.pdf.

48. US INDOPACOM, "US INDOPACOM Area of Responsibility," September 2023, https://www.pacom.mil/About-USINDOPACOM/USPACOM-Area-of-Responsibility/.

49. The sanctions, in retaliation for Australia's call for an inquiry into the possible Chinese origins of the coronavirus, involved suspension of Chinese imports of Australian beef, barley, wine, timber, and lobsters, among other products, although China remained Australia's largest trading partner. See Zaheena Rasheed, "What Is the Quad and Can It Counter China's Rise?," Al Jazeera, November 25, 2020, https://www.aljazeera.com/news/2020/11/25/what-is-the-quad-can-us-india-japan-and-australia-deter-china.

50. Particularly notable steps included provocative actions in the South China Sea, imposition of a draconian National Security Law to quell dissent in Hong Kong, and military provocations against India in disputed areas along the Line of Control. See Abraham Denmark, Charles Edel, and Siddharth Mohandas, "The Same as Ever: China's Pandemic Opportunism on its Periphery," *War on the Rocks*, April 16, 2020, https://warontherocks.com/2020/04/same-as-it-ever-was-chinas-pandemic-opportunism-on-its-periphery/.

51. All four, together with Singapore, participated in the 2007 Malabar exercises on a one-time basis. Japan joined permanently in 2015, while Australia became an established member in 2020. See Salvatore Babones, "The Quad's Malabar Exercises Point the Way to an Asian NATO," *Foreign Policy*, November 25, 2020, https://foreignpolicy.com/2020/11/25/india-japan-australia-u-s-quad-alliance-nato/.

52. See Jagannath P. Panda, "India, the Blue Dot Network, and the 'Quad Plus' Calculus," *Journal of Indo-Pacific Affairs* 3, no. 3 (Fall 2020), 3–21, https://www.airuniversity.af.edu/JIPA/Display/Article/2278057/india-the-blue-dot-network-and-the-quad-plus-calculus/.

53. See Jason Scott, "Japan, Australia, and India to Launch Supply Chain Initiative," Bloomberg, September 1, 2020, https://www.bloomberg.com/news/articles/2021-04-27/supply-chain-initiative-from-japan-india-australia-under-way.

54. Patrick Gerard Buchan and Benjamin Rimland, "Defining the Diamond: The Past, Present, and Future of the Quadrilateral Security Dialogue," CSIS, March 16, 2020, https://www.csis.org/analysis/defining-diamond-past-present-and-future-quadrilateral-security-dialogue.

55. One such project is the joint US-Australia naval-base initiative on Papua New Guinea's Manus Island, announced by US Vice President Mike Pence in November 2018. The prospective base, more than 4,000 kilometers southeast of China, is arguably safer from Chinese outreach than Guam, located only 3,000 kilometers from China. Long-range Chinese weapons, such as the Dong Feng–26 intermediate-range ballistic missile and the cruise-missile-armed H–6K bomber, reportedly can now hit targets close to 4,000 kilometers

away. See CSIS Missile Threat Project, "DF-26," April 23, 2024, https://missilethreat.csis.org/missile/dong-feng-26-df-26/.

56. Kunal Prohit, "India Joins French-Led Naval Exercise, Revealing Clues about Quad's Plans to Contain China in Indo-Pacific," *South China Morning Post*, April 4, 2021, https://www.scmp.com/week-asia/politics/article/3128236/india-joins-french-led-naval-exercise-revealing-clues-about.

57. Buchan and Rimland, "Defining the Diamond."

58. White House, "Fact Sheet: Quad Leaders' Summit," September 24, 2021, https://www.whitehouse.gov/briefing-room/statements-releases/2021/09/24/fact-sheet-quad-leaders-summit/; and White House, "Quad Leaders' Summit Fact Sheet," May 20, 2023, https://www.whitehouse.gov/briefing-room/statements-releases/2023/05/20/quad-leaders-summit-fact-sheet/.

59. France, Britain, and Germany have all recently participated in Indo-Pacific naval exercises, and are engaging on economic matters as well. See Jagannath P. Panda, "Quad Plus: Form Versus Substance," *Journal of Indo-Pacific Affairs* 3, no. 5 (2020), 3–13, https://media.defense.gov/2021/Feb/06/2002577570/-1/-1/1/JIPA_QUAD_PLUS_SPECIAL_ISSUE.PDF.

60. Ken Moriyasu, "Philippines First, India Later, as US Prioritizes 'Squad' Allies," *Nikkei Asia*, May 8, 2024, asia.nikkei.com/Politics/Internationalr.elations/Indo-Pacific/Philippines-first-India-later-as-US-prioritizes-Squad-allies.

61. Prohit, "India Joins French-Led Naval Exercise."

62. India's continuing strategic relationships with Russia and Iran could be considered cases of "multi-alignment." See, for example, Franz-Stefan Gady, "Russia Confirms Delivery of S-400 Air Defense Systems to India Will Begin in 2020," *The Diplomat,* July 3, 2019, https://thediplomat.com/2019/07/russia-confirms-delivery-of-s-400-air-defense-systems-to-india-will-begin-in-2020/; also Bobo Lo, *Once More With Feeling: Russia and the Asia Pacific*, Lowy Institute Analysis (Sydney: The Lowy Institute, 2019), 10, https://www.lowyinstitute.org/publications/once-more-feeling-russia-and-asia-pacific; and Tanvi Madan, "Trump Tightens Sanctions on Iran's Oil Exports — How India Will Respond," *Order from Chaos* (blog), Brookings, April 23, 2019, https://www.brookings.edu/blog/order-from-chaos/2019/04/23/trump-tightens-sanctions-on-irans-oil-exports-how-india-will-respond/.

63. The November 2019 Cross-Strait Summit between Xi Jinping and Ma Ying-jeou, as well as the June 2018 US–North Korea summit between Donald Trump and Kim Jong-un, were held in Singapore. On Singapore's diplomatic role, see Calder, *Singapore*, 97–105; and Kent E. Calder, *Global Political Cities: Actors and Arenas of Influence in International Affairs* (Washington, DC: Brookings Institution Press, 2021), 129–31.

64. The Republic of China, as Taiwan presents itself internationally, is recognized by only fourteen countries, including the Vatican, compared to twenty-three in 2011. It was derecognized by two strategically important South Pacific nations, the Solomon Islands and Kiribati, in 2019, and by Nicaragua in 2021.

65. On the "Island China" concept, see Ralph Clough, *Island China* (Cambridge, MA: Harvard University Press, 2014).

66. See "How Taiwan Beat China to Be Asia's Top-Performing Economy," DW, February 26, 2021, https://www.dw.com/en/how-taiwan-beat-china-to-be-asias-top-performing-economy/a-56710096.

67. During 2020–2024, Taiwanese real GDP increased around 3.5 percent annually, compared to around 5.3 percent for mainland China. For the comparative figures, see the Statista website at https://www.statista.com/statistics.

68. The Biden administration, for example, sent a guided-missile destroyer through the Taiwan Strait on February 24, 2021, for the second time in two months. In 2020, the US Navy conducted thirteen Taiwan Strait transits, breaking its previous record of twelve during 2016. See Oriana Skylar Mastro, "How China Is Bending the Rules in the South China Sea," *The Interpreter* (blog), Lowy Institute, February 17, 2021, https://www.lowyinstitute.org/the-interpreter/how-china-bending-rules-south-china-sea.

69. "US Approves $100 Million Arms Sale to Taiwan for Missile Upgrades," France 24, February 8, 2022, https://www.france24.com/en/asia-pacific/20220208-us-approves-100-million-arms-sale-to-taiwan-for-missile-upgrades.

70. See Cindy Wang, "Number of Hong Kongers Moving to Taiwan Hits a Record," Bloomberg, January 26, 2022, https://www.bloomberg.com/news/articles/2022-01-27/number-of-hong-kongers-moving-to-taiwan-hits-a-record.

71. In 2020, for example, Indian parliamentarians attended (albeit virtually) the swearing-in ceremony of a Taiwanese president for the first time. In October 2021, former Australian Prime Minister Tony Abbott spoke at Taiwan's Yushan Forum. See Sana Hashmi, "India-Taiwan Relations: Time Is Ripe to Bolster Ties," *Indian Foreign Affairs Journal* 15, no. 1 (January–March 2020): 33–47, https://www.jstor.org/stable/48630158.

72. Kennedy, *Rise and Fall of British Naval Mastery.*

73. European Commission, "Association of Southeast Asian Nations," accessed March 20, 2024, https://policy.trade.ec.europa.eu/eu-trade-relationships-country-and-region/countries-and-regions/association-south-east-asian-nations-asean_en.

74. Katerina Ang, "Europe Pivots to Indo-Pacific with 'Multipolar' Ambitions," *Nikkei Asia*, February 2, 2021, https://asia.nikkei.com/Spotlight/Asia-Insight/Europe-pivots-to-Indo-Pacific-with-multipolar-ambitions.

75. Frederic Grare, "France, the Other Indo-Pacific Power," Carnegie Endowment for International Peace, October 21, 2020, https://carnegieendowment.org/2020/10/21/france-other-indo-pacific-power-pub-83000. The United States has the largest EEZs in aggregate.

76. Ang, "Europe Pivots to Indo-Pacific."

77. This agreement provides Australia with access to French bases in Reunion and New Caledonia, while also increasing intelligence sharing and defense-industrial cooperation. See "Two Years After AUKUS, Australia and France Reach Base-Sharing Agreement," *The Maritime Executive*, December 5, 2023, at: https://maritime-executive.com/article/two-yers-after-aukus-australia-and-france-reach-base-sharing-agreement.

78. The Five Power Defense Arrangements are a series of defense relationships among Australia, Malaysia, New Zealand, Singapore, and the United Kingdom, signed in 1971, whereby the five powers are to consult immediately in the event of an armed attack on any of them.

79. European Commission, "The EU Strategy for Cooperation in the Indo-Pacific," September 16, 2021, https://www.eeas.europa.eu/sites/default/files/jointcommunication_2021_24_1_en.pdf.

80. Grare, "France, the Other Indo-Pacific Power."

81. On the Gulf states and their Asia policies, see Kent E. Calder, *The United States, Japan, and the Gulf Region* (Tokyo: Sasakawa Peace Foundation, August 2015).

82. See Embassy of the People's Republic of China in the Kingdom of Saudi Arabia, "His Majesty King Abdullah to Visit China," January 19, 2006, http://sa.china-embassy.gov. cn/eng/xwdt/200601/t20060119_1647041.htm.

83. Jonathan Fulton, *Stranger to Strategic Partnership: Thirty Years of the Sino-Saudi Relationship* (Washington, DC: Atlantic Council, August 2020), https://www.atlanticcouncil.org/wp-content/uploads/2020/08/Sino-Saudi-Relations_WEB.pdf.

84. Ma continued as ambassador for many years, and after leaving his post as ambassador when Saudi Arabia derecognized Taiwan, he retired to Saudi Arabia, where he continued to be influential.

85. Lo Tien-pin and Jonathan Chin, "Air Force Highlights Secret North Yemen Operations," *Taipei Times*, January 29, 2019, http://www.taipeitimes.com/News/taiwan/archives/2019/01/29/2003708858.

86. Under the act, for the first time in India, religion is established as a basis for granting citizenship. India has the world's third-largest Muslim population, at around 200 million people. See Lindsay Maizland, "India's Muslims: An Increasingly Marginalized Population," Council on Foreign Relations, July 14, 2022, https://www.cfr.org/backgrounder/india-muslims-marginalized-population-bjp-modi.

87. This formulation leads to fears that millions of Indian Muslims, including many families who have lived in the country for generations, could be stripped of their citizenship rights and disenfranchised. See "'Shoot the Traitors': Discrimination Against Muslims under India's New Citizenship Policy," Human Rights Watch, April 9, 2020, https://www.hrw.org/report/2020/04/09/shoot-traitors/discrimination-against-muslims-under-indias-new-citizenship-policy.

88. Bernard Orr and Aziz El Yaakoubi, "Top Iranian, Saudi Envoys Meet in China in Restoration of Diplomatic Ties," Reuters, April 6, 2023, https://www.reuters.com/world/foreign-ministers-iran-saudi-meet-china-2023-04-06/.

89. See Alyssa Ayres, "India's Stakes in the Middle East," *Forbes*, February 26, 2014, https://www.forbes.com/sites/alyssaayres/2014/02/26/indias-stakes-in-the-middle-east/?sh=55d0a0e91a5.

90. "8.9 Million Indians Live in UAE, Saudi Arabia, Kuwait, Qatar, Oman, and Bahrain," *Arabian Business*, March 22, 2024, https://www.arabianbusiness.com/culture-society/8-9m-indians-live-in-uae-saudi-arabia-kuwait-qatar-oman-and-bahrain.

91. Kabir Taneja, "The India and France Bonhomie Has Potential for Expansion with the Gulf," Raisina Debates, Observer Research Foundation, January 23, 2021, https://www.orfonline.org/expert-speak/india-france-bonhomie-potential-expansion-gulf.

92. Mohammad Pervez Bilgrami, "GCC and India's Indo-Pacific Strategy," Al Sharq Strategic Research, August 21, 2020, https://research.sharqforum.org/2020/08/21/gcc-and-indias-indo-pacific-strategy/; and Jonathan Fulton, "The Gulf between the Indo-Pacific and the Belt and Road Initiative," *Rising Powers Quarterly* 3, no. 2 (August 2018): 175–93, https://rpquarterly.kureselcalismalar.com/wp-content/uploads/2018/10/vol3.2-fulton.pdf. The port, however, was built by a Chinese consortium, at an ultimate expected cost of nearly $11 billion.

93. See the Indian Ocean Rim Association website at https://www.iora.int/en.

94. See the Organization of Islamic Cooperation website at https://www.oic-oci.org.

95. See the Pacific Environmental Security Forum website at https://pesforum.org.
96. Grare, "France, the Other Indo-Pacific Power."

CHAPTER 8

1. On the methodological rationale, see Pierre Wack, "Scenarios: Uncharted Waters Ahead," *Harvard Business Review* 63, no. 5 (September–October 1985), https://hbr.org/1985/09/scenarios-uncharted-waters-ahead.

2. For a previous application of these concepts, see Calder, *Super Continent*, 185–205.

3. China also has the largest economy in the world in purchasing-power parity (PPP) terms. See World Bank, "GDP, PPP (current international $)," World Development Indicators, accessed January 29, 2024, https://data.worldbank.org/indicator/NY.GDP.MKTP.PP.CD.

4. See Samuel P. Huntington, *The Third Wave: Democracy in the Late 20th Century* (Norman: University of Oklahoma Press, 1993).

5. See Minxin Pei, *From Reform to Revolution: The Demise of Communism in China and the Soviet Union* (Cambridge, MA: Harvard University Press, 1994).

6. See Nicholas R. Lardy, *The State Strikes Back: The End of Economic Reform in China?* (Washington, DC: The Peterson Institute for International Economics, 2019).

7. See Nathaniel Taplin and Jacky Wong, "Profits and Politics in China's Tech Crackdown," *Wall Street Journal*, April 30, 2021, https://www.wsj.com/articles/profits-and-politics-in-chinas-tech-crackdown-11619781614. Recent crackdowns have focused on the financial-sector influence of high-tech firms like Alibaba, rather than on the e-commerce, logistics, or cloud-computing functions.

8. See, for example, Alexandra Stevenson, "China Evergrande Must Be Liquidated, a Judge Said. What Happens Next?," *New York Times*, January 29, 2024, https://www.nytimes.com/2024/01/29/business/china-evergrande-explainer.html.

9. United Nations Department of Economic and Social Affairs Population Division, *World Population Prospects 2019* (New York: United Nations, June 2019), https://www.un.org/development/desa/pd/news/world-population-prospects-2019-0.

10. Graham Allison and Eric Schmidt, "The U.S. Needs a Million Talents Program to Retain Technology Leadership," *Foreign Policy*, July 16, 2022, https://foreignpolicy.com/2022/07/16/immigration-us-technology-companies-work-visas-china-talent-competition-universities/.

11. Jinghan Zeng, *The Chinese Communist Party's Capacity to Rule: Ideology, Legitimacy, and Party Cohesion* (London: Palgrave Macmillan, 2014); and Francis Fukuyama, "China's Bad Emperor Returns," *Washington Post*, March 6, 2018, https://www.washingtonpost.com/news/theworldpost/wp/2018/03/06/xi/.

12. On Wolf Warrior diplomacy, see Peter Martin, *China's Civilian Army: The Inside Story of China's Quest for Global Power* (New York: Oxford University Press, 2021).

13. See, for example, Hal Brands and Michael Beckley, *Danger Zone: The Coming Conflict with China* (New York: W.W. Norton, 2022), especially 24–51.

14. Calder, *Super Continent*, 140–84.

15. By 2020, China had surpassed the United States to possess the world's largest naval fleet, with 350 warships and submarines, as compared to 293 for the United States. See US Department of Defense, *Military and Security Developments Involving the People's Republic of China 2020: Annual Report to Congress*, September 1, 2020, 47, https://media.defense.gov/2020/Sep/01/2002488689/-1/-1/1/2020-DOD-CHINA-MILITARY-POWER-REPORT-FINAL.PDF.

16. Calder, *Global Political Cities*, 61–90.

17. United Nations Population Fund - Asia and the Pacific, "Population Trends," April 2024, https://asiapacific.unfpa.org/en/populationtrends. In East Asia, for example, the total fertility rate is only 1.7 children per woman—below the replacement rate—while in South Asia the rate is 2.5. By 2050, nearly one in three East Asians will be over the age of sixty.

18. In Bangladesh, for example, 20 percent of the population is between the ages of fifteen and twenty-four, in a country of 165 million people, that is expected to number 220 million by the year 2050. See United Nations Population Fund Bangladesh, "Population Trends," accessed February 6, 2024, https://bangladesh.unfpa.org/en/node/24314.

19. Hal Brands and Michael Beckley, "China Is a Declining Power—and That's the Problem," *Foreign Policy*, September 24, 2021, https://foreignpolicy.com/2021/09/24/china-great-power-united-states/; as well as Brands and Beckley, *Danger Zone*.

20. See Jean-Paul Rodrigue, *The Geography of Transport Systems*, 5th ed. (London: Routledge, 2020).

21. James Manyika et al., *Digital Globalization: The New Era of Global Flows* (New York: McKinsey, 2016).

22. See World Bank, *Crossing Borders: World Development Report 2021*, March 24, 2021, https://wdr2021.worldbank.org/stories/crossing-borders/.

23. Digitally driven trade on a global scale was worth between $800 billion and $1.5 trillion in 2019. See World Bank, *Crossing Borders*; and Christian Ketels and Arindam Bhattacharya, "Global Trade Goes Digital," Boston Consulting Group, August 12, 2019, https://www.bcg.com/publications/2019/global-trade-goes-digital.

24. Calder, *Global Political Cities*, 44. Among the new platforms have been LinkedIn (2003), Facebook (2004), YouTube (2006), Twitter (2007), Instagram (2010), WhatsApp (2011), and TikTok (2016).

25. Tim Stronge, "Do $10 Trillion of Financial Transactions Flow Over Sub Cables Each Day?," *TeleGeography* (blog), April 6, 2023, https://blog.telegeography.com/2023-mythbusting-part-1.

26. On Sunni-Shia relations, see Vali Nasr, *The Shi'a Revival: How Conflicts within Islam will Shape the Future* (New York: W.W. Norton, 2007).

27. India operationalized its first SSBN in November 2018, and plans to ultimately deploy four to five SSBNs and six SSNs. In response, Pakistan has established a Naval Strategic Force Command Headquarters and plans to develop a sea-based deterrent, possibly supported by China. See Iskander Rehman, *Murky Waters: Naval Nuclear Dynamics in the Indian Ocean* (Washington, DC: Carnegie Endowment for International Peace, March 9, 2015), https://carnegieendowment.org/research/2015/03/murky-waters-naval-nuclear-dynamics-in-the-indian-ocean?lang=en.

28. David Sacks, "Taiwan Announced a Record Defense Budget: But Is It Enough to Deter China?," *Asia Unbound* (blog), Council on Foreign Relations, August 30, 2023, https://www.cfr.org/blog/taiwan-announced-record-defense-budget-it-enough-deter-china.

29. In 2023, China accounted for 43 percent of Asian regional defense spending. Japan was second at 11 percent. See Karl Dewey, "Asian Defense Spending Ambitions Outstrip Growth," *Military Balance* (blog), International Institute for Strategic Studies, February 5, 2024, https://www.iiss.org/online-analysis/military-balance/2024/02/asian-defence-spending-ambitions-outstrip-growth/.

30. Recently, analysts, have questioned this policy of "strategic ambiguity," emphasizing the political-military dangers generated by the lack of charity itself. See, for example,

Richard Haas and David Sacks, "American Support for Taiwan Must Be Unambiguous," *Foreign Affairs* 100, no. 4 (September/October 2020), https://www.foreignaffairs.com/articles/united-states/american-support-taiwan-must-be-unambiguous.

31. For a review of the strategic issues, see Aaron L. Friedberg, *Beyond Air-Sea Battle: The Debate over US Military Strategy in Asia* (London: International Institute for Strategic Studies, 2014), especially 73–104.

32. On this pattern, especially prominent with respect to energy demand, see Calder, "Asia's Empty Tank"; and Calder, *Pacific Defense*.

33. For customs clearance statistics for 2023, see the People's Republic of China General Administration of Customs website, accessed June 3, 2024, http://stats.customs.gov.cn/indexEn.

34. IEA, "World Energy Outlook 2019," November 2019, https://www.iea.org/reports/world-energy-outlook-2019. and "The Great Well of China: Oil Is Bringing China and the Arab World Closer Economically," *The Economist*, June 18, 2015, https://www.economist.com/middle-east-and-africa/2015/06/18/the-great-well-of-china.

35. Columbia University Center on Global Energy Policy, "The Future of the Power of Siberia 2 Pipeline," Columbia University School of International and Public Affairs, May 15, 2024, https://www.energypolicy.columbia.edu/publications/the-future-of-the-power-of-siberia-2-pipeline/.

36. Hussein Moghaddam, "Role of Natural Gas in China 2050," Gas Exporting Countries Forum, October 23, 2019, https://www.gecf.org/_resources/files/events/gecf-expert-commentary---the-role-of-natural-gas-in-china-2050/gecf_expertcommentary_role_naturalgaschina2050.pdf.

37. Dale Aluf, "China's Reliance on Middle East Oil, Gas to Rise Sharply," *Insights Global*, January 11, 2022, https://www.insights-global.com/chinas-reliance-on-middle-east-oil-gas-to-rise-sharply/.

38. See the 2022 figures in EDGAR (Emissions Database for Global Atmospheric Research), *GHG Emissions of All World Countries: 2023 Report* (Brussels: European Commission 2023), https://edgar.jrc.ec.europa.eu/report_2023.

39. See Daniel Yergin, *The New Map: Energy, Climate, and the Clash of Nations* (New York: Penguin Press, 2020), 327–46.

40. Gresh, *To Rule Eurasia's Waves*, 246.

41. According to the US Geological Survey, the Arctic has more than 24 percent of the world's current natural-gas reserves. See Kenneth Bird et al., "Factsheet: Circum-Arctic Resource Appraisal: Estimates of Undiscovered Oil and Gas North of the Arctic Circle," US Geological Survey, 2008, https://pubs.usgs.gov/fs/2008/3049/fs2008-3049.pdf.

42. Gresh, *To Rule Eurasia's Waves*, 251.

43. On this phenomenon, see Calder, *Super Continent*, especially 140–84.

44. "Chinese Navy Ships Conduct a Live-Fire Drills in Mediterranean," *Military Times*, July 12, 2017, https://www.militarytimes.com/news/pentagon-congress/2017/07/12/chinese-navy-ships-conduct-live-fire-drills-in-mediterranean.

45. Franz-Stefan Gady, "China, Russia Conduct First Ever Joint Strategic Bomber Patrol Flights in Indo-Pacific Region," *The Diplomat*. July 2019, https://thediplomat.com/2019/07/china-russia-conduct-first-ever-joint-strategic-bomber-patrol-flights-in-indo-pacific-region/; and Justin McCurry, "Japan and South Korea Scramble Jets to Track Russian and Chinese Bomber Patrol," *Guardian*, December 22, 2020, https://www.theguardian.com/world/2020/dec/22/russia-and-china-fly-joint-bomber-patrol-over-the-pacific.

46. See Kosuke Takahashi, "China, Russia Fly 6 Bombers Near Japan Amid Quad Summit," *The Diplomat*, May 25, 2022, https://the diplomat.com/2022/05/China-russia-fly-6-bombers-near-japan-amid-quad-summit/.

47. Yew Lun Tian, "China, Russia to Start Joint Air and Sea Drill in Sea of Japan," Reuters, July 16, 2023, https://www.reuters.com/world/china-russia-start-joint-air-sea-drill-sea-of-japan-2023-07-6/.

48. Ethan Meick, *China-Russia Military-to-Military Relations: Moving Toward a Higher Level of Cooperation* (Washington, DC: U.S.-China Economic and Security Review Commission, March 20, 2017), 14, https://www.uscc.gov/sites/default/files/Research/China-Russia%20Mil-Mil%20Relations%20Moving%20Toward%20Higher%20Level%20of%20Cooperation.pdf.

49. Rick Joe, "The FC-31, China's 'Other' Stealth Fighter," *The Diplomat*, February 18, 2021, https://thediplomat.com/2021/02/the-fc-31-chinas-other-stealth-fighter/.

50. The Sunburn antiship cruise missiles are direct counterthreats to the US Navy's Aegis air-defense system. See Huang Panyue, "With Modified Fire Control System, China's Su–30 Fighter Jets Might Be Aircraft Carrier's Nightmare," *China Military Online*, February 2, 2019, http://eng.chinamil.com.cn/CHINA_209163/TopStories_209189/9420175.html; and US Department of Defense, *Annual Report to Congress: Military and Security Developments Involving the People's Republic of China 2019* (May 2, 2019), 47, https://media.defense.gov/2019/May/02/2002127082/-1/-1/1/2019_CHINA_MILITARY_POWER_REPORT.pdf.

51. Congressional Budget Office, "The 2021 Long-term Budget Outlook," March 4, 2021, https://www.cbo.gov/publication/56977#data.

52. Sarah Almukhtar and Ron Nordland, "What Did the US Get for $2 Trillion in Afghanistan?," *New York Times*, December 9, 2019, https://www.nytimes.com/interactive/2019/12/09/world/middleeast/afghanistan-war-cost.html; and Neta C. Crawford, "The Iraq War Has Cost the US Nearly $2 Trillion," *Military Times*, February 6, 2020, https://www.militarytimes.com/opinion/commentary/2020/02/06/the-iraq-war-has-cost-the-us-nearly-2-trillion/.

53. The March 2020 Cares Act involved expenditures of $2.2 trillion, and a $900 billion stimulus package was added in December 2020. Yuka Hayashi, "Pandemic Spending Boosts Global Government Debt to 98% of Economic Output," *Wall Street Journal*, January 28, 2021, https://www.wsj.com/articles/pandemic-spending-boosts-global-government-debt-to-98-of-economic-output-imf-says-11611838809.

54. See the federal debt tracker at US Department of the Treasury, "What Is the National Debt?," April 10, 2024, https://fiscaldata.treasury.gov/americas-finance-guide/national-debt/.

55. Congressional Budget Office, "The 2021 Long-term Budget Outlook," 2.

56. Larry Summers, "The Biden Stimulus Is Admirably Ambitious. But It Brings Some Big Risks, Too," *Washington Post*, February 4, 2021, https://www.washingtonpost.com/opinions/2021/02/04/larry-summers-biden-covid-stimulus/.

57. Aila Slisco, "Larry Summers, Who Predicted Biden's Inflation Missteps, Expects Recession," *Newsweek*, July 22, 2022, https://www.newsweek.com/larry-summers-who-predicted-bidens-inflation-missteps-expects-recession-1727335.

58. IMF, "Database of Fiscal Policy Responses to COVID19," updated October 2021, accessed September 28, 2024, https://www.imf.org/en/Topics/imf-and-covid19/Fiscal-Policies-Database-in-Response-to-COVID-19.

59. Ministry of Finance, Japan, "International Reserves/Foreign Currency Liquidity (as of May 31, 2024)," June 7, 2024, https://www.mof.go.jp/english/international_policy/reference/official_reserve_assets/e0303.html; and China State Administration of Foreign Exchange, "Official Reserve Assets," May 2024, http://www.safe.gov.cn/safe/2022/0207/23934.html.

60. In 2012, China's annual export-import trade totaled $3.87 trillion, compared to $3.82 trillion for the United States Since then, according to the US Department of Commerce, the gap in favor of China has persisted. See "China Eclipses US as Biggest Trading Nation," *Bloomberg News*, February 10, 2013, https://www.bloomberg.com/news/articles/2013-02-09/china-passes-u-s-to-become-the-world-s-biggest-trading-nation.

61. Lowy Institute. "The US-China Trade War: Who Dominates Global Trade?," Lowy Institute, May 10, 2024. https://interactives.lowyinstitute.org/charts/china-us-trade-dominance/us-china-competition/.

62. In 2020, the US dollar fell below 50 percent of Sino-Russian trade for the first time. By early 2023, Russia's President Vladimir Putin could declare that two-thirds of Sino-Russian trade was settled in roubles or yuan; virtually all bilateral resource trade is now settled in yuan. See Chen Aizhu, "Vast China-Russia Resources Trade Shifts to yuan from Dollars in Ukraine Fallout," Reuters, May 10, 2023, https://www.reuters.com/markets/currencies/vast-china-russia-resources-trade-shifts-yuan-dollars-ukraine-fallout-2023-05-11/.

63. Since mid-2022, the renminbi's share of IMF Special Drawing Rights has been 12.28 percent, compared to 43.38 percent for the US dollar. See IMF, "Press Release – IMF Determines New Currency Amounts for the SDR Valuation Basket," July 29, 2022, https://www.imf.org/en/News/Articles/2022/07/29/%20pr22281-press-release-imf-determines-new-currency-amounts-for-the-sdr-valuation-basket.

64. David P. Goldman, "Digital Yuan Could Bust the United States," *Asia Times*, February 6, 2021, https://asiatimes.com/2021/02/digital-yuan-could-bust-the-united-states/.

65. "Yuan's Share Hits Record High in Global Payments in March: SWIFT," *Global Times*, April 8, 2024, https://www.globaltimes.cn/source/index.html. Yuan cross-border receipts and payments increased 24 percent in 2023, to 25 percent of total trade settlements in 2023, with the shift to yuan in Sino-Russian trade representing an important dimension.

66. Susanne Barton, "Yuan's Popularity for Global Payments Hits Five-Year High," Bloomberg, February 17, 2021, https://www.bloomberg.com/news/articles/2021-02-18/yuan-s-popularity-for-cross-border-payments-hits-five-year-high.

67. Rashid Husain Syed, "One Day, Oil Might Not Be Bought With Dollars Anymore, but With Yuan," *Globe and Mail*, January 17, 2023, https://www.theglobeandmail.com/business/commentary/article-one-day-oil-might-not-be-bought-with-dollars-anymore-but-with-yuan/.

68. Jose Miguel Alonso-Trabanco, "Ukraine War: A Reshuffling of the Global Monetary Order?," *Geopolitical Monitor*, May 17, 2022, https://www.geopoliticalmonitor.com/ukraine-war-a-reshuffling-of-the-global-monetary-order/.

69. See, for example, Samuel P. Huntington, *Political Order in Changing Societies* (New Haven, CT: Yale University Press, 1968).

70. Darshana M. Baruah, "India in the Indo-Pacific: New Delhi's Theater of Opportunity," Carnegie Endowment for International Peace, June 30, 2020, https://carnegieendowment.org/2020/06/30/india-in-indo-pacific-new-delhi-s-theater-of-opportunity-pub-82205. Tensions with China have persisted, of course, since the 1962 Sino-Indian border war.

71. In March 2022, Germany and Qatar concluded a long-term energy partnership agreement, and Germany began building its first-ever LNG terminal to receive seaborne gas shipments. See Beniot Faucon, Summer Said, and Stephen Kalin, "Europe Woos Qatar for an Alternative to Russian Gas," *Wall Street Journal*, March 30, 2022, https://www.wsj.com/articles/europe-woos-qatar-as-alternative-to-russian-gas-11648649463.

72. For the European Union, American LNG amounted to more than 50 percent of imports in 2023. Intra–European Union imports, mainly from Norway to Central Europe, also largely were by sea. See European Council, "Where Does the EU's Gas Come From?," March 21, 2024, https://www.consilium.europa.eu/en/infographics/eu-gas-supply/.

73. Foreign Agricultural Service, "The Ukraine Conflict and Other Factors Contributing to High Commodity Prices and Food Insecurity," US Department of Agriculture, April 6, 2022, https://www.fas.usda.gov/data/ukraine-conflict-and-other-factors-contributing-high-commodity-prices-and-food-insecurity.

74. Giovanna Faria, "War in Ukraine Causes Global Food Shortage," Radio Free Europe–Radio Liberty, March 28, 2022, https://www.rferl.org/a/war-ukraine-global-food-shortage/31872861.html.

75. Between 2018 and 2020, for example, more than 40 percent of Africa's wheat imports came from Russia and Ukraine, flowing almost entirely across sea lanes impeded south of Odesa by the 2022 Ukraine war. See Anders Åslund, "Russia's War on Global Food Security," Issue Brief, Atlantic Council, June 1, 2022, https://www.atlanticcouncil.org/in-depth-research-reports/issue-brief/russias-war-on-global-food-security/.

76. Matina Stevis-Gridneff, "Russia Agrees to Let Ukraine Ship Grain, Easing World Food Shortage," *New York Times*, July 22, 2022, https://www.nytimes.com/2022/07/22/world/europe/ukraine-russia-grain-deal.html. With the use of largely domestically produced drones, Ukrainian forces by the spring of 2024 had destroyed or incapacitated more than 20 percent of the Russian Black Sea fleet. See "Ukrainian Attacks Increasingly Sap the Power of Russia's Black Sea Fleet," Associated Press, March 5, 2024, https://apnews.com/article/russia-ukraine-war-black-sea-12e2219192caaae1b20044584fb5816d.

77. See Yoshihara and Holmes, *Red Star Over the Pacific*, 83–87; as well as Brandan Rittenhouse Green and Caitlin Talmadge, "Then What? Assessing Military Implications of Chinese Control of Taiwan," *International Security* 47, no. 1 (Summer 2022): 7–45, https://doi.org/10.1162/isec_a_00437.

78. On the technical details, see Green and Talmadge, "Then What?," 19–23.

79. Loren Thompson, "Why Taiwan Has Become the 'Geographical Pivot of History' in the Pacific Age," *Forbes*, September 29, 2020, https://www.forbes.com/sites/lorenthompson/2020/09/29/why-taiwan-has-become-the-geographical-pivot-of-history-in-the-pacific-age/?sh=2472e3471921.

80. China's official 2021 defense budget, often considered understated, was $206 billion, compared to Taiwan's $15.4 billion—6.8 percent of China's spending. Chinese coast guard ships outnumbered their Taiwanese counterparts by more than 10 to 1, as did China's fleet of jet fighters. See US Department of Defense, *Annual Report to Congress: Military and Security Developments Involving the People's Republic of China 2021*, September 1, 2021, 140, https://media.defense.gov/2021/Nov/03/2002885874/-1/-1/0/2021-CMPR-FINAL.PDF.

81. On global shipping capacities, see "Alphaliner Top 100," accessed June 17, 2024, alphaliner.axmarine.com/PublicTop100/.

82. Matthew Fulco, "Amid a Changing World Economy, Taiwanese Manufacturers Return Home," *Am Cham Taiwan*, February 9, 2021, https://topics.amcham.com.tw/2021/02/changing-world-economy-taiwanese-manufacturers-return/.

83. Fulco, "Amid a Changing World Economy."

84. Ralph Jennings, "Why Taiwanese Firms Are Scaling Back Their China Operations," *Forbes*, November 20, 2018, https://www.forbes.com/sites/ralphjennings/2018/11/20/why-taiwanese-firms-are-scaling-back-their-china-operations/?sh=4ba4a25e2ef5.

85. Ralph Jennings, "Taiwan Is Finally Luring Companies Back from China After More Than 15 Years of Trying," *South China Morning Post*, March 21, 2019, https://www.scmp.com/economy/china-economy/article/3002699/taiwan-finally-luring-companies-back-china-after-more-15.

86. James Pomfret, Jessie Pang, and Greg Torode, "New Hong Kong Security Law Comes into Force Amid Fears for Freedoms," Reuters, March 23, 2024, https://www.reuters.com/world/asia-pacific/new-hong-kong-national-security-law-comes-into-force-amid-international-2024-03-22/.

87. Yu Nakamura, "Google Embraces Taiwan as Asia Hub with Third Data Center," *Nikkei Asia*, September 4, 2020, https://asia.nikkei.com/Business/Technology/Google-embraces-Taiwan-as-Asia-hub-with-third-data-center.

88. Lauly Li and Cheng Ting-fang, "Microsoft to Build Taiwan Data Center amid US-China Tech War," *Nikkei Asia*, October 26, 2020, https://asia.nikkei.com/Economy/Trade-war/Microsoft-to-build-Taiwan-data-center-amid-US-China-tech-war.

89. Statistics from the Johns Hopkins University Coronavirus Resource Center website at https://coronavirus.jhu.edu.

90. "Taiwan Emerges as Pioneer in Strengthening Global Healthcare," *Biospectrum Asia*, December 21, 2019, https://www.biospectrumasia.com/news/55/15136/taiwan-emerges-as-pioneer-in-strengthening-global-healthcare.html.

91. Taiwan in 2022 had only fourteen diplomatic partners remaining. Kiribati and the Solomon Islands switched their recognition to China in 2019, and Nicaragua followed suit in late 2021. See Lily Kuo, "Taiwan Loses Another Diplomatic Partner as Nicaragua Recognizes China," *Washington Post*, December 9, 2021, https://www.washingtonpost.com/world/asia_pacific/nicaragua-taiwan-china/2021/12/09/741098d8-5954-11ec-8396-5552bef55c3c_story.html. On Taipei's fluctuating political fortunes in Washington, and the reasons for this fluctuation, see Kent E. Calder, *Asia in Washington: Exploring the Penumbra of Transnational Power* (Washington, DC: Brookings Institution Press, 2014), 154–70.

92. Chen, who has a science doctorate from the Bloomberg School of Public Health at Johns Hopkins University, served as leader of Taiwan's Department of Health (2003–2005) during the SARS epidemic. He then led Taiwan's response to COVID-19 as vice president to Tsai Ing-wen (2016–2020).

93. Javier Hernandez and Chris Horton, "Taiwan's Weapon Against Coronavirus: An Epidemiologist as Vice President," *New York Times*, May 21, 2020, https://www.nytimes.com/2020/05/09/world/asia/taiwan-vice-president-coronavirus.html. See also Kent E. Calder and Neave Denny, eds., *Asia and the Covid Crisis* (Washington, DC: Edwin O. Reischauer Center for East Asian Studies, 2022).

94. The Taiwan Relations Act codified the de facto, nondiplomatic relationship between the United States and Taiwan since the formal recognition of the People's Republic of China. It went into law in 1979. For the text of the Taiwan Relations Act (Public Law 96–8, January 1, 1979), see the Congress.gov website at https://www.congress.gov/bill/96th-congress/house-bill/2479.

95. For the text of S.1678, Taiwan Allies International Protection and Enhancement Initiative (TAIPEI) Act of 2019 (Public Law No. 116–135 (March 26, 2020)), see the Congress.gov website at https://www.congress.gov/bill/116th-congress/senate-bill/1678/text.

96. Calder, *Asia in Washington*, 162.

97. Elaine Chao, for example, served as US secretary of transportation under President Donald Trump (2017–2021), while Katherine Tai (2021–) served as US special trade representative under President Joe Biden.

98. Stanley Kao was influential in increasing the Trump administration's consciousness of Taiwan's waning diplomatic presence in the Pacific and Latin America, leading to the TAIPEI Act. Hsiao Bi-Khim continued with this congressional activism. See "Taiwan's US Envoy Acknowledges Support from Biden Administration," *Taiwan News*, April 9, 2021, https://www.taiwannews.com.tw/en/news/4172613.

99. James Johnson, "Pelosi Becomes Highest-Ranking U.S. Official to Visit Taiwan in 25 Years," *Japan Times*, August 3, 2022, https://www.japantimes.co.jp/news/2022/08/03/asia-pacific/nancy-pelosi-taiwan-visit-us-china/.

100. See, for example, Yoshihara and Holmes, *Red Star Over the Pacific*; Ian Easton, *The Chinese Invasion Threat: Taiwan's Defense and American Strategy in Asia* (Manchester, UK: Eastbridge Books, 2019); Richard C. Bush, *Uncharted Strait: The Future of China-Taiwan Relations* (Washington, DC: Brookings Institution Press, 2013); and Fravel, *Active Defense*.

101. "Sixty Percent in Taiwan Poll Want U.S. Military Alliance to Counter China," *Newsweek*, November 28, 2023, https://www.nwskweek.com/poll-says-most-taiwans-favor-amrica-military-allianc-1847593.

102. Other islands held by the Kuomintang off the coast of China's Zhexiang Province—the Yijiangshan and Dachen Islands, actually were taken by the PLA in 954, while the islands of Quemoy and Matsu, in the harbor of the major Chinese city of Xiamen, were heavily bombarded in 1958.

103. Ishaan Tharoor, "China Shifts the Military Status Quo on Taiwan After Pelosi Visit," *Washington Post*, August 9, 2022, https://www.washingtonpost.com/world/2022/08/09/military-beijing-china-pla-taiwan-pelosi/; as well as Bonny Lin et al., "How China Could Quarantine Taiwan: Mapping Out Two Possible Scenarios," CSIS, June 5, 2024, http://www.csis.org/analysis/how-china-could-quarantine-taiwan-mapping-out-two-possible-scenarios.

104. Friedberg, *Beyond Air-Sea Battle*, 73–132.

105. Easton, *Chinese Invasion Threat*, 149–51.

106. See, for example, John Culver, "The Unfinished Chinese Civil War," *The Intercept*, September 30, 2020, https://www.lowyinstitute.org/the-interpreter/unfinished-chinese-civil-war; as well as Robert Blackwill and Philip Zelikow, *The US, China, and Taiwan: A Strategy to Prevent War* (Washington, DC: Council on Foreign Relations, February 2021).

107. The PLA response to the Pelosi Taiwan visit in August 2022 has been characterized as a "dry run" for this sort of "soft" attack on Taiwan. See Gilbert Rozman, "20 Ways China Is Losing the Ukraine War," *The Asan Forum*, May 23, 2022, https://theasanforum.org/20-ways-china-is-losing-the-ukraine-war/; and Lin et al., "How China Could Quarantine Taiwan."

108. On this dimension, see Erickson and Martinson, *China's Maritime Gray Zone Operations*.

109. On the coast guard law and its implications, see Hadano, "China Fires Opening Salvo at Biden."

110. On this topic, see Easton, *Chinese Invasion Threat*.

111. For a full-throated exposition, see Michael Beckley, *Unrivaled: Why America Will Remain the World's Sole Superpower* (Ithaca, NY: Cornell University Press, 2018).

112. Relative to the United States, China is disadvantaged by geography, especially in the early twenty-first century. China has land borders with fourteen nations, several of them adversarial, while the United States is bordered by only two smaller, relatively benign nations. China also is heavily dependent on the Eurasian sea lanes for energy and markets, while being constrained by the First Island Chain. Beyond its land borders with fourteen

nations, it has maritime borders with another eight countries. China has engaged in actual military conflict with five countries—Russia, Japan, the Koreas, Vietnam and India. Among its overall twenty-two bordering nations (land plus sea), China has territorial and maritime disputes with seventeen of them.

CHAPTER 9

1. See Calder, *New Continentalism*; and Calder, *Super Continent*.

2. US Geological Survey, "How Much Water Is There on Earth?," November 13, 2019, https://www.usgs.gov/special-topics/water-science-school/science/how-much-water-there-earth.

3. For one example, see the exploratory work on the geopolitical role of Indian Ocean islands by Darshana Baruah. Darshana M. Baruah and Yogesh Joshi, "India's Policy on Diego Garcia and Its Quest for Security in the Indian Ocean," *Australian Journal of International Affairs* 75, no. 1 (2021): 36–59, https://doi.org/10.1080/10357718.2020.1769550; and Darshana M. Baruah, "Geopolitics of Indian Ocean Islands in 2019: Takeaways for Traditional Powers," Carnegie Endowment for International Peace. January 9, 2020, https://carnegieendowment.org/posts/2020/01/geopolitics-of-indian-ocean-islands-in-2019-takeaways-for-traditional-powers.

4. Among such pioneer studies, see Peter M. Haas, *Saving the Mediterranean: The Politics of International Environmental Cooperation* (New York: Columbia University Press, 1992); Sunil S. Amrith, *Crossing the Bay of Bengal: The Furies of Nature and the Fortunes of Migrants* (Cambridge, MA: Harvard University Press, 2013); Michael North, *The Baltic: A History* (Cambridge, MA: Harvard University Press, 2016); and Kent E. Calder, *Transformation in the Bay of Bengal: Implications for Economics and Security* (Tokyo: Sasakawa Peace Foundation, July 2018).

5. Japan in particular has become a trusted ally and "partner of choice" for many Southeast Asian and Pacific island countries, as well as external great powers such as France and Britain that are looking to expand their Indo-Pacific presence.

6. On the concrete operational dimensions, see Michael J. Green, Zack Cooper, and Kathleen H. Hicks, "Federated Defense in Asia," CSIS, December 11, 2014. https://www.csis.org/analysis/federated-defense-asia.

7. Peter C. Oleson, "Employing 'Smart Power' to Counter Chinese Efforts in Oceania," *Pacnet* 56, Pacific Forum International September 30, 2022, https://pacforum.org/publication/pacnet-56-employing-smart-power-to-counter-prc-efforts-in-oceania.

8. The traditional equation rigorously compartmentalizes economic and military matters, creating an "Economic Asia" and a "Security Asia" which so far has precariously coexisted. See Evan A. Feigenbaum and Robert A. Manning, "A Tale of Two Asias," *Foreign Policy*, October 31, 2012, https://foreignpolicy.com/2012/10/31/a-tale-of-two-asias.

9. In 2021, more than 2.7 million immigrants from India were living in the United States—the largest number from a single Asian country, and 6 percent of all US immigrants. This number, however, was much smaller in the 1970s; the 1965 repeal of US country quotas led to a major expansion of the South Asian community. Even in 2000, there were only 1.02 million Indians in the United States, comprising 3.3 percent of total immigrants. See "Largest US Immigrant Groups over Time, 1960–Present," Migration Policy Institute Data Hub, data for 1960–2022, accessed June 17, 2024, http://migrationpolicy.org/programs/data-hub/charts/largest-immigrant-groups-over-time.

10. Taiwan, for example, is becoming an increasingly important international data hub, with well-known US technology companies like Google and Microsoft building new data centers there.

11. See, for example, the pronouncements of the late Japanese Prime Minister Abe Shinzo, as well as his brother, former Defense Minister Kishi Nobuo, as in Ryo Nemoto, "Abe: Taiwan Must Never Repeat Hong Kong Experience," *Nikkei Asia*, July 30, 2021, https://asia.nikkei.com/Politics/International-relations/Abe-Taiwan-must-never-repeat-Hong-Kong-experience.

12. On the concept of "Peak China," implying early and urgent Chinese incentives to revise the Taiwan status quo, and the strategic implications for US-China relations, see Brands and Beckley, *Danger Zone*, 24–51. For a contrary view, suggesting less urgent revisionist pressure but a sustained Chinese buildup, see Oriana Skylar Mastro and Derek Scissors, "China Hasn't Reached the Peak of Its Power," *Foreign Affairs*, August 22, 2022, https://www.foreignaffairs.com/china/china-hasnt-reached-peak-its-power.

13. In the Pacific Island region, for example, the configuration of local communications infrastructure raises significant geopolitical concerns. Chinese-built dual-use sites or ports in the South Pacific could give Chinese commercial ships and naval vessels access to a much wider area of Pacific waters for surveillance and monitoring purposes in an area historically considered predominantly under US strategic control.

14. The "Davidson window" refers to the argument of Admiral Philip Davidson, outgoing US Indo-Pacific combatant commander, in his valedictory testimony before the Senate Armed Services Committee in March 2021. He argued that China might seek to achieve its ambition of integrating Taiwan with the Chinese mainland within six years (2021–2027). Adm. Philip Davidson, "US Indo-Pacific Command Posture," US Senate Committee on Armed Services testimony, March 9, 2021, https://www.armed-services.senate.gov/imo/media/doc/Davidson_03-09-21.pdf. On the argument, see Jerry Hendrix, "Closing the Davidson Window," Real Clear Defense, July 3, 2021, https://www.realcleardefense.com/articles/2021/07/03/closing_the_davidson_window_784100.html. See also Andrew Erickson, "Make China Great Again: Xi's Truly Grand Strategy," *War on the Rocks*, October 30, 2019, https://warontherocks.com/2019/10/make-china-great-again-xis-truly-grand-strategy/.

15. The US Navy has begun to develop a new guided-missile destroyer class, DDG(X), to serve as its backbone into the twenty-first century. It will have "an efficient Integrated Power System and greater endurance" and be able to carry new hypersonic missiles and long-range weapons. If all goes as planned, the first destroyer would be commissioned around 2032, and the *Columbia*-class SSBNs would also become operational during the early 2030s. See Megan Eckstein, "US Navy Creates DDG(X) Program Office after Years of Delays for Large Combatant Replacement," *Defense News*, June 4, 2021, https://www.defensenews.com/naval/2021/06/04/navy-creates-ddgx-program-office-after-years-of-delays-for-large-combatant-replacement/.

16. China has created an early monopoly in many emerging digital economies, which makes it more difficult for US and Japanese firms to compete and expand market share. This situation could lead to Chinese-like authoritarian technology standards becoming more widely adopted around the world, compromising allied digital infrastructure, as Chinese equipment and standards become more dominant in the marketplace. Supporting this analysis, JETRO (Japan External Trade Organization) has found that China targets the telecommunications business in strategically chosen developing nations, particularly in Africa, such

as Algeria, Egypt, Tunisia, Morocco, and South Africa. Many of these are coastal nations located along central shipping lanes and maritime chokepoints. China's penetration into the emerging digital world within such countries gives it enhanced access to broader continental and maritime regions as well. See Institute of Developing Economies, JETRO, "China's Telecommunications Footprint in Africa," 2009, https://www.ide.go.jp/English/Data/Africa_file/Manualreport/cia_09.html.

17. The 2021 Quad Vaccine Partnership delivered almost 800 million COVID-19 vaccine doses globally, despite implementation problems along the way. It was superseded in May 2023 by a broader Quad Health Security Partnership, designed to respond to future disease outbreaks with pandemic potential. See White House, "Quad Leaders' Joint Statement," May 20, 2023, https://www.whitehouse.gov/briefing-room/statements-releases/2023/05/20/quad-leaders-joint-statement/.

18. See US Department of Defense, "Readout of Under Secretary of Defense Dr. William LaPlante's Visit to Japan," June 10, 2024, https://defense.gov/News/Releases/Release/Article/3800838/readout-of-under-secretary-of-defense-dr-william-laplantes-visit-to-japan/

19. Julia Kollewe, "Friend Shoring: What Is It and Can It Solve Our Supply Problems?," *Guardian*, August 6, 2022, https://www.theguardian.com/business/2022/aug/06/friendshoring-what-is-it-and-can-it-solve-our-supply-problems.

20. The 2021 Cornwall G-7 summit generated a bold communique highlighting quality infrastructure, and maintaining that wealthy nations have a responsibility to promote transparent, values-driven projects by helping to close the finance gap in developing nations. In support of this initiative, the Biden administration unveiled its "Build Back Better World" (B3W) program. For details, see White House, "President Biden and G-7 Leaders Launch Build Back Better World (B3W) Partnership," June 12, 2021, https://www.whitehouse.gov/briefing-room/statements-releases/2021/06/12/fact-sheet-president-biden-and-g7-leaders-launch-build-back-better-world-b3w-partnership/.

21. See JBIC, "JBIC Signs MOU with US International Development Finance Corporation," January 14, 2021, https://www.jbic.go.jp/en/information/press_00005.html.

22. See Keith Johnson, "Belt and Road Meet Build Back Better," *Foreign Policy*, October 4, 2021, https://foreignpolicy.com/2021/10/04/belt-and-road-initiative-bri-build-back-better-us-china-competition-west?/.

23. IMEC would provide a hybrid maritime-overland link between India and Europe via the GCC. See "Fact Sheet: World Leaders Launch a Landmark India-Middle East-Europe Economic Corridor," White House, September 9, 2023, https://www.whitehouse.gov/briefing-room/statements-releases/2023/09/09/fact-sheet-world-leaders-launch-a-landmark-india-middle-east-europe-economic-corridor/; and Alberto Rizzi, "The Infinite Connection: Make the India-Middle East-Europe Economic Corridor Happen," European Council on Foreign Relations Policy Brief, April 23, 2024, https://www.ccfr.eu/publications/the-infinite-connection-how-to-make-the-india-middle-east-europe-economic-corridor-happen/.

24. The Japan Bank for International Cooperation (JBIC) and the US International Development Finance Corporation (DFC) both help to mobilize private investment in support of economic development in emerging Indo-Pacific economies and around the world. On bilateral US-Japan initiatives, see JBIC, "JBIC Signs MOU with US DFC," April 2, 2024, https://www.jbic.go.jp/en/information/press/press-2024/press_00005.html. Also, Tobias Harris, "Quality Infrastructure: Japan's Robust Challenge to China's Belt and

Road," *War on the Rocks*, April 9, 2019, https://warontherocks.com/2019/04/quality-infrastructure-japans-robust-challenge-to-chinas-belt-and-road/; Masafumi Iida, "Japan's Reluctant Embrace of BRI?," German Institute for International and Security Affairs, October 3, 2018, https://www.swp-berlin.org/publications/products/projekt_papiere/Iida_BCAS_2018_BRI_Japan_6.pdf; and Jennifer Hillman and David Sacks, *How the U.S. Should Respond to China's Belt and Road* (New York: Council on Foreign Relations, March 2021), https://www.cfr.org/report/chinas-belt-and-road-implications-for-the-united-states/.

25. To this end, Japan's establishment of a parallel structure to the US DARPA (Defense Advanced Research Projects Agency) could well increase possibilities for bilateral US-Japan defense-related applications, with such maritime applications as optical wireless underwater communication and underwater drones. See Ryo Nemoto, "Japan Eyes US-Style Defense Research Agency as Tech Pace Heats Up," *Nikkei Asia*, October 20, 2022, https://asia.nikkei.com/Politics/Japan-eyes-U.S.-style-defense-research-agency-as-tech-race-heats-up.

26. US policy in recent years has been slow to create policy incentives for low-polluting hydrocarbons, but Japan has been much more supportive. See, for example, Masaya Kato and Juntaro Arai, "Japan Considers Financial Support to Boost US LNG Output," *Nikkei Asia*, May 4, 2022, https://asia.nikkei.com/Business/Energy/Japan-considers-financial-support-to-boost-U.S.-LNG-output.

27. That would not, however, preclude Japan's technological cooperation at later stages, which could in some areas be mutually valuable. See "Japan to Discuss AUKUS Defense Technology Partnership: US Diplomat," *Japan Times*, March 22, 2024, https://www.japantimes.co.jp/news/2024/03/22/japan/politics/japan-to-discuss-aukus-with-us/.

28. Ken Moriyasu, "US Seeks to Revive Idled Shipyards with Help of Japan, South Korea," *Nikkei Asia Review*, March 4, 2024, https://asia.nikkei.com/Politics/Defense/U.S.-seeks-to-revive-idled-shipyards-with-help-of-Japan-South-Korea.

29. Ko Hirano, "Japan Begins Cybersecurity Push in the Pacific," *Japan Times*, March 23, 2024. https://www.japantimes.co.jp/news/2024/03/22/japan/politics/japan-cybersecurity-pacific/

30. On details, see Oleson, "Employing 'Smart Power' to Counter Chinese Efforts in Oceania."

Bibliography and Further Readings

Abu-Lughod, Janet L. *Before European Hegemony: The World System A.D. 1250–1350.* New York: Oxford University Press, 1989.

Allison, Graham. *Destined for War: Can America and China Escape Thucydides's Trap?* New York: Houghton Mifflin Harcourt, 2018.

Alpers, Edward A. *The Indian Ocean in World History.* Oxford: Oxford University Press, 2014.

Amrith, Sunil S. *Crossing the Bay of Bengal: The Furies of Nature and the Fortunes of Migrants.* Cambridge, MA: Harvard University Press, 2013.

Black, Jeremy. *Naval Warfare: A Global History since 1860.* Lanham, MD: Rowman and Littlefield, 2017.

Bonacich, Edna, and Jake B. Wilson. *Getting the Goods: Ports, Labor, and the Logistics Revolution.* Ithaca, NY: Cornell University Press, 2008.

Bradford, James C. *America, Sea Power, and the World.* Malden, MA: John Wiley and Sons, 2016.

Brewster, David, ed. *India and China at Sea: Competition for Naval Dominance in the Indian Ocean.* New Delhi: Oxford University Press, 2018.

Calder, Kent E. (coeditor with Francis Fukuyama). *East Asian Multilateralism: Prospects for Regional Stability.* Baltimore, MD: Johns Hopkins University Press, 2008.

Calder, Kent E. *Embattled Garrisons: Comparative Base Politics and American Globalism.* Princeton, NJ: Princeton University Press, 2007.

———. *The New Continentalism: Energy and Twenty-First Century Eurasian Geopolitics.* New Haven, CT: Yale University Press, 2012.

———. *Pacific Alliance: Reviving U.S.-Japan Relations.* New Haven, CT: Yale University Press, 2009.

———. *Pacific Defense: Arms, Energy, and America's Future in Asia.* New York: William Morrow, 1996.

———. *Singapore: Smart City, Smart State.* Washington, DC: Brookings Institution Press, 2016.

———. *Super Continent: The Logic of Eurasian Integration.* Stanford, CA: Stanford University Press, 2019.

Calder, Kent E., and Min Ye, *The Making of Northeast Asia*. Stanford, CA: Stanford University Press, 2010.

Cole, Bernard D. *China's Quest for Great Power: Ships, Oil, and Foreign Policy*. Annapolis, MD: Naval Institute Press, 2016.

———. *The Great Wall at Sea: China's Navy in the Twenty-First Century*, 2nd ed. Annapolis, MD: Naval Institute Press, 2010.

Corbett, Julian Stafford. *Maritime Operations in the Russo-Japanese War, 1904–1905*, vols. I and II. Annapolis, MD: Naval Institute Press, 1994.

———. *Some Principles of Maritime Strategy*. Annapolis, MD: Naval Institute Press, 1988.

Easton, Ian. *The Chinese Invasion Threat: Taiwan's Defense and American Strategy in Asia*. Manchester, UK: Camphor Press, 2017.

Erickson, Andrew S. *Chinese Naval Shipbuilding: An Ambitious and Uncertain Course*. Annapolis, MD: Naval Institute Press, 2016.

Erickson, Andrew S., Lyle J. Goldstein, and Nan Li, eds. *China, the United States, and 21st Century Sea Power: Defining a Maritime Security Partnership*. Annapolis, MD: Naval Institute Press, 2010.

Erickson, Andrew S., and Ryan D. Martinson, eds. *China's Maritime Gray Zone Operations*. Annapolis, MD: Naval Institute Press, 2019.

Feldman, Noah. *Cool War: The United States, China, and the Future of Global Competition*. New York: Random House, 2015.

Frankopan, Peter. *The Silk Roads: A New History of the World*. New York: Alfred A. Knopf, 2016.

Fravel, M. Taylor. *Active Defense: China's Military Strategy since 1949*. Princeton, NJ: Princeton University Press, 2019.

Friedberg, Aaron L. *Beyond Air-Sea Battle: The Debate over US Military Strategy in Asia*. London: International Institute for Strategic Studies, April 2014.

Gresh, Geoffrey F. *To Rule Eurasia's Waves: The New Great Power Competition at Sea*. New Haven, CT: Yale University Press, 2020.

Griffiths, Richard T. *The Maritime Silk Road: China's Belt and Road at Sea*. Leiden, Netherlands: International Institute of Asian Studies, 2020.

Harvey, Neil. *The Modern Chinese Navy*, 2nd ed. Bristol, UK: Morley Press, 2018.

———. *The Modern Japanese Navy and the Modern South Korean Navy*, 2nd ed. Bristol, UK: Morley Press, 2019.

Hayton, Bill. *The South China Sea: The Struggle for Power in Asia*. New Haven, CT: Yale University Press, 2014.

Heydarian, Richard Javad. *Asia's New Battlefield: The USA, China, and the Struggle for the Western Pacific*. London: Zed Books, 2015.

Hillman, Jonathan E. *The Emperor's New Road: China and the Project of the Century*. New Haven, CT: Yale University Press, 2020.

Holmes, James R. *A Brief Guide to Maritime Strategy*. Annapolis, MD: Naval Institute Press, 2019.

Kaplan, Robert D. *Asia's Cauldron: The South China Sea and the End of a Stable Pacific*. New York: Random House, 2014.

———. *Monsoon: The Indian Ocean and the Future of American Power*. New York: Random House, 2010.

Kardon, Isaac B. *China's Law of the Sea: The New Rules of Maritime Order*. New Haven, CT: Yale University Press, 2023.

Kennedy, Paul M. *The Rise and Fall of British Naval Mastery*. London: Allen Lane, 1976.

Khan, Sulmaan Wasif. *Haunted by Chaos: China's Grand Strategy from Mao Zedong to Xi Jinping*. Cambridge, MA: Harvard University Press, 2018.

Kissinger, Henry. *On China*. New York: The Penguin Press, 2011.

Krasner, Stephen D. *Defending the National Interest: Raw Materials Investments and U.S. Foreign Policy*. Princeton, NJ: Princeton University Press, 1978.

Lambert, Andrew. *Sea Power States*. New Haven, CT: Yale University Press, 2018.

Lardy, Nicholas R. *The State Strikes Back: The End of Economic Reform in China?* Washington, DC: Peterson Institute for International Economics, 2019.

Levinson, Marc. *Outside the Box: How Globalization Changed from Moving Stuff to Spreading Ideas*. Princeton, NJ: Princeton University Press, 2020.

———. *The Box: How the Shipping Container Made the World Smaller and the World Economy Bigger*. Princeton, NJ: Princeton University Press, 2006.

Li, Qingxin. *Maritime Silk Road*. William W. Wang, trans. Beijing: China Intercontinental Press, 2006.

Lintner, Bertil. *The Costliest Pearl: China's Struggle for India's Ocean*. London: C. Hurst and Co., 2019.

Mackinder, Halford. *Heartland: Three Essays on Geopolitics*. Katoomba, NSW: Spinebill Press, 2022.

Mahan, Alfred Thayer. *The Influence of Sea Power on History, 1660–1783*. Boston, Little Brown, 1890.

———. *The Problem of Asia: Its Effect upon International Politics*. New Brunswick, NJ: Transaction Publishers, 2003.

Mahbubani, Kishore. *Has China Won? The Chinese Challenge to American Primacy*. New York: Perseus Books, 2020.

Mahnken, Thomas G. *Technology and the American Way of War Since 1945*. New York: Columbia University Press, 2008.

Markey, Daniel S., *China's Western Horizon: Beijing and the New Geopolitics of Eurasia*. New York: Oxford University Press, 2020.

McDevitt, Michael A. *China as a Twenty-First Century Naval Power: Theory, Practice, and Implications*. Annapolis, MD: Naval Institute Press, 2020.

McGregor, Richard, *Xi Jinping: The Backlash*. Sydney: Penguin Random House Australia, 2019.

Medcalf, Rory. *Contest for the Indo-Pacific: Why China Won't Map the Future*. Carlton, Victoria, Australia: La Trobe University Press, 2020.

———. *Indo-Pacific Empire: China, America, and the Contest for the World's Pivotal Region*. Manchester, UK: Manchester University Press, 2020.

Nitze, Paul H. *From Hiroshima to Glasnost: At the Center of Decision*. New York: Grove Weidenfeld, 1989.

Palmer, Michael A. *Guardians of the Gulf: A History of America's Expanding Role in the Persian Gulf, 1833–1992*. New York: Simon and Schuster, 1992.

Parello-Plesner, Jonas, and Mathiew Duchatel. *China's Strong Arm: Protecting Citizens and Assets Abroad*. London: Routledge, 2015.

Paterson, Lawrence. *Hitler's Gray Wolves: U-Boats in the Indian Ocean*. New York: Carrel Books, 2004.

Prestowitz, Clyde. *The World Turned Upside Down: America, China, and the Struggle for Global Leadership*. New Haven, CT: Yale University Press, 2021.

Rachman, Gideon. *Easternization: Asia's Rise and America's Decline*. New York: Other Press, 2016.

Reed, W. Craig. *Red November: Inside the Secret U.S.-Soviet Submarine War*. New York: Harper Collins, 2010.

Rhode, Grant F. *Great Power Clashes Along the Maritime Silk Road: Lessons from History to Shape Current Strategy.* Annapolis, MD: Naval Institute Press, 2023.

Rodrigue, Jean-Paul. *The Geography of Transport Systems*, 5th ed. New York: Routledge, 2020.

Rowley, Anthony H. *Foundations of the Future: The Global Battle for Infrastructure.* Singapore: World Scientific Publishing Company, Ltd., 2020.

Seagrave, Sterling. *Lords of the Rim 2010: China's Renaissance.* Middletown, DE: Bowstring Books, 2010.

Shambaugh, David. *Where Great Powers Meet: America and China in Southeast Asia.* New York: Oxford University Press, 2021.

Speller, Ian. *Understanding Naval Warfare*, 2nd ed. New York: Routledge, 2019.

Starosielski, Nicole. *The Undersea Network.* Durham, NC: Duke University Press, 2015.

Stavridis, James. *Sea Power: The History and Geopolitics of the World's Oceans.* New York: Penguin Books, 2017.

Strangio, Sebastian. *In the Dragon's Shadow: Southeast Asia in the Chinese Century.* New Haven, CT: Yale University Press, 2020.

Till, Geoffrey. *Sea Power: A Guide for the Twenty-First Century*, 4th ed. London: Routledge, 2018.

Wachman, Alan M. *Why Taiwan? Geostrategic Rationales for China's Territorial Integrity.* Stanford, CA: Stanford University Press, 2007.

Wang, Dennis. *Reigning the Future: AI, 5G, and the Next 30 Years of US-China Rivalry.* Middletown, DE: New Degree Press, 2020.

Westcott, Allan, ed. *Mahan on Naval Warfare: Selections from the Writings of Rear Admiral Alfred T. Mahan.* Mineola, NY: Dover Publications, Inc., 1999.

Ye, Min. *The Belt Road and Beyond: State-Mobilized Globalization in China: 1998–2018.* Cambridge, UK: Cambridge University Press, 2020.

Yergin, Daniel. *The New Map: Energy, Climate, and the Clash of Nations.* New York: Penguin Press, 2020.

Yoshihara, Toshi, and James R. Holmes. *Red Star over the Pacific: China's Rise and the Challenge to U.S. Maritime Strategy*, 2nd ed. Annapolis, MD: Naval Institute Press, 2018.

Zheng, Chongwei, Chongyin Li, Hailang Wu, and Min Wang. *21st Century Maritime Silk Road: Construction of Remote Islands and Reefs.* Singapore: Springer Nature Singapore, 2019.

Zimmerman, Stan. *Submarine Technology for the 21st Century*, 2nd ed. Victoria, BC: Trafford Publishing, 2000.

Index

www.ingramcontent.com/pod-product-compliance
Lightning Source LLC
Chambersburg PA
CBHW021212270326
41929CB00010B/1090